H. Albert Napier, Ph.D.
Professor of Management
Jesse H. Jones Graduate School of Management
Rice University
Houston, TX

~

Philip J. Judd
Napier & Judd, Inc.
Houston, TX

~

Jack P. Hoggatt, Ed.D.
Professor of Business Communication
University of Wisconsin - Eau Claire
Eau Claire, WI

THOMSON
SOUTH-WESTERN

Australia · Canada · Mexico · Singapore · Spain · United Kingdom · United States

Learning with Computers

H. Albert Napier, Philip J. Judd, Jack Hoggatt

VP/Editorial Director:
Jack W. Calhoun

VP/Editor-in-Chief:
Karen Schmohe

Acquisitions Editor:
Jane Congdon

Project Manager:
Dave Lafferty

Contributing Author:
Ollie Rivers, Napier & Judd, Inc.

Development:
Victory Productions, Inc.,
Janet Stone, Developmental Editor

VP/Director of Marketing:
Carol Volz

Marketing Manager:
Michael Cloran

Marketing Coordinator:
Linda Kuper

Review Coordinator:
Karen Hein

Senior Production Editor:
Martha Conway

Production Manager:
Patricia Boies

Senior Manufacturing Coordinator:
Charlene Taylor

Manager of Technology - Editorial:
Liz Prigge

Technology Project Editor:
Mike Jackson

Web Coordinator:
Ed Stubenrauch

Art Director:
Stacy Jenkins Shirley

Permissions Editor:
Linda Ellis

Copyeditor:
Beth Anderson

Production House:
New England Typographic Service

Cover and Internal Design and Illustrations:
Grannan Graphic Design, Ltd.

Cover Images:
Grannan Graphic Design, Ltd.

Photo Researcher:
Darren Wright

Printer:
Quebecor World – Versailles
Versailles, KY

Printed in the United States of America
1 2 3 4 5 09 08 07 06 05

ISBN: 0-538-43971-8

For more information about our products, contact us at:

Thomson Higher Education
5191 Natorp Boulevard
Mason, Ohio 45040
USA

ASIA (including India)
Thomson Learning
5 Shenton Way
#01-01 UIC Building
Singapore 068808

AUSTRALIA/NEW ZEALAND
Thomson Learning Australia
102 Dodds Street
Southbank, Victoria 3006
Australia

CANADA
Thomson Nelson
1120 Birchmount Road
Toronto, Ontario
Canada M1K 5G4

UK/EUROPE/MIDDLE EAST/AFRICA
Thomson Learning
High Holborn House
50-51 Bedford Road
London WC1R 4LR
United Kingdom

Learning With Computers: *A Features Safari*

Explorers' Guide defines what files are needed to complete the project, provides an outline of skills to be learned, and identifies cross-curricular subjects covered.

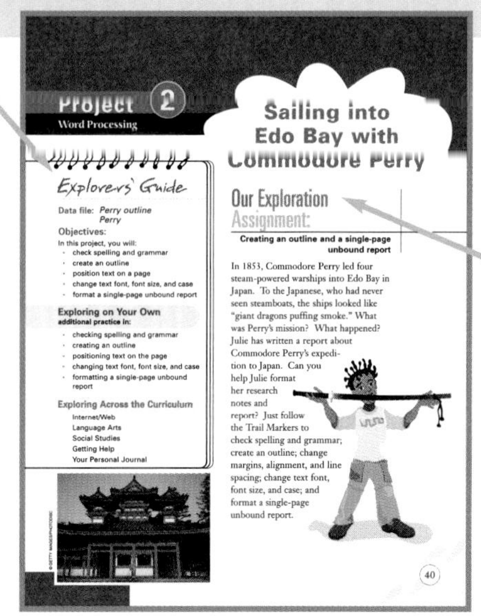
Project 2
Word Processing

Sailing into Edo Bay with Commodore Perry

Explorers' Guide

Data file: Perry outline
Perry

Objectives:
In this project, you will:
- check spelling and grammar
- create an outline
- position text on a page
- change text font, font size, and case
- format a single-page unbound report

Exploring on Your Own
additional practice in:
- checking spelling and grammar
- creating an outline
- positioning text on the page
- changing text font, font size, and case
- formatting a single-page unbound report

Exploring Across the Curriculum
Internet/Web
Language Arts
Social Studies
Getting Help
Your Personal Journal

Our Exploration Assignment:
Creating an outline and a single-page unbound report

In 1853, Commodore Perry led four steam-powered warships into Edo Bay in Japan. To the Japanese, who had never seen steamboats, the ships looked like "giant dragons puffing smoke." What was Perry's mission? What happened? Julie has written a report about Commodore Perry's expedition to Japan. Can you help Julie format her research notes and report? Just follow the Trail Markers to check spelling and grammar; create an outline; change margins, alignment, and line spacing; change text font, font size, and case; and format a single-page unbound report.

40

Our Exploration Assignment is introduced by one of the young explorers and gives a scenario of what students will do in each project.

Starting Out! gets students moving on a project by having them open the data file and rename it.

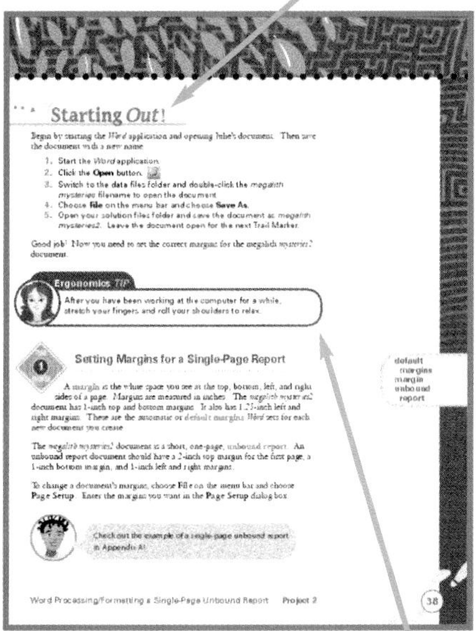
Starting Out!

Begin by starting the Word application and opening Julie's document. Then save the document with a new name.

1. Start the *Word* application.
2. Click the **Open** button.
3. Switch to the data files folder and double-click the *megalith mysteries* filename to open the document.
4. Choose **File** on the menu bar and choose **Save As**.
5. Open your solution files folder and save the document as *megalith mysteries2*. Leave the document open for the next Trail Marker.

Good job! Now you need to set the correct margins for the megalith *mysteries2* document.

Ergonomics TIP
After you have been working at the computer for a while, stretch your fingers and roll your shoulders to relax.

1 Setting Margins for a Single-Page Report

A margin is the white space you see at the top, bottom, left, and right sides of a page. Margins are measured in inches. The *megalith mysteries2* document has 1-inch top and bottom margins. It also has 1.25-inch left and right margins. These are the automatic or default margins *Word* sets for each new document you create.

The *megalith mysteries2* document is a short, one-page, unbound report. An unbound report document should have a 2-inch top margin for the first page, a 1-inch bottom margin, and 1-inch left and right margins.

To change a document's margins, choose **File** on the menu bar and choose **Page Setup**. Enter the margins you want in the **Page Setup** dialog box.

default margins margin unbound report

Check out the example of a single-page unbound report in Appendix A!

Word Processing/Formatting a Single-Page Unbound Report Project 2 38

Each project is divided into numbered tasks called **Trail Markers,** which explain how to perform computer functions using menu commands, toolbar buttons, and keyboard shortcuts.

Ergonomics Tips are introduced by Julie and stress how to use the computer properly.

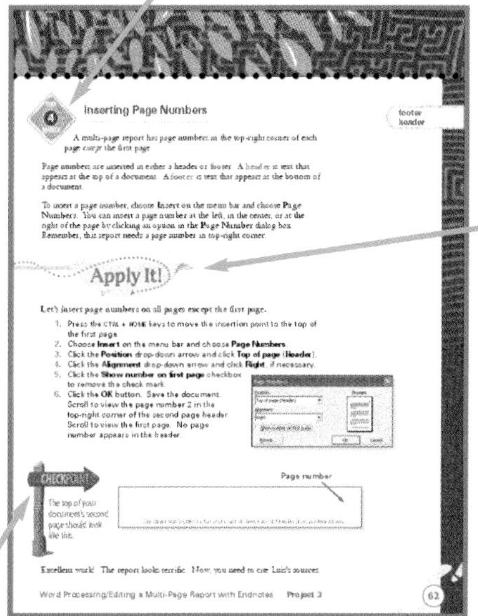
4 Inserting Page Numbers

A multi-page report has page numbers in the top-right corner of each page *except* the first page.

Page numbers are inserted in either a header or footer. A header is text that appears at the top of a document. A footer is text that appears at the bottom of a document.

To insert a page number, choose **Insert** on the menu bar and choose **Page Numbers**. You can insert a page number at the left, in the center, or at the right of the page by clicking an option in the **Page Number** dialog box. Remember, this report needs a page number in top-right corner.

footer header

Apply It!

Let's insert page numbers on all pages except the first page.

1. Press the CTRL + HOME keys to move the insertion point to the top of the first page.
2. Choose **Insert** on the menu bar and choose **Page Numbers**.
3. Click the **Position** drop-down arrow and click **Top of page (Header)**.
4. Click the **Alignment** drop-down arrow and click **Right**, if necessary.
5. Click the **Show number on first page** checkbox to remove the check mark.
6. Click the **OK** button. Save the document. Scroll to view the page number 2 in the top-right corner of the second page header. Scroll to view the first page. No page number appears in the header.

CHECKPOINT
The top of your document's second page should look like this.

Page number

Excellent work! The report looks terrific. Now you need to cite Luis's sources.

Word Processing/Editing a Multi-Page Report with Endnotes Project 3 62

Apply It! contains step-by-step instructions to give hands-on practice on the skill learned in the Trail Marker.

Checkpoints featured throughout the project provide students with visual examples of how their work should appear.

Margin notes—introduced by the explorers—offer tips, additional information, and encouragement.

Project Skills Review is a table of software commands that summarizes the skills learned in the project.

Exploring on Your Own is a critical-thinking, cross-curricular activity that students complete independently, applying computer skills learned.

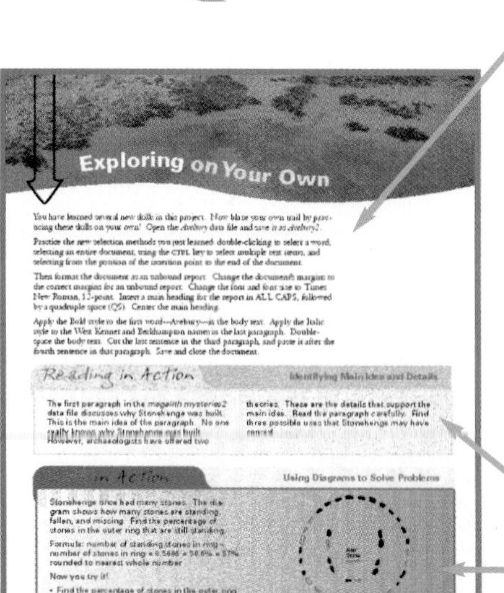

Reading in Action and **Math in Action** are short projects that enhance core curricular skills.

Exploring Across the Curriculum end-of-project exercises integrate practice in computer skills with language arts, social studies, science, math, art, and Internet skills.

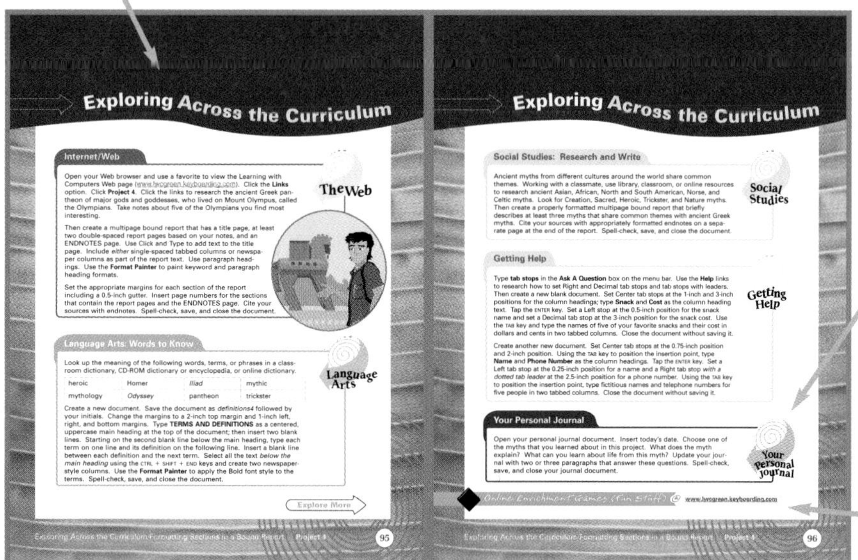

Exploring Across the Curriculum

Internet/Web

Open your Web browser and use a favorite to view the Learning with Computers Web page (www.lwcgreen.keyboarding.com). Click the **Links** option. Click **Project 4**. Click the links to research the ancient Greek pantheon of major gods and goddesses, who lived on Mount Olympus, called the Olympians. Take notes about five of the Olympians you find most interesting.

Then create a multipage bound report that has a title page, at least two double-spaced report pages based on your notes, and an ENDNOTES page. Use Click and Type to add text to the title page. Include *either* single-spaced tabbed columns or newspaper columns as part of the report text. Use paragraph headings. Use the **Format Painter** to paint keyword and paragraph heading formats.

Set the appropriate margins for each section of the report including a 0.5-inch gutter. Insert page numbers for the sections that contain the report pages and the ENDNOTES page. Cite your sources with endnotes. Spell-check, save, and close the document.

The Web

Language Arts: Words to Know

Look up the meaning of the following words, terms, or phrases in a classroom dictionary, CD-ROM dictionary or encyclopedia, or online dictionary.

heroic	Homer	*Iliad*	mythic
mythology	*Odyssey*	pantheon	trickster

Create a new document. Save the document as *definitions4* followed by your initials. Change the margins to a 2-inch top margin and 1-inch left, right, and bottom margins. Type **TERMS AND DEFINITIONS** as a centered, uppercase main heading at the top of the document; then insert two blank lines. Starting on the second blank line below the main heading, type each term on one line and its definition on the following line. Insert a blank line between each definition and the next term. Select all the text *below the main heading* using the CTRL + SHIFT + END keys and create two newspaper-style columns. Use the **Format Painter** to apply the Bold font style to the terms. Spell-check, save, and close the document.

Language Arts

Explore More

Exploring Across the Curriculum Formatting Sections in a Bound Report Project 4 95

Exploring Across the Curriculum

Social Studies: Research and Write

Ancient myths from different cultures around the world share common themes. Working with a classmate, use library, classroom, or online resources to research ancient Asian, African, North and South American, Norse, and Celtic myths. Look for Creation, Sacred, Heroic, Trickster, and Nature myths. Then create a properly formatted multipage bound report that briefly describes at least three myths that share common themes with ancient Greek myths. Cite your sources with appropriately formatted endnotes on a separate page at the end of the report. Spell-check, save, and close the document.

Social Studies

Getting Help

Type **tab stops** in the **Ask A Question** box on the menu bar. Use the **Help** links to research how to set Right and Decimal tab stops and tab stops with leaders. Then create a new blank document. Set Center tab stops at the 1-inch and 3-inch positions for the column headings; type **Snack** and **Cost** as the column heading text. Tap the ENTER key. Set a Left stop at the 0.5-inch position for the snack name and set a Decimal tab stop at the 3-inch position for the snack cost. Use the TAB key and type the names of five of your favorite snacks and their cost in dollars and cents in two tabbed columns. Close the document without saving it.

Create another new document. Set Center tab stops at the 0.75-inch position and 2-inch position. Using the TAB key to position the insertion point, type **Name** and **Phone Number** as the column headings. Tap the ENTER key. Set a Left tab stop at the 0.25-inch position for a name and a Right tab stop *with a dotted tab leader* at the 2.5-inch position for a phone number. Using the TAB key to position the insertion point, type fictitious names and telephone numbers for five people in two tabbed columns. Close the document without saving it.

Getting Help

Your Personal Journal

Open your personal journal document. Insert today's date. Choose one of the myths that you learned about in this project. What does the myth explain? What can you learn about life from this myth? Update your journal with two or three paragraphs that answer these questions. Spell-check, save, and close your journal document.

Your Personal Journal

Online Enrichment Games (Fun Stuff) www.lwcgreen.keyboarding.com

Exploring Across the Curriculum Formatting Sections in a Bound Report Project 4 96

Your Personal Journal gives students the opportunity to record their thoughts and ideas regarding project topics.

Online Enrichment Games (Fun Stuff) direct students to the *Learning with Computers* website for fun activities that enhance learning.

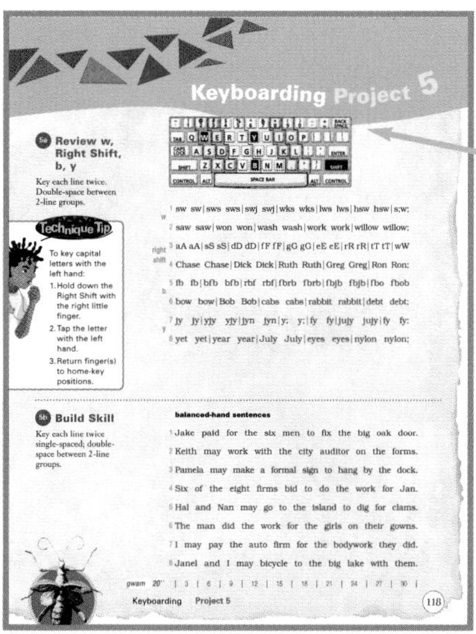

Keyboarding Project 5

5a Review w, Right Shift, b, y

Key each line twice. Double-space between 2-line groups.

Technique Tip

To key capital letters with the left hand:

1. Hold down the Right Shift with the right little finger.
2. Tap the letter with the left hand.
3. Return finger(s) to home-key positions.

w
1 sw sw|sws sws|swj swj|wks wks|lws lws|hsw hsw|s;w;
2 saw saw|won won|wash wash|work work|willow willow;

right shift
3 aA aA|sS sS|dD dD|fF fF|gG gG|eE eE|rR rR|tT tT|wW
4 Chase Chase|Dick Dick|Ruth Ruth|Greg Greg|Ron Ron;

b
5 fb fb|bfb bfb|rbf rbf|fbrb fbrb|fbjb fbjb|fbo fbob
6 bow bow|Bob Bob|cabs cabs|rabbit rabbit|debt debt;

y
7 jy jy|yjy yjy|jyn jyn|y; y;|fy fy|jujy jujy|fy fy;
8 yet yet|year year|July July|eyes eyes|nylon nylon;

5b Build Skill

Key each line twice single-spaced; double-space between 2-line groups.

balanced-hand sentences

1 Jake paid for the six men to fix the big oak door.
2 Keith may work with the city auditor on the forms.
3 Pamela may make a formal sign to hang by the dock.
4 Six of the eight firms bid to do the work for Jan.
5 Hal and Nan may go to the island to dig for clams.
6 The man did the work for the girls on their gowns.
7 I may pay the auto firm for the bodywork they did.
8 Janel and I may bicycle to the big lake with them.

gwam 20" | 3 | 6 | 9 | 12 | 15 | 18 | 21 | 24 | 27 | 30 |

Keyboarding Project 5 118

Keyboarding page at the end of every project offers practice and reinforcement of keyboarding skills and features a Technique Tip.

About the Authors

About the Authors

H. Albert Napier, Ph.D. is a Professor of Management at the Jesse H. Jones Graduate School of Management, Rice University. The author and co-author of several books about using desktop applications, Al has been involved in computer education for more than 20 years.

Philip J. Judd is the former Director of the Research and Instructional Computing Service and an instructor in the Management Department at the University of Houston. Phil currently focuses on consulting as a principal of Napier & Judd, Inc. His consulting activities include the analysis and design of automated business systems, planning for large-scale computer operations, the design and implementation of local area networks, and the development of integrated Web sites.

Dr. Jack P. Hoggatt is Department Chair for the Department of Business Communications at the University of Wisconsin-Eau Claire. He has taught courses in Business Writing, Advanced Business Communications, and the communication component of the university's Master in Business Administration (MBA) program. Dr. Hoggatt has held offices in professional organizations and has been received the Outstanding Post-Secondary Business Educator Award in Wisconsin. He has served as an advisor to local and state business organizations. Dr. Hoggatt is involved with his community and the school activities of his four children.

Dedication

Al Napier: To my family.

Phil Judd: To my wife, Valerie; and my children, Michelle, Jacob, and Heather; for their support and understanding.

Jack Hoggatt: This book is dedicated to Glenda (my wife), Ashley, Logan, Erika, Cody (my children), and to Maxine Vermillion Hoggatt (my mother), who was a master teacher at providing the informal portion of my early education.

Acknowledgements

Comments from reviewers of *Learning with Computers* have been valuable in the development of this book. Special thanks to the following individuals:

Karen Bean, Instructor,
Office Technology
Blinn Community College
Brenham, Texas

Terri Lynn Cole
Hamilton Middle School,
Cypress-Fairbanks ISD
Cypress, Texas

Jennifer Gipp
DC Everest Middle School
Weston, Wisconsin

Janet Grayson
Tichenor Middle School
Erlanger, Kentucky

Charles Motley
Cypress Fairbanks ISD
Houston, Texas

Sue Nash
DC Everest Junior High
Schofield, Wisconsin

Tracy Sanders
Walhalla Middle School
Walhalla, South Carolina

Tom Thompson
Lakota Plains Junior School
Liberty Township, Ohio

Jen Wegner
Mishicot Middle School
Mishicot, Wisconsin

Connie Williams
Virginia State Department
of Education
Richmond, Virginia

To the Student

The Explorers Club Preview

Hi! Welcome to *Learning with Computers*, Level Green. My name is Ray and this is Julie and Luis. We belong to the **Explorers Club** where we learn how to use the computer while exploring interesting and exciting things about our world. Join us and together we will:

- **Create** and format *Word* documents
- **Solve** problems using *Excel* worksheets
- **Present** ideas and facts in *PowerPoint* slide shows
- **Organize** information in *Access* databases

Julie, Luis, and I will be your guides through the 18 projects in this book. Just like the trail markers that help you follow a forest trail, each project has Trail Markers to guide you through learning new skills. There are many activities at the end of every project to let you practice your new skills. You will explore the World Wide Web and share your research using documents, workbooks, presentations, and databases. Throughout your explorations, you will record your thoughts about what you've learned in your own personal journal.

Are you ready to set out on our Explorers Club trail? Let's go!

Getting Started

Can you name the parts of your computer? Do you know the difference between computer hardware and software? Do you know how to protect your body by sitting correctly at your computer?

In the Getting Started project, you will find the answer to these and other basic computer questions. You will learn how to use the *Windows* desktop and create files and folders. You will also visit the *Learning with Computers* Middle School Web pages.

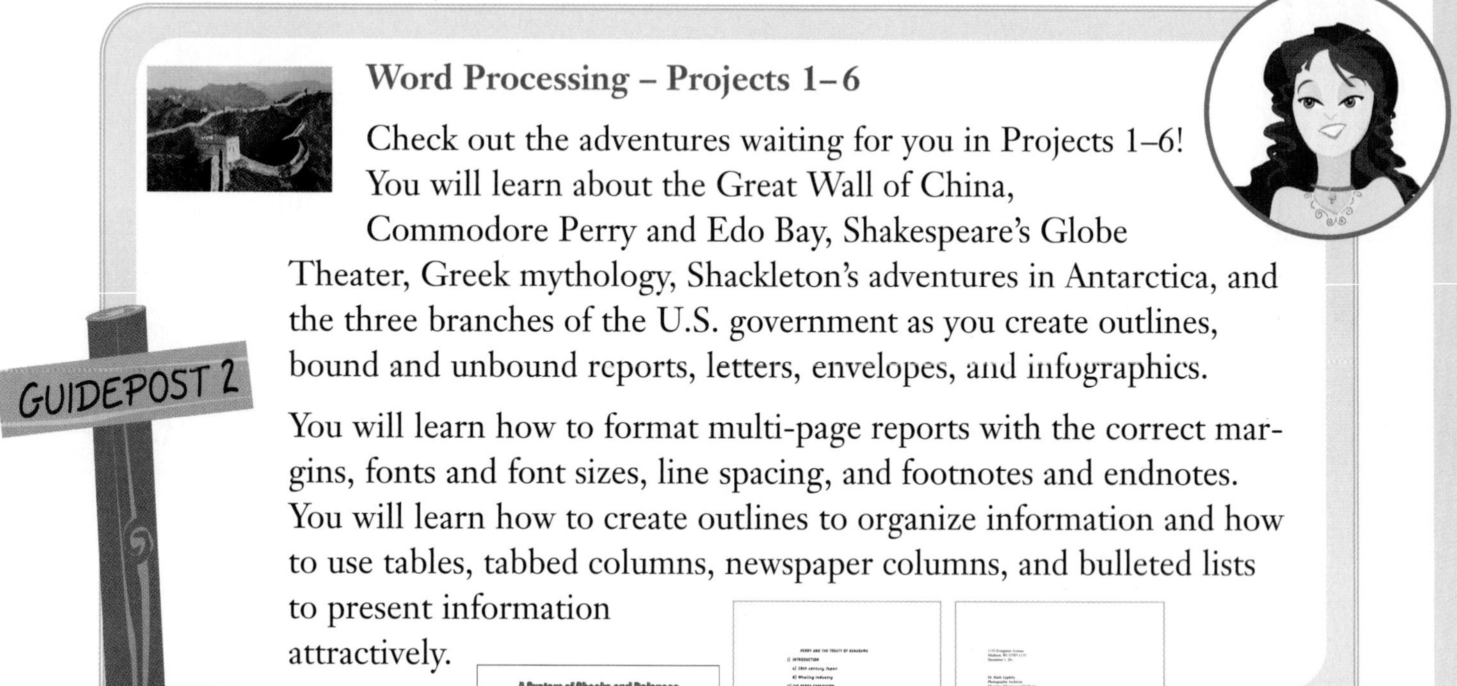

Word Processing – Projects 1–6

Check out the adventures waiting for you in Projects 1–6! You will learn about the Great Wall of China, Commodore Perry and Edo Bay, Shakespeare's Globe Theater, Greek mythology, Shackleton's adventures in Antarctica, and the three branches of the U.S. government as you create outlines, bound and unbound reports, letters, envelopes, and infographics.

You will learn how to format multi-page reports with the correct margins, fonts and font sizes, line spacing, and footnotes and endnotes. You will learn how to create outlines to organize information and how to use tables, tabbed columns, newspaper columns, and bulleted lists to present information attractively.

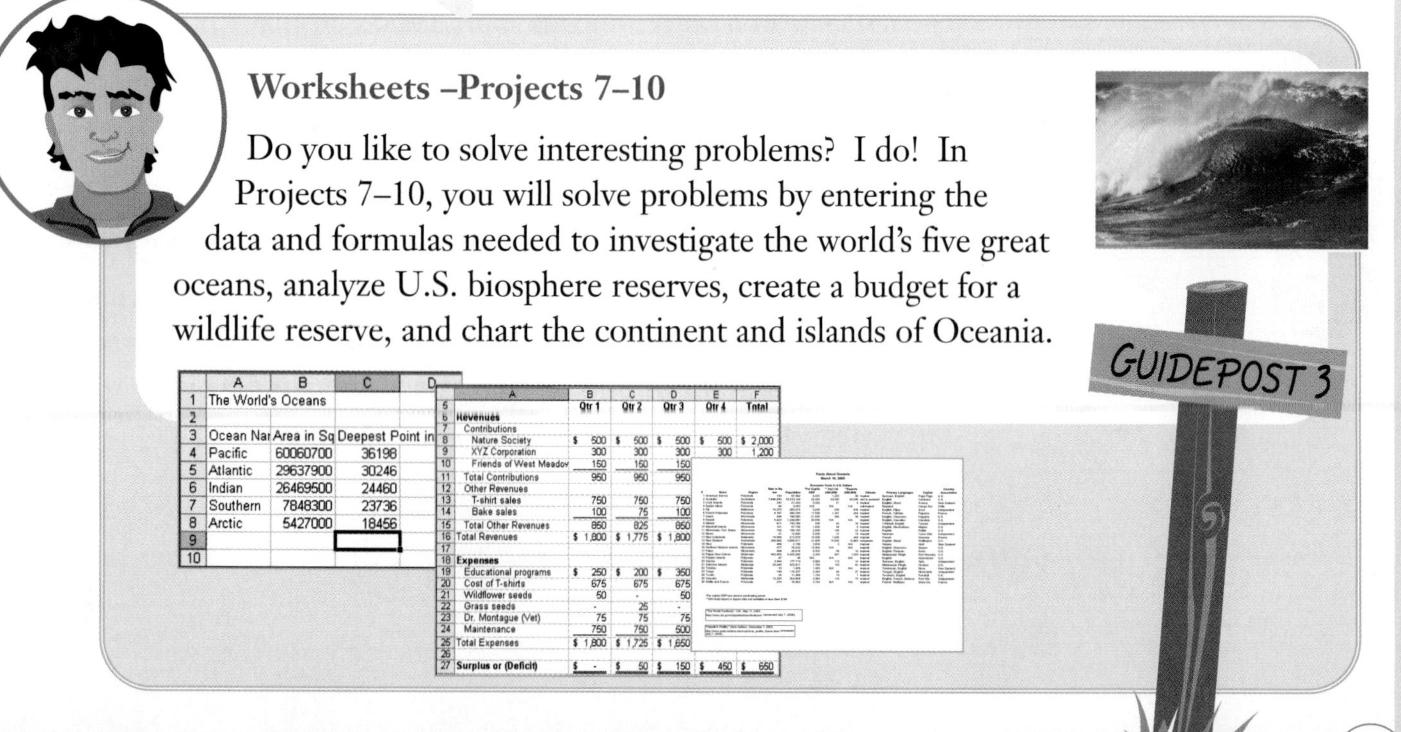

Worksheets –Projects 7–10

Do you like to solve interesting problems? I do! In Projects 7–10, you will solve problems by entering the data and formulas needed to investigate the world's five great oceans, analyze U.S. biosphere reserves, create a budget for a wildlife reserve, and chart the continent and islands of Oceania.

	A	B	C
1	The World's Oceans		
2			
3	Ocean Nar	Area in Sq	Deepest Point in
4	Pacific	60060700	36198
5	Atlantic	29637900	30246
6	Indian	26469500	24460
7	Southern	7848300	23736
8	Arctic	5427000	18456
9			
10			

	A	B	C	D	E	F
5		Qtr 1	Qtr 2	Qtr 3	Qtr 4	Total
6	Revenues					
7	Contributions					
8	Nature Society	$ 500	$ 500	$ 500	$ 500	$ 2,000
9	XYZ Corporation	300	300	300	300	1,200
10	Friends of West Meadov	150	150	150		
11	Total Contributions	950	950	950		
12	Other Revenues					
13	T-shirt sales	750	750	750		
14	Bake sales	100	75	100		
15	Total Other Revenues	850	825	850		
16	Total Revenues	$ 1,800	$ 1,775	$ 1,800		
17						
18	Expenses					
19	Educational programs	$ 250	$ 200	$ 350		
20	Cost of T-shirts	675	675	675		
21	Wildflower seeds	50	-	50		
22	Grass seeds	-	25	-		
23	Dr. Montague (Vet)	75	75	75		
24	Maintenance	750	750	500		
25	Total Expenses	$ 1,800	$ 1,725	$ 1,650		
26						
27	Surplus or (Deficit)	$ -	$ 50	$ 150	$ 450	$ 650

Presentations and Multimedia – Projects 11–15

Exploring science and art is really great fun—especially when you can share what you learn in a slide show.

In Projects 11–15, you will create slide show presentations with lots of different slide layouts, design templates, and color schemes. You will also add transitions, animations, sound, motion clips, and hyperlinks to make your slide shows more exciting. Finally, you even learn how to work in two applications at once by adding worksheet data to a slide show!

Database – Projects 16–18

Do you need help to organize your research? Databases are really useful for organizing data! In Projects 16–18, you will organize research data about the famous siege of the Alamo; art created by the indigenous people of North America, Central America, and South America; and foods you should eat for a well-balanced diet. You learn to open and create database files; create tables; enter data in your tables; sort and filter your data; and print your data in a Datasheet or as a report.

GUIDEPOST 5

Now that you have reached the end of this trail, we hope you are excited about joining our Explorers Club. Go to the Getting Started project to begin blazing your own trail!

Contents

Presentations and Multimedia
Unit 3

Project 13 Describing the Scientific Method

Explorers' Guide

Project 14 Making Sourdough Bread

Explorers' Guide

Project 15 Exploring the Mind of Leonardo

Explorers' Guide

Project 16 Remembering the Alamo

Explorers' Guide

Getting Started

Explorers' Guide

Data file: *none*

Objectives:

In this project, you will:

- learn about computer ergonomics
- describe computer hardware and software
- review the *Windows* desktop and use the mouse
- work with windows and folders
- explore a Web page
- send and receive e-mail

Our Exploration Assignment:

Learn about computer basics

Welcome to the Explorers Club. Follow the Trail Markers with us—Julie, Luis, and Ray—as we explain the right way to sit at the computer and describe computer hardware and software. Then you will review the *Windows* desktop, use the mouse, and work with windows and folders. Finally, you will explore a Web page and send and receive e-mail.

18a Build Skill

Key each line twice. Double-space between 2-line groups.

balanced-hand sentences

1 When he turns in the audit, he may go to the lake.

2 When did the widow make the gown for the neighbor?

3 I may go downtown to fix the problem with the bus.

4 Diana and Enrique paid for the rug for the chapel.

5 Alan and I may go to the social for the six firms.

6 Six men may dismantle the signs by the big chapel.

7 I wish to pay the man for the six bushels of corn.

gwam *20″* | 3 | 6 | 9 | 12 | 15 | 18 | 21 | 24 | 27 | 30 |

18b Speed Building

1. Key a 1' timing on paragraph 1.
2. Determine the number of words you keyed.
3. Key another 1' timing on paragraph 1. Try to go three words a minute faster.
4. Repeat steps 1–3 for paragraph 2.

all letters used *gwam* *1′*

Taxes are the means used by the government to raise money 12
for its expenditures. Taxes have never been popular. The legislative 26
branches of the government devote a lot of time and energy trying to 40
devise a system that requires everyone to pay their just and fair 53
share. Tax assessments are typically based on the benefits realized 67
and on an individual's ability to pay. Two of the most common 79
taxes are the personal income tax and the sales tax. 90

The personal income tax is the assessment individuals are 101
required to pay on their earnings. Employers deduct this tax from 115
employees' paychecks. The sales tax is another assessment with 128
which the majority of people are familiar. It is a tax that is added 142
to the retail price of a good or service. While the income tax is an 156
assessment based on an individual's ability to pay, the general sales 170
tax is based on the benefits a person receives. 179

gwam *1′* | 1 | 2 | 3 | 4 | 5 | 6 | 7 | 8 | 9 | 10 | 11 | 12 | 13 |

Learning About Computer Ergonomics

TRAIL 1 MARKER

computer ergonomics

Before you begin to work at your computer, you must check your posture. It is very important that you sit properly at your computer and position your hands correctly on the keyboard to avoid injury to your back, wrists, or fingers. See how Ray is sitting at his computer? This is the way you should sit at your computer to avoid injury.

Computer Ergonomics

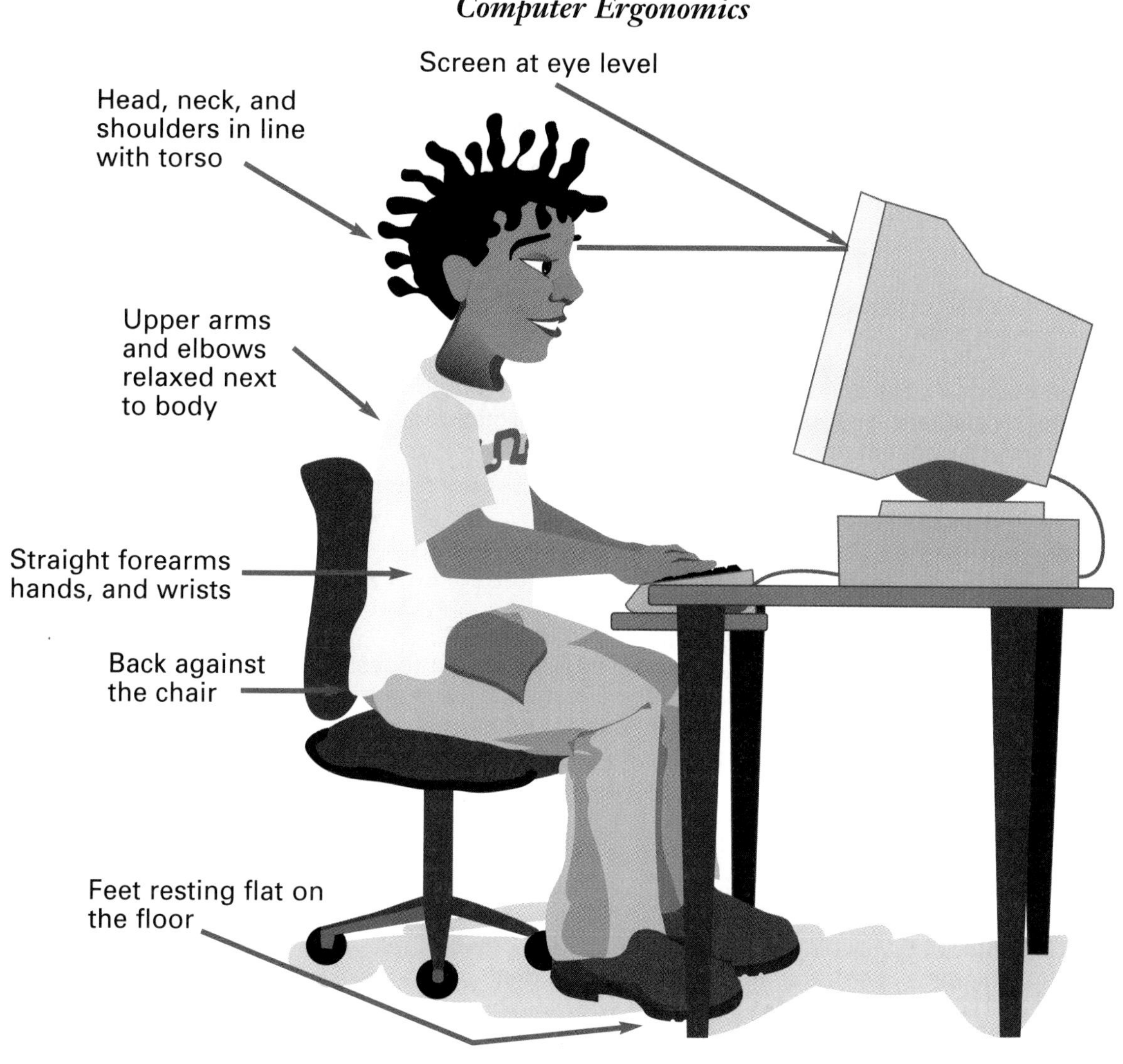

The rules for using a computer correctly to avoid personal injury are called **computer ergonomics**. Computer ergonomics includes using appropriate posture as well as placing and correctly using the keyboard, mouse, and monitor.

Exploring Across the Curriculum

Health and Fitness: Record and Organize

A good way to learn more about the nutritional value of the food you commonly eat each day is to keep a food log. Create a new database and save it as *food log18*. Then create a new table in the database using the Table Wizard and the Diet Log personal sample table. Add all the sample fields to the new table and save the table as *My Food Log*.

Open the table in Datasheet view and switch to Design view. Make the following design changes to the table: Rename the *DietLogID* field as *RecordID* and change the caption to *ID*. Delete the *PersonID* field. Rename the *DietType* field as *Description* and change its caption to *Food Consumed*. Save the table and close it.

Then write down everything you eat each day for seven days and record the data in the *My Food Log* table. Use classroom, library, or online sources to find the approximate carbohydrate, protein, and fat grams, and total calories for each item you record. At the end of the seven days, use the data in the *My Food Log* table to calculate the total carbohydrates, total protein, total fat, and total calories you consumed each day.

Getting Help

Start *Access*, if necessary, and type **Data Type Property** in the **Ask A Question** box and tap the ENTER key. Research the different field data types and write down a brief description of each data type. Create a *PowerPoint* presentation that briefly describes each data type. Format and animate the presentation as desired. Save, preview, print, and close the presentation.

Your Personal Journal

Open your personal journal document. Insert today's date and two blank lines. Do you think you eat a nutritional and well-balanced diet? If yes, why? If no, why not? If no, how could you improve your diet? Update your journal with one or two paragraphs that answer these questions. Spell-check, save, and close your journal.

Online Enrichment Games (Fun Stuff) @ www.lwcgreen.keyboarding.com

Let's check out your posture and the position of your computer.

1. Are you sitting straight with your back against the chair?
2. Are your forearms, wrists, and hands straight and in line on the keyboard?
3. Are your feet resting flat on the floor or on a footrest?
4. Are your neck and head and shoulders in line with your body and facing the computer?
5. Are your upper arms and elbows relaxed next to your body?
6. Is your computer monitor's screen at eye level?
7. Is your mouse next to the keyboard and within easy reach?

Super! When you can answer yes to each of these questions, you are ready to start working at your computer.

TRAIL 2 MARKER

Describing Computer Hardware and Software

hardware
software

A computer has both hardware and software. Computer hardware includes the computer parts that you can see and touch. Computer software provides instructions the computer needs to operate.

Hardware

cable
CD
CPU
diskette
hard drive
keyboard
monitor
mouse
printer
screen
storage device
USB flash drive

Hardware includes the monitor, keyboard, mouse, internal and external storage devices, and CPU. These parts are connected by insulated wires called cables. The CPU is the computer's "brain." It sends and receives electronic instructions to and from the other hardware parts, such as a disk drive, across these cables.

The documents you type on your computer's keyboard can be stored electronically on the computer's internal hard drive storage device. If your computer is part of a network, you may be able to save your documents to a network storage device, called a server, which is shared by everyone on the network. You may also be able to store your documents on external storage media, such as a diskette, USB flash drive, or a CD.

You view your documents on the monitor's screen and print them using a printer. If your computer has a microphone and speakers, you can also record and listen to sounds.

Exploring Across the Curriculum

Internet/Web

Open your Web browser and use a favorite to view the Learning with Computers Web page (www.lwcgreen.keyboarding.com). Click the **Links** option. Click **Project 18**. Use the links, together with information in the *nutrition18* and *fast food18* databases you created in this project, to learn more about food choices that provide good nutrition as part of a well-balanced diet. Take notes about what you learn. Then, using your notes, plan three nutritious and well-balanced meals—breakfast, lunch, and dinner—plus two snacks per day for seven days.

Record your seven-day meal and snack plan in a Word document or an *Excel* workbook or a *PowerPoint* presentation, and save it as *my meal plan18*. Format your document, worksheet, or presentation as desired. With permission, give an oral presentation to your class, describing your research and the reasons for your meal plan choices.

Language Arts: Words to Know

Look up the meaning of the following terms using a classroom, library, CD-ROM, or online encyclopedia or dictionary.

protein	carbohydrate	nutrient	vitamin
fiber	antioxidant	calorie	fat

Create a new database and save it as *definitions18*. Create a new table in Design view. Add the following fields:

Field Name	Data Type	Field Size	Caption
TermID	AutoNumber	Long Integer	ID
Term	Text	15	None
Definition	Text	50	None

Set the *TermID* field as the primary key. Save the table as *Terms and Definitions*. Switch to Datasheet view and enter each term and its definition. *Remember—each definition can be no longer than 50 characters!* Resize the columns, if necessary. Sort the table in ascending order by term. Spell-check the table and save it.

Explore More

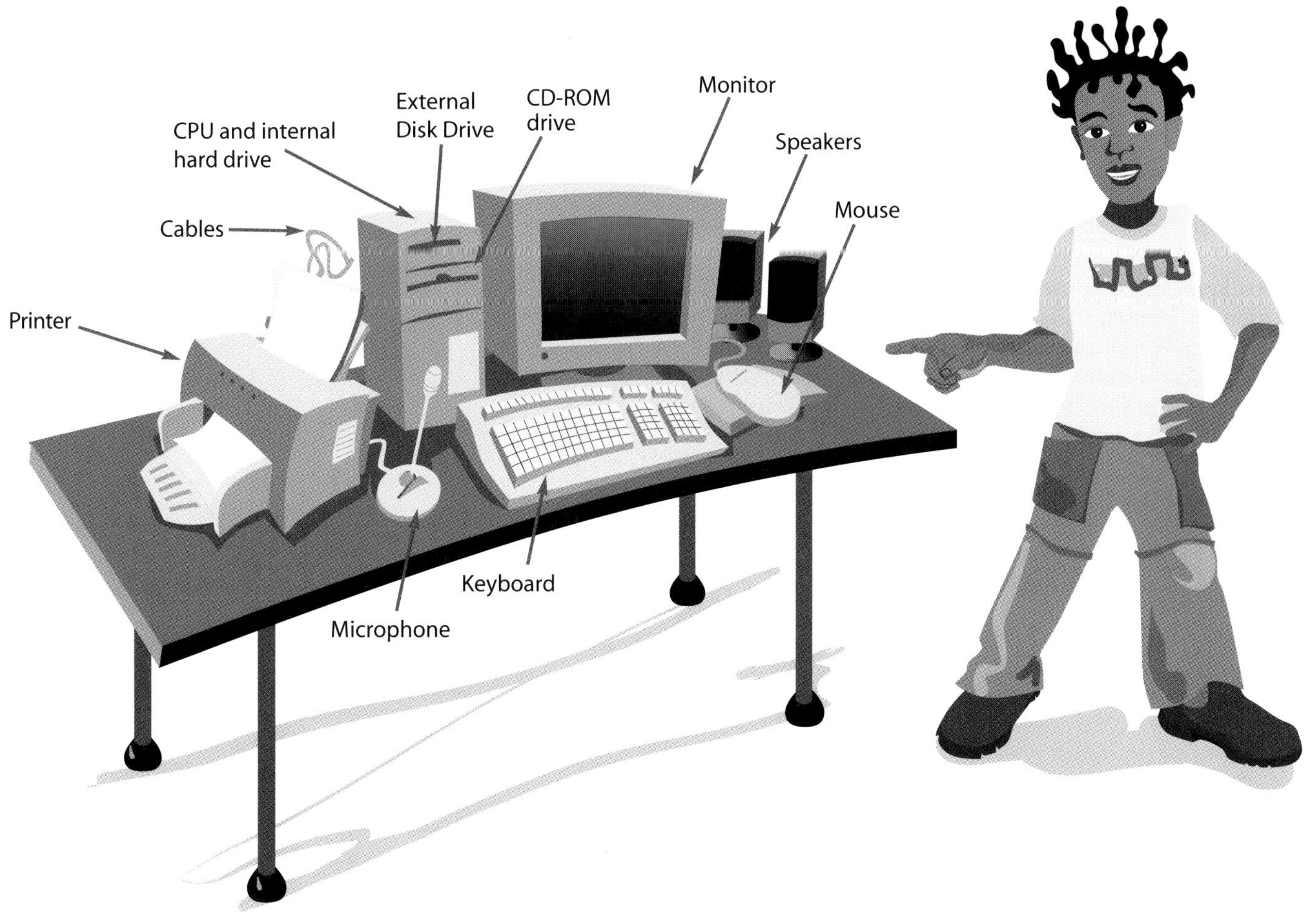

CPU and internal hard drive
External Disk Drive
CD-ROM drive
Monitor
Speakers
Mouse
Cables
Printer
Keyboard
Microphone

Let's find the hardware components on your computer.

1. Find these hardware components on your computer: the CPU, the monitor, the storage devices (internal and external disk drive, CD-ROM drive, flash drive), the cables, the keyboard, and the mouse.
2. Look to see if your computer also has the following hardware components: a printer, microphone, and speakers.

You also need computer software to use your computer.

Exploring on Your Own

Reading in Action

Making Inferences

When you make an inference, you use facts to make a generalization or draw a conclusion. Your inferences can also be based on your personal experience and knowledge. Review the data in the *nutrition18* database and the Math in Action. Use the information in them to make inferences about nutrition and exercise.

Examples:

The more strenuously you exercise, the more calories you burn.

Fried foods contain more calories than other types of foods.

Math in Action

Using Algebra to Solve Problems

In nutrition, the calorie is the unit used to measure how much energy is contained in food. Different exercises burn calories at different rates. How many hours do you have to walk to burn the calories from a meal of 3 ounces of beef and 1 cup of rice?

<u>Rate of calories burned</u>
Swimming: 500 calories/hour
Walking: 250 calories/hour
Sitting: 100 calories/hour

<u>Calories</u>
1 apple: 72 calories
1 scrambled egg: 101 calories
1 cup of orange juice: 110 calories
1 cup of rice: 169 calories
3 ounces of beef: 220 calories

220 calories (3 ounces of beef) + 169 calories (1 cup of rice) = 389 calories

Let x = number of hours walking

(rate of calories burned per hour) * (number of hours exercising) = # of calories in food
(250 calories) * (x) = 389 calories
divide each side by 250 calories
x = 1.556
It will take about 1.5 hours of walking to burn off the meal.

Now you try it!

How long do you have to swim to burn off the calories from a meal of 1 scrambled egg, 1 apple, and 1 cup of orange juice? How long would you have to sit to burn off the same meal?

Software

Computer software is grouped into two categories: application software and system software. Application software is used for a specific purpose. In the projects in this text, you will learn to use the *Microsoft Word, Excel, PowerPoint,* and *Access* application software.

application software
system software

Word is used to create text documents. *Excel* is used to create worksheets, sometimes called spreadsheets. *PowerPoint* is used to create multimedia presentations. *Access* is used to organize data in databases.

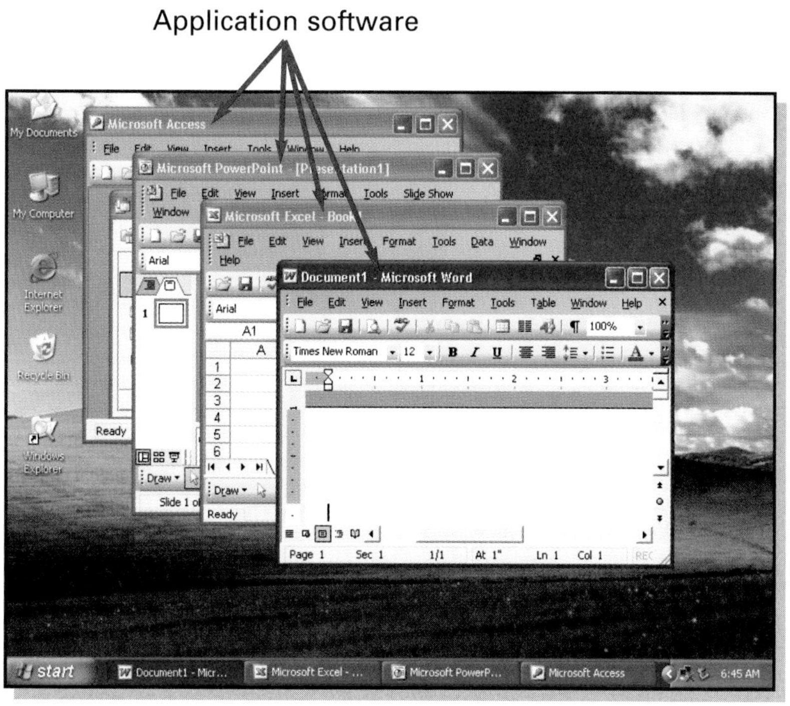

Application software

System software is the operating system that runs your computer. *Microsoft Windows XP* or *Microsoft Windows 2000,* often just called *Windows,* are two versions of popular operating system software. Your computer probably uses a *Windows* operating system.

Let's start your computer and look at the *Windows* desktop.

Exploring on Your Own

Blaze your own trail! Create a new database and save it as *fast food18*. Then create a new table in Design view. Add the following fields to the table.

Field Name	Data Type	Field Size	Caption	Default Value
FoodID	AutoNumber	Long Integer	ID	None
FoodType	Text	50	Description	None
FoodGroup	Text	25	Meal	None
Notes	Text	25	None	None
TotalCalories	Number	Long Integer, zero decimal places	Calories	None
Website	Hyperlink	N/A	Hyperlink	None

Set the *FoodID* field as the primary key. Save the table as *Fast Food Calories*. Modify the table to add the following field before the *Website* field. (Hint: Select the Website field row and click the *Insert Rows* button on the Table Design toolbar to insert a row for the new field.)

Field Name	Data Type	Field Size	Caption	Default Value
Source	Text	30	None	Nutrient Data Laboratory

Delete the *Notes* field and save the table. Switch to Datasheet view. Add the following records to the table.

FoodID	Description	Group	Calories
1	1 biscuit, egg and bacon	Breakfast	477
2	1 burrito, beans and cheese	Lunch or Dinner	378
3	1 brownie	Dessert	405
4	1 double cheeseburger	Lunch or Dinner	704
5	1 chicken sandwich	Lunch or Dinner	632
6	6 chicken nuggets	Lunch or Dinner	285
7	1 medium fries	Lunch or Dinner	458
8	1 large taco	Lunch or Dinner	568
9	1 small strawberry shake	Beverage	113
10	salad with chicken and no dressing	Lunch or Dinner	105
11	1 medium baked potato with cheese	Lunch or Dinner	482
12	1 submarine sandwich with cold cuts	Lunch or Dinner	456
13	1 hot fudge sundae	Dessert	284
14	1 croissant with egg, cheese, sausage	Breakfast	523
15	1 medium vanilla shake	Beverage	370

Type http://www.nal.usda.gov/fnic/foodcomp/search/ in the *Hyperlink* field for the first record. Copy the URL to the Hyperlink field in the remaining records using a keyboard shortcut. Resize the datasheet columns to fit. Spell-check the datasheet and save it. *Save the table.*

Filter the records to view only those records where the *Meal* is **Breakfast**. With your teacher's permission, preview and print the datasheet. Remove the filter. Close the table without saving it.

Then, using the Simple Query Wizard, create a simple query to list all the records in the table but show only the *FoodType* and *TotalCalories* fields. Save the query as **Calories List**. With your teacher's permission, preview and print the query datasheet. Close the database.

Reviewing the *Windows* Desktop and Using the Mouse

Now, it is time to turn on your computer. Your teacher may modify the following Apply It! instructions, if necessary.

desktop
icon
Internet Explorer
My Computer folder
My Documents folder
notification area
Recycle Bin folder
Start button
taskbar

Be certain to follow all classroom or lab rules when you are working at your school computer. Always respect other students' work that might also be stored on the computer you are using.

Let's turn on your computer.

1. Turn on your computer.

If you must log on to your computer using a password, complete steps 2–4.

2. Press the CTRL + ALT + DELETE keys, if necessary, and type your user name and password. Click the **OK** button.

CHECKPOINT

Your monitor's screen should look similar to this.

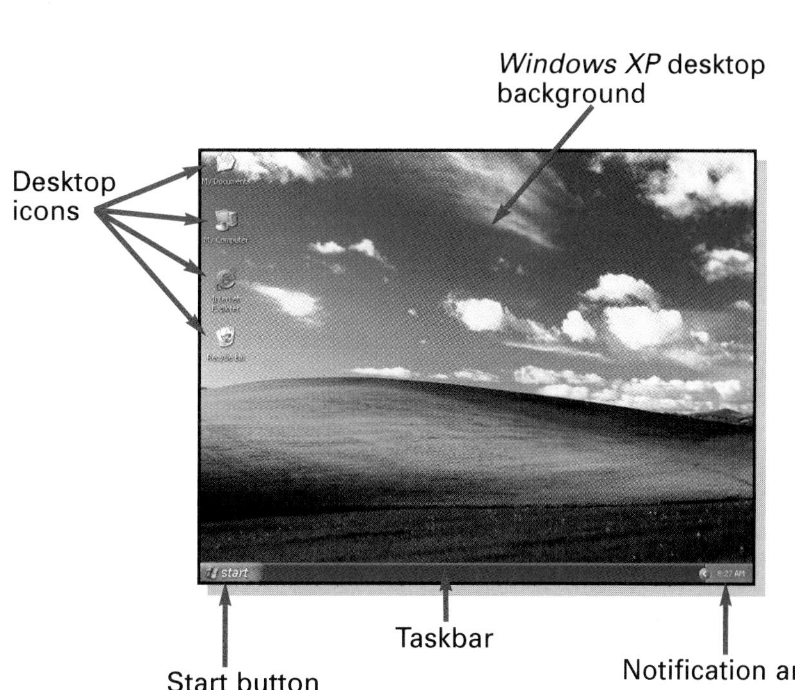

Project | *Skills Review*

You learned a lot in this project! We are very impressed with your progress. Let's take a few minutes to review the skills that you learned.

Create a table in Design view	Double-click the **Create table in Design** view shortcut.
Move from text box to text box in the Fields pane or Field Properties pane to define field properties	Tap the TAB, ENTER, or arrow keys. Click the text box.
Move between the Fields pane and the Field Properties pane to define field properties	Tap the F6 key.
Set the primary key	Select the field name.
Save a new table	Choose **File** on the menu bar and choose **Save As.**
Switch between table Design view and Datasheet view	Choose **View** on the menu bar and choose **Design View** or **Datasheet View.**
Add a new field	Type the field name and set the properties in the Fields and Field Properties panes.
Delete a field	Click the field selector to select the entire field, choose **Edit** on the menu bar, and choose **Delete** or tap the DELETE key.
Filter records by selection and then remove the filter	Move the insertion point into the field to be filtered.
Spell-check a table in Datasheet view	
Create a simple query	

The Windows Desktop

The *Windows* desktop is the work area that covers your monitor's screen after you turn on your computer. The *Windows* desktop has five main elements:

1. a background picture or color that covers the work area
2. the taskbar, which displays a button for each open application
3. the Start button, which opens the Start menu
4. small graphic symbols called icons. An icon can represent an electronic file or folder, or it can represent application software.
5. the notification area or tray, which displays the current time as well as small icons for system software or applications that are running in the computer's background memory.

Always take good care of your diskettes, flash drives, and CDs to make sure you do not damage your stored documents.

The *Windows* desktop can have many different icons. The most common are these: My Documents folder, My Computer folder, Recycle Bin folder, and *Internet Explorer* application icons.

The My Documents folder is used to store documents and other folders. Documents you delete from your hard drive are temporarily stored in the Recycle Bin folder until you permanently delete them. The My Computer folder displays icons that help you locate your computer's resources, such as printers and memory.

By clicking the *Internet Explorer* icon, you can use the Web browser to visit the Internet and view Web pages.

The Start menu contains commands you can use to open folders and to start applications.

The Mouse Pointer

Your mouse is a very useful and important tool. For example, you use it to click a desktop icon to open a folder or to start an application. You also use the mouse to perform tasks inside an application. Moving the mouse on the mouse pad also moves a pointer, called the mouse pointer, across the screen. You use the mouse pointer to *point* to items on the screen.

click
double-click
drag
point
right-click
triple-click

As you work in the projects in this text, you will perform the following basic mouse actions.

3. Click the **Next** button to go to the next wizard step. You can specify a detail list or a summarization of the data in this step. You want a detail list, and the **Detail** option button is selected by default.
4. Click the **Next** button to go to the next wizard steps. Type **Name and Calories** in the **What title do you want for your query?** text box to give the query a name. Click the **Finish** button to complete the wizard process, save the query, and run it.

CHECKPOINT

The results of your *Name and Calories* query should look like this.

Records queried to show only three fields

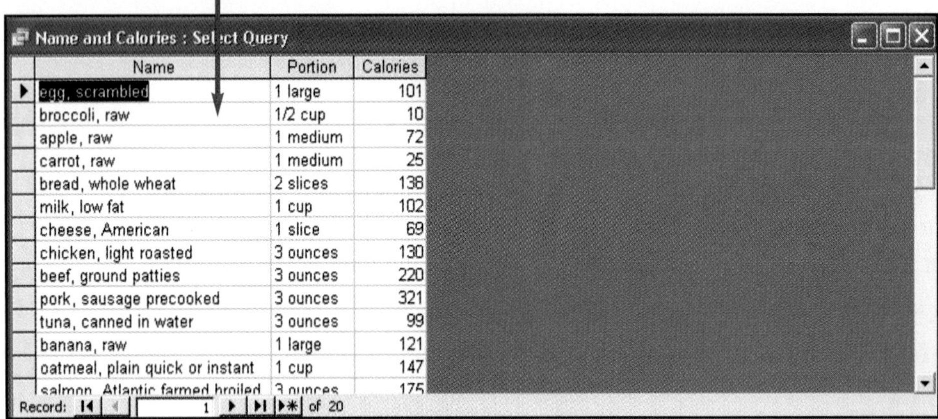
Name and Calories : Select Query

Name	Portion	Calories
egg, scrambled	1 large	101
broccoli, raw	1/2 cup	10
apple, raw	1 medium	72
carrot, raw	1 medium	25
bread, whole wheat	2 slices	138
milk, low fat	1 cup	102
cheese, American	1 slice	69
chicken, light roasted	3 ounces	130
beef, ground patties	3 ounces	220
pork, sausage precooked	3 ounces	321
tuna, canned in water	3 ounces	99
banana, raw	1 large	121
oatmeal, plain quick or instant	1 cup	147
salmon, Atlantic farmed broiled	3 ounces	175

Record: 1 of 20

5. Close the query datasheet. The Name and Calories query is now shown in the Database window. You can run the query again whenever you need to by double-clicking the query name.
6. Double-click the **Name and Calories** query to run the query again. Then close the query datasheet and close the database.

Congratulations! Luis's notes are now organized and ready for use in planning his well-balanced diet.

Mouse Action	Description
Point	Place the mouse pointer on a specific area of the screen.
Click	Point to a specific area on the screen and press the left mouse button once.
Double-click	Point to a specific area on the screen and press the left mouse button twice very quickly.
Triple-click	Point to a specific area on the screen and press the left mouse button three times very quickly.
Right-click	Point to a specific area on the screen and press the right mouse button once.
Drag	Press and hold down the left mouse button and move the mouse pointer across the screen.

Fantastic! Now, let's use the *Windows* desktop and the mouse pointer to work with windows and folders.

TRAIL 4 MARKER

Working with Windows and Folders

file
folder

All the documents that you create on your computer can be saved electronically as files on diskettes, a CD, a flash drive, your computer's hard drive, or on a network server.

It is important to keep your files organized so that you can easily find them. To organize your files, store them in electronic folders. An electronic folder is similar to a paper folder that fits inside a file cabinet drawer; you can store many electronic files within one electronic folder.

Let's check out the My Documents folder. To open the folder, double-click the My Documents folder icon on the *Windows* desktop or click the My Documents folder icon on the Start menu.

Creating a Query Using the Simple Query Wizard

query
Simple Query Wizard

Luis wants to print a datasheet that lists only the *FoodName*, *PortionSize*, and *Calories* fields for all the records in the *Food Values* table. You can create a database query object to do this. A query is an object that looks at the records in a table and then displays only those records that meet specific criteria. Queries are very powerful and you can create queries in many different ways. But when you want a simple query—such as one that lists only two or three fields for all the records in a table—use the Simple Query Wizard.

Similar to the Table Wizard you learned to use in Project 17, the Simple Query Wizard is a step-by-step process that allows you identify a table and then specify individual fields in that table to be shown in a query datasheet. To start the Simple Query Wizard, first select a table in the Database window. Then click the **New Object** button drop-down arrow on the Database toolbar and choose **Query** to open the **New Query** dialog box. In the dialog box, double-click **Simple Query Wizard** to start the wizard.

Did you know? Executing a query is called *running the query*! After you save a query object, you can run it again as often as needed.

Let's use the Simple Query Wizard to create a query that lists only the *FoodName*, *PortionSize*, and *Calories* fields in the *Food Values* table.

1. Select the *Food Values* table in the Database window, if necessary. Click the **New Object** button drop-down arrow and choose **Query**. Double-click **Simple Query Wizard** in the **New Query** dialog box. The Simple Query Wizard opens. The first step is to select the fields from the *Food Values* table to be listed by the query.
2. Double-click the **FoodName**, **PortionSize**, and **Calories** field names in the **Available Fields** list to add each field to the **Selected Fields** list.

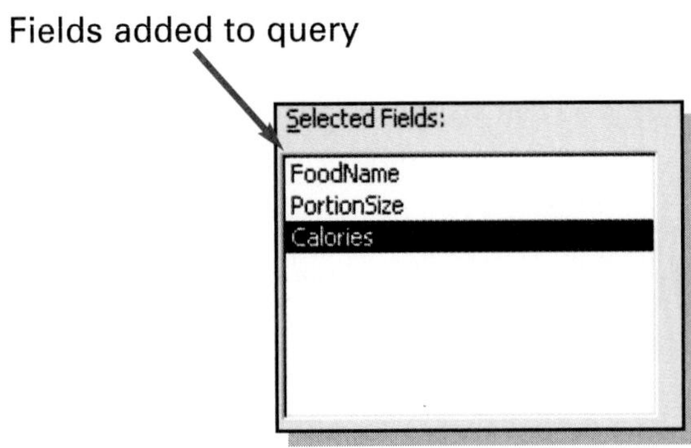

Let's open the My Documents folder.

1. Point to the **My Documents** folder on the *Windows* desktop.
2. Double-click the **My Documents** folder icon.

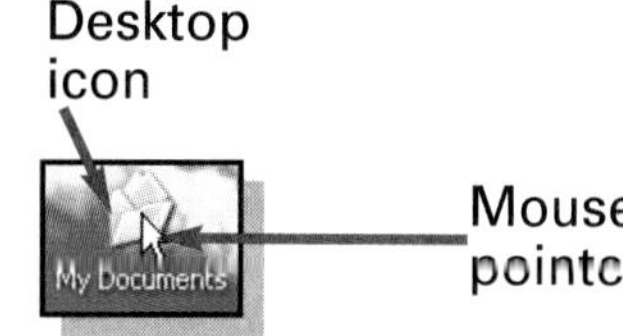

The My Documents folder opens in a window on the desktop. Let's see how we can use the mouse pointer to hide, show, and resize the My Documents window.

Hiding, Showing, and Resizing a Window

A window is a special area on the desktop in which files, folders, and applications are opened. Open desktop windows share these common features:

- Title bar—shows the name of the window
- Minimize button—hides the window
- Maximize button—sizes the window so that it covers the entire desktop
- Restore Down button—sizes the window smaller
- Close button—closes the window
- Taskbar button—unhides a hidden window

Close button
Maximize button
Minimize button
Restore Down button
taskbar button
title bar
window

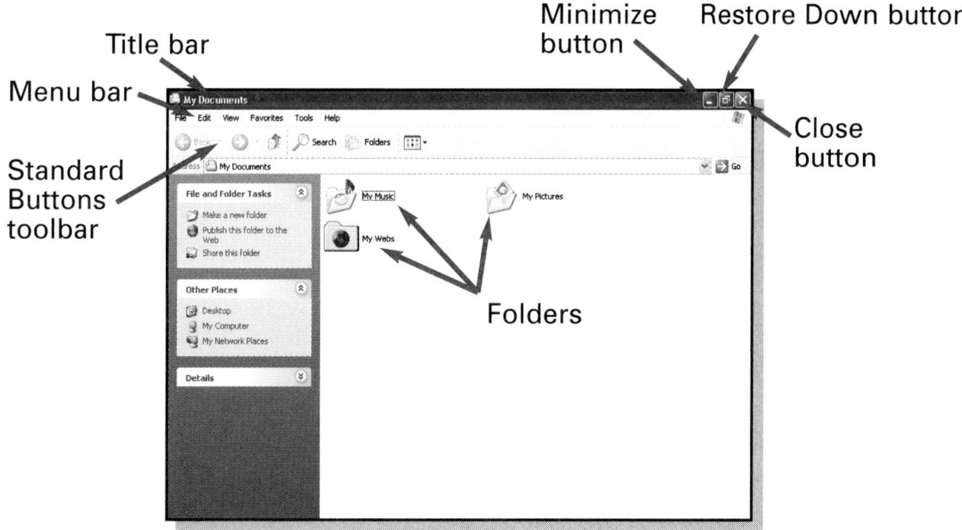

An open window also has a button on the taskbar. Use a taskbar button to unhide a hidden window or switch between open windows. Desktop windows can be hidden, unhidden, and resized using the mouse pointer.

TRAIL 4 MARKER

Filtering Records by Selection

filter
filtering by selection

In the *Excel* unit, you learned how to filter a list to see specific records. You can also filter a table in Datasheet view to find all the records that have the same data in a specific field. This is called filtering by selection. For example, suppose you want to see only the records in the *Grains* category. To filter the table to show only those records in the *Grains* category, move the insertion point into the *Category* field for any record that has the word *Grains* in the field. This selects the data on which the records are to be filtered. Then click the **Filter by Selection** button on the Table Datasheet toolbar.

To see all the records again, you must remove the filter by clicking the **Remove Filter** button on the Table Datasheet toolbar. Applying a filter to a table changes the table's design to add the filter. When you close the table, you are prompted to save the design changes. In this project, *do not* save the table after you filter it.

Apply It!

Let's filter the records and then remove the filter.

1. Click the **Category** field for record 5, whole wheat bread. This record has *Grains* as the category.
2. Click the **Filter by Selection** button on the Table Datasheet toolbar. 

CHECKPOINT
Your filtered data should look like this.

Table filtered to show records in Grains category

Food Values : Table

	Record ID	Name	Food Category	Portion	Calories	Source	Link
▶	5	bread, whole wheat	Grains	2 slices	138	USDA	www.nal.usda.gov/fnic/foodcomp
	13	oatmeal, plain quick or instant	Grains	1 cup	147	USDA	www.nal.usda.gov/fnic/foodcomp
	17	rice, white	Grains	1 cup	169	USDA	www.nal.usda.gov/fnic/foodcomp
	18	pasta, spaghetti cooked	Grains	3 ounces	112	USDA	www.nal.usda.gov/fnic/foodcomp
*	ıtoNumber)				0	USDA	

3. Click the **Remove Filter** button to view all the records.
4. Filter the table to see all the records in the **Dairy** category. Then remove the filter and close the table *without saving* it.

Nice work! Now let's find specific information in the *Food Values* table by querying it.

Let's hide, unhide, and resize the My Documents window.

1. Click the **Minimize** button on the My Documents window title bar to hide the window. The window is still open, but it is hidden, or minimized, to a button on the taskbar.
2. Click the **My Documents** button on the taskbar to unhide the window. The window is again visible on the desktop.
3. Click the **Restore Down** button on the My Documents window title bar to size the window smaller.
4. Click the Maximize button on the title bar to size the window larger so that it covers the entire desktop.

If a window is not maximized, you can resize and reposition it. To resize a window, drag the top, bottom, left, or right edge of the window with the black double-headed arrow mouse pointer. To reposition a window, drag the window's title bar with the mouse pointer.

Great! Now, let's practice creating and deleting a folder inside the My Documents window.

Creating and Deleting Folders

Sometimes you want to organize your files by placing them in a folder inside another folder. For example, you might want to place all the school reports you create on your computer in a folder named *Reports* inside the My Documents folder.

To create a folder inside the My Documents folder, choose **File** on the My Documents window menu bar, point to **New**, and choose **Folder**.

Let's create a new folder inside the My Documents folder.

1. Choose **File** on the menu bar, point to **New**, and choose **Folder**. Type **Reports** in the **folder name** text box and tap the ENTER key.
2. Click in the white area away from the new folder icon.

Your new *Reports* folder icon and name should look like this.

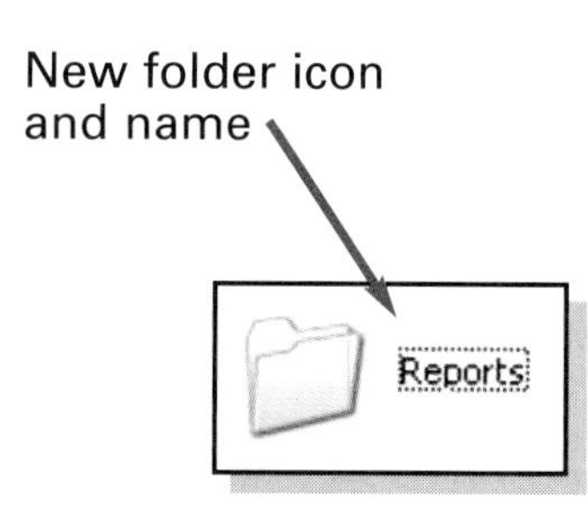

Luis used the same website source for all his data. Instead of typing the website's URL in the Link field in each record, you can type it in the first record's Link field and then copy it to the remaining records using a keyboard shortcut.

2. Move the insertion point into the **Link** field for record 1, scrambled egg. Type www.nal.usda.gov/fnic/foodcomp/ and tap the **Down** arrow. Resize the column to fit.
3. Press the CTRL + apostrophe (') keys to copy the URL from the previous entry to the current field. Tap the **Down** arrow. Copy the URL to the remaining records using the CTRL + apostrophe keyboard shortcut keys.
4. Click the **Spelling** button on the Table Datasheet toolbar and make any necessary spelling corrections. Save the table.

Your datasheet should now look like this.

Named and saved table with data

Food Values : Table

Record ID	Name	Food Category	Portion	Calories	Source	Link
1	egg, scrambled	Poultry	1 large	101	USDA	www.nal.usda.gov/fnic/foodcomp
2	broccoli, raw	Vegetables	1/2 cup	10	USDA	www.nal.usda.gov/fnic/foodcomp
3	apple, raw	Fruit	1 medium	72	USDA	www.nal.usda.gov/fnic/foodcomp
4	carrot, raw	Vegetables	1 medium	25	USDA	www.nal.usda.gov/fnic/foodcomp
5	bread, whole wheat	Grains	2 slices	138	USDA	www.nal.usda.gov/fnic/foodcomp
6	milk, low fat	Dairy	1 cup	102	USDA	www.nal.usda.gov/fnic/foodcomp
7	cheese, American	Dairy	1 slice	69	USDA	www.nal.usda.gov/fnic/foodcomp
8	chicken, light roasted	Poultry	3 ounces	130	USDA	www.nal.usda.gov/fnic/foodcomp
9	beef, ground patties	Beef and Pork	3 ounces	220	USDA	www.nal.usda.gov/fnic/foodcomp
10	pork, sausage precooked	Beef and Pork	3 ounces	321	USDA	www.nal.usda.gov/fnic/foodcomp
11	tuna, canned in water	Fish	3 ounces	99	USDA	www.nal.usda.gov/fnic/foodcomp
12	banana, raw	Fruit	1 large	121	USDA	www.nal.usda.gov/fnic/foodcomp
13	oatmeal, plain quick or instant	Grains	1 cup	147	USDA	www.nal.usda.gov/fnic/foodcomp
14	salmon, Atlantic farmed broiled	Fish	3 ounces	175	USDA	www.nal.usda.gov/fnic/foodcomp
15	chicken, breast fried	Poultry	1/2 large	364	USDA	www.nal.usda.gov/fnic/foodcomp
16	orange juice, unsweetened	Fruit	1 cup	110	USDA	www.nal.usda.gov/fnic/foodcomp
17	rice, white	Grains	1 cup	169	USDA	www.nal.usda.gov/fnic/foodcomp
18	pasta, spaghetti cooked	Grains	3 ounces	112	USDA	www.nal.usda.gov/fnic/foodcomp
19	spinach, cooked	Vegetables	1/2 cup	21	USDA	www.nal.usda.gov/fnic/foodcomp
20	milk, chocolate whole fat	Dairy	1 cup	208	USDA	www.nal.usda.gov/fnic/foodcomp
utoNumber)				0	USDA	

Record: 1 of 20

What a terrific effort! All the records are now entered in the table. Let's filter the table to view specific records.

When you no longer need the *Reports* folder, you can delete it. A quick way to delete a folder is with a shortcut menu. A **shortcut menu** is a brief list of commands. To open a shortcut menu, right-click the folder or item.

To delete the *Reports* folder, right-click the folder icon and choose **Delete** on the shortcut menu. When you choose **Delete**, a dialog box opens. A **dialog box** generally asks you a question or provides options you can choose to continue your task.

You can also delete a file inside a folder by right-clicking the file's icon and choosing **Delete** on the shortcut menu.

How can you tell the difference between a window and a dialog box? Unlike a window, a dialog box *does not* have **Minimize**, **Maximize**, or **Restore Down** buttons on its title bar!

The dialog box that opens when you delete a file or folder asks you to confirm your deletion. This confirmation helps make sure that you do not accidentally delete the wrong file or folder!

Let's delete the new *Reports* folder using a shortcut menu.

1. Right-click the **Reports** folder icon in the My Documents window. Choose **Delete** to open the **Confirm Folder Delete** dialog box.
2. Click **Yes** to confirm your deletion.

Choose **View** on the menu bar, point to **Toolbars**, and choose **Standard Buttons** to see the toolbar, if necessary.

As you work on your computer, you will likely create many files and folders. Occasionally, you may need help in finding a specific file or folder.

Finding Files and Folders

In the projects in this text, you will either create and save a new document or you will open and work on an existing document, called a **data file**. Your teacher will place your data files in a folder on your computer's hard drive or network drive.

data file
dialog box
shortcut menu

You can search for your data files folder by clicking the **Search** button on the Standard Buttons toolbar in the My Documents folder window.

Don't worry if you accidentally delete an item from your hard drive! Items deleted from the *hard drive* are temporarily stored in the **Recycle Bin** folder. You can double-click the **Recycle Bin** folder to open it. Then right-click the deleted item and click **Restore**.

Let's add records to the table.

1. Click the **View** button face on the Table Design toolbar to switch to Datasheet view. Enter the following records in the table's datasheet. Because the Source field has a default value (USDA) you will not enter data in the field. You will add the URL to the Link field in later steps. Resize the columns to fit after you enter the data.

Record ID	Name	Category	Portion	Calories
1	egg, scrambled	Poultry	1 large	101
2	broccoli, raw	Vegetables	1/2 cup	10
3	apple, raw	Fruit	1 medium	72
4	carrot, raw	Vegetables	1 medium	25
5	bread, whole wheat	Grains	2 slices	138
6	milk, low fat	Dairy	1 cup	102
7	cheese, American	Dairy	1 slice	69
8	chicken, light roasted	Poultry	3 ounces	130
9	beef, ground patties	Beef and Pork	3 ounces	220
10	pork, sausage precooked	Beef and Pork	3 ounces	321
11	tuna, canned in water	Fish	3 ounces	99
12	banana, raw	Fruit	1 large	121
13	oatmeal, plain quick or instant	Grains	1 cup	147
14	salmon, Atlantic farmed broiled	Fish	3 ounces	175
15	chicken, breast fried	Poultry	1/2 large	364
16	orange juice, unsweetened	Fruit	1 cup	110
17	rice, white cooked	Grains	1 cup	169
18	pasta, spaghetti cooked	Grains	3 ounces	112
19	spinach, cooked	Vegetables	1/2 cup	21
20	milk, chocolate whole fat	Dairy	1 cup	208

Let's find your data files. Before you begin, make sure that the My Documents folder is still open.

1. Click the **Search** button.
2. Click **All Files and Folders** in the **Search Companion** pane on the left side of the window.
3. Type the name of your data files folder in the **All or part of the file name** text box. (Your teacher will tell you the name of the folder.) Click the **Look in:** drop-down arrow and click the folder that contains your data files folder. Your teacher will tell you where to look.
4. Click **Search** on the **Search Companion** pane.

CHECKPOINT

Your search results should look similar to this.

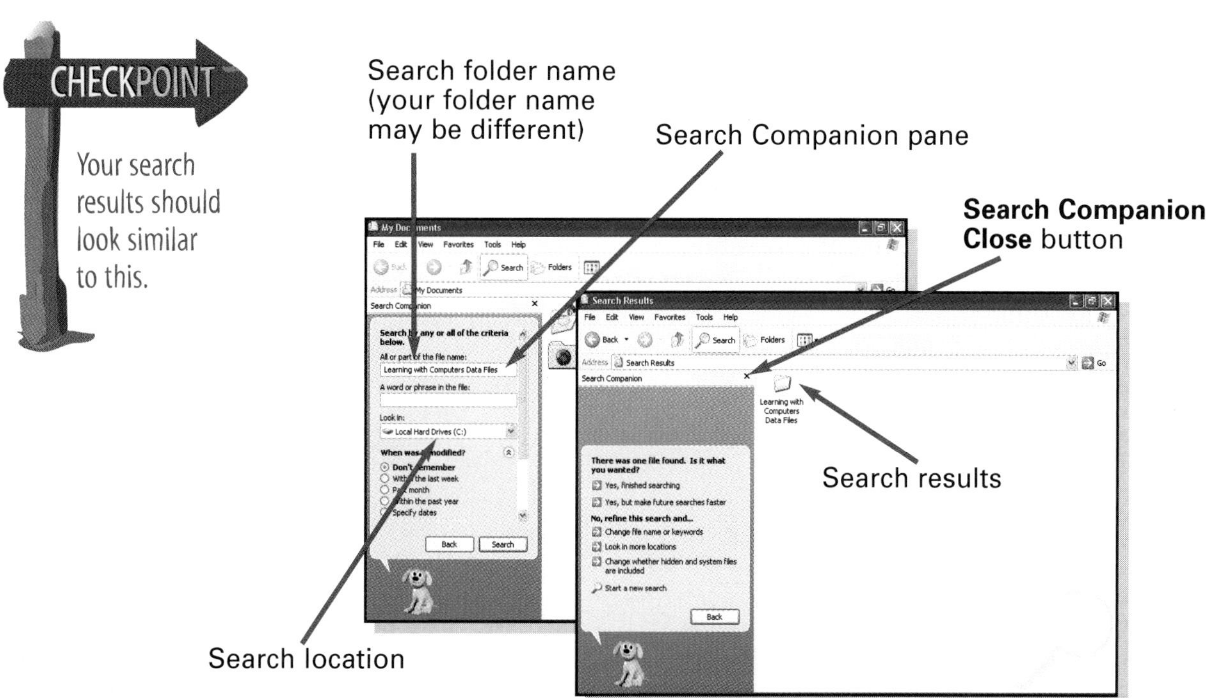

5. Click the **Close** button on the **Search Companion** pane. Double-click the folder icon to see the data files. Click the **Close** button on the window's title bar.

Fantastic! Now you are ready to learn about the Internet, the World Wide Web, and Web pages.

Warning! Be careful adding or deleting fields *after* you enter records in the table. Deleting a field also deletes all the data entered in that field! Adding fields means you must update existing records with the new data.

Luis has decided not to use the **Description** field. To delete the **Description** field, click the field selector button to the left of the field name and tap the DELETE key. Remember to save the changes to your table after you add or delete a field!

Apply It!

Let's add a new field with a Hyperlink data type and delete the Description field.

1. Click in the first blank text box in the **Field Name** column and type **SourceURL**. Tap the TAB key. Change the data type to **Hyperlink**. Switch to the Field Properties pane and add **Link** as the caption. Then switch back to the Fields pane.
2. Click the **Field selector** button to the left of the **Description** field name to select the entire field and tap the DELETE key. The **Description** field is removed from the table.
3. Click the **RecordID** field name to position the insertion point.

   Click the **Save** button on the Table Design toolbar. 

You can also delete a field in Design view by selecting the field, choosing **Edit** on the menu bar, and choosing **Delete** or right-clicking the field and choosing **Delete Row**.

CHECKPOINT
Your Fields pane should look like this.

Description field is deleted

Food Values : Table

Field Name	Data Type
RecordID	AutoNumber
FoodName	Text
CategoryName	Text
PortionSize	Text
Calories	Number
Source	Text
SourceURL	Hyperlink

New field added to Fields pane

Nice job! Now you are ready to switch to Datasheet view and enter the records in the table.

Exploring a Web Page

TRAIL 5 MARKER

Address bar
browser home page
favorite
Go button
home page
hyperlink
Internet
link
URL (Uniform Resource Locator)
Web
Web browser
Web page
website
World Wide Web

The Internet is a worldwide network that links computers together. The World Wide Web, sometimes just called the Web, is a part of the Internet. The Web consists of servers that store multimedia documents containing text, pictures, sound, and animation. These documents are called Web pages.

A group of related Web pages that are stored together is called a website. The primary Web page at a website is called its home page.

You can view Web pages by using application software called a Web browser. The two most popular Web browsers are *Microsoft Internet Explorer* and *Netscape Navigator*. It is likely that one of these two browsers is available on your computer.

The Apply It! activities in this project assume that you are using the *Internet Explorer* browser. If you are using a different browser, your teacher may modify the steps.

When you open a Web browser application, the browser's starting Web page, called the browser home page, is visible in the browser window. To view a different Web page, you type its address, called a Uniform Resource Locator, or URL, in the browser's Address bar and tap the ENTER key or click the Go button. The new Web page then opens in the browser window.

Web pages are connected by hyperlinks. A Web page hyperlink, often just called a link, is text or a picture that you click with the mouse to *jump* to another page.

Stay safe! Only view Web pages approved by your teacher or parents. Never enter any personal information on a Web page you might visit and never exchange personal information with others you might meet online.

Let's start the Web browser and view a Web page.

1. Double-click your Web browser icon on the desktop or use the **Start** menu to open your Web browser. Your teacher will help you find your Web browser icon, if necessary.
2. Type www.lwcgreen.keyboarding.com/ in the **Address bar** and tap the ENTER key.

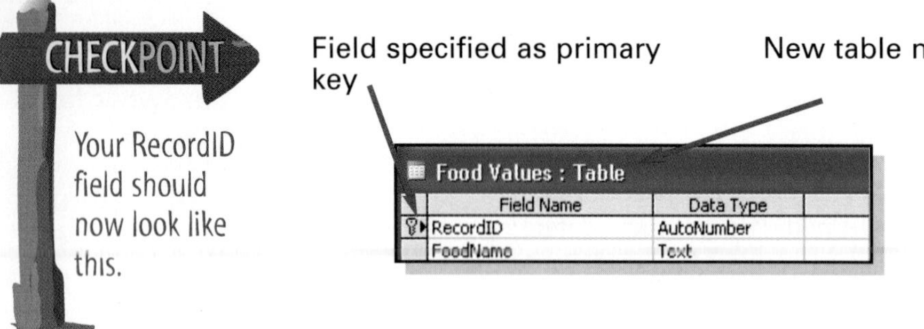

When working in a table in Design view, the default option for the **View** button on the Table Design toolbar is Datasheet view.

Well done! To see the new table you created, let's switch to Datasheet view.

Let's switch to Datasheet view, and then return to Design view.

1. Click the **View** button face on the Table Design toolbar.

   You are now viewing the new table in Datasheet view. Look carefully at the **View** button on the Table Datasheet toolbar. When you are working in a table in Datasheet view, the default option for the **View** button is Design view.
2. Click the **View** button face on the Table Design toolbar to switch back to Design view.

Great! Now let's modify the table by adding a new field and deleting an existing field.

TRAIL 3 MARKER

Adding and Deleting Fields in Design View

You can add a new field to a table by clicking the first blank text box in the Fields pane and then typing the field name, specifying the data type, and setting the field's other properties. If you want to insert a new field above an existing field, select the existing field's row and click the **Insert Rows** button on the Table Design toolbar. Then type the field name and set its other properties. Luis wants to be able to click a hyperlink to view his online sources' websites whenever he opens the new table in Datasheet view. To do this, you must add the following new field with a Hyperlink data type.

Field Name	Data Type	Field Size	Caption	Default Value
SourceURL	Hyperlink	N/A	Link	None

Another way to switch between Design view and Datasheet view is to choose **View** on the menu bar and then choose **Design View** or **Datasheet View**.

Your Web browser window should look similar to this.

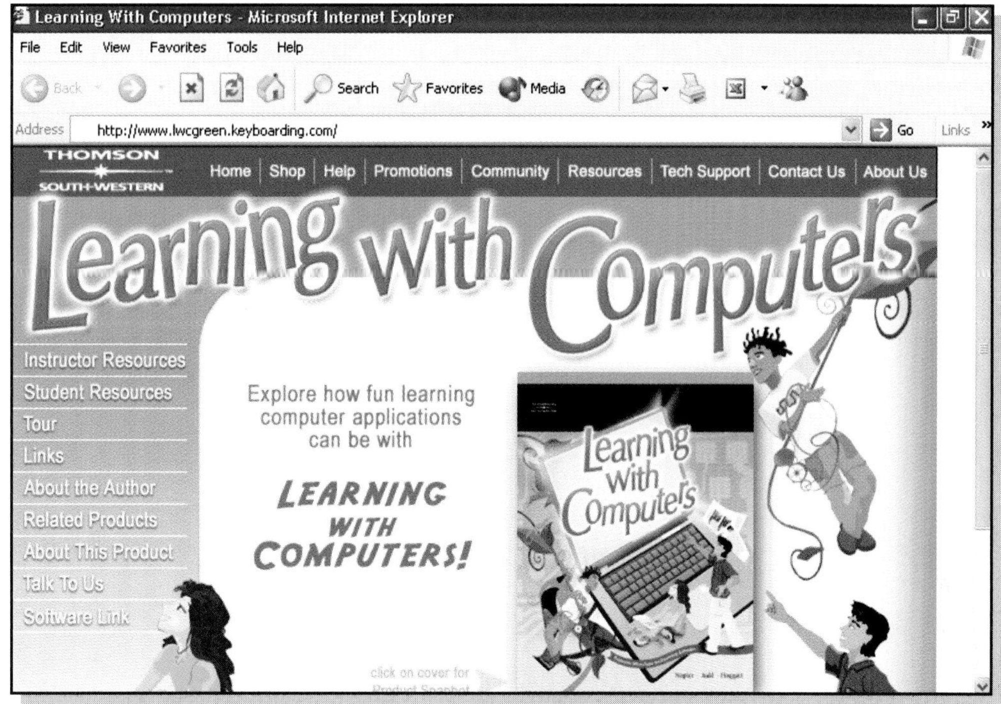

3. Click the **Links** option. Click the **Getting Started** link. Click the links to learn about the history of computers.

Use the **Back** and **Forward** buttons on the Web browser's toolbar to revisit recently viewed Web pages. Try it!

When you find a Web page that you want to return to at another time, you can save it as a favorite. A favorite is the URL and name of a Web page you visit frequently. To create a favorite, choose **Favorites** on the menu bar. Then choose **Add to Favorites.**

8. Switch back to the Fields pane and add the **Source** field with the **Text** data type. Switch to the Field Properties pane, type **20** in the **Field Size** text box, and tap the ENTER key four times to move the insertion point into the **Default Value** text box. Type **USDA** and tap the F6 key.

CHECKPOINT

Your completed Fields pane should look like this.

Completed Fields pane

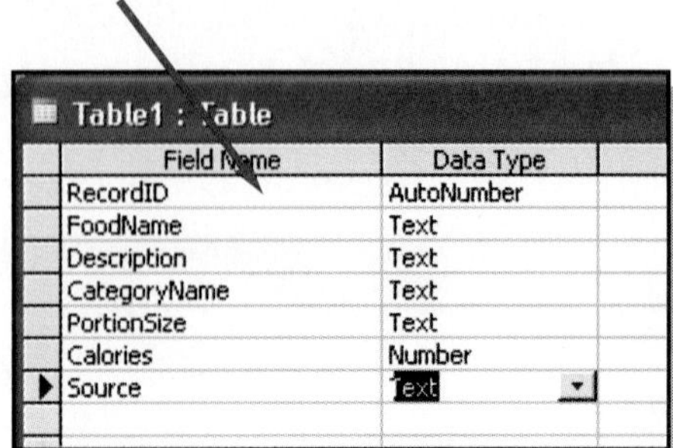
Table1 : Table

Field Name	Data Type
RecordID	AutoNumber
FoodName	Text
Description	Text
CategoryName	Text
PortionSize	Text
Calories	Number
Source	Text

Fantastic! Now you need to set the table's primary key.

Setting the Primary Key, Saving the Table, and Changing Views

In the previous project, you learned that each record in the table has a unique identifier called its primary key. You allowed *Access* to set the primary key for you when you created a table using the Table Wizard.

When you create a table in Design view, you can let Access set the primary key when you save the table or you can manually set the primary key by selecting a field and clicking the **Primary Key** button on the Table Design toolbar.

A Help tip appears in the lower-right corner of the Field Properties pane when you move to a text box in the Fields or Field Properties pane. For extra Help, you can tap the F1 key. Check it out!

Let's set RecordID as the primary key and save the table.

1. Click the **RecordID** field name text box to position the insertion point in the field name. Then click the **Primary Key** button on the Table Design toolbar. The primary key icon appears in the **Field selector** button to the left of the field name.
2. Click the **Save** button on the Table Design toolbar to open the **Save As** dialog box. Type **Food Values** in the **Table Name** text box and click the **OK** button.

Web pages are full of useful information. But you should always carefully review any information you find on a Web and make certain you can confirm the information from multiple sources before you use it.

Let's save the *Learning with Computers* Web page as a favorite.

1. Click the **Back** button to view the *Learning with Computers* Web page.
2. Choose **Favorites** on the menu bar and choose **Add to Favorites**.

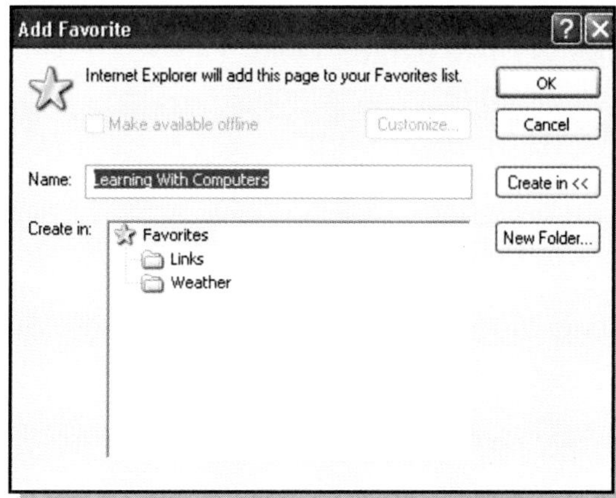

3. Click the **OK** button to save the page as a favorite.

The next time you want to visit the *Learning with Computers* page, just choose **Favorites** on the menu bar and then choose the *Learning with Computers* favorite in the **Favorites** list.

TRAIL 6 MARKER

Sending and Receiving E-mail

Another very popular Internet feature is electronic mail, or e-mail. You can very quickly correspond with a friend, family member, or teacher by sending an e-mail message to an electronic mail box using an e-mail address.

An e-mail address has three parts:

- The name of the person using the mail box, called the user name.
- The @ symbol, which stands for *at*.
- The name of the computer where the user's mail box is stored, called the host name.

e-mail
e-mail address
e-mail etiquette
host name
user name

Apply It!

Let's add the RecordID field with an AutoNumber data type.

1. Type **RecordID** in the first blank text box in the **Field Name** column; then tap the TAB key to move to the **Data Type** column. Click the **Data Type** drop-down arrow to view the available data types; then click **AutoNumber**.
2. Tap the F6 key to move the insertion point into the first text box in the Field Properties pane, the **Field Size** property. The default Field Size property for the AutoNumber data type is **Long Integer**, which means that the field size can be a very large positive or negative number. *Do not* change the default Field Size property for the AutoNumber data type.
3. Tap the ENTER key three times to move to the **Caption** text box and then type **Record ID**. *Don't forget to type the space.*
4. Tap the F6 key to move the insertion point back into the Fields pane. Tap the TAB key twice to move the insertion point to the second blank text box in the **Field Name** column.

CHECKPOINT
The first field in the Fields pane should look like this.

New field added to table

Table1 : Table

Field Name	Data Type
RecordID	AutoNumber

Let's continue by defining the remaining fields.

5. Type **FoodName** in the second blank text box in the **Field Name** column. Tap the TAB key. The default **Text** data type is automatically selected. Tap the F6 key. Move the insertion point into the Caption field and type **Name**. Tap the F6 key to return to the Fields pane. Tap the TAB key twice.
6. Using the previous steps and Luis's notes as your guide, add the **Description**, **CategoryName**, and **PortionSize** fields.
7. Add the **Calories** field with the **Number** data type. Switch to the Field Properties pane and tap the ENTER key twice to move the insertion point into the **Decimal Places** text box. Click the **Decimal Places** text box drop-down arrow (on the right edge of the text box) and click **0** in the list to set zero decimal places.

Here is an example of an e-mail address.

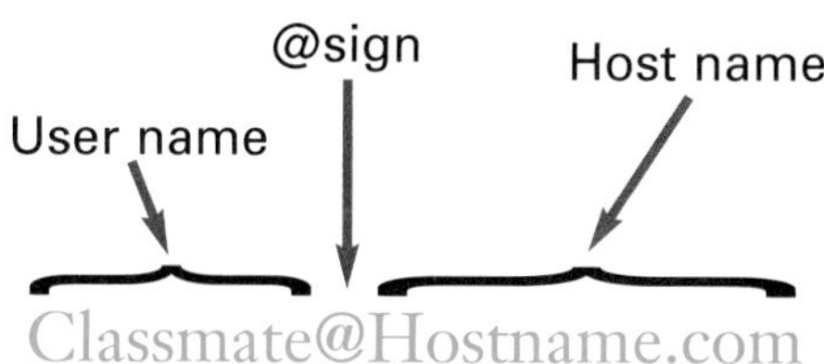

Classmate@Hostname.com

When you are sending or receiving an e-mail message, you should remember a few simple rules of good behavior, called **e-mail etiquette**. Let's share some e-mail etiquette rules with a friend or classmate! With your teacher's permission, send a classmate or friend an e-mail message listing a few e-mail etiquette rules.

The following Apply It! steps assume you are using *Outlook Express* as your e-mail application. If you are using a different e-mail application, your teacher will modify the steps.

Let's send an e-mail message.

1. Open your e-mail application using the **Start** menu or a desktop icon. Your teacher will tell you the name of your e-mail application. Your e-mail application window should look something like this.

Create Mail button

Send/Recv button

Inbox folder to store incoming messages

Outbox folder to temporarily store outgoing messages

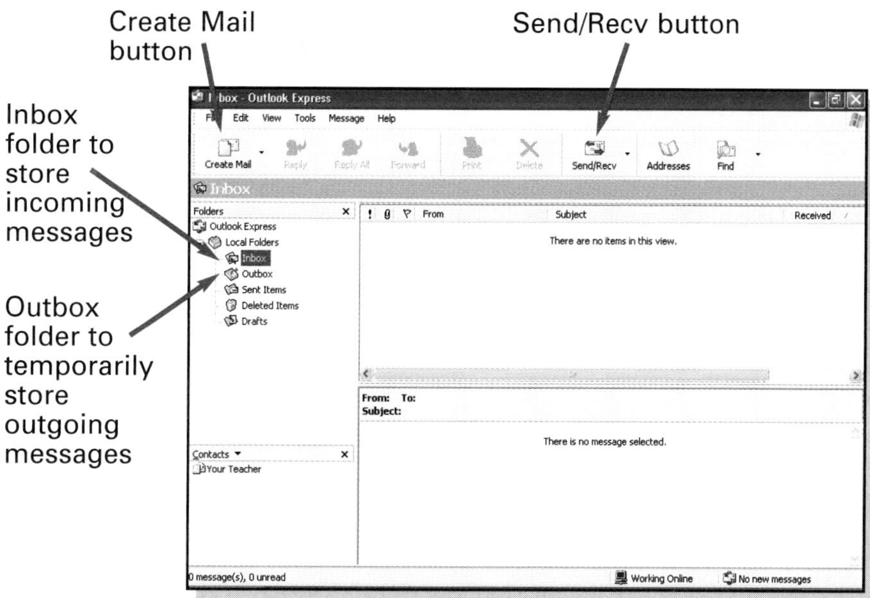

You should think carefully about the data to be stored in the table before you begin to create it. Write down each field name, the type and size of the data to be entered in the field, and any other field properties you want to set. Luis organized his notes into table fields and gave you the following information:

Field Name	Data Type	Field Size	Caption	Default Value
RecordID	AutoNumber	Long Integer	Record ID	N/A
FoodName	Text	50 characters	Name	None
Description	Text	50 characters	None	None
CategoryName	Text	15 characters	Food Category	None
PortionSize	Text	15 characters	Portion	None
Calories	Number	Long Integer, zero decimal places	None	None
Source	Text	20 characters	None	USDA

To create the fields for the table, you type the field name and select the data type in the Fields pane. The default data type for each field is Text. To change the data type, click the **Data Type** drop-down arrow in the Fields pane and click a different data type.

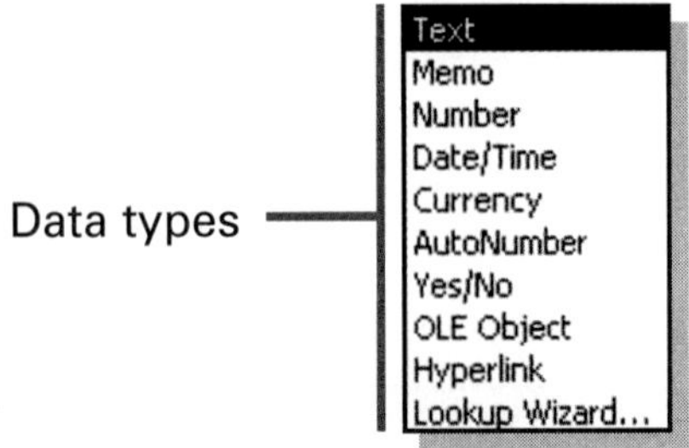

Next, switch to the Field Properties pane by tapping the F6 key and change the Field Size property, if necessary, by entering a different number of characters in the Field Size text box; type a caption or default value in their respective text boxes, if required. Move the insertion point from text box to text box in the Fields pane or the Field Properties pane by clicking a text box or by tapping the TAB, ENTER, or arrow keys.

2. Click the **Create Mail** button on the toolbar to open the **New Message** window.

3. Type the e-mail address of a classmate or friend in the **To** text box. (Your teacher may tell you the e-mail address to use.) Tap the TAB key twice to move to the **Subject** text box. Type **E-mail Etiquette**. Tap the TAB key once to move to the message area. Type the message just as you see it in the following figure. Type your name instead of *Student Name* at the end of the message.

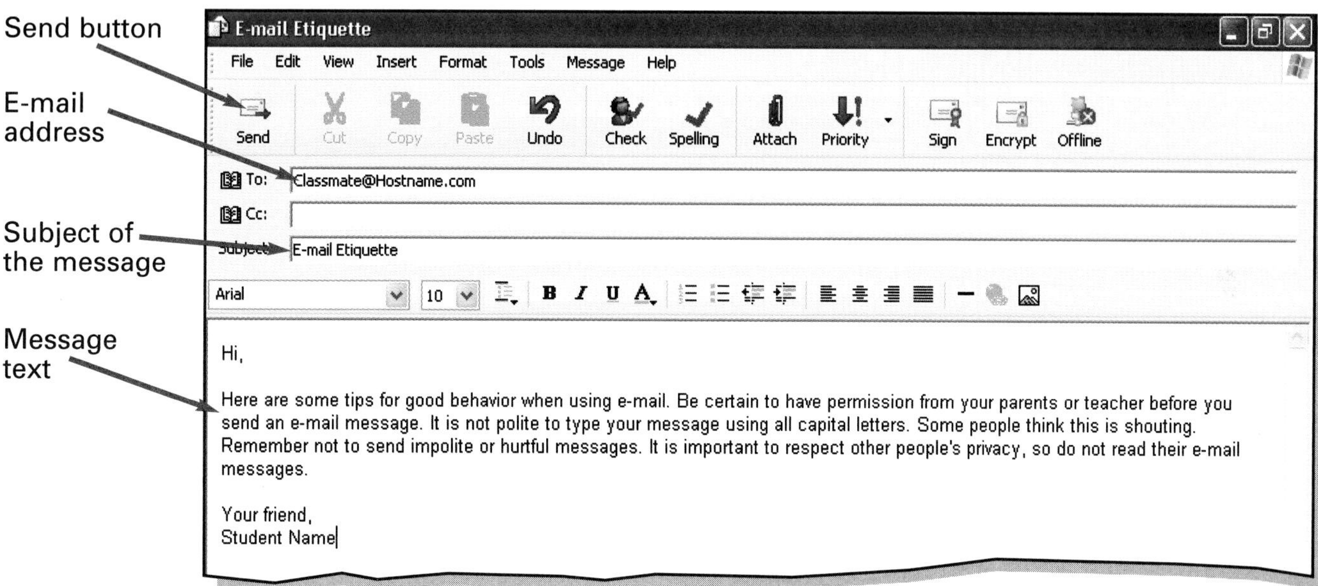

Send button
E-mail address
Subject of the message
Message text
E-mail Etiquette
File Edit View Insert Format Tools Message Help
Send Cut Copy Paste Undo Check Spelling Attach Priority Sign Encrypt Offline
To: Classmate@Hostname.com
Cc:
E-mail Etiquette
Arial 10
Hi,
Here are some tips for good behavior when using e-mail. Be certain to have permission from your parents or teacher before you send an e-mail message. It is not polite to type your message using all capital letters. Some people think this is shouting. Remember not to send impolite or hurtful messages. It is important to respect other people's privacy, so do not read their e-mail messages.
Your friend,
Student Name

4. Click the **Send** button on the toolbar.

You can check for new e-mail messages at any time. Messages you receive from others are stored in the Inbox folder. You can see the Inbox folder and its contents when you open your e-mail application.

To quickly answer an e-mail message, click the **Reply** button on the toolbar. The e-mail address of the person who sent you the message is automatically placed in the **To** box. The **Subject** box automatically fills in. Just type your reply and send it!

Let's check for new e-mail messages.

1. Click the **Send/Recv** button on the toolbar.
2. Look in the message area for any new messages. Double-click a message to open and read it. Click the **Close** button on the message window title bar.
3. Click the **Close** button on the e-mail application title bar.

Congratulations! You are ready to begin exploring!

Another way to create a table in Design view is to view the table objects and double-click the **Create table in Design view** new object shortcut.

The Field Name, Data Type, and Field Size properties must be set for every field. The Caption and Default Value properties are set as needed.

You work back and forth between two panes—the Fields pane and the Field Properties pane—when you create a table in Design view. Use the **Fields pane** to set the Field Name and Data Type properties. Use the **Field Properties pane** to specify the field's other properties, such as Field Size or Caption.

To create a table in Design view in an empty database, view the table objects in the Database window and click the **Design** button on the Database window toolbar. Then add fields to the table, identify the primary key, and save the table inside the database.

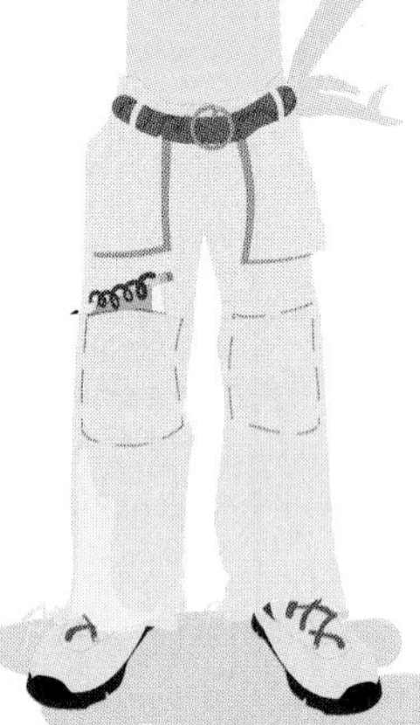

Let's create a table in Design view.

1. View the table objects in the Database window, if necessary, to see that currently there are no tables in the database.
2. Click the **Design View** button on the Database window toolbar. A new, blank table temporarily named *Table1* opens in Design view. The first row in the Fields pane is active and the insertion point is in the first blank text box in the Field Name column.

CHECKPOINT

Your new, blank table in Design view should look like this.

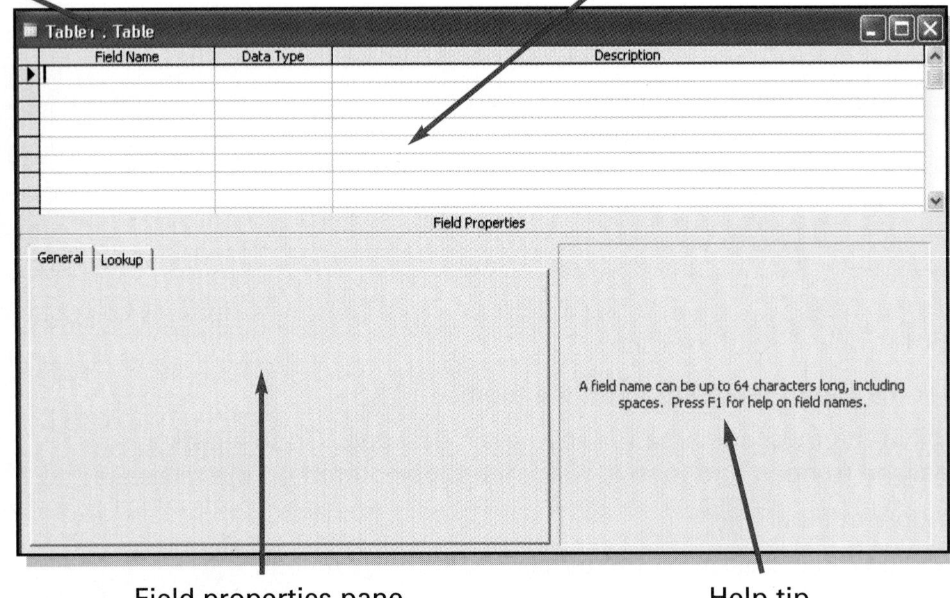

Word Processing

Unit 1

Welcome to the Explorers Club! Are you ready to join us as we examine some great accomplishments by people throughout time? Fantastic! Come with us to:

* Explore the Great Wall of China
* Sail into Edo Bay with Commodore Perry
* Tour Shakespeare's Globe
* Explore Greek Mythology
* Battle Antarctica with Shackleton
* Balance the Three Branches of Government

As you explore these great adventures in history, you will learn to use a word processing application called *Word* to create letters and multipage reports with cover sheets, endnotes, and footnotes. You will learn how to organize information in outlines, tables, tabbed columns, and newspaper columns. You will also learn how to create an eye-catching infographic with colored fonts and borders, symbols, text boxes, pictures, and WordArt. Let's go!

Starting *Out*!

Begin by starting the *Access* application and then creating and saving a new database.

1. Start the *Access* application, if necessary, create a new database, and save it as *nutrition18*.

Super! Let's create a table object from scratch and save it in the empty *nutrition18* database.

Ergonomics *TIP*

Need a break? Stand, stretch, roll, and flex to relax your muscles when you have been working at the computer for a long time! Now you are relaxed and ready to go!

TRAIL 1 MARKER

Creating a Table in Design View

In the previous project you used the Table Wizard to create a new table from predefined fields taken from sample tables. You can also create a table by manually defining each field in Design view.

Defining a field means to set the field's special characteristics, called field properties. For example, you must name the field; specify what type of data can be typed in the field; and specify how many characters can be typed in the field by setting the Field Name, Data Type, and Field Size properties. A field can have many different properties; but in this project, you will set only the five field properties listed in the following table.

Field Property	Description
Field Name	a descriptive name up to 64 characters
Data Type	the kind of data to be stored in the field such as text or AutoNumbers
Field Size	the number of characters that can be typed in the field
Caption	text that appears in the datasheet or form instead of the field name
Default Value	text or a value that automatically appears in the field

Caption property
Data Type property
Default Value property
Design view
Field Name property
field properties
Field Properties pane
Field Size property
Fields pane

Project 1
Word Processing

Exploring the Great Wall of China

Explorers' Guide

Data file: *Great Wall*
China

Objectives:

In this project, you will:

- open and save an existing document
- switch editing views and view formatting marks
- select, replace, and delete text
- preview and print a document
- create and save a new document
- insert a date and type text

Exploring on Your Own
additional practice in:

- opening and closing the word processing application
- opening, saving, and closing an existing document
- inserting, selecting, and deleting text
- previewing and printing a document
- closing a document

Exploring Across the Curriculum

Internet/Web
Language Arts
Science
Getting Help
Your Personal Journal

Our Exploration Assignment:

Editing a document and creating a personal journal

Did you know that the Great Wall of China is a fortress that was built over 2,000 years ago? Julie wrote a report about the Great Wall for the next Explorers Club meeting and now she needs your help to make a few changes to it. Follow the Trail Markers to open, rename, and save a document; switch between editing views and turn on the view of formatting marks; select, replace, and delete text; and preview and print the document. Finally, create a new document for your own personal journal!

Project 18

Database

Planning a Well-Balanced Diet

Explorers' Guide

Data files: *none*

Objectives:

In this project, you will:

- create a table in Design view
- set the primary key, save the table, and change views
- add and delete fields in Design view
- filter records by selection
- create a query using the Simple Query Wizard

Exploring on Your Own

additional practice in:

- creating a table in Design view
- setting the primary key, saving the table, and changing views
- adding and deleting fields in Design view
- filtering records by selection
- creating a query using the Simple Query Wizard

Exploring Across the Curriculum

Internet/Web

Language Arts

Health and Fitness

Getting Help

Your Personal Journal

Our Exploration Assignment:

Create a new table from scratch in Design view, add and filter records in a datasheet, and query a table

Which food has the most carbohydrates: a slice of cheese or an apple? Which has the lowest number of calories: three ounces of tuna or a piece of fried chicken? Which is a better source of protein: a banana or a glass of low-fat milk? The Explorers Club is learning about the nutritional value of different foods, and Luis needs your help to organize his notes. Follow the Trail Markers to create a new table in Design view; add and delete table fields in Design view and then add records to the table; filter the records to find similar data; and then query the table to view specific fields.

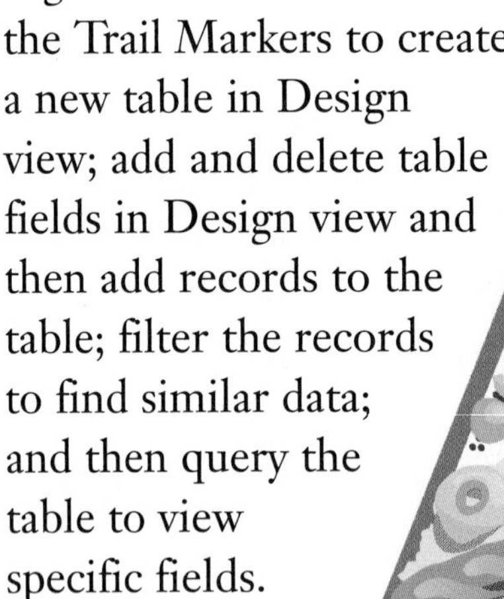

Starting Out!

Let's turn on your computer and use the *Windows* Start menu to start the *Word* application.

1. Turn on your computer, if necessary.
2. Click the **Start** button on the taskbar.
3. Point to **All Programs** on the Start menu.
4. Point to ***Microsoft Office.***
5. Click ***Microsoft Word*** to open the application.

Well done! Let's review the *Word* window and then open and save an existing document.

If you have a *Microsoft Word* icon on your desktop, double-click it to start the application. If your computer is on a network, follow the login process outlined by your teacher.

Ergonomics *TIP*

Check your posture! Your elbows should be relaxed at your sides; your wrists should be low and not resting on the keyboard frame; and your feet should be flat on the floor or on a footrest.

TRAIL 1 MARKER

Opening and Saving an Existing Document

The *Word* application window that opens on your screen contains great features to help you open, edit, and save existing documents or create and save new ones.

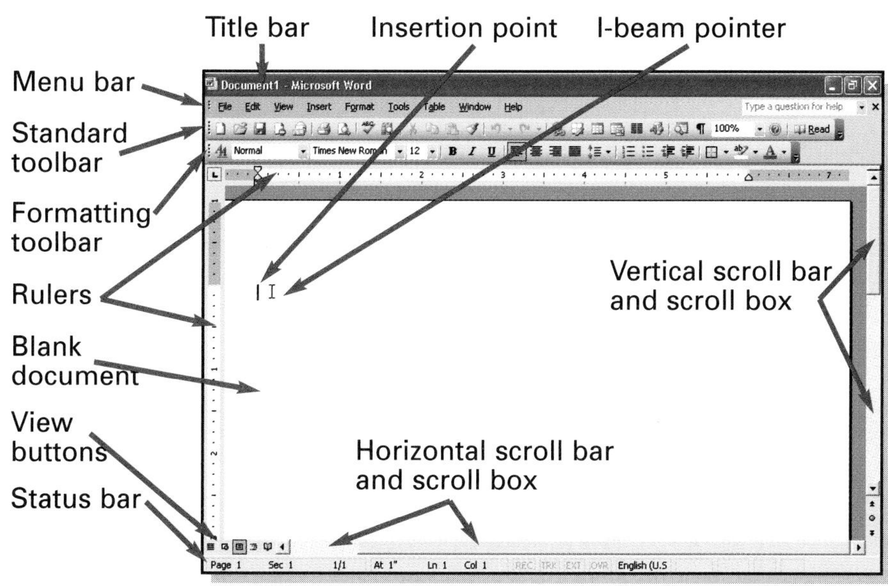

Formatting toolbar
I-beam pointer
insertion point
menu bar
rulers
scroll bar
scroll box
Standard toolbar
status bar
title bar
View button

17a Build Skill

Key each line twice. Double-space between 2-line groups.

Remember to keep your eyes on the copy as you key.

balanced-hand sentences

1 She may pay them to handle the work on the claims.
2 I kept the eight signs for the firm on the island.
3 The amendment by the girl was cut down by the men.
4 Keith is the big man to the right of the big bush.
5 Diana may pay the eight men to dismantle the dock.
6 The goal of the eight men is to make a big profit.
7 The men may visit the cozy island to fish for cod.

gwam 20'' | 3 | 6 | 9 | 12 | 15 | 18 | 21 | 24 | 27 | 30 |

17b Speed Building

1. Key a 1' timing on paragraph 1.
2. Determine the number of words you keyed.
3. Key another 1' timing on paragraph 1. Try to go three words a minute faster.
4. Repeat steps 1–3 for paragraph 2.
5. Key a 2' timing on the two paragraphs combined.

all letters used gwam 2'

The Bill of Rights includes the changes to the Constitution that 7
deal with human rights of all people. The changes or amendments 13
were to improve and correct the original document. They were made 20
to assure the quality of life and to protect the rights of all citizens. 27

One of the changes provides for the right to religious choice, 33
free speech, and free press. Another addresses the right to keep 40
and bear firearms. Another deals with the right of the people with 47
regard to unreasonable search and seizure of person or property. 53
Two others deal with the right to an immediate and public trial by a 60
jury and the prevention of excessive bail and fines. 65

gwam 2' | 1 | 2 | 3 | 4 | 5 | 6 |

Word Feature	Description
title bar	contains the name of your document, the name of the application in which you are working, and the application **Minimize, Restore Down, Maximize,** and **Close** buttons
menu bar	contains menus, each having a drop-down list of commands used to complete tasks
Standard toolbar	has button shortcuts for common tasks, such as creating, opening, saving, and printing documents
Formatting toolbar	has button shortcuts for editing tasks such as underlining text
rulers	used to identify the typing position in a document and to set tabs
View buttons	used to switch between editing views, such as Normal view and Print Layout view
insertion point	vertical line that indicates the typing position in a document
I-beam pointer	the mouse pointer shape used to position the insertion point in a text area
scroll bars and scroll box	used to view different parts of a document
status bar	contains information about the open document as well as the location of the insertion point

A new blank document with the temporary name *Document1* opens each time you start *Word.* If you are creating a new document, you can start typing in *Document1.* Then you save it with its own unique name. If you open an existing document without typing in *Document1*, the blank *Document1* automatically closes.

Now that you are familiar with the *Word* window, you are ready to open and edit an existing document. You open a document by clicking the **Open** button on the Standard toolbar.

Exploring Across the Curriculum

Language Arts: Words to Know

Look up the meaning of the following terms using a classroom, library, CD-ROM, or online encyclopedia or dictionary.

ritual	clan	Mesoamerica	culture
pre-Columbian	indigenous	totem	tribe

Create a new database and save it as *definitions17*. Create a new table using the Table Wizard and the *Categories* sample table in the Personal group. Add the *CategoryID* field to the new table and rename it as **ID**. Add two *CategoryName* fields and rename them as **Term** and **Definition**. Save the table as *Definitions* and let *Access* set the primary key for you. Finish the table and close it.

Use AutoForm to create a new data entry form for the *Definitions* table. Save the form as **Data Entry Form**. Use the form to enter eight records containing the terms and definitions. Close the form. Open the *Definitions* table in Datasheet view, resize the columns, and sort the Term column in ascending alphabetical order. Save and close the table. Close the database.

Getting Help

Type **creating a table** in the **Ask A Question** box and tap the ENTER key. Research how to create a table by entering data in a datasheet. Then create a new database. Using what you learned, create a new table in the database by entering the names of five indigenous groups who live in the Americas and the region in which they live. Save the table and let *Access* set the primary key. Close the table and close the database.

Your Personal Journal

Open your personal journal document. Insert today's date and two blank lines. Choose an artwork created by one of the cultures you studied. Describe it in a paragraph. Tell what you can see and name. What colors and materials did the artist use? Does the work have a pattern that creates rhythm and movement? Then in another paragraph, tell why you like this artwork. Spell-check, save, and close your journal.

Online Enrichment Games (Fun Stuff)  www.lwcgreen.keyboarding.com

Let's open an existing document and save it with a new name.

1. Click the **Open** button to open the **Open** dialog box.
2. Switch to the folder that contains your data files. Your teacher will tell you the name and location of your data files folder, if necessary.

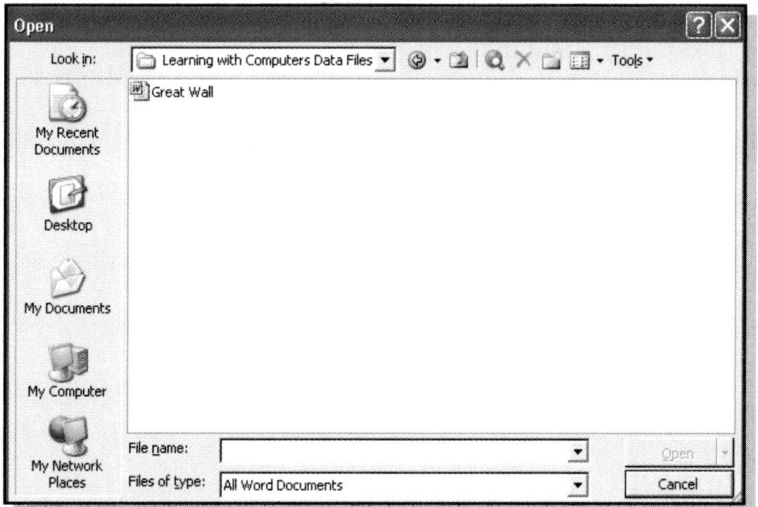

3. Double-click the *Great Wall* filename to open the document.

You can also open an existing document by choosing **File** on the menu bar and choosing **Open**.

CHECKPOINT

The *Great Wall* document on your screen should look like this.

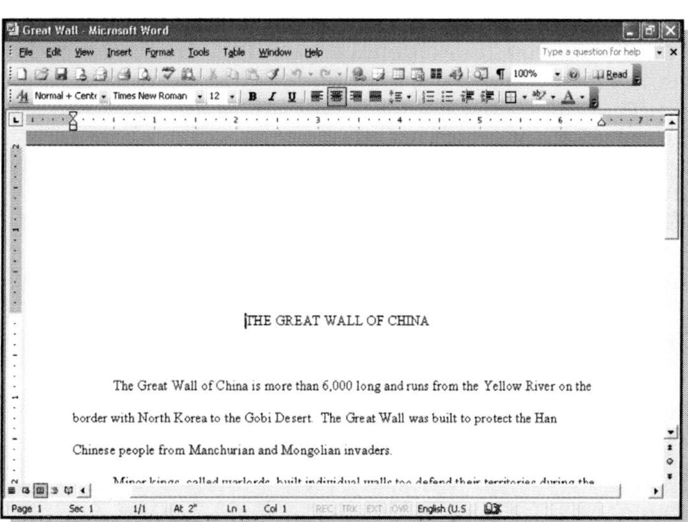

Exploring Across the Curriculum

Internet/Web

TheWeb

You can learn more about the indigenous people of the Americas on the Web. Open your Web browser and use a favorite to view the Learning with Computers Web page (www.lwcgreen.keyboarding.com). Click the **Links** option. Click **Project 17**. Use the links to research facts about the indigenous people listed in the following table. Take notes about the region of the Americas and the specific area in which each group originally lived or lives. Write a description of each group and note the source of your information. Use no more than 50 characters for the description or source.

Name	Name	Name	Name
Aleut	Paiute	Wyandot	Navaho
Modoc	Klamath	Shawnee	Zuni
Abenaki	Haida	Arawak	Aztec
Mohawk	Caddo	Toltec	Tehuelche
Passamaquoddy	Cherokee	Apache	Choctaw

Now create a new database and save it as *indigenous people17*. Create a new table using the Table Wizard and the *Categories* sample table in the Personal group. Add the *CategoryID* and four *CategoryName* fields to the table. Rename the *CategoryID* field as **ID** and the five *CategoryName* fields as **Name**, **Region**, **Area**, **Description**, and **Source**. Save the table as *Indigenous People*, let *Access* set the primary key, finish the table, and close the datasheet.

Using AutoForm, create a data entry form for the *Indigenous People* table and save it as **Data Entry Form**. Use the form to enter the name, region, area, description, and source for the 20 indigenous groups listed in the table above. Close the form. Open the *Indigenous People* table in Datasheet view. Then resize the columns, sort the data in ascending alphabetical order by the Name field, and save the table.

Using AutoReport, create a report for the *Indigenous People* table and save it as **Indigenous People Report**. With your teacher's permission, print the report. Close the table and close the database.

Social Studies: Research, Draw, and Map It!

Social Studies

Work with a classmate on this activity. Draw maps of North America, Central America, and South America. Then using library and online resources and the databases you created in this project, indicate on the maps the location of the following indigenous people: Inuit, Haida, Caddo, Navaho, Toltec, Maya, Inca, Lakota, Modoc, and Tehuelche.

Explore More

Each time you open a project data file, you must save the document with a unique name before you begin to work on it. You must also tell *Word* where the document should be saved: to your hard drive, to a network drive, or to some other location, such as a flash drive.

To name a document and specify its location, open the **Save As** dialog box by choosing **File** on the menu bar and choosing **Save As.**

As you type in and edit a document, save your changes frequently. To save a document—without renaming or saving it to a new location—just click the **Save** button on the Standard toolbar.

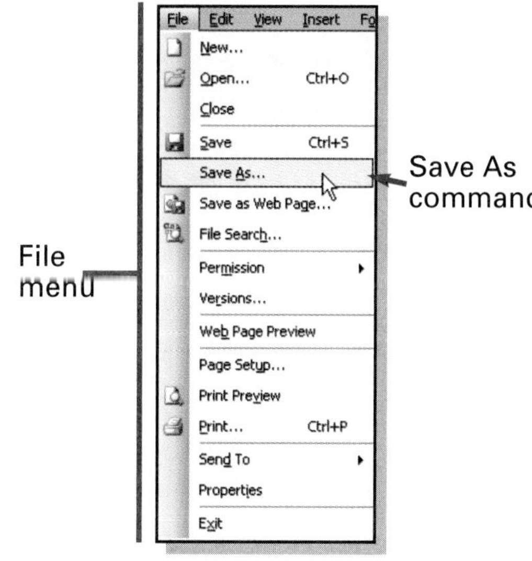

To change the name or location, open the **Save As** dialog box, rename the document, select a new location, and save it.

Let's rename and save the *Great Wall* document.

1. Choose **File** on the menu bar and choose **Save As** to open the **Save As** dialog box.
2. Click the **Save in** drop-down arrow. Locate and open the folder in which you will save your work. Ask your teacher which folder to use, if necessary.
3. Type *Great Wall1* followed by your initials in the **File name** text box.

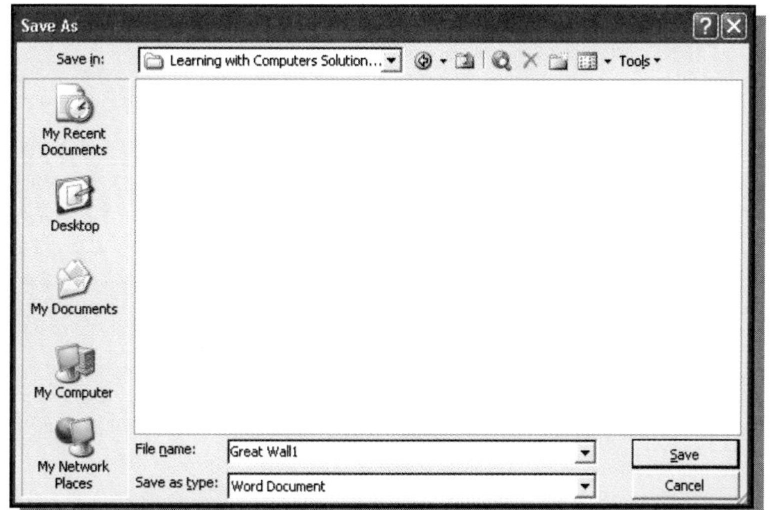

You can also click the **Save** button on the Standard toolbar to open the **Save As** dialog box the first time you save a document.

Exploring on Your Own

Reading in Action

Understanding Sequence

When you read a passage about a process, take notes about the sequence of steps. Read the following paragraph. Take notes by numbering each step and jotting down the main points in your own words.

The coil method can be used to make clay pots in almost any shape and size. Coils of clay are rolled to a desired thickness, attached to a base, and added on top of each other until the pot is completed. The form can be curved outward or inward by making the coils progressively wider or narrower in circumference. While most artists smooth the coils on the inside for strength, some artists leave coils visible on the exterior.

Math in Action

Using Scientific Notation

Scientific notation is used to express very large numbers in simpler terms. The population of Native Americans in the United States in 2000 was 4,249,000. Using scientific notation, this number can be written as 4.249×10^6.

4.249 is called the base.

10^6 is called the exponent. The raised number 6 is equal to the number of places you moved the decimal point left. 10^6 is "10 raised to the 6th power" and is the exponent form of $(10 \times 10 \times 10 \times 10 \times 10 \times 10) = 1{,}000{,}000$.

Now you try it! Write the following numbers in scientific notation.

The population of Cherokee in the United States in 2000 was 730,000.

The population of Navajo in the United States in 2000 was 298,000.

4. Click the dialog box **Save** button.
5. Drag the scroll box on the vertical scroll bar down to view the bottom of the document. Then drag the scroll box back up to view the top of the document.

Well done! Word has multiple views in which you can edit a document. Let's practice switching between editing views.

Switching Editing Views and Viewing Formatting Marks

formatting mark
Normal view
Print Layout view
ScreenTip

When you edit a document, you can view it in different ways on your screen. These different ways to look at your document are called editing views. The two most used *Word* editing views are Normal view and Print Layout view. You work in one of these two views to type, select, edit, and delete text.

Print Layout view allows you to see the top, bottom, left, and right edges of the page. Normal view hides the page edges. The *Word* application automatically opens in Print Layout view.

To switch between Print Layout and Normal views, click a **View** button in the lower-left corner of the *Word* window. To locate the **View** buttons, you can use a ScreenTip.

A ScreenTip is a small yellow flag that gives the name of buttons and other screen elements. To see a ScreenTip, just put the mouse pointer on a button!

Your *Great Wall1* document may have opened in either Print Layout or Normal view. In the illustrations in this text, all documents are opened in the default Print Layout view.

Let's switch editing views.

1. Use the mouse pointer and **ScreenTips** to locate the **Normal View** and **Print Layout View** buttons in the lower-left corner of the *Word* window.
2. Click the **Normal View** button to view the document in the Normal editing view.
3. See how the top and bottom page edges are hidden.
4. Click the **Print Layout View** button to view the document in the Print Layout editing view.

Exploring on Your Own

Blaze your own trail by practicing the skills you have learned! Create a new database and save it as *Explorers Club17*. Start the Table Wizard and create a new table using fields in the **Addresses** sample table in the **Personal** group. Add the following fields from the sample table to your new table: *AddressID*, *FirstName*, *LastName*, *EmailAddress*, and *HomePhone*. Rename the *AddressID* field to *ID*. Save the table as **Members** and let *Access* set the primary key for you. Finish the table and close the datasheet.

Select the *Members* table in the Database window and create a simple data entry form using AutoForm. Save the form as **Members Data Entry Form**. Use the new form to add the following records to the table. Add your name, e-mail address, and phone number as the last record.

First Name	Last Name	Email Address	Home Phone
Luis	Gonzales	lgonzales@navx.net	608-555-8841
Julie	Wilson	juliew@odzok.com	608-555-6578
Tanisha	Jones	tjones@nztk.com	608-555-1579
Liz	Wang	lw@xeon.net	608-555-6654
Your first name	Your last name	Your e-mail address	Your phone number
Ray	Jackson	rayjackson@xeon.net	608-555-2608

Close the form and open the table in Datasheet view. Resize the datasheet columns to fit. Sort the records in ascending order by the *Last Name* field and save the table. Close the datasheet.

Select the *Members* table in the Database window and create a new report using AutoReport. Save the report as **Members List**. With your teacher's permission, print the report. Close Print Preview and close the database.

Explore More

The top, bottom, left, and right edges of the page are visible. Unless otherwise instructed, work in Print Layout view to type, select, replace, and delete text.

As you type text or edit text in a document, *Word* adds special nonprinting characters to the document called formatting marks. For example, *Word* automatically inserts a dot each time you tap the Space Bar, a paragraph formatting mark each time you tap the ENTER key, and a tab formatting mark each time you tap the TAB key. You will learn more about setting tabs and using the TAB key in a later project.

It is often useful to see these formatting marks so that you can find extra spaces between words or find the end of a paragraph. You can turn on or off the view of formatting marks by clicking the **Show/Hide** button on the Standard toolbar.

Let's turn on the view of formatting marks in the *Great Wall1* document.

You can also turn on or off the view of formatting marks in the **Options** dialog box. Choose **Tools** on the menu bar and choose **Options** to open the dialog box. Click the **View** tab to see the formatting mark options in the **Formatting marks** group.

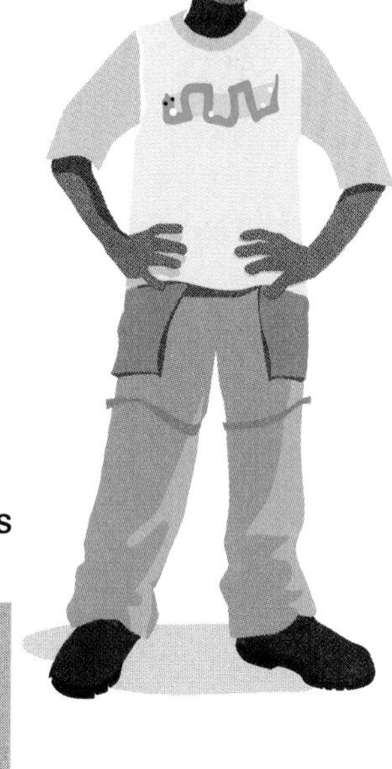

Let's turn on the view of formatting marks.

1. Use ScreenTips to locate the **Show/Hide** button on the Standard toolbar.
2. Click the **Show/Hide** button. ¶

CHECKPOINT

Your *Great Wall1* document with formatting marks should look like this.

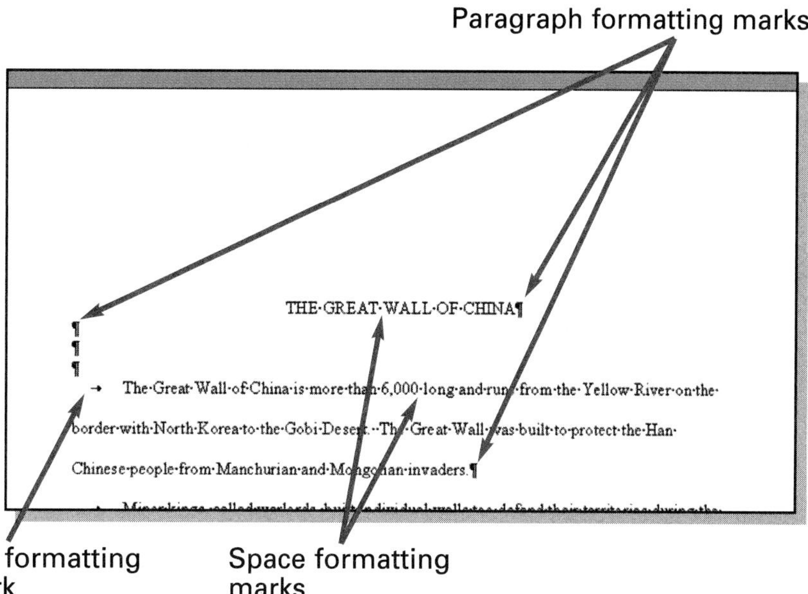

Project *Skills Review*

You learned a lot in this project! We are very impressed with your progress. Let's take a few minutes to review the skills that you learned.

Create a table using the Table Wizard	Select the table in the Database window and then double-click the **Create table by using wizard** shortcut. View the table objects and then click the **New** button on the Database toolbar.
View sample tables in the Table Wizard	Click the **Business** or **Personal** option buttons in the **Table Wizard.**
Add a field from a sample table to the new table	Select the field in the **Sample Fields** list and click the single right arrow (>) button.
Add all the fields from a sample table to the new table	Click the double right arrow (>>) button.
Rename a field in the Table Wizard	Click the **Rename Field** button and type the new name.
Create a simple data entry form or report	Select a table in the Database window, choose **Insert** on the menu bar, and choose **AutoForm** or **AutoReport.**
Navigate in a form	Tap or press the ENTER, TAB, SHIFT + TAB, or arrow keys. Click the text box to position the insertion point.
Sort records in the datasheet	In Datasheet view, after moving the insertion point to the appropriate field, choose **Records** on the menu bar, point to **Sort**, and choose **Sort Ascending** or **Sort Descending**.

Fantastic! Can you see the dots between the words and the paragraph mark symbols? The dots represent spaces between the words and sentences. The paragraph mark symbols represent the end of a paragraph. To turn off the view of formatting marks, simply click the **Show/Hide** button again.

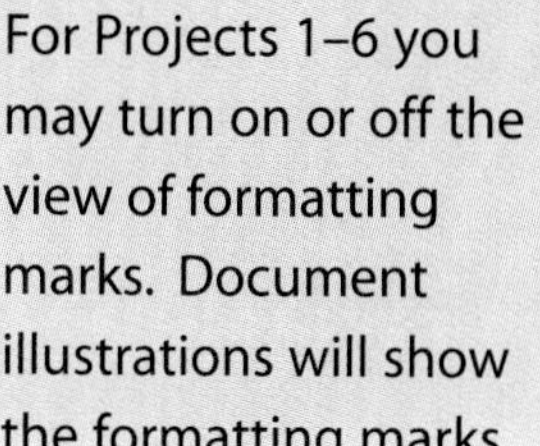
For Projects 1–6 you may turn on or off the view of formatting marks. Document illustrations will show the formatting marks.

Now you are ready to make some changes to the document.

TRAIL 3 MARKER

Selecting, Replacing, and Deleting Text

The mouse pointer changes shape and looks like a very large capital I—called an I-beam pointer—when placed in a text area. You use the I-beam pointer to position the insertion point in the text area of the document.

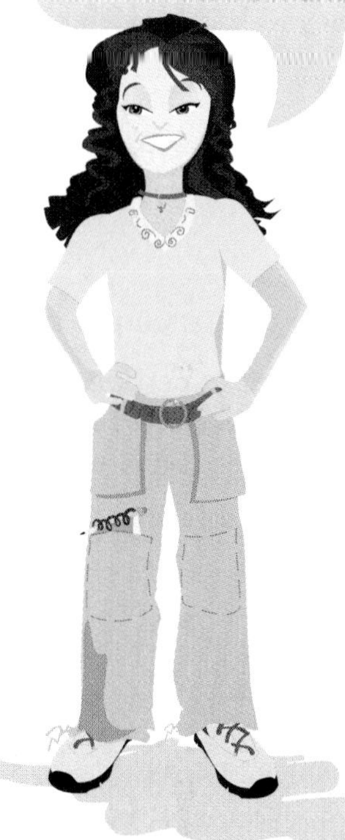

Positioning the Insertion Point with the I-Beam Pointer

The abbreviation for kilometers—km—is missing from the first sentence in the *Great Wall1* document. Let's use the I-beam pointer to reposition the insertion point and insert the abbreviation.

Apply It!

Let's reposition the insertion point using the I-beam pointer and type the missing text.

1. Move the I-beam pointer until it is exactly at the end of the number 6,000 in the first sentence.

I-beam pointer

The·Great·Wall·of·China·is·more·than·6,000 long·and

2. Click the mouse button to reposition the insertion point.
3. Move the I-beam pointer out of the way so you can clearly see the insertion point.
4. Tap the Space Bar and type **km**.
5. Click the **Save** button.

TRAIL 6 MARKER

Create a Report Using AutoReport

A quick way to create a simple report object, like the one you reviewed in Project 16, is to use AutoReport. AutoReport creates a report for a selected table and then opens the report in Print Preview.

To create a report using AutoReport, first select a table. Then click the drop-down arrow on the **New Object** button on the Database toolbar and choose **AutoReport**.

You can create a report using AutoReport by choosing **Insert** on the menu bar and choosing **AutoReport**.

Let's create a simple report using AutoReport and then save it.

1. Make certain that the **Tables** option is selected in the Objects pane and the *Art Exhibit* table is selected in the Database window.
2. Click the **New Object** button drop-down arrow and choose **AutoReport**.

CHECKPOINT

Your report in Print Preview should be similar to this.

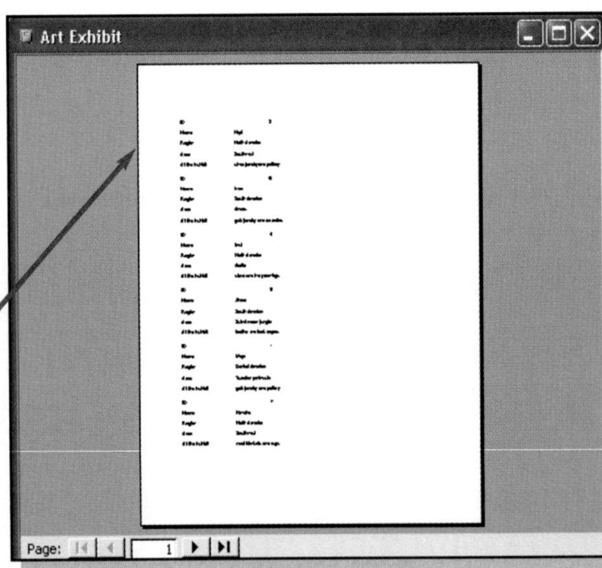

Art Exhibit report in Print Preview

3. Choose **File** on the menu bar and choose **Save As** to open the **Save As** dialog box. Type **Art Exhibit Report** in the **Save Report 'Report1' To** text box and click the **OK** button.
4. With your teacher's permission, click the **Print** button on the Print Preview toolbar to print the report. Then close the Print Preview window and close the database.

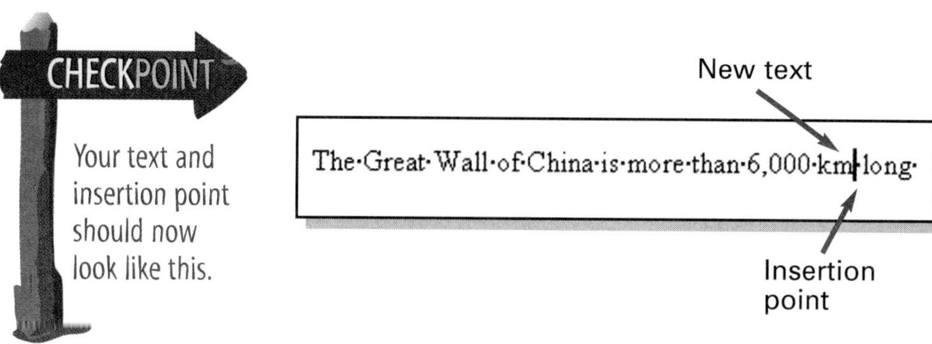
CHECKPOINT
Your text and insertion point should now look like this.
New text
The·Great·Wall·of·China·is·more·than·6,000·km·long·
Insertion point

Great job! A few more corrections still need to be made.

Positioning the Insertion Point with Keyboard Keys

Use the arrow keys to reposition the insertion point and then make the following corrections:

- Remove the extra letter *o* from the word *too* in the first sentence of the second body paragraph.
- Remove the extra letter *e* from the word *bee* in the first sentence in the third body paragraph.
- Insert the letter *g* between the letters *n* and *d* in the word *Huandi* in the third sentence of the second body paragraph.

Use the BACKSPACE and DELETE keys to make these corrections after you reposition the insertion point.

Apply It!

Let's reposition the insertion point using the arrow keys and correct the words *too, bee,* and *Huandi.*

1. Tap the **Down** arrow and **Right** arrow keys until the insertion point is exactly between the two letters *o* in *too.*

Insertion point

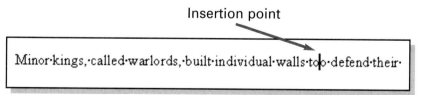

Minor·kings,·called·warlords,·built·individual·walls·to|o·defend·their·

2. Tap the BACKSPACE key to remove the extra *o.*

TRAIL 5 MARKER

Sorting Records in a Datasheet

You can sort records in a datasheet just like you sort data in an *Excel* list. First, move the insertion point into the field you want to sort and then click the **Sort Ascending** or **Sort Descending** buttons on the Table Datasheet toolbar.

To keep the records in the new sorted order, save the table before you close it. If you want to keep the records in their original order, close the table *without* saving it.

You can also choose **Records** on the menu bar, point to **Sort**, and choose **Sort Ascending** or **Sort Descending** to sort records in a datasheet.

Apply It!

Let's sort the data in ascending order and then save the sort order.

1. Click the **Name** field *in any record* to select this field as the sort criteria. Click the **Sort Ascending** button on the Table Datasheet toolbar. The data is rearranged in ascending alphabetical order by last name.
2. Click the **Save** button on the Table Datasheet toolbar and the close the datasheet.

CHECKPOINT

Your sorted data should look like this.

Records sorted in Name order

Art Exhibit : Table

	ID	Name	Region	Area	At the Exhibit
▶	3	Hopi	North America	Southwest	silver jewelry and pottery
	10	Inca	South America	Andes	gold jewelry and ceramics
	4	Inuit	North America	Arctic	stone and ivory carvings
	9	Jivaro	South America	Sub-Andean jungle	feather and bark capes
	1	Maya	Central America	Yucatan peninsula	gold jewelry and pottery
	7	Navaho	North America	Southwest	wool blankets and rugs
	5	Nez Perce	North America	Plateau	beaded baskets and clothing
	6	Ojibwa	North America	Eastern woodlands	soapstone and wood carvings
	8	Seminole	North America	Southeast	patchwork dresses
	2	Yupik	North America	Arctic	storytelling and ritual masks
*	(AutoNumber)				

Outstanding! Now you are ready to create a hard copy of the *Art Exhibit* data as a handout for Explorers Club members who are going on the field trip. Instead of printing the datasheet, you are going to print the data as a report.

3. Tap the **Down** arrow and **Left** arrow keys until the insertion point is exactly in between the two letters *e* in the word *bee.*

Insertion point

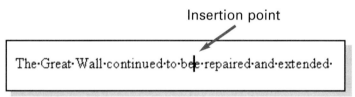

The·Great·Wall·continued·to·bee·repaired·and·extended·

4. Tap the DELETE key to remove the extra *e.*
5. Tap the **Up** arrow and **Right** arrow keys until the insertion point is between the letters *n* and *d* in the word *Huandi.* Type the letter **g.**
6. Click the **Save** button. 

Here is a great rule to remember! If the text to be deleted is to the left of the insertion point, tap the BACKSPACE key. If the text is to the right of the insertion point, tap the DELETE key.

Fantastic! The *Great Wall1* document is looking better and better. Next, you will select text and replace it by typing new text. You will also select and delete text.

Selecting Text

keyboard shortcut
select

As you edit a document, you may need to replace or delete text. To do this, you should first select the text.

An easy way to select text is to drag the I-beam mouse pointer across it. You can also use the mouse pointer by itself or in combination with the CTRL and SHIFT keys to select text in a variety of ways.

You can even use a keyboard shortcut to select text. A keyboard shortcut is a set of keystrokes you use to perform a task. Here is a list of very useful ways to select text.

Don't worry if you forget to save a table after you change the datasheet column widths. Access will prompt you to save the table when you close it!

Let's enter data in the table using the new form.

1. Tap the ENTER key to move the insertion point to the *Name* field text box. Type **Maya** and tap the ENTER key. Type **Central America** and tap the ENTER key. Continue to enter the data for the first record using Ray's list.
2. Click the **New record** button in the navigation buttons to view a new blank record in the form. Click the **Name** field text box, type **Yupik**, and tap the TAB key. Type **North America** and tap the TAB key. Continue to enter the data for the second record using Ray's list.
3. Tap the ENTER key to view a new blank record in the form. Using Ray's list, enter the remaining records. Close the form when you have entered the data for all ten records.
4. Open the *Art Exhibit* table in Datasheet view.

Now, let's widen the columns and save the table.

5. Double-click the right boundary of the *Region*, *Area*, and *At the Exhibit* field selectors (column headings) to resize the columns to fit.
6. Click the **Save** button on the Table Datasheet toolbar to save the layout changes to the table.

Your *Art Exhibit* datasheet should look like this.

Records in *Art Exhibit* table

Art Exhibit : Table

ID	Name	Region	Area	At the Exhibit
1	Maya	Central America	Yucatan peninsula	gold jewelry and pottery
2	Yupik	North America	Arctic	storytelling and ritual masks
3	Hopi	North America	Southwest	silver jewelry and pottery
4	Inuit	North America	Arctic	stone and ivory carvings
5	Nez Perce	North America	Plateau	beaded baskets and clothing
6	Ojibwa	North America	Eastern woodlands	soapstone and wood carvings
7	Navaho	North America	Southwest	wool blankets and rugs
8	Seminole	North America	Southeast	patchwork dresses
9	Jivaro	South America	Sub-Andean jungle	feather and bark capes
10	Inca	South America	Andes	gold jewelry and ceramics
(AutoNumber)				

Terrific! Now let's sort the data in ascending alphabetical order by the contents of the *Name* field.

Selection	Action
A single word and its following space	Double-click the word.
A single line	Move the mouse pointer to the white area to the left of the line and click.
A sentence and its following spaces	Move the I-beam into the sentence, press and hold the CTRL key, and click at the beginning of the sentence.
A complete paragraph	Move the I-beam into the paragraph and triple-click.
An entire document	Move the mouse pointer into white area to the left of the text and triple-click.
From the insertion point to the end of the document	Press the CTRL + SHIFT + END keys.
From the insertion point to the top of the document	Press the CTRL + SHIFT + HOME keys.
A large area of text	Move the insertion point to the beginning of the selection, press and hold the SHIFT key, and click where the selection ends.
Nonadjacent characters, words, or phrases	Press and hold the CTRL key, and click or drag to make the selections.

You can deselect text by clicking anywhere in your document. You can also deselect text by tapping an arrow key.

When you select text, you can always replace it by typing new text. This feature is called *typing replaces selection.*

You need to make two final changes to the *Great Wall1* document. First, replace the word *Yellow* in the first sentence of the document with the word *Yalu.* Then delete the duplicate word *over* in the first sentence of the third body paragraph.

Remember! You must frequently save the changes to your documents by clicking the **Save** button on the Standard toolbar.

2. Click the **Save** button on the Form view toolbar.

3. Type **Art Exhibit Data Entry** in the **Form Name** text box and click the **OK** button. Leave the form open for the next Trail Marker.

Excellent! Now that the form is saved, let's use it to enter Ray's data.

TRAIL 4 MARKER

Adding Records to a Table Using a Form

Here is Ray's list of the cultures and their artworks that are included in the museum's exhibit. Let's enter the records in the *Art Exhibit* table using the new data entry form.

Name	Region	Area	At the Exhibit
Maya	Central America	Yucatan peninsula	gold jewelry and pottery
Yupik	North America	Arctic	storytelling and ritual masks
Hopi	North America	Southwest	silver jewelry and pottery
Inuit	North America	Arctic	stone and ivory carvings
Nez Perce	North America	Plateau	beaded baskets and clothing
Ojibwa	North America	Eastern woodlands	soapstone and wood carvings
Navaho	North America	Southwest	wool blankets and rugs
Seminole	North America	Southeast	patchwork dresses
Jivaro	South America	Sub-Andean jungle	feather and bark capes
Inca	South America	Andes	gold jewelry and ceramics

You can navigate from field to field in the form just like you do in a datasheet by tapping the ENTER, TAB, SHIFT + TAB, or arrow keys. Click the **New record** navigation button at the bottom of the form when you are ready to enter the data for a new record.

Don't forget! Each time you move to a new record, the record you added or edited is automatically saved.

Let's select and replace the word *Yellow* and select and delete the duplicate word *over*.

1. Double-click the word *Yellow* in the first sentence of the first body paragraph. The word and its following space are selected.

Selected word and following space

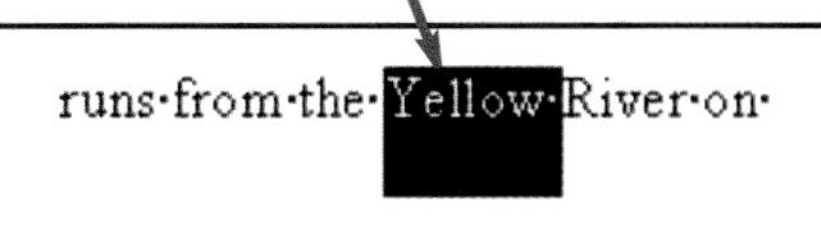

2. Type **Yalu**.
3. Drag the I-beam pointer over the duplicate word *over* in the first sentence of the third body paragraph. The word is selected.
4. Tap the DELETE key.

CHECKPOINT

Your corrected document text should look similar to this.

Corrections

THE·GREAT·WALL·OF·CHINA¶

¶
¶
¶

→ The·Great·Wall·of·China·is·more·than·6,000·km·long·and·runs·from·the·Yalu·River·on·the·border·with·North·Korea·to·the·Gobi·Desert.··The·Great·Wall·was·built·to·protect·the·Han·Chinese·people·from·Manchurian·and·Mongolian·invaders.¶

→ Minor·kings,·called·warlords,·built·individual·walls·to·defend·their·territories·during·the·period·of·the·Warring·States·(403·BCE·to·220·BCE).··These·individual·walls·were·connected·into·one·Great·Wall·by·the·first·Chinese·emperor,·Qin·Shi·Huangdi,·during·the·latter·part·of·his·reign·(246·BCE·to·208·BCE).·¶

→ The·Great·Wall·continued·to·be·repaired·and·extended·over·the·next·several·centuries·by·

Don't worry if you accidentally delete the wrong text! Just click the **Undo** button on the Standard toolbar to quickly undo the delete action. To redo the undone action, click the **Redo** button.

New *Art Exhibit* table in Datasheet view

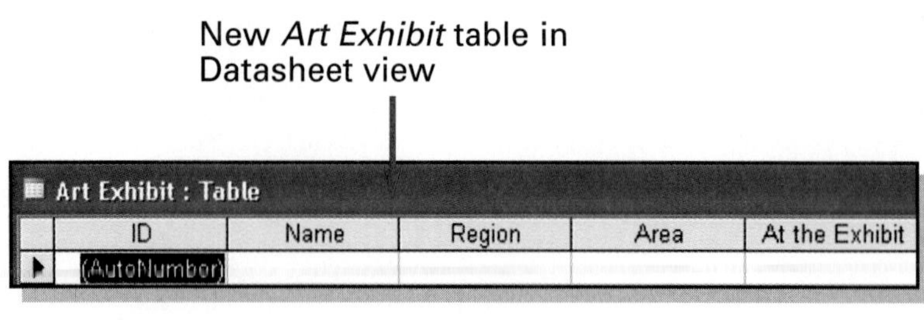

3. Close the table.

What a great job! Now you are ready to enter data about the exhibit into the table. Instead of entering data directly in the table using the datasheet, let's create and use a data entry form.

TRAIL 3 MARKER

Creating a Form Using AutoForm

AutoForm

In Project 16, you learned that a database form object is an easy-to-use tool for adding new records to a table or editing existing records. You can use AutoForm to quickly create a form for the *Art Exhibit* table. To create a form using AutoForm, first select a table. Then click the drop-down arrow on the **New Object** button on the Database toolbar and choose **AutoForm**.

AutoForm creates a simple form, like the one you reviewed in Project 16, that lists all of the fields in a selected table. When you create a form using AutoForm, the form automatically opens in Form view, ready for your data entry! Then save the form so that you can use it whenever you need to enter or edit data in the table. To save it, click the **Save** button on the Form View toolbar.

Let's use AutoForm to create and save a data entry form for the *Art Exhibit* table.

1. View the Tables objects and click the *Art Exhibit* table to select it, if necessary. Then click the **New Object** button drop-down arrow on the Database toolbar. Click **AutoForm**. The new form opens in Form view.

Art Exhibit
ID (AutoNumber)
Name
Region
Area
At the Exhibit
Record: 1 of 1

Repositioning the Insertion Point with a Keyboard Shortcut

You can also use keyboard shortcut keys to reposition the insertion point. For example, pressing the CTRL + HOME keys moves the insertion point to the top of the document. Pressing the CTRL + END keys moves the insertion point to the bottom of the document.

Warning! Scrolling a document does not reposition the insertion point! It just changes your view of the document.

Let's reposition the insertion point at the top of the document and then save the document.

1. Press the CTRL + HOME keys to move the insertion point to the top of the document.
2. Click the **Save** button.

Excellent! You are now ready to preview and print the edited *Great Wall1* document.

TRAIL 4 MARKER

Previewing and Printing a Document

Print Preview

Print Preview is the view that allows you to see what your document will look like on the printed page—before you print it!

Previewing a document before it is printed is very important. It helps you avoid wasting paper and printer toner or ink. If the document does not look right, you can make your changes, preview it again, and print it.

To view a document in Print Preview, click the **Print Preview** button on the Standard toolbar.

Let's preview the *Great Wall1* document.

1. Use the mouse pointer and ScreenTips to locate the **Print Preview** button on the Standard toolbar.
2. Click the **Print Preview** button. 

3. Click the **CategoryName** field in the **Fields in my new table** list to select it. Then click the **Rename Field** button; type **Name** in the **Rename field** text box; and click the **OK** button. The CategoryName field is renamed.

4. Double-click the **CategoryName** field in the **Sample Fields** list to add another field to the new table. Rename the new field as **Region**. Using the **CategoryName** field in the **Sample Fields** list, add two additional fields and rename them **Area** and **At the Exhibit** respectively.

Remember! An AutoNumber is a unique record number automatically assigned by *Access* for each new record you enter in a table.

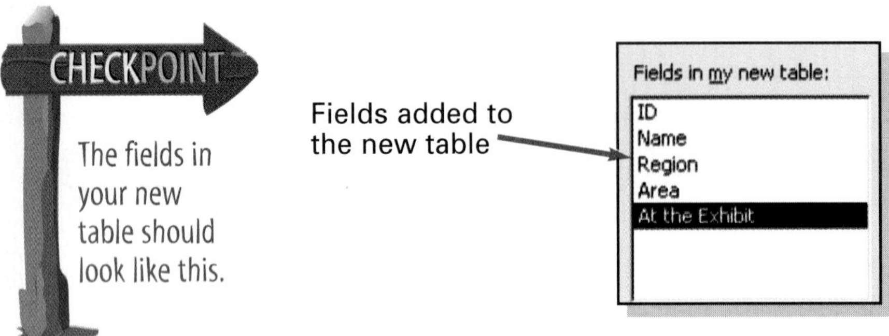

Excellent! In the second Table Wizard step, you will give the new table a name and set the table's primary key. A primary key is a special field that contains the unique identifier for each record in the table. You can let *Access* set the primary key for you. In the new table, *Access* will use the *ID* field as the primary key and insert an AutoNumber for each record.

Let's name the table, let *Access* set the primary key, and finish the table.

1. Click the **Next** button to go to the next Table Wizard step.
2. Type **Art Exhibit** in the **What do you want to name your table?** text box. Click the **Yes, set a primary key for me.** option button, if necessary. Click the **Finish** button. The new *Art Exhibit* table opens in Datasheet view.

Your document in Print Preview should look similar to this.

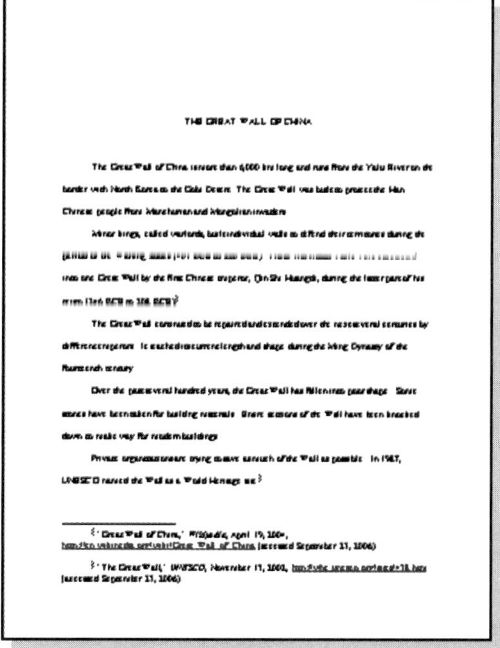

THE GREAT WALL OF CHINA

Another way to preview or print a document is to choose **File** on the menu bar and choose **Print Preview** or **Print.** You can also print a document by clicking the **Print** button on the Standard toolbar.

Excellent! To print the document, click the **Print** button on the Print Preview toolbar. After your document is printed, you can close Print Preview by clicking the **Close Preview** button on the Print Preview toolbar.

Be certain to ask your teacher for permission before you print any documents in this text!

You can close a document by clicking the **Close Window** button on the menu bar or by choosing **File** on the menu bar and choosing **Close**.

Let's print the document, close Print Preview, and close the document.

1. Use the mouse pointer and ScreenTips to locate the **Print** and **Close Preview** buttons on the Print Preview toolbar.
2. Click the **Print** button.
3. Click the **Close Preview** button. Close
4. Click the **Close Window** button on the menu bar to close the *Great Wall1* document. ✕

Outstanding! Now that you have finished editing the *Great Wall1* document, you will create a new document—your very own personal journal!

2. Click the **Personal** option button. The **Addresses** sample table is selected in the **Sample Tables** list. The **AddressID** field is selected in the **Sample Fields** list. Scroll the **Sample Fields** list to view all the fields in the *Addresses* sample table.
3. Click **Household Inventory** in the **Sample Tables** list. Scroll to view the fields in the table. Now select two other sample tables so that you can view and become familiar with their fields.
4. Click **Categories** in the **Sample Tables** list.

You will add fields from the *Categories* sample table to your new table and then rename the fields. To add fields from a sample table to a new table, select the field name in the **Sample Fields** list and click the single right arrow (>) button. You can also double-click the field name to add the field to the new table.

Clicking the double right arrow button (>>) places all of the fields from the sample table into the new table. Clicking the single or double left arrow buttons (< or <<) removes the selected field(s) from the table. Check it out!

Let's add the sample fields to our new table and then rename them.

1. Click the **double right arrow** (>>) button. Both fields from the *Categories* sample table are added to the new table.

2. Click the **CategoryID** field in the **Fields in my new table** list to select it, if necessary. Then click the **Rename Field** button to open the **Rename Field** dialog box. Type **ID** in the **Rename field** text box and click the **OK** button. The CategoryID field is renamed.

Creating and Saving a New Document

null screen

When you close the *Great Wall1* document, you will see the *Word* application window but no open document. This view of the *Word* application is called the null screen. When you see the null screen, you must either open another document or create a new, blank one.

To create a new, blank document, click the **New Blank Document** button on the Standard toolbar. Then save it with a unique name in the location specified by your teacher.

Let's create a new document.

1. Click the **New Blank Document** button.
2. Click the **Save** button.
3. Type **My Personal Journal** followed by your initials in the **File name** text box. Switch to the location and folder where your solution files are stored.
4. Click the dialog box **Save** button.

Good work! Now let's add today's date and a brief paragraph to the document.

Inserting a Date and Typing Text

wordwrap

Begin the first entry in your personal journal by inserting today's date instead of typing it. Insert a date by choosing **Insert** on the menu bar and choosing **Date and Time** to open the **Date and Time** dialog box. This dialog box offers you different date and time formats.

TRAIL 2 MARKER

Creating a Table Using the Table Wizard

primary key
Table Wizard

In the *Excel* unit, you learned to use a step-by-step process called the Chart Wizard. In *Access*, you can use a similar step-by-step process, called the Table Wizard, to create a table.

The Table Wizard has two groups of sample tables—Business and Personal—that you can use to create your own tables. Each sample table contains the fields commonly used to organize specific kinds of data, such as names and addresses, exercise activities, photos, books, or movie videos. You can add one or more fields from a sample table to your new table. You can even change the name of a field after you add it to your table.

To start the Table Wizard, double-click the **Create table by using wizard** shortcut in the Database window.

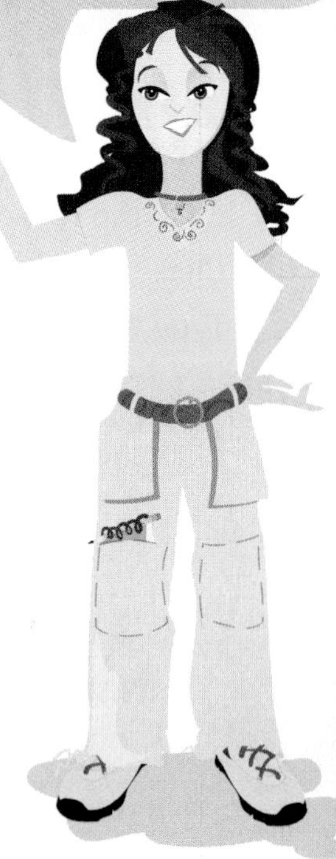

Apply It!

Let's start the Table Wizard and look at the Personal group sample tables and their sample fields.

1. Click the **Tables** button in the Objects pane, if necessary, to view the table objects. Then double-click the **Create table by using wizard** shortcut in the Database window. The Table Wizard opens.

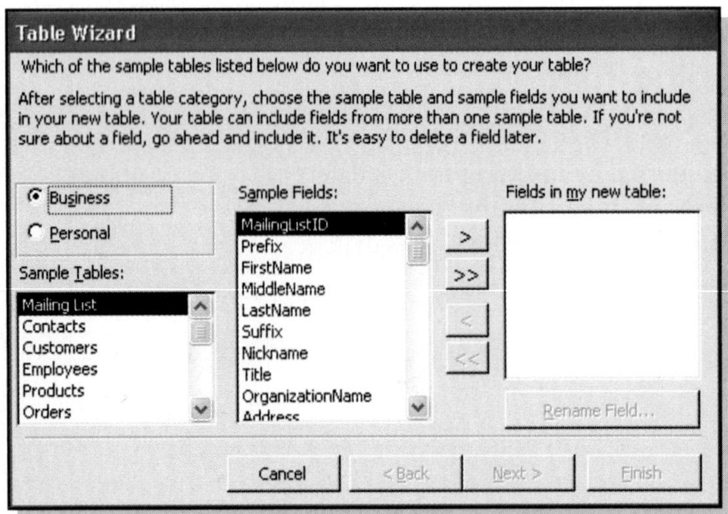

Let's insert today's date in your journal.

1. Choose **Insert** on the menu bar and choose **Date and Time**.
2. Click the third date format in the list.
3. Click the **OK** button.
4. Tap the ENTER key twice to insert two lines below the date.

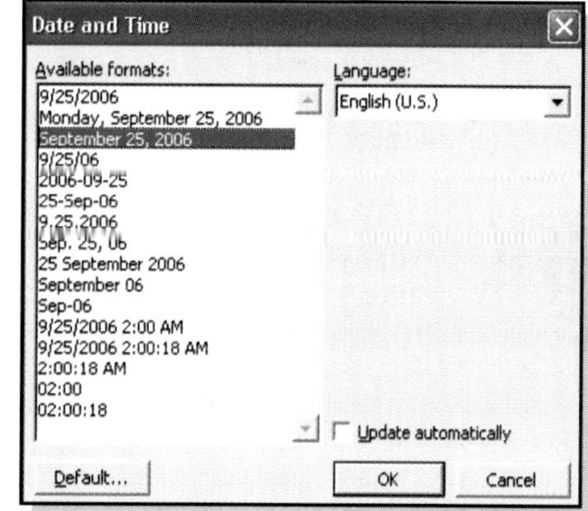

Terrific! As you type text in the document, the insertion point moves across the line to the right until there is no more room on the line; then it moves down to the next line. This process is called **wordwrap**.

As you type in your personal journal document, let *Word* wrap your text to the next line when necessary! Tap the ENTER key only after typing a text paragraph or when you want to insert lines between text paragraphs.

If you see a series of tiny purple dots below dates and addresses, just ignore them! These dots are called SmartTags and indicate that the text can be used to create an item in another application, such as *Microsoft Outlook*.

Let's type a short paragraph.

1. Type **three or four sentences** about facts that you know about China.
2. Notice that the insertion point and the text move to the right as you type and that *Word* automatically wraps the text to the next line when necessary.
3. Use the I-beam or other method to select and change or delete words as necessary.
4. Save the document. With your teacher's permission, preview and print the document.
5. Click the **Close** button on the title bar to close the document and the application.

Word automatically checks a document for unsaved changes when you close it. If the document has unsaved changes, a warning dialog box opens. Click **Yes** to save the changes before the document closes, click **No** if you do not want to save the changes, or click **Cancel** to stop the Close process.

Starting Out!

Begin by starting the *Access* application.

1. Start the *Access* application, if necessary, using the Start menu or a desktop shortcut.

Great! Now let's create a new database.

Ergonomics *TIP*

Are you sitting up straight with your back against your chair? Thumbs up!

TRAIL 1 MARKER

Creating a New Database

To create a new database, first open the **New File** task pane by clicking the **New** button on the Database toolbar or choosing **File** on the menu bar and choosing **New**. Click **Blank Database** in the **New File** task pane to open the **File New Database** dialog box.

Unlike creating a new file in *Word*, *Excel*, or *PowerPoint*, in *Access* you must save a new database before you can work in it. In the **File New Database** dialog box, switch to the folder in which you store your database files, type the new filename, and click the **Create** button.

Apply It!

Let's create a new database.

1. Click the **New** button on the Database toolbar. Click **Blank Database** in the **New File** task pane to open the **File New Database** dialog box.
2. Switch to the folder that contains your database files. Type **art17** in the **File name** text box and click the **Create** button. Your empty *art17* database opens in the Database window inside the *Access* window.

What a great start! Next, you will create a table for your data.

Project | *Skills Review*

You learned a lot in this project! We are very impressed with your progress. Let's take a few minutes to review the skills that you learned.

Open an existing document	Choose **File** on the menu bar and choose **Open**.
Save a document for the first time or with a new name or location	Choose **File** on the menu bar and choose **Save As**.
Switch between Normal view and Print Layout view	Choose **View** on the menu bar and choose **Normal** or **Print Layout**.
Undo an action	Choose **Edit** on the menu bar and choose **Undo** (action).
Save a document with the same name and in the same location	Choose **File** on the menu bar and choose **Save**.
Create a new, blank document	Choose **File** on the menu bar and choose **New**.
Insert a formatted date	Choose **Insert** on the menu bar and choose **Date and Time**.
Print Preview a document	Choose **File** le on the menu bar and choose **Print Preview**.
Print a document	Choose **File** on the menu bar and choose **Print**.
Close a document	Choose **File** on the menu bar and choose **Close**. ✕

Project 17

Database

Cataloging the Native Arts of the Americas

Explorers' Guide

Data files: *none*

Objectives:

In this project, you will:

- create a new database
- create a table using the Table Wizard
- create a form using AutoForm
- add records to a table using a form
- sort records in a datasheet
- create a report using AutoReport

Exploring on Your Own
additional practice in:

- creating a new database
- creating a table using the Table Wizard
- creating a form using AutoForm
- adding records to a table using a form
- sorting records
- creating a report using AutoReport

Exploring Across the Curriculum

Internet/Web
Social Studies
Language Arts
Getting Help
Your Personal Journal

Our Exploration Assignment:

Create a new database, table, form, and report

The Explorers Club is going on a field trip! Everyone is excited about the chance to see the new *Arts of the Americas* exhibit at the local museum. Ray has gathered data on the artwork created by the indigenous people of North, Central, and South America. Can you help him put his data in a database? Super! Just follow the Trail Markers to create a new database; create a table using the Table Wizard; create a form using AutoForm and enter data using the form; sort the data; and then create, preview, and print a report using AutoReport.

Exploring on Your Own

You have learned several new skills in this project. Now blaze your own trail by practicing these skills on your own!

First, open *Word*. Then open the *China* data file and save it as *China1*. Make the following corrections, using the selection methods you learned in this project.

Remove the extra *s* in the word *iss* in the first sentence of the first body paragraph. Select the abbreviation *sq* in the second sentence of the first body paragraph and type the word *square*. Select and delete the duplicate word in in the first sentence of the fourth body paragraph. Insert the word *dam* following the word *hydroelectric* in the last sentence of the fourth body paragraph. Select the word *Yalu* in the last sentence of the fourth body paragraph and type *Yangtze*.

Save the document. With permission, preview and print it. Close the document and close *Word*.

Reading in Action

Asking Questions

As you read information about the Great Wall of China, look for answers to questions that begin with *Who? What? Where? When?* and *Why?* First, write your questions. Then read the data file *Great Wall1,* and find answers to each question.

Example: *Who built the Great Wall of China?*

Qin Shi Huangdi built the Great Wall by connecting individual walls built by warlords.

Math in Action

Finding the Volume

You want to build a wall 20 feet long, 2 feet wide, and 10 feet high. Your blocks are 2 feet long, 1 foot wide, and 1 foot high. Use volume to find out how many blocks you will need. Divide the volume of the wall by the volume of each block.

Volume = Length × Width × Height

Volume of wall = 20 ft × 2 ft × 10 ft = 400 ft^3

Volume of block = 2 ft × 1 ft × 1 ft = 2 ft^3

400 ft^3 ÷ 2 ft^3 per block = 200 blocks

Now you try it!

How many blocks will it take to build the same wall if the blocks are 2 feet long, 2 feet wide, and 2 feet high? What if the blocks are 1 foot long, 1 foot wide, and 1 foot high?

16a Build Skill

Key each line twice. Double-space between 2-line groups.

Keep the insertion point moving steadily across each line without pausing.

balanced-hand sentences

1 If the town amends the bills, the problem may end.
2 Orlando and Diana may make six signs for the city.
3 Their firm may sign the form for the big oak door.
4 The chapel is to be down the road by the big lake.
5 They may cut the lens to make it fit my right eye.
6 Henry is the man Helen got to fix the chapel door.
7 Glen may make a big profit for the big oak panels.

gwam 20'' | 3 | 6 | 9 | 12 | 15 | 18 | 21 | 24 | 27 | 30 |

16b Speed Check

1. Key a 1' timing on paragraph 1.
2. Determine the number of words you keyed.
3. Key another 1' timing on paragraph 1. Try to go two words a minute faster.
4. Repeat steps 1–3 for paragraph 2.
5. Key a 2' timing on paragraphs 1–2. Determine words keyed.

all letters used *gwam* 2'

What is it that makes one person succeed and another fail 6
when the two seem to have about equal ability? Some have said 12
that the difference is in the degree of motivation and effort each 19
brings to the job. Others have said that an intent to become 25
excellent is the main difference. 28

At least four items are likely to have a major effect on 34
success: basic ability, a desire to excel, an aim to succeed, and 41
zestful effort. If any one of these is absent or at a low point, our 48
chances for success are lessened. These features, however, can be 55
developed if we wish. 57

gwam 2' | 1 | 2 | 3 | 4 | 5 | 6 |

Exploring Across the Curriculum

Internet/Web

To learn more about the Great Wall of China, you can use the Web. Open your Web browser and use a favorite to view the Learning with Computers Web page (www.lwcgreen.keyboarding.com). Click the **Links** option. Click **Project 1**. Click the links to learn more about the history of the Great Wall of China.

Create a new, blank document. Save the document as *history1.* Insert today's date at the top of the document. Type your name on the second line below the date. Insert two blank lines. Type at least three short paragraphs describing the history of the Great Wall. Explain when the Great Wall was built and by whom. Discuss when it was modified into the Great Wall we see today. Describe the current conservation efforts to save the Great Wall.

Save the document. With permission, preview and print it. Close the document.

Language Arts: Words to Know

Look up the meaning of the following words, terms, or phrases in a classroom dictionary, CD-ROM dictionary or encyclopedia, or online dictionary.

fortress	hydropower	Ming Dynasty	Qin Shi Huangdi
UNESCO	World Heritage site	Yalu	Yangtze

Create a new document. Save the document as *definitions1* followed by your initials. Insert today's date at the top of the document. Type your name on the second line below the date and insert two blank lines. Type each term on one line and its definition on the next line. Save the document. With permission, preview, and print it. Close the document.

Explore More

Exploring Across the Curriculum

Social Studies: Research and Write

Use library or online resources plus the *Alamo16* and *Texians16* databases to research the Texas Revolution. What were the social, political, and economic factors that led to the Texas Revolution? Who were the important players? How long did the Republic of Texas exist? When did Texas become a state? Then write a multi-page bound report about the Texas Revolution. Include a cover sheet and endnotes in your report. Use Appendix A to review the formatting for a multi-page bound report, if necessary. Spell-check the report and save it. With your teacher's permission, preview and print it.

Getting Help

In the *Access* window, type **check spelling** in the **Ask A Question Box** and tap the ENTER key. Research how to check the spelling of data in a datasheet. Then open the *Alamo16* database you updated in this project. Using what you learned, open the *At the Alamo* table in Datasheet view and check the spelling. Make any necessary corrections. Do not add any proper names to the dictionary. Close the table and close the database.

Your Personal Journal

Open your personal journal document. Insert today's date and two blank lines. Think about what you have learned about the siege of the Alamo and the Texas Revolution. Why do you think we still *Remember the Alamo*? Update your journal with one or two paragraphs that answer this question. Spell-check, save, and close your journal.

Online Enrichment Games (Fun Stuff)  www.lwcgreen.keyboarding.com

Exploring Across the Curriculum

Science: Research and Write

Use library, classroom, or online resources including maps to locate information about the building of the Three Gorges Dam on the Yangtze River in China. Create a new document containing three paragraphs describing the Three Gorges Dam. What are its benefits? What problems does it pose for the people living and traveling on the Yangtze River? Save the document. With permission, preview and print it. Then close the document.

Getting Help

Type **viewing *Word* documents** in the **Ask A Question** box and tap the ENTER key. Research different ways to view a *Word* document. Then create a new document, insert today's date, and type four paragraphs describing Web Page view, Outline view, Document Map, and Full Screen view. Save the document. With permission, preview and print it. Close the document.

Your Personal Journal

Open your personal journal document. Insert today's date. Beginning on the second line below the date, type a few sentences about why you think it is important to preserve the Great Wall of China. Save and close your journal document.

Online Enrichment Games (Fun Stuff)  www.lwcgreen.keyboarding.com

Exploring Across the Curriculum

Internet/Web

In Project 15, you learned that you can create hyperlinks on a slide and then click the hyperlinks during a slide show to open your Web browser and load a Web page. You can also use hyperlinks created in a *Word* document, an *Excel* worksheet, or an *Access* database table to access the Web.

Open the *Alamo16* database and open the *At the Alamo* table in Datasheet view. Locate the hyperlinks in the *Source 1* and *Source 2* fields. You will use these hyperlinks to start your browser and load Web pages containing more information about some of the men and women who were at the siege of the Alamo. *Warning! Each time you click a datasheet hyperlink, a new copy of your browser opens. Be sure to close the browser window before you click the next hyperlink.*

Use the datasheet hyperlinks to learn more about the following men and women. Take notes about what you learn.

- The Defenders: Davy Crockett, Jim Bowie, William Travis, and Juan Seguin
- The Survivors: Susanna Dickerson and the Esparza family
- The Attackers: General Antonio Lopez de Santa Anna

Close the database. Then create a new *Word* document and type and format your notes as a three-level outline. Save the outline document as *outline16* and close it.

Language Arts: Words to Know

Look up the following terms, names, or phrases using a classroom, library, CD-ROM, or online encyclopedia or dictionary.

barricade	Bowie knife	courier	Goliad massacre
siege	Texas Revolution	Texian	the Alamo

Open the *definitions16* database. Open the *Terms* table and enter a brief definition or fact for each record in the *Definition* field. Use no more than 50 characters for the definitions and facts. Print Preview the datasheet and, with your teacher's permission, print it. Close Print Preview and close the database.

Explore More

1a Home-Row Review

Key each line twice. Double-space between 2-line groups.

1 a s d f j k l ; | as df jk l; | as df jk l; | asdf jkl;;

2 aa kk ss ;; dd jj ff ll | kk dd ;; aa jj ss ll ff jj

3 aja aja | dld dld | f;f f;f | sks sks | jaj jaj | ldl ldl | kk

4 as as | ask ask | ad ad | lad lad | all all | fall fall | j;j;

5 add add | dad dad | sad sad | fad fad | lad lad | add; adds;

6 lass lass | salad salad | asks asks | flak flak | dad dad;

Technique Tip

- body erect
- sit back in chair
- fingers curved and upright

1b Speed Check

1. Key a 1' timing on paragraph 1.
2. Determine the number of words you keyed.
3. Key another 1' timing on paragraph 1. Try to go two words a minute faster.
4. Key a 2' timing on paragraphs 1–2 combined.
5. Determine the number of words you keyed.

all letters used *gwam* 2'

Set goals that will challenge you to reach them. When you 6
set them high enough, you will have to put in time and effort to 12
accomplish them. When you have to really work hard to reach a 19
goal, it is one worth having. 22

To realize your keying goals, you need to use good tech- 27
niques. Be sure to keep your feet on the floor, your eyes on the 34
copy, and each arm relaxed by your side. As difficult as it may 40
seem, you can enjoy working hard to be successful. 45

gwam 2' | 1 | 2 | 3 | 4 | 5 | 6 |

Exploring on Your Own

Open the *Texians16* database. View the table, form, and report objects. Then open the *Famous Texians* table in Datasheet view and add the following record:

Title=Colonel **First Name=Benjamin R.** **Last Name=Milam**
Description=Commanded Texian volunteers at the Battle of Bexar
Source=http://www.tsha.utexas.edu/handbook/online/articles/view/MM/fmi3.html

Use the **Find** command to locate **Houston** in the *Last Name* field. Change the first name to **Sam**. Delete the duplicate record for Hendrick Arnold. Print Preview the datasheet and, with your teacher's permission, print it. Close the Print Preview window, close the *Famous Texans* table, and close the *Texians16* database.

Reading in Action

Generate Questions

As you read historical nonfiction, ask yourself questions about people, events, and other details. For example, as you read the passage below, you might ask, *Who was at the Alamo? When did the battle take place?* Look for answers to your questions. List three more questions you may have about the Alamo.

In February 1836, the Alamo was defended by about 150 men. Most of them were not born in Texas. They came from almost every American state, and some even came from Europe. One famous defender was David Crockett, an expert rifleman who had served six terms in Congress.

On February 23, 1836, Santa Anna's army arrived outside of San Antonio. His army began a siege that lasted 12 days. During the siege, 32 volunteers arrived to help the defenders.

On March 6, at 5 A.M., about 1,800 Mexican soldiers advanced on the Alamo. By 9 A.M., the battle was over. Although they fought bravely, the Texians were defeated. The handful of survivors were executed at once by the Mexicans. However, the battle gave Texians a rallying cry—*Remember the Alamo*—that spurred Texians to win the Texas Revolution.

Math in Action

Drawing an Object to Scale

The dimensions of the Alamo are shown in the photograph. Make a scale drawing of the Alamo. A scale is the ratio that compares a length in a drawing to the length in the actual object. In your drawing, use the ratio of 1:7. This means that 1 inch in the drawing will equal 7 feet of the actual Alamo. Round the numbers, if necessary.

For example, the length of the base is 63 feet 9 inches. Round up to 64 feet. The length of the base in your scale drawing will be 9 inches. Complete the scale drawing of the Alamo. Draw the height of each side, the arched cap, and the door to scale.

Project 2

Word Processing

Sailing into Edo Bay with Commodore Perry

Explorers' Guide

Data file: *Perry outline*
Perry

Objectives:

In this project, you will:

- check spelling and grammar
- create an outline
- position text on a page
- change text font, font size, and case
- format a single-page unbound report

Exploring on Your Own

additional practice in:

- checking spelling and grammar
- creating an outline
- positioning text on the page
- changing text font, font size, and case
- formatting a single-page unbound report

Exploring Across the Curriculum

Internet/Web
Language Arts
Social Studies
Getting Help
Your Personal Journal

Our Exploration Assignment:

Creating an outline and a single-page unbound report

In 1853, Commodore Perry led four steam-powered warships into Edo Bay in Japan. To the Japanese, who had never seen steamboats, the ships looked like "giant dragons puffing smoke." What was Perry's mission? What happened? Julie has written a report about Commodore Perry's expedition to Japan. Can you help Julie format her research notes and report? Just follow the Trail Markers to check spelling and grammar; create an outline; change margins, alignment, and line spacing; change text font, font size, and case; and format a single-page unbound report.

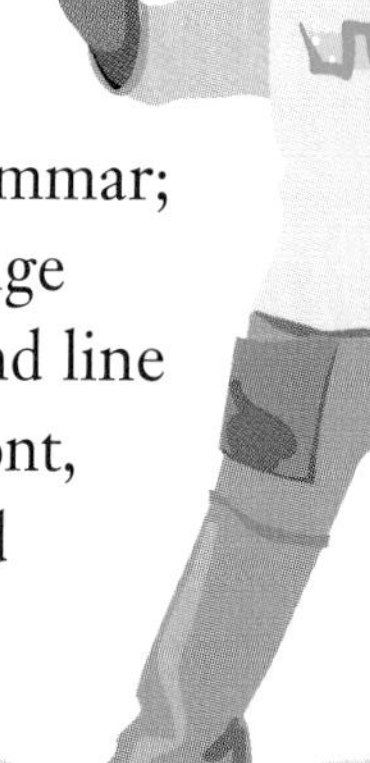

Project | *Skills Review*

You learned a lot in this project! We are very impressed with your progress. Let's take a few minutes to review the skills that you learned.

Open a database file	Choose **File** on the menu bar and choose **Open**.
View table, form, or reports objects in the Database window	Tables Forms Reports
Open a database object	Double-click the object's icon or name in the Database window. Open
Insert a new record in Datasheet view	Open the table in Datasheet view. Enter the data for each field. Move to a different record to save the new record.
Delete a record in Datasheet view	Open the table in Datasheet view. Click the record selector for the record to be deleted. Choose **Edit** on the menu bar and choose **Delete Record**.
Find specific data in Datasheet view	Choose **Edit** on the menu bar and choose **Find**.
Preview and print a datasheet	Choose **File** on the menu bar and choose **Print Preview** or **Print**.

Starting *Out*!

Start the *Word* application, if necessary, and open the *Perry outline* document. Then save the document with a new name.

1. Start the *Word* application.
2. Click the **Open** button on the Standard toolbar.
3. Switch to your data files folder.
4. Open the *Perry outline* document.
5. Choose **File** on the menu bar and choose **Save As**.
6. Switch to your solution files folder.
7. Save the document as *Perry outline2*.

Excellent! Now, let's begin by correcting the spelling errors in the *Perry outline2* document.

Ergonomics *TIP*

Can you easily see what is on your monitor's screen without tilting your head up or down? If not, reposition the monitor until you can look straight ahead to see the *Word* application window and the open document.

TRAIL 1 MARKER

Checking Spelling and Grammar

Always check the spelling and grammar in all of your documents. To help you find misspelled or misused words, use *Word*'s built-in dictionary and grammar checker. It makes checking spelling and grammar a snap! But remember, it will not find all your errors. You still have to read your document carefully!

To check the spelling and grammar of an entire document, click the **Spelling and Grammar** button on the Standard toolbar or choose **Tools** on the menu bar and choose **Spelling and Grammar**. *Word* begins the spell-checking process at the insertion point. Remember to press CTRL + HOME to move the insertion point to the top of the document before you start the spell-checking process.

A wavy red line appears under a suspected mistyped word, and a wavy green line appears under a word or phrase that may be a grammar error. Right-click the word and use the shortcut menu to correct the error. Try it!

TRAIL 5 MARKER

Previewing a Datasheet

A printed datasheet is a great tool you can use to visually verify your data entry. You can preview and print a datasheet just like an *Excel* worksheet. Click the **Print Preview** button on the Table Datasheet toolbar to switch to Print Preview. Then click the **Print** button on the Print Preview toolbar to print the datasheet.

***Warning!* The *At the Alamo* table datasheet contains more than 200 records; therefore, you will only preview it. Do not print the datasheet unless your teacher tells you to do so.**

You can also preview and print a datasheet by choosing **File** on the menu bar and choosing **Print Preview** or **Print**.

Apply It!

Let's preview the datasheet.

1. Click the **Print Preview** button on the Table Datasheet toolbar to switch to Print Preview.
2. Use the zoom pointer to magnify the report. Click the **Next page** button in the navigation buttons to view page 2 of the report. Use the zoom pointer to reduce the magnification. Click the **Close** button on the Print Preview window. A confirmation dialog box appears asking if you want to save changes to the table's layout. *Remember!* You changed the layout of the table's datasheet when you widened the column. Now you need to save those changes. Click **Yes** to save the layout changes. Close the *Alamo16* database. Close *Access*.

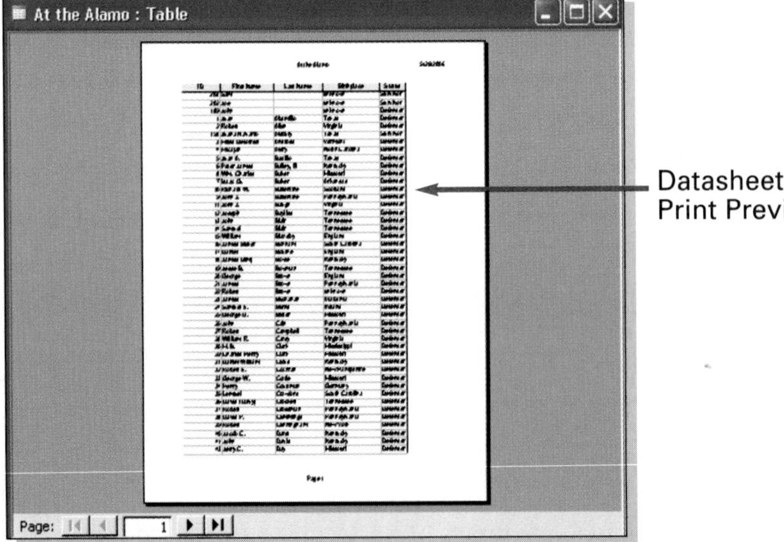

Let's spell-check the entire *Perry outline2* document.

1. Press the CTRL + HOME keys, if necessary, to position the insertion point at the top of the document.
2. Click the **Spelling and Grammar** button to open the **Spelling and Grammar** dialog box.
3. Click the **Change** button to change the misspelled word *Expedtion* to *Expedition.*
4. Click the **Change** button to change the misspelled word *responsee* to *response.*
5. Click the **OK** button.

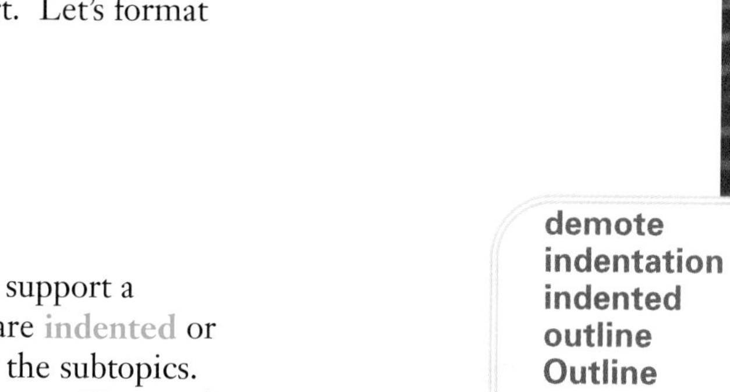

Fantastic! The *Perry outline2* document includes a list of topics that Julie used to write the paragraphs of her report. Let's format the notes as an outline.

TRAIL 2 MARKER

Creating an Outline

An outline has main topics, subtopics, and details that support a subtopic. This is called a three-level outline. Subtopics are indented or *moved* inward under the main topic. Details are indented under the subtopics. Each outline level is numbered or lettered according to a set system. Here is the most common numbering system for a three-level outline:

demote
indentation
indented
outline
Outline Numbered list
promote

Outline Topic	Numbering System
Main topics—first outline level	Roman numerals (I, II, III)
Subtopics—second outline level	Uppercase letters (A, B, C)
Details—third outline level	Arabic numerals (1, 2, 3)

The most efficient way to create a document in *Word* is to first type all the text. Then select and format the text.

TRAIL 4 MARKER

Finding Specific Data

You can use the **Find** and **Replace** commands in *Access* in much the same way as you do in *Word*. To find specific data in a field or in the entire table, choose **Edit** on the menu bar and choose **Find**. Then specify the data and where *Access* should look—in the current field or in the whole table. Before you begin, be sure you are looking at the *At the Alamo* table in Datasheet view. Then move the insertion point into the field that has the data you want to find.

Let's find the record for David (Davy) Crockett and change the Status to Defender.

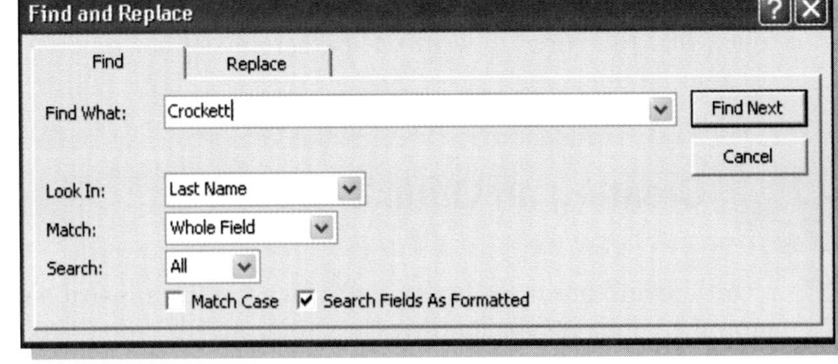

1. Click the *Last Name* field in any record to position the insertion point in the field. Then choose **Edit** on the menu bar and choose **Find** to open the **Find and Replace** dialog box. Type **Crockett** in the **Find What** text box. The *Last Name* field appears in the **Look In** list.
2. Click the **Find Next** button to find the record for David (Davy) Crockett. The *Last Name* field in the David (Davy) Crockett record is selected. Cancel the **Find and Replace** dialog box. Tap the TAB key twice to select the contents of the *Status* field. Type **Defender** and tap the **Down** arrow to move off the record and save the changes.

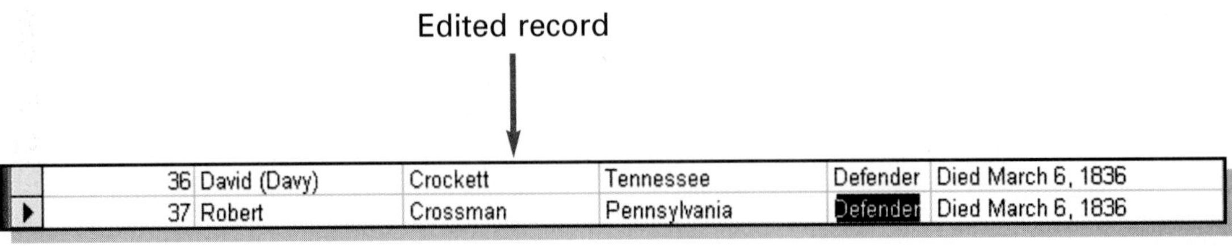

Edited record
36 David (Davy) Crockett Tennessee Defender Died March 6, 1836
37 Robert Crossman Pennsylvania Defender Died March 6, 1836

Outstanding! The final step is to preview the datasheet.

In the *Perry outline2* document, each paragraph is a main topic, a subtopic, or a detail. To turn Julie's list into an outline, you can use the *Word* Outline Numbered list feature. You do not have to type the Roman numerals, letters, or numbers; or indent the text! *Word* will do this for you!

First, select all the text below the title using the CTRL + SHIFT + END keyboard shortcut. Next, choose **Format** on the menu bar and choose **Bullets and Numbering**. Click the **Outline Numbered** tab in the **Bullets and Numbering** dialog box and select a numbering style. Finally, you will customize the numbering format. Let's get started!

Did you know that each topic line in the *Perry outline2* document is really a separate paragraph? Turn on the **Show/Hide** feature, if necessary, and check it out!

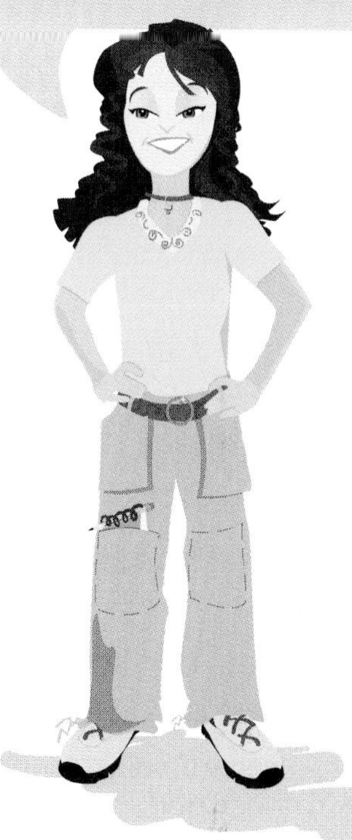

Let's select all the text below the title paragraph. Then we will set the numbering formats we want for the three levels.

1. Move the insertion point immediately in front of *Introduction.*
2. Press the CRTL + SHIFT + END keys to select all the text from the insertion point to the end of the document.

Perry·and·the·Treaty·of·Kanagawa¶
¶
Introduction¶
19th·century·Japan¶
Whaling·industry¶
The·Perry·Expedition¶
Expedition·size¶
Perry's·task¶
Entering·Edo·Bay¶
Japan's·response·to·treaty·request¶
Perry's·determination¶
Signing·the·Treaty·of·Kanagawa¶
Treaty·provisions¶
Opening·Japan·to·the·world¶

3. Choose **Format** on the menu bar and choose **Bullets and Numbering.** Click the **Outline Numbered** tab in the **Bullets and Numbering** dialog box. Click the first numbering option.

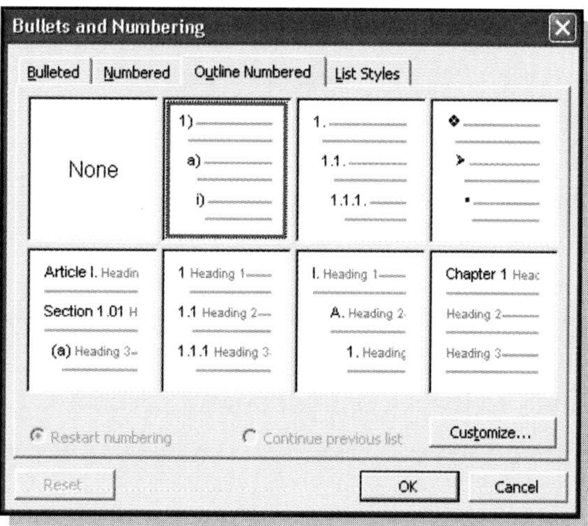

The first five fields in your two new records should look like this.

New records

209	Juan	Seguin	Texas	Survivor
210	Antonio Lopez de	Santa Anna	Mexico	Attacker

Fantastic! Now let's delete a duplicate record.

Deleting a Record

To delete a record, first select it by clicking its record selector. Then click the **Delete Record** button on the Table Datasheet toolbar. When you delete a record with an AutoNumber ID field, all the remaining records keep their AutoNumber ID; the AutoNumber ID of the deleted record is not reused.

Let's delete the duplicate record for James Bowie.

1. Scroll to view the two records for James (Jim) Bowie. Click the **record selector** for the second record (ID=208) to select the entire record.
2. Click the **Delete Record** button on the Table Datasheet toolbar and then click **Yes** to confirm the deletion. The duplicate Bowie record is deleted.

Another way to delete a selected record is to choose **Edit** on the menu bar and choose **Delete Record**. You can also tap the DELETE key.

Terrific! Now let's look for data in a specific field.

Do not forget! Your mouse and mouse pad should be positioned within easy reach immediately to the left or right of your keyboard.

4. Click the **Customize** button to set the numbering system in the **Customize Outline Numbered List** dialog box. Set the numbering system for Levels 1–3. *Do not* set the numbering system for Levels 4–9.
5. Click **1** in the **Level** list, if necessary. Click the **Number style** drop-down arrow and click **I, II, III**.... Uppercase Roman numerals are selected for Level 1.

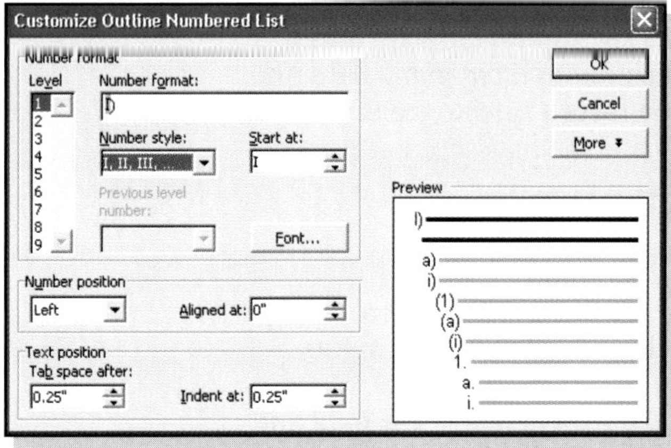

6. Click **2** in the **Level** list. Click the **Number style** drop-down arrow and click **A, B, C**....
7. Click **3** in the **Level** list. Click the **Number style** drop-down arrow and click **1, 2, 3**....
8. Click the **OK** button. Deselect the list. Save the document.

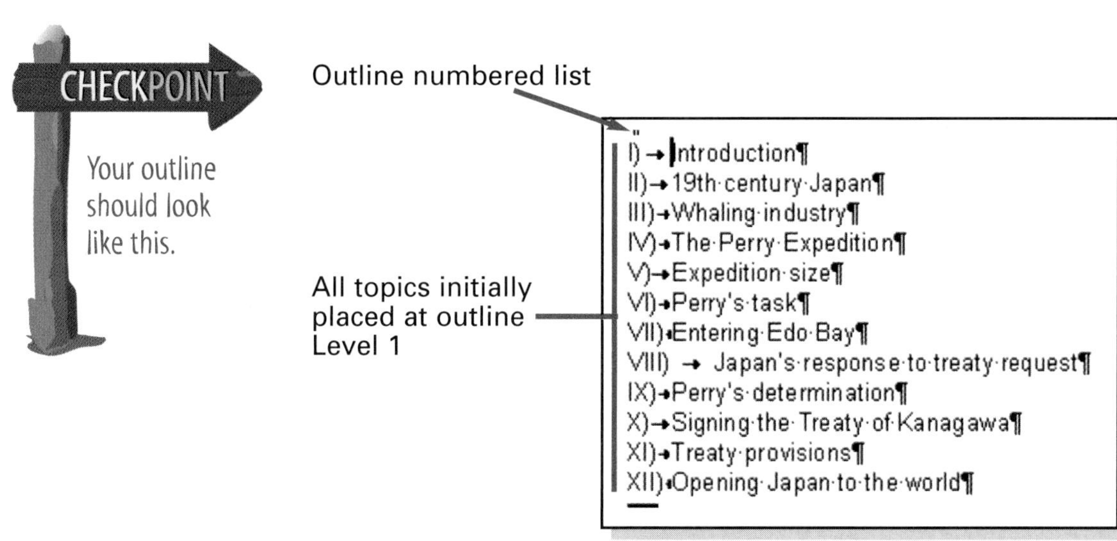

Let's add two new records: one for Juan Seguin and one for General Santa Anna. ***Type the URLs very carefully using underscores for spaces. Then proof the two new records.***

1. Click the **New Record** navigation button to move to the blank row at the bottom of the datasheet. Tap the TAB key to move the insertion point into the *First Name* field. Type **Juan** in the *First Name* field and tap the TAB key. The pencil symbol in the record selector tells you that you are editing the record and the changes have not been saved.

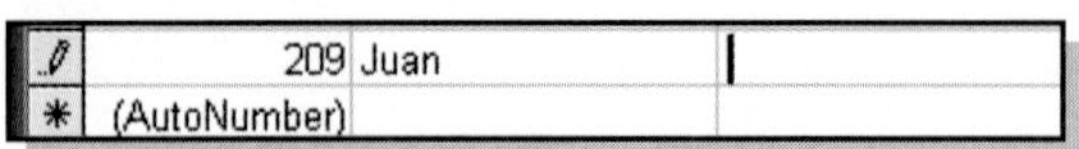

2. Type **Seguin** in the *Last Name* field and tap the TAB key. Type **Texas** in the *Birthplace* field and tap the ENTER key. Type **Survivor** in the *Status* field and tap the ENTER key.
3. Type **Left for reinforcements before final battle** in the *Notes* field and tap the **Right** arrow key. Type http://www.pbs.org/weta/thewest/people/s_z/seguin.htm in the *Source 1* field and tap the **Right** arrow key. *Be careful when you type the URL and remember to proof it. Use the underscore for a space.*
4. Type http://www.tsha.utexas.edu/handbook/online/articles/view/SS/fse8.html in the Source 2 field. Tap the **Right** arrow key to move off the current record and save it.
5. Enter the following data for General Santa Anna. Use the ENTER, TAB, or **Right** arrow key to move from field to field. Remember to move off the Santa Anna record to save the data.

   First Name=Antonio Lopez de
   Last Name=Santa Anna
   Birthplace=Mexico
   Status=Attacker
   Notes=Mexican general and president
   Source 1=http://www.pbs.org/weta/thewest/people/s_z/santaanna.htm
   Source 2=http://www.tsha.utexas.edu/handbook/online/articles/view/SS/fsa29.html

   You can resize a datasheet column by dragging a column boundary or double-clicking a column boundary, just like you do in an *Excel* worksheet.
6. Move the mouse pointer to the boundary between the *Source 1* and *Source 2* column headers then double-click the *Source 1* boundary to resize the column to fit.

By default, *Word* places all of the selected paragraphs at the main topic level—Level 1. Now that the number format for each level is set, you are ready to change each line to a main topic, subtopic, or detail by clicking the **Increase Indent** button on the Formatting toolbar.

When you select an outline topic and click the **Increase Indent** button, the topic is indented and moved down to the next outline level. This is called demoting a topic. Clicking the **Decrease Indent** button moves the topic up to a higher outline level. This is called promoting a topic. *Word* automatically applies the correct outline number or letter to the demoted or promoted topic.

In the *Perry outline2* document, you can demote several topics at once. You do this by first selecting multiple topics using the CTRL key and then clicking the **Increase Indent** button.

Another way to promote or demote selected topics in an outline is by displaying the Outlining toolbar. Choose **View** on the menu bar, point to **Toolbars**, and choose **Outlining**. Then click the **Promote** or **Demote** buttons.

Let's demote several topics to outline Levels 2 and 3.

1. Use the I-beam to select the *19th century Japan* topic.
2. Press and hold the CTRL key. Use the I-beam to select the following topics: *Whaling industry, Expedition size, Perry's task, Japan's response to treaty request,* and *Perry's determination.* Release the CTRL key.
3. Click the **Increase Indent** button. The selected topics are demoted to outline Level 2. These topics are subtopics. Deselect the text.
4. Use the I-beam to select the *Signing the Treaty of Kanagawa* topic. Press and hold the CTRL key and select the *Treaty provisions* topic. Release the CTRL key.
5. Click the **Increase Indent** button twice. The selected topics are demoted twice to outline Level 3. These topics are details.

I)→Introduction¶
II)→19th·century·Japan¶
III)→Whaling·industry¶
IV)→The·Perry·Expedition¶
V)→Expedition·size¶
VI)→Perry's·task¶
VII)→Entering·Edo·Bay¶
VIII)→Japan's·response·to·treaty·request¶
IX)→Perry's·determination¶
X)→Signing·the·Treaty·of·Kanagawa¶
XI)→Treaty·provisions¶
XII)→Opening·Japan·to·the·world¶

Let's edit the record for Peter James Bailey to change his birthplace from Texas to Kentucky.

1. Move the mouse pointer to the left edge of the Birthplace field for the Peter James Bailey, III record. The mouse pointer becomes a large white plus pointer.

	6	Peter James	Bailey, III	Texas
	8	Wm. Charles	Baker	Missouri

2. Click the field to select its contents and then type **Kentucky**. Look at the record selector for the record. It still has a pencil symbol meaning that the change to the record is not yet saved.

	6	Peter James	Bailey, III	Kentucky
	8	Wm. Charles	Baker	Missouri

3. Tap the **Down** arrow key to move to the next record. The change to the Bailey record is saved.

Well done! Next, let's add two new records.

Adding Records

AutoNumber

Each record in a table must have a unique identifying number. In the *At the Alamo* table, this number appears in the first column, the ID field. When you add a new record to the *At the Alamo* table, *Access* automatically assigns it a unique record number called an AutoNumber. You will see the new identifying number as you begin entering data in the blank row below the last record.

Look carefully at the ID field in the *At the Alamo* datasheet. The *At the Alamo* table has been saved with the data sorted in alphabetical order by last name; therefore, the identifying numbers you see in the ID field *are not* in order. Each time you add new records to the *At the Alamo* datasheet, *Access* will automatically resort the data alphabetically by the *Last Name* field.

Remember! You must move to a different record after all the data is entered in order to save the new record.

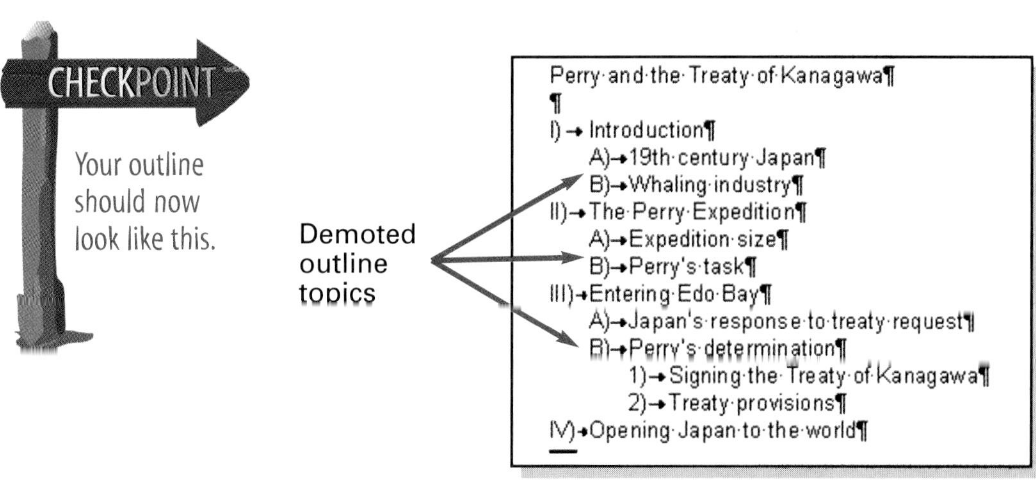
CHECKPOINT
Your outline should now look like this.
Demoted outline topics

Perry·and·the·Treaty·of·Kanagawa¶
¶
I)→Introduction¶
A)→19th·century·Japan¶
B)→Whaling·industry¶
II)→The·Perry·Expedition¶
A)→Expedition·size¶
B)→Perry's·task¶
III)→Entering·Edo·Bay¶
A)→Japan's·response·to·treaty·request¶
B)→Perry's·determination¶
1)→Signing·the·Treaty·of·Kanagawa¶
2)→Treaty·provisions¶
IV)→Opening·Japan·to·the·world¶

Terrific! Next, you will position the document's text more attractively on the page by setting margins, indents, and horizontal alignment.

TRAIL 3 MARKER

Positioning Text on a Page

line spacing
margin
paragraph formatting

To position text attractively on the page, you can change the document's margins, center paragraphs horizontally, and change line spacing.

Margins are the amount of white space between the edge of the top, bottom, left, and right sides of a page and the typed text. *Word* automatically sets 1-inch top and bottom margins and 1.25-inch left and right margins for each new document. You can change a document's margins in the **Page Setup** dialog box. Open the dialog box by choosing **File** on the menu bar and choosing **Page Setup**.

You can also change horizontal alignment and line spacing options in the **Paragraph** dialog box by choosing **Format** on the Standard toolbar and choosing **Paragraph**.

Positioning text on the page by indenting paragraphs, aligning paragraphs horizontally, or setting line spacing is all part of paragraph formatting. To select a single paragraph for paragraph formatting, simply move the insertion point into the paragraph. To apply paragraph formatting to multiple paragraphs, you must select them with the I-beam or other selection method.

Selected paragraphs can be aligned at the left side, center, or at the right side of the page by clicking the **Align Left**, **Center**, or **Align Right** buttons on the Formatting toolbar.

Line spacing specifies the amount of white space between the lines of text. *Word* automatically single-spaces paragraphs. To double-space selected paragraphs, click the **Line Spacing** button drop-down arrow and click 2.0. Other options are 1.5, 2.5, 3.0, or more lines of space.

An outline document should have 2-inch top, left, and right margins and a 1-inch bottom margin. Its title paragraph should be centered between the left and right margins. A short outline should have double-spaced paragraphs.

- Press the CTRL + HOME keys to select the first field in the first record (the top of the table)
- Press the CTRL + END keys to select the last field in the last record (the end of the table)
- Click the field selector (column heading) to select the entire column
- Click the record selector (row heading) to select the entire row

When you are working in a specific record, several different symbols can appear in its record selector. For example, the black right-pointing arrow symbol indicates the current record, and a pencil symbol indicates changes that have been made to the record have not yet been saved. To save the changes, move to a different record.

Let's open the *At the Alamo* table and navigate through different records and fields.

1. Double-click the **At the Alamo** table icon or name to open the table in Datasheet view.
2. Press the CTRL + END keys to move to the last field (Source 2) in the last record. Press the CTRL + HOME keys to move to the first field (ID) in the first record. Tap the TAB key four times to move to the fifth field (Status) in the record.
3. Tap the **Down** arrow key three times to move to fifth field (Status) in the fourth record. Press the SHIFT + TAB keys twice to move to the third field (Last Name) in the record.
4. Move the I-beam to the second field (First Name) in the next record and click to position the insertion point in the field.
5. Click the *Notes* **field selector** to select the entire *Notes* column. Click the **record selector** for any record (row) to select the entire row. Press the CTRL + HOME keys.
6. Click the **Last record** button in the navigation buttons to move to the last record. Click the **Previous record** button in the navigation buttons to move to the previous record. Type **10** in the **Record number** box in the navigation buttons and tap the ENTER key to move to the tenth record. Press the CTRL + HOME keys.

Super! Now let's edit a record.

Editing a Record

To select the entire contents of a field, you can double-click the field or move the mouse pointer to the left edge of the field where it becomes a large white plus pointer. Click the field with the large white plus pointer to select its contents.

Let's set the margins, center the main heading, and change the line spacing for the *Perry outline2* document.

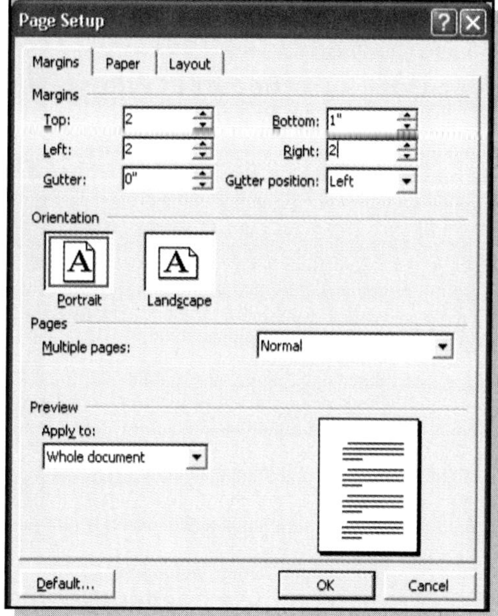

1. Choose **File** on the menu bar and choose **Page Setup**. Click the **Margins** tab, if necessary. Type **2** in the **Top**, **Left**, and **Right** text boxes. Leave the bottom margin at 1 inch.
2. Click the **OK** button.
3. Click in the title paragraph at the top of the page to position the insertion point. This selects the title paragraph for formatting.
4. Click the **Center** button.
5. Move the insertion point to the left margin immediately in front of the word *Introduction*. Press the CTRL + SHIFT + END keys to select all the text below the title.
6. Click the **Line Spacing** button drop-down arrow and click **2.0**. Deselect the text and save the document.

CHECKPOINT

The double-spaced outline on your screen should look like this.

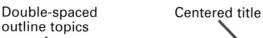

Double-spaced outline topics

Centered title

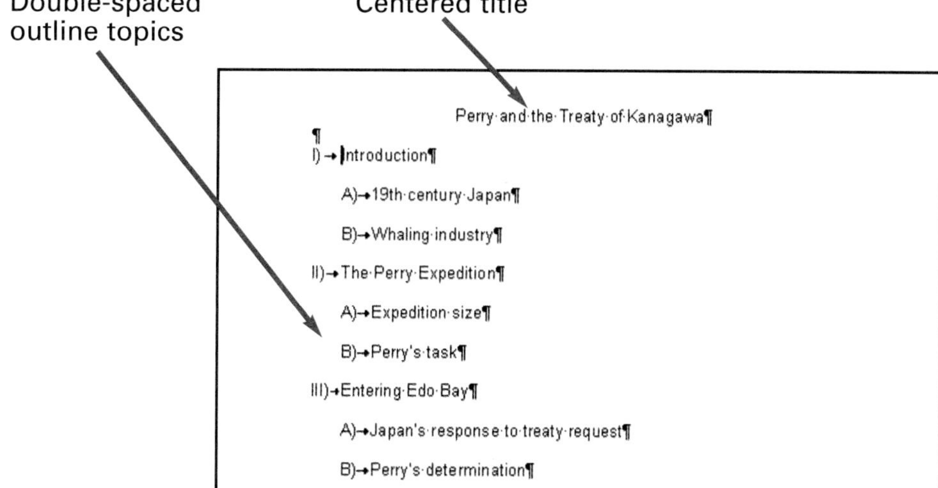

Perry·and·the·Treaty·of·Kanagawa¶
¶
I)→Introduction¶
A)→19th·century·Japan¶
B)→Whaling·industry¶
II)→The·Perry·Expedition¶
A)→Expedition·size¶
B)→Perry's·task¶
III)→Entering·Edo·Bay¶
A)→Japan's·response·to·treaty·request¶
B)→Perry's·determination¶
1)→Signing·the·Treaty·of·Kanagawa¶
2)→Treaty·provisions¶
IV)→Opening·Japan·to·the·world¶

Fantastic! Next, you will make the outline more attractive and easier to read by changing the text's shape, size, and case.

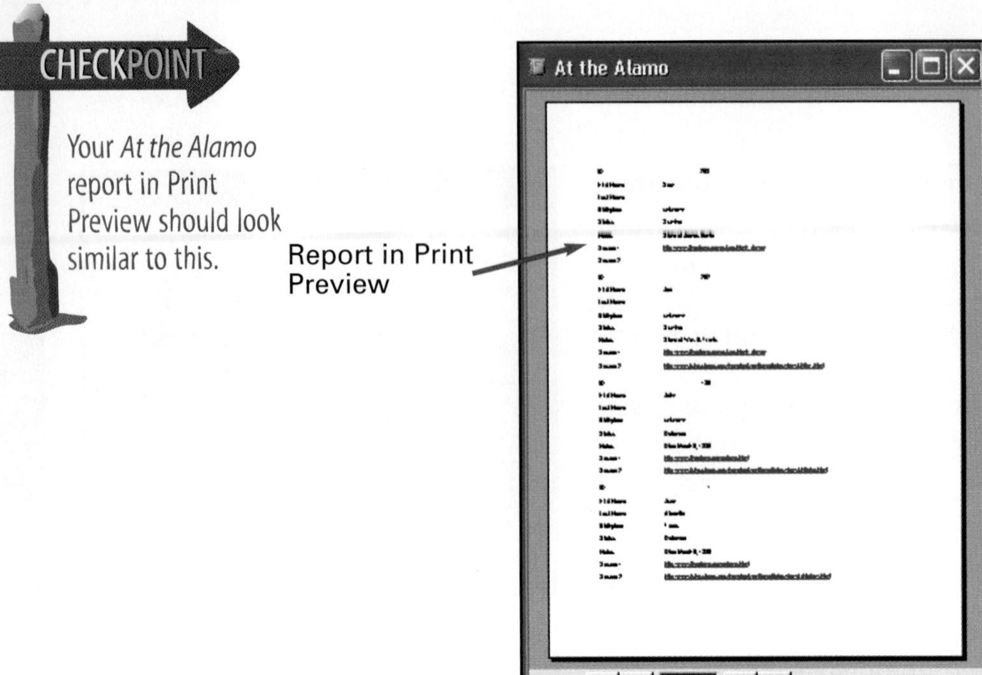
CHECKPOINT
Your *At the Alamo* report in Print Preview should look similar to this.
Report in Print Preview
At the Alamo
Page: 1

Remember, an *Access* database is a relational database that can contain multiple table, form, and report objects all saved together in one file.

2. Move the mouse pointer over the report in the Print Preview window. The mouse pointer becomes a zoom pointer. Click the report to increase the magnification so that you can read its contents. Click the report to decrease the magnification. Then, click the **Close** button on the Print Preview window. Click the **Tables** button in the Objects pane.

Terrific! You have finished checking out all the objects in the *Alamo16* database. Now let's make a few changes to the data in the *At the Alamo* table.

TRAIL 3 MARKER

Editing, Adding, and Deleting Records

field selector
pencil symbol
record selector
right-pointing arrow symbol

You can add, edit, and delete records in a datasheet, much like you can add, edit, or delete data in an *Excel* worksheet. Additionally, navigating in a datasheet is very much like navigating in an *Excel* worksheet. For example, you can:

- Use the I-beam to position the insertion point in a field or select field contents
- Select the contents of a field by clicking the field's left boundary with the large white mouse pointer
- Move right and left from field to field in the same record using the TAB, ENTER, SHIFT + TAB, or arrow keys
- Move up and down from record to record using the Up or Down arrow keys

Changing Text Font, Font Size, and Case

TRAIL 4 MARKER

Changing the way one or more text characters, or letters, appear is called character formatting. Character formatting includes changing the font, font size, and case.

character formatting
font
font size
point
typeface

Font and Font Size

A font or typeface is the way letters and numbers are shaped. Commonly used fonts are Times New Roman and Arial. Font size is measured in points. The larger the point size, the larger the text will look.

Julie originally formatted the *Perry outline2* document with the Arial 10 point font. Changing the font and font size to Times New Roman 12 point makes the outline document easier to read.

To change the font and font size for an entire document, select all the text in the document by pressing the CTRL + A keyboard shortcut keys or by choosing **Edit** on the menu bar and choosing **Select All**. Then click the **Font** and **Font Size** box drop-down arrows on the Formatting toolbar to choose the new font and font size.

You can change the font and font size with options in the **Font** dialog box. Open the dialog box by choosing **Format** on the menu bar and choosing **Font**.

Did you know? *Word* automatically uses the Times New Roman 12 point font for all new documents you create.

Apply It!

Let's select the entire *Perry outline2* document and change the font and font size.

1. Press the CTRL + A keys to select the entire document.
2. Click the **Font** box drop-down arrow and click **Times New Roman**.

   Times New Roman ▾ Scroll the font list, if necessary, to see the font name.
3. Click the **Font Size** box drop-down arrow and click 12. 12 ▾ Deselect the text. Save the document.

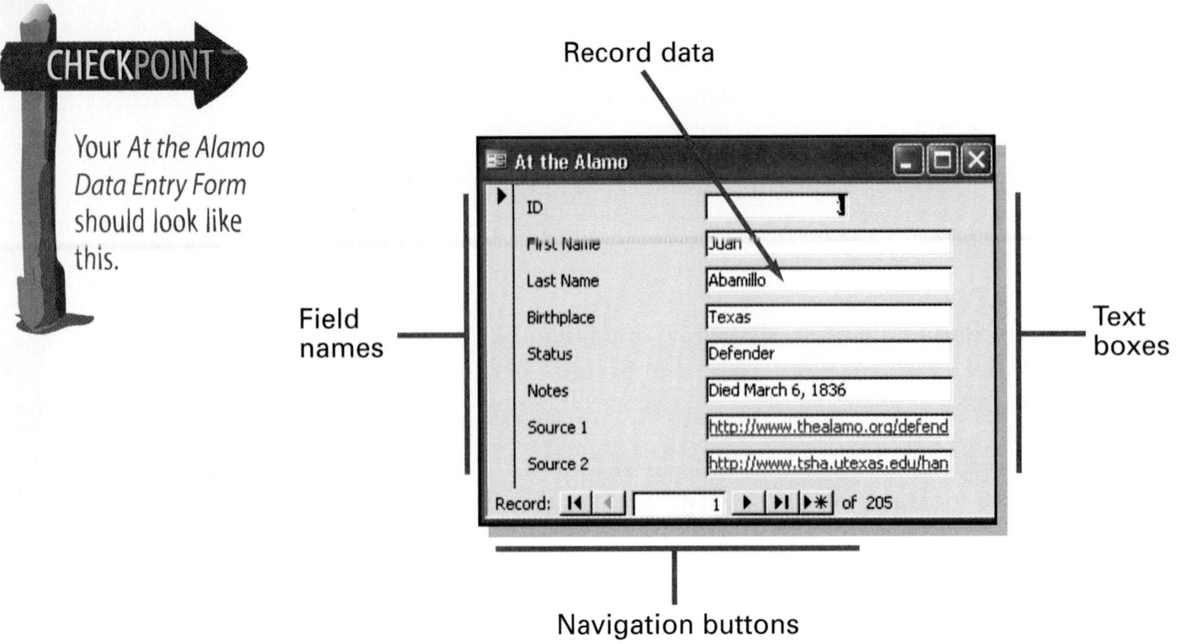

2. Locate the field names, the text boxes containing data for a record, and the navigation buttons. Then, click the **Close** button on the form window's title bar.

Now, let's view the *Alamo16* report object.

Report Objects

A report is a hard copy or printout of a table's records. You can create a report that shows some or all of the data in a table. Use Print Preview to see and print the report.

Let's view the *Alamo16* database's report object.

1. Click the **Reports** button in the Objects pane in the Database window. Reports

   The *Alamo16* database contains one report named *At the Alamo.* Double-click the **At the Alamo** report icon or name to open the report in Print Preview. The *At the Alamo* report uses data from the *At the Alamo* table to create a list of each record and the data in each field in the record.

Times New Roman
12 point font

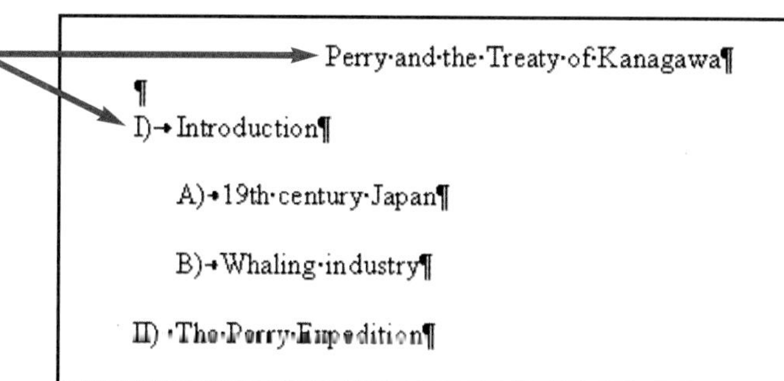

Text Case

lowercase
uppercase

Capital letters are called uppercase characters. Letters that are not capitals are called lowercase characters. You type uppercase characters by holding down the SHIFT key as you type. If you are typing more than just one or two uppercase characters, press the CAPS LOCK key before you begin typing and then press it again after you finish typing.

But what if text has already been typed in lowercase and you want to change it to uppercase? Just select the text and then choose **Format** on the menu bar and choose **Change Case**. In the **Change Case** dialog box, click the **Uppercase** option.

Let's change the case of the title and Level 1 topics to uppercase.

1. Use the I-beam to select the title at the top of the page.
2. Press and hold the CTRL key. Select all the Level 1 topics. Release the CTRL key.
3. Choose **Format** on the menu bar and choose **Change Case**. The **Uppercase** option in the **Change Case** dialog box is already selected. Click the **OK** button. Deselect the text.

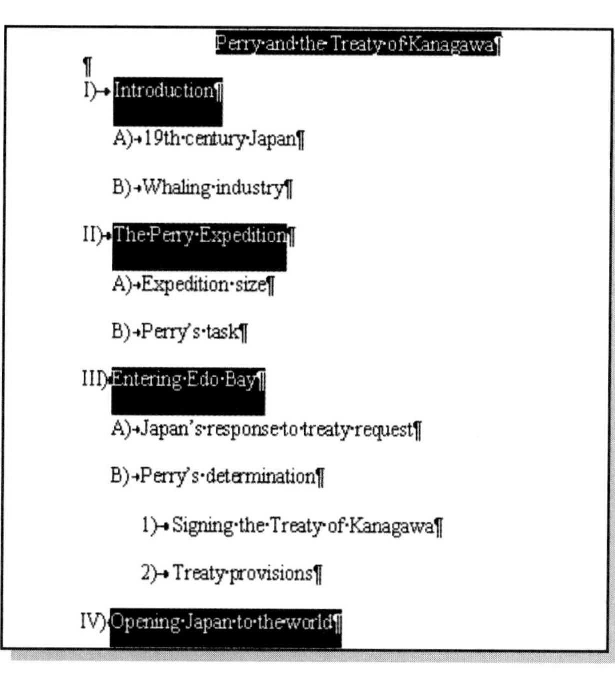

2. Scroll the datasheet vertically to see all 205 records. Scroll the datasheet horizontally to see all 8 fields in each record.
3. Locate the navigation buttons in the lower-left corner of the datasheet. The navigation buttons include a **First record**, **Previous record**, **Next record**, **Last record**, and **New record** button and the **Record number** text box.
4. Click the **Close** button on the *datasheet window's* title bar.

Next, let's view a form object in the *Alamo16* database.

Be careful! Remember to click the **Close** button on a *datasheet window's* title bar to close a table. Clicking the **Close** button on the *Database window's* title bar will close the entire database!

Form view

Form Objects

A form is used to add a new record or edit data in an existing record. You likely have completed *paper forms* to join a club or register for a special activity at school. A database form is an electronic version of a paper form.

Look carefully at the Objects pane on the left side of the Database window. You click Object pane buttons to view the different object types stored in the database. For example, to view the form object stored in the *Alamo16* database, you can click the **Forms** button in the Objects pane.

A form object opens in its own window in Form view and lists the fields in a record. Each field has a text box you can use to enter data for a new record or edit data in an existing record. Like a datasheet, a form has a set of navigation buttons you can click to navigate through existing records or create a new record. Unlike a datasheet, you can see only one record at a time in a form.

Let's view the *Alamo16* database's form object.

1. Click the **Forms** button in the Objects pane in the Database window.

   Forms The *Alamo16* database contains one form named *At the Alamo Data Entry Form*. The form's name is selected. Double-click the **At the Alamo Data Entry Form** icon or name to open the form object.

CHECKPOINT
Your outline's title and Level 1 topics should look like this.

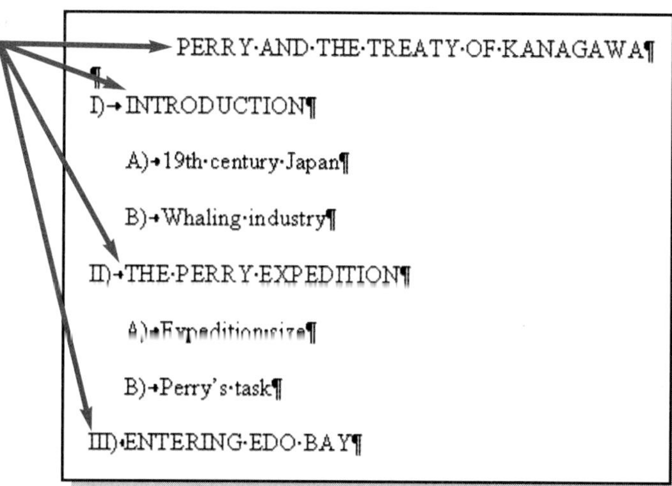
Uppercase title and topic paragraphs

PERRY·AND·THE·TREATY·OF·KANAGAWA¶

¶

I)→INTRODUCTION¶

A)→19th·century·Japan¶

B)→Whaling·industry¶

II)→THE·PERRY·EXPEDITION¶

A)→Expedition·size¶

B)→Perry's·task¶

III)·ENTERING·EDO·BAY¶

4. Save the document and close it.

Congratulations! Julie's notes are now formatted as an outline. All that remains is to format her report.

TRAIL 5 MARKER

Formatting a Single-Page Unbound Report

A single-page **unbound report** has a 2-inch top margin and 1-inch left, right, and bottom margins. An uppercase title or **main heading** is centered at the top of the report followed by a quadruple space (three blank lines). The font should be Times New Roman 12 point and the body text paragraphs should be double-spaced.

Julie used her outline to write her report. Let's open her report and change the margins, text font, font size, case, and line spacing, just as you did in the *Perry outline2* document.

First Line Indent marker
Hanging Indent marker
Left Indent marker
main heading
Right Indent marker
unbound report

Apply It!

Let's open Julie's *Perry* document and format it.

1. Open the *Perry* document and save it as *Perry2.*
2. Spell-check the entire document. Change *Treety* to *Treaty;* change *Ledd* to *Led;* and delete the duplicate word *the.*

When you open a table in Datasheet view, the primary toolbar becomes the Table Datasheet toolbar. Check it out!

Navigation buttons at the bottom of the datasheet allow you to view the first record, the previous record, the next record, a specific record, the last record, or create a new record. To the right of the navigation buttons you can see the total number of records in the table. A datasheet can be scrolled both vertically and horizontally to see all the rows (records) and columns (fields).

Let's open the *At the Alamo* table, check out its records and fields, and then close the table.

1. Click the **Open** button on the Database window toolbar. Open

   The *At the Alamo* table opens in a datasheet in its own window in Datasheet view.

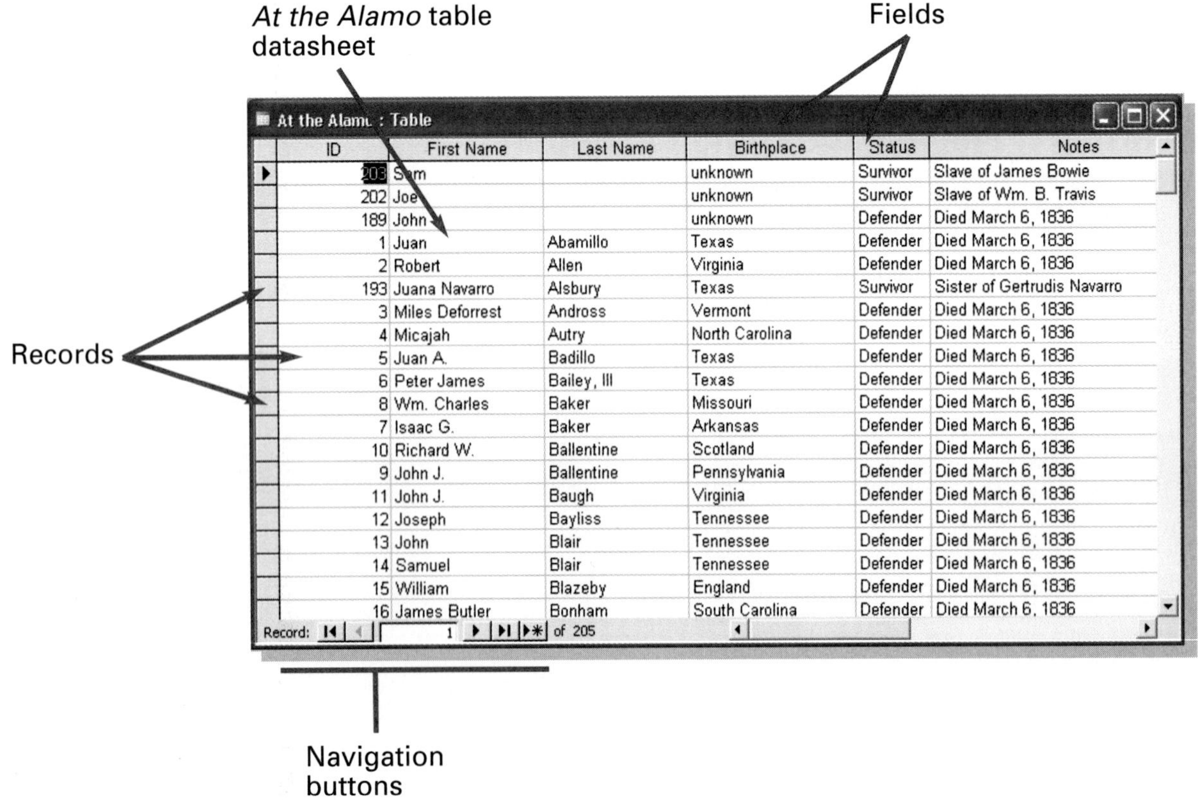

ID	First Name	Last Name	Birthplace	Status	Notes
203	Sam		unknown	Survivor	Slave of James Bowie
202	Joe		unknown	Survivor	Slave of Wm. B. Travis
189	John		unknown	Defender	Died March 6, 1836
1	Juan	Abamillo	Texas	Defender	Died March 6, 1836
2	Robert	Allen	Virginia	Defender	Died March 6, 1836
193	Juana Navarro	Alsbury	Texas	Survivor	Sister of Gertrudis Navarro
3	Miles Deforrest	Andross	Vermont	Defender	Died March 6, 1836
4	Micajah	Autry	North Carolina	Defender	Died March 6, 1836
5	Juan A.	Badillo	Texas	Defender	Died March 6, 1836
6	Peter James	Bailey, III	Texas	Defender	Died March 6, 1836
8	Wm. Charles	Baker	Missouri	Defender	Died March 6, 1836
7	Isaac G.	Baker	Arkansas	Defender	Died March 6, 1836
10	Richard W.	Ballentine	Scotland	Defender	Died March 6, 1836
9	John J.	Ballentine	Pennsylvania	Defender	Died March 6, 1836
11	John J.	Baugh	Virginia	Defender	Died March 6, 1836
12	Joseph	Bayliss	Tennessee	Defender	Died March 6, 1836
13	John	Blair	Tennessee	Defender	Died March 6, 1836
14	Samuel	Blair	Tennessee	Defender	Died March 6, 1836
15	William	Blazeby	England	Defender	Died March 6, 1836
16	James Butler	Bonham	South Carolina	Defender	Died March 6, 1836

3. Set the document's margins to 2-inch top margin and 1-inch left, right, and bottom margins.
4. Select the report's main heading. Center it and change its case to uppercase.
5. Select the entire document. Change the font and font size to Times New Roman 12 point.
6. Select all the paragraphs below the main heading and double-space them. Save the document.

Indenting Text

The last step is to indent each paragraph. Can you see the indent markers on the left and right edges of the Horizontal Ruler? Use ScreenTips, if necessary, to find them. You can indent a paragraph in several ways using the mouse pointer and the indent markers.

Left Indent marker	Indents all the lines of a paragraph inward from the left margin.
Right Indent marker	Indents all the lines of a paragraph inward from the right margin.
First Line Indent marker	Indents *only* the first line of a paragraph inward from the left margin.
Hanging Indent marker	Indents all the lines of a paragraph inward from the left margin *except* the first line.

You can indent a paragraph with options in the **Paragraph** dialog box. To open the dialog box, choose **Format** on the menu bar and then choose **Paragraph**. Click the **Indents and Spacing** tab, if necessary.

Because the report is double-spaced, the first line of each paragraph should be indented 0.5 inch from the left margin.

Reviewing Database Objects

TRAIL 2 MARKER

An *Access* database is a *single* file that can contain many different objects. The *Alamo16* database contains three objects: a table, a form, and a report.

datasheet
Datasheet view
field
form
navigation button
record
report
table

Database Object	Description
table	An object that contains data
form	An object used to enter or edit table data
report	An object used to preview and print table data

Table Objects

Before you begin, make sure that you are viewing the Table objects and that the *At the Alamo* table name is selected in the Database window.

Open the *At the Alamo* table in Datasheet view by clicking the **Open** button on the Database toolbar or by double-clicking the table name in the Database window. In Datasheet view, the data is organized in rows and columns in a datasheet, which is similar to an *Excel* worksheet.

Each row in the datasheet is a record. Each record in the *At the Alamo* table contains all of the data for a person who was known to be at the Alamo during the siege. Each column in the datasheet is a field. Each field contains specific data found in each record as follows:

Field	Data
ID	A unique identifying number
First Name and Last Name	A person's name
Birthplace	Person's birthplace
Status	A person's status: Alamo defender, survivor, Mexican army attacker
Notes	Additional notes about the person
Source 1 and Source 2	Online sources for the data

Database objects are often referred to just by their name and object type. For the rest of this unit, the term *object* will be omitted when referencing a specific table, form, or report.

Let's indent the paragraphs using the First Line Indent marker.

1. Select all the paragraphs below the main heading.
2. Move the mouse pointer to the **First Line Indent** marker.

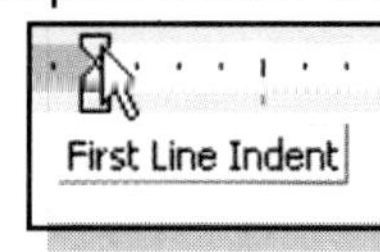

3. Drag the **First Line Indent** marker to the 0.5-inch position on the Horizontal Ruler.

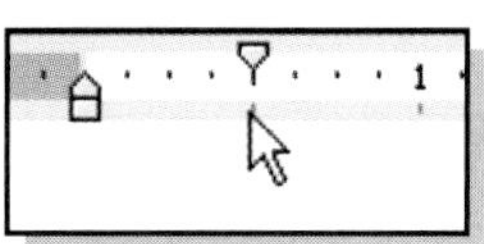

4. Deselect the text. Save the document.

Well done! Julie's formatted document should look like this.

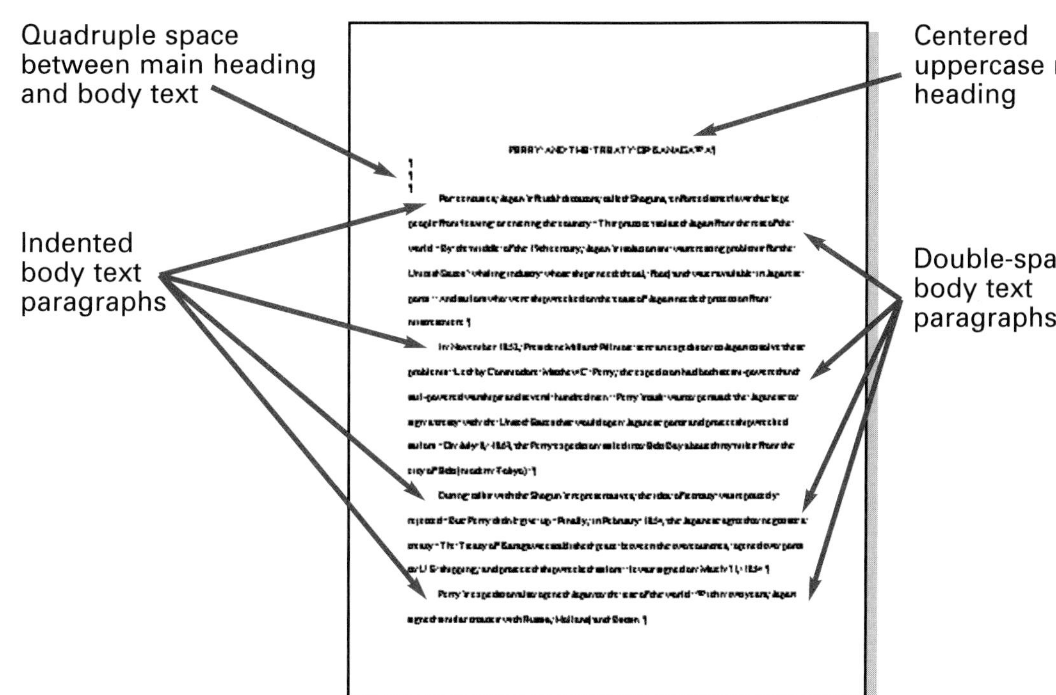

5. Close the document.

In this and the remaining projects in this unit, there are no instructions to print your documents. Your teacher will tell you which documents to print.

Let's open Julie's database and take a closer look at the *Access* and Database windows.

1. Click the **Open** button on the Database toolbar and switch to the folder that contains your *Access* data files.
2. Open the *Alamo16* database. The database file opens in a smaller Database window inside the *Access* window.

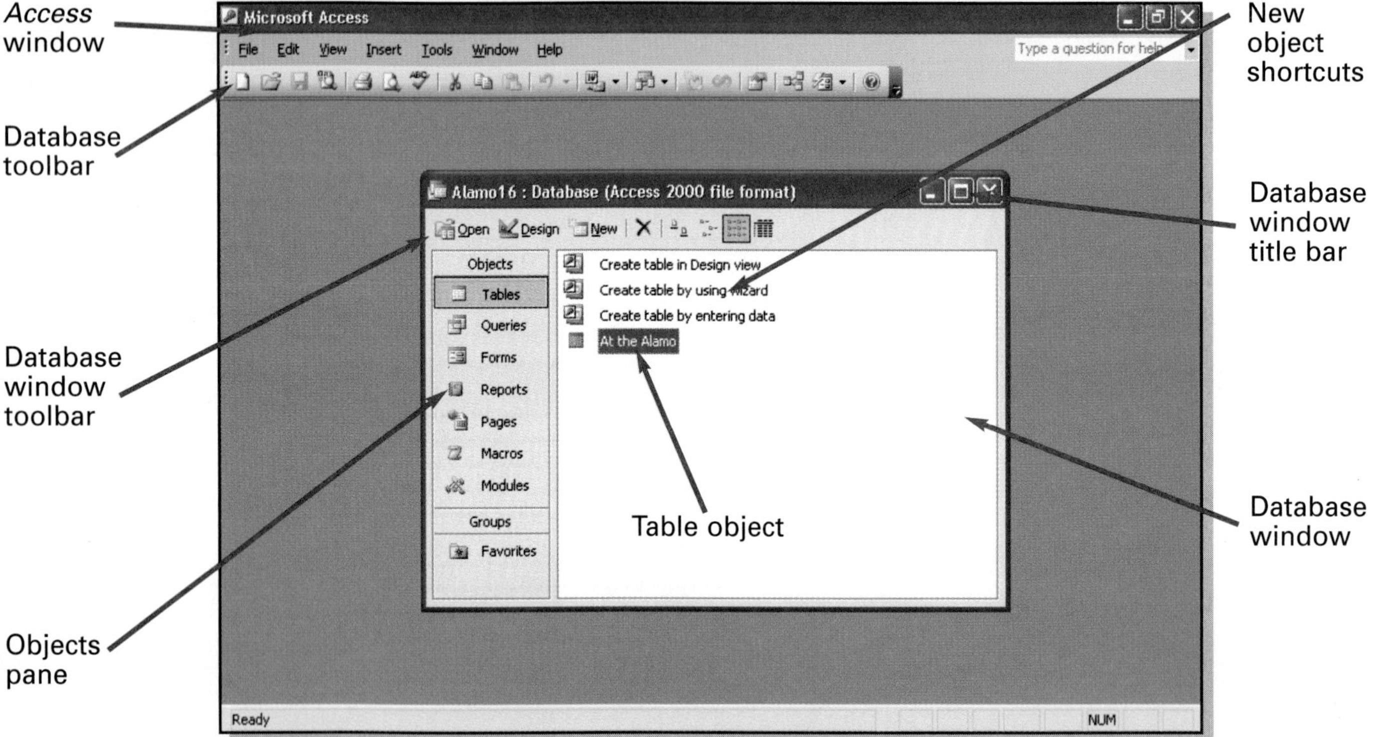

3. Look closely at the smaller Database window to find the following elements:
   - A title bar with the name and file type of the database and **Minimize**, **Maximize**, and **Close** buttons
   - The Database window toolbar with buttons to open, create, delete, and view database objects
   - New object shortcuts that offer multiple ways to create new objects in the database
   - Existing database objects
   - An Objects pane with buttons to view the different types of objects in the database

Next, let's check out the different database objects inside the *Alamo16* database.

Project | *Skills Review*

You learned a lot in this project! We are very impressed with your progress. Let's take a few minutes to review the skills that you learned.

Check spelling and grammar	Choose **Tools** on the menu bar and choose **Spelling and Grammar.**
Create an outline	Choose **Format** on the menu bar and choose **Bullets and Numbering**. Click the **Outline Numbered** tab.
Promote and demote topics in an outline	Click the **Increase Indent** and **Decrease Indent** buttons on the Formatting toolbar.
Set document margins	Choose **File** on the menu bar and choose **Page Setup**. Click the **Margins** tab.
Align paragraphs horizontally between the left and right margins	Choose **Format** on the menu bar and choose **Paragraph.**
Change paragraph line spacing	Choose **Format** on the menu bar and choose **Paragraph.**
Change the font and font size	Choose **Format** on the menu bar and choose **Font.** Times New Roman 12
Change text case	Choose **Format** on the menu bar and choose **Change Case.**
Indent text using the mouse pointer and the indent markers	Drag an indent marker to the desired place on the Horizontal Ruler.

Starting *Out*!

Begin by starting the *Access* application.

1. Click the **Start** button on the taskbar. Point to **All Programs**, point to ***Microsoft Office***, and click ***Microsoft Access***.

If you have a desktop icon for *Access*, just double-click it to open the application.

Good job! Look at the *Access* window. The *Access* application *does not* start with a blank document like *Word*, *Excel*, or *PowerPoint*. After you start *Access*, you must create a new database or open an existing database. Let's open an existing database.

TRAIL 1 MARKER

Opening an Existing Database

database
database object
Database window
electronic database
relational database

A database is used to organize related data in a structured way. One common example of a database is the White Pages telephone book! The White Pages organizes the same type of data—name, address, and telephone number—in ascending alphabetical order for each person or business listed.

Database files that are stored on electronic media, such as your hard drive, a flash drive, or a network drive, are called electronic databases. Electronic databases allow you to easily add, edit, delete, and reorganize data. An example of a simple electronic database is an *Excel* worksheet *list* like the ones you sorted or filtered in the *Excel* unit.

You use the *Access* application to create a more complex type of electronic database, called a relational database. A relational database is a *single* file that contains multiple related items called database objects. For example, a relational database stores its data in a single table object or in multiple, linked table objects. Other *Access* database objects include reports and forms. You will learn more about database tables, forms, and reports as you work in this unit.

As you work in *Access*, you will not see the familiar Standard and Formatting toolbars you worked with in *Word*, *Excel*, and *PowerPoint*. The primary toolbar in the *Access* window is the Database toolbar. Each different type of database object—table, form, and report—has its own toolbars. Do not forget to use ScreenTips to identify the buttons on all the new toolbars you see as you work in an *Access* database!

An *Access* database opens in its own Database window inside the *Access* window and is generally not maximized with the *Access* window.

Warning! You cannot save an *Access* database with a new name. In this unit, the database files you open automatically become your solution files. Also, you can open only one *Access* database at a time.

Exploring on Your Own

Using classroom, library, CD-ROM, or online resources, research modern Japan. Take brief notes about what you learn. Organize your research notes for an outline you can use to write a report. Then complete Part 1 and Part 2.

Part 1: Create a new document and save it as *Japan outline2.* Type an uppercase title, tap the ENTER key, and type your brief research notes in a list. Change the document's margins to the appropriate margins for an outline. Select the title and center it. Select the text below the title and format it as an outline using the **Outline Numbered** list feature. Use the I, II, III, A, B, C, 1, 2, 3 number system for Levels 1, 2, and 3. Demote the subtopics and detail paragraphs in the outline using the **Increase Indent** button. Select the Level 1 topics and change the case to uppercase, if necessary. Double-space the outline. Spell-check, save, and close the document.

Part 2: Create a new blank document and save it as *Japan2.* Change the margins to the appropriate margins for a single-page unbound report. Type a main heading in uppercase, tap the ENTER key four times (QS), and type the text for a single-page report about Japan using your outline as your guide. Select the main heading and center it. Double-space the body text and indent the first lines of the paragraphs 0.5 inch from the left margin. Spell-check, save, and close the document.

Reading in Action

Taking Notes in Outline Form

Read the following passage on Japanese samurai. Use the **Outline Numbered** list feature to complete the outline below with specific details.

The samurai class arose in a time in Japanese history when civil battle was continual and emperors needed highly skilled and faithful warriors to secure their power and empire. Samurai warriors carried two weapons—a long sword and a short sword. They wore colorful armor including a helmet, breastplate, and limb protectors. The samurai was a master of sword-fighting and unarmed combat.

The samurai was not just a skilled warrior. He was also a poet and an artist. The samurai was well-educated and equally devoted to both the martial arts and the fine arts. Often a samurai would write a poem before going to battle.

I) The Samurai
  A) Samurai as warrior
  B)
    1) Carried two swords and wore armor
    2)
II)

Math in Action

Converting Currencies

A samurai sword costs 23,200 yen. How much does the sword cost in U.S. dollars? If the conversion rate is 116 yen for each U.S. dollar, divide the cost in yen by 116 to find the cost in dollars. To convert the cost of an item from U.S. dollars to yen, multiply the cost in dollars times 116 yen.

cost of the samurai sword = 23,200 yen ÷ 116 = $200

Now you try it! How many yen would you need to purchase a $50 textbook? How many U.S. dollars would you need to purchase a textbook that costs 5,000 yen?

Project 16

Database

Remembering the Alamo

Explorers' Guide

Data files: *Alamo16*
Texians16

Objectives:

In this project, you will:

- open an existing database
- review database objects
- edit, add, and delete records
- find specific data
- preview a datasheet

Exploring on Your Own

additional practice in:

- opening an existing database
- reviewing database objects
- editing, adding, and deleting records
- finding specific data
- previewing a datasheet

Exploring Across the Curriculum

Internet/Web
Language Arts
Social Studies
Getting Help
Your Personal Journal

Our Exploration Assignment:

Review database objects, update a table, and preview a datasheet

Remember the Alamo! That famous rallying cry helped the Texians win the fight to found the Republic of Texas. Julie researched the people who were at the siege of the Alamo, an old Spanish mission in San Antonio, Texas. She saved her data in a database. Now she needs your help to update the data and then preview it. Just follow the Trail Markers to open an existing database; add, edit, and delete records; find specific data; and then preview a datasheet.

Exploring Across the Curriculum

Internet/Web

The Web

A search engine uses software, called a spider or robot, to find Web pages. Google is an example of a search engine. A directory is an online search tool that lists websites by category. To use a directory, click links from page to page until you find the page you want. Yahoo! is an example of a directory.

The first Englishman to live in Japan was Will Adams, a seventeenth century sailor. To learn about Will Adams, search the Web. Open your Web browser and use a favorite to view the Learning with Computers Web page (www.lwcgreen.keyboarding.com). Click the **Links** option. Click **Project 2**. Click the **Google** and **Yahoo!** links to open each search tool's Web page. Type the keywords *"Will Adams" + Japan* in the **Search** text box. *Do not forget to type the open and closing quotation marks and the plus sign.* Click the **Search** button to find a list of Web pages that describe Adams and his adventures. Click the links to those pages and take brief notes you can use to create an outline and a single-page unbound report.

Part 1: Create a new blank document and save it as *Adams outline2.* Change the margins to the appropriate margins for an outline. Center an uppercase title at the top of the document. Double-space after the title. Type your brief notes as a list. Format the list as an outline using the **Outline Numbered** list feature. Use the **Increase Indent** button to demote subtopics and details. Select the Level 1 topics and change the case to uppercase, if necessary. Double-space the outline. Spell-check the document. Then save and close it.

Part 2: Create a second new document and save it as *Adams2.* Change the margins to the appropriate margins for a single-page unbound report. Add an uppercase, centered main heading. Insert a quadruple space (three blank lines) and then type at least three paragraphs describing Will Adams and his adventures. Double-space the body text paragraphs and indent the first lines 0.5 inch from the left margin. Spell-check, save, and close the document.

Explore More

Database

Unit 4

A database is a great way to store information that you can access quickly and easily. The Explorers Club is going to create databases about history, art, and nutrition. Join Julie, Luis, and me to:

- **Remember the Alamo**
- **Catalog the Native Arts of the Americas**
- **Plan a Well-Balanced Diet**

The application that we will use to create our databases is called *Access*. You will learn how to use *Access* to review data about the siege of the Alamo; organize data about art created by people who live in North, Central, and South America; and organize and arrange data about nutritional value of different foods. You will open and create database files and then create tables to contain your data. Then you will learn how to add and edit the data. After you have entered all your data, you will learn some neat ways to find just the facts you want by sorting, filtering, and querying the data in the databases. Come on! We cannot wait!

Exploring Across the Curriculum

Language Arts: Words to Know

Look up the meaning of the following words, terms, or phrases in a classroom dictionary, CD-ROM dictionary or encyclopedia, or online dictionary.

commodore	emissary	isolationism	Japanese archipelago
samurai	shogun	steamship	treaty

Create a new document. Save the document as *definitions2* followed by your initials. Change the margins to a 2-inch top margin and 1-inch left, right, and bottom margins. Type **Terms and Definitions** as a centered main heading at the top of the document and insert two blank lines. Change the main heading font to Arial 14 point and the case to uppercase.

Then, starting on the second blank line below the main heading, type each term on one line and its definition on the following line. Insert a blank line between each definition and the next term. Select all the terms using the CTRL key and change the font to Arial 12 point. Check the spelling. Then save and close the document.

Social Studies: Research and Write

Work with a classmate to use library, classroom, or online resources to research Japanese society during the nineteenth century. Why was Japan isolated from the rest of the world? Did the Japanese emperor actually rule Japan? What roles did a daimyo, shogun, and a samurai play in the Japanese feudal society? What major event helped to open Japan to foreigners?

Part 1: Using the *Word* **Outline Numbered** list feature, create an outline for a single-page report that answers these questions. Set the appropriate margins for an outline. Center an uppercase title. Change the Level 1 topics to uppercase. Demote subtopics and details using the **Increase Indent** button. Double-space the outline. Spell-check, save, and close the outline.

Part 2: Create a single-page report based on the outline. Set the appropriate margins; add a centered, uppercase main heading; and insert a quadruple space (three blank lines) between the main heading and the body text. Type at least three body paragraphs. Indent the paragraphs 0.5 inch from the left margin and double-space them. Spell-check, save, and close the report.

Explore More

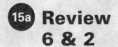

15a Review 6 & 2

Key each line twice. Double-space between 2-line groups.

1 j 6 j 6 | j u 6 j u 6 | ju76 ju76 | 6jy6 6jy6 | juy6 juy6;

2 a6z b6y c6x d6w e6v f6u g6t h6s i6r j6q k6p l6o mn

3 s 2 s 2 | s w 2 s w 2 | xsw2 xsw2 | 2sx2 2sx2 | w2x2 w2x2;

4 z2a y2b x2c w2d v2e u2f t2g s2h r2i q2j p2k o2l nm

5 Of the 1,527 students enrolled, 486 were freshmen.

6 Karla scored 28, 36, and 19 points in three games?

7 Joe lives at 390 Lake Street; Kay at 207 Broadway.

8 The ZIP Code for 2158 Coolidge Boulevard is 54720.

Technique Tip
Do not stop or pause between words.

15b Build Skill: Paragraphs with Numbers

Key each paragraph twice; double-space between paragraphs.

Delaware became the first of the United States on December 7, 1787. The second state, Pennsylvania, became a state five days later on December 12, 1787. The last two states admitted were Alaska, January 3, 1959, and Hawaii, August 21, 1959.

The smallest state in the U.S. is Rhode Island. It is approximately 1,200 square miles. Alaska is the largest state. It is about 572,000 square miles.

The population of the states varies a great deal. Based on 2002 estimates, California is the most heavily populated state with 35,116,033 residents. Wyoming is the least with an estimated 498,703 residents.

Exploring Across the Curriculum

Getting Help

Type **indenting** in the **Ask A Question** box and tap the ENTER key. Using the online Help links, research how to use Left and Right indents to make paragraphs stand out from the rest of the body text. Then open the *Perry2* document and practice what you learned. Close the document without saving it.

Getting Help

Your Personal Journal

Open your personal journal document. Insert today's date. Think about what you learned about Commodore Perry and his expedition to Japan. What persuasive reasons would you have given Japan's emperor to persuade him to open Japan to the Western world? Beginning on the second line below the date, write your response in one or two brief paragraphs. Spell-check, save, and close your journal document.

Online Enrichment Games (Fun Stuff) @ www.lwcgreen.keyboarding.com

Exploring Across the Curriculum

Getting Help

Type **send slides to Microsoft Word** in the **Ask A Question** box and tap the ENTER key. Research how to send an entire presentation to *Microsoft Word* to create a *Word* document that can be used for audience handouts. Then, open the *Leonardo15* presentation you completed in this project. Use your research to send the presentation to *Word* to create a *Word* document that has blank lines to the right of each slide and pasted slide objects. Preview the new *Word* document and then close it without saving. Close the presentation without saving it.

Your Personal Journal

Open your personal journal document. Insert today's date and two blank lines. Update your journal with a brief biography of Leonardo da Vinci and his important contributions to science, engineering, and art. Spell-check, save, and close your journal.

Online Enrichment Games (Fun Stuff)  www.lwcgreen.keyboarding.com

Keyboarding Project 2

2a Review h, e, i, r

Key each line twice. Double-space between 2-line groups.

h
1 jh jh|hjh hjh|ha ha|hs hs|hd hd|hf hf|hj hj|hk hk;
2 has has|had had|half half|hall; halls;|dash; dash;

e
3 de de|ede ede|el el|ea ea|es es|ek ek|ef ef|ej ej;
4 seek seek|fell fell|ease ease|feed feed|jell jell;

i
5 ki ki|iki iki|i; i;|il il|ik ik|ij ij|ia ia|id id;
6 is is|his his|ill ill|kid kid|hike hike|side side;

r
7 fr fr|rfr rfr|rd rd|rj rj|rs rs|rk rk|ra ra|rl rl;
8 jar jar|hair hair|ride ride|hear hear|cards cards;

2b Technique: ENTER

Key each line twice single-spaced; double-space between 2-line groups.

1 if;
2 if he;
3 if he did
4 if he did see
5 if he did see her

6 ask
7 ask her
8 ask her if
9 ask her if he
10 ask her if he has

Exploring Across the Curriculum

Language Arts: Words to Know

Look up the meaning of the following terms or phrases using a classroom, library, CD-ROM, or online encyclopedia or dictionary.

anatomy	botany	fresco	horizon line
Italian Renaissance	linear perspective	realism	sketchbook

Create a new presentation. Save it as *definitions15*. Type **Leonardo da Vinci** as the title and **Definitions** as the subtitle on the Title Slide. Apply the slide design with the color scheme of your choice. Insert eight new slides and apply the Title and Text layout to each slide.

Type a single term in the title placeholder and the related definition in the bulleted-list placeholder on each of the eight slides. Add slide numbers to all the slides *except* the Title Slide. Switch to Slide Sorter view and create a Summary Slide for the first four Title and Text slides. Create a second Summary Slide for the last four Title and Text slides. Add the slide transitions of your choice; then save and close the presentation.

Art: Research, Write, and Present

Leonardo da Vinci and other Italian Renaissance artists were among the first to use *linear perspective* to create realistic paintings and drawings. Using library or online resources, research the linear perspective technique and how it is used to create the illusion of depth and distance. Identify five examples of linear perspective in Italian Renaissance paintings. List the date, artist, and painting name in an *Excel* workbook. Then create a new presentation and apply the design template and color scheme of your choice. Add a Title and Text slide, and use it to define linear perspective. Add a Title Only slide; then copy and paste your list of paintings on it as a table, an embedded workbook object, or a picture object. Cite your sources on Title and Text slides. Insert a Summary Slide as a new slide 2 and use the bulleted list text to create hyperlinks to each related slide. Add action buttons back to slide 2. Run the slide show. Save and close the presentation.

Explore More

Project 3
Word Processing

Touring Shakespeare's Globe

Data file: *Globe Theater*

Objectives:

In this project, you will:

- apply the Bold, Italic, and Underline font styles
- use the thesaurus
- create a bulleted list
- cut, copy, and paste text
- insert page breaks, section breaks, and page numbers
- add footnotes

Exploring on Your Own
additional practice in:

- applying the Bold, Italic, and Underline font styles
- using the thesaurus
- creating a bulleted list
- cutting, copying, and pasting text
- inserting page breaks, section breaks, and page numbers
- adding footnotes

Exploring Across the Curriculum

Internet/Web
Language Arts
Social Studies
Getting Help
Your Personal Journal

© PAWEL LIBERA/CORBIS

Our Exploration Assignment:

Formatting a multi-page unbound report

"All the world's a stage." An actor spoke these words by William Shakespeare on the stage of the Globe 400 years ago. Today, actors perform Shakespeare's plays at the new Globe, which was rebuilt in the 1990s to look just as it did in 1599. Follow the Trail Markers to help Ray finish his report on Shakespeare's Globe. You will apply the Bold, Italic, and Underline font styles; use *Word*'s thesaurus; create a bulleted list; cut, copy, and paste text; insert page breaks, section breaks, and page numbers; and cite sources with footnotes.

Exploring Across the Curriculum

Internet/Web

You can learn more about Leonardo by using the Web. Open your Web browser and use a favorite to view the Learning with Computers Web page (www.lwcgreen.keyboarding.com). Click the **Links** option. Click **Project 15**. Click the links to research facts about the life of Leonardo da Vinci. When and where was he born? When did he die? Who was his family? What was his education? Why is he called a Renaissance man? For whom did he work as an engineer? What are some of his most famous achievements? Then create a new workbook and save it as *facts15*. Rename the Sheet1 sheet tab as **Leonardo da Vinci**. Add a worksheet title and the column names **Date** and **Fact**. Record eight to ten important facts in the worksheet. Resize the columns as necessary and sort the data in ascending order by the **Date** column.

Then, create a new presentation and save it as *Renaissance15*. Apply the design template and color scheme of your choice. Add an appropriate title and subtitle to the Title Slide. Insert a **Title Only** slide as slide 2 and type **Facts About Leonardo** as the title. Insert one or more **Title and Text** slides at the end of your presentation and cite your sources on them. Add slide numbers and your name as footer text.

Make certain that the *Renaissance15* presentation and the *facts15* workbook are both open. Select and copy all the data on the *Leonardo da Vinci* worksheet and paste it on slide 2 as either a table, an embedded workbook object, or a picture object. Format the table, embedded workbook object, or picture object as desired.

Insert a Summary Slide as the new slide 2. Change the title to **About Leonardo**. Use the slide 2 text to create hyperlinks to the appropriate slides. Add action buttons back to slide 2.

Add your own speaker notes to slide 2. Add the slide transitions of your choice to all the slides and the custom animation of your choice to the Title Slide. Then run the slide show and navigate using the hyperlinks and action buttons. Use the slide 3 hyperlinks to open your Web browser and access the Web sites. Save and close the presentation.

Explore More

Starting Out!

Begin by opening the *Globe Theater* document and saving it with a new name.

1. Open the *Globe Theater* document and save it as *Globe Theater3.*

Great! Ray's *Globe Theater3* document is a two-page unbound report. The first step in finalizing the report is to emphasize some important text.

Ergonomics *TIP*

Check the position of your mouse and mouse pad! Be certain they are located immediately to the right or left of your keyboard so you do not have to reach too far to use the mouse.

TRAIL 1 MARKER

Applying the Bold, Italic, and Underline Font Styles

font style
side heading

The Bold, Italic, and Underline font styles are used to add emphasis to individual characters, entire words, or phrases. Applying font styles is part of character formatting.

- **The Bold style makes text darker.**
- *The Italic style slants text to the right.*
- The default Underline style adds a line below words and spaces.

Apply font styles to selected text by clicking the **Bold**, **Italic**, and **Underline** buttons on the Formatting toolbar. It is easy to remove a font style! Just select the text and click the **Bold**, **Italic**, or **Underline** button on the Formatting toolbar to turn off the font style.

The phrase *Elizabethan Era* appears three times in the *Globe Theater3* document. To make the text stand out from the other text, Ray wants you to apply the Bold font style. Remember—you can use the CTRL key to select text in different places in the document and then apply the same formatting all at once!

A side heading is a short, underlined phrase that begins at the left margin and introduces a section of a report. Apply the default Underline style to the three side headings in the *Globe Theater3* document.

In a report, the names of plays, books, magazines, and journals are italicized. Apply the Italic font style to the names of the four plays listed near the bottom of page 1.

To select a single word for the Bold, Underline, or Italic style, just move the insertion point into the word. Then apply the style you want. Try it!

Exploring on Your Own

Blaze your own trail by practicing the new skills learned in this project! Open the *High Renaissance* data file and save it as *High Renaissance15*. Apply the design template and color scheme of your choice and view slide 2. Then open the *artists* workbook from the data files. Copy the range **A1:D11** and paste it on slide 2 as a table; on slide 3 as an embedded object; and on slide 4 as a picture object. Reposition, resize, and format the table and objects as desired.

Switch to Slide Sorter view and insert a Summary Slide using all the slides. Change the title of the Summary Slide to **Ways to Paste *Excel* Data**. Create text hyperlinks on the new slide 2 (the Summary Slide) to the relevant slides 3–6. Add action buttons on slides 3–5 that return to slide 2.

Create your own speaker notes for the new slide 2. Preview the speaker notes and, with permission, print them. Add your name as footer text, and add slide numbers to all slides except the Title Slide. Add slide transitions *of your choice* to all the slides and add the custom animation *of your choice* to the Title Slide. Run the slide show; then save and close the presentation.

Reading in Action

Multiple-meaning words

The terms *High Renaissance*, *medium*, and *work* have specific meanings when they are used in the context of art. Read the passage below. Use the context clues to write a definition of these three terms.

The Renaissance, which literally means *rebirth*, refers to a period in the 1400s, when art and science flourished. At the end of the 1400s, art entered a phase called High Renaissance, which lasted about twenty years. Perhaps the two most famous artists of this period are Leonardo da Vinci and Michelangelo. Although they are both recognized as great painters, paint was not their only medium. Their works include sculpture and architecture. Michelangelo's *The Pietà* was his first work for the Vatican, and is an excellent example of High Renaissance sculpture.

Math in Action

The Golden Ratio

Leonardo da Vinci used the golden ratio in his artwork. The golden ratio is 1.618. Why is this ratio special? If $\frac{a}{b} = 1.618$, then it is always true that $\frac{a + b}{a} = 1.618$.

A rectangle is a golden rectangle if the ratio of its length to its width is 1.618. To make a golden rectangle, multiply the width by 1.618.

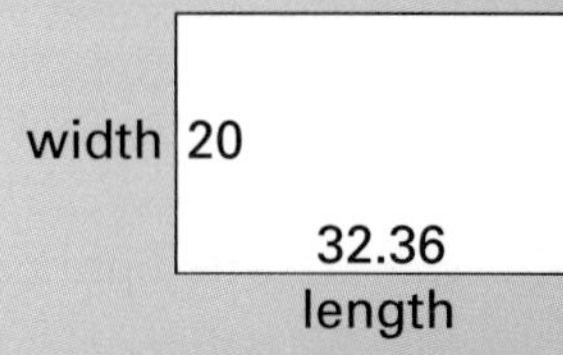

For example, if the width is 20 inches, then the length is 20 inches x 1.618 = 32.36 inches.

Now you try it! The width of a golden rectangle is 50 inches. What is the length?

Let's apply the Bold style to the phrase *Elizabethan Era;* the Underline style to the side headings; and the Italic style to the play names.

1. Use the I-beam to select the phrase *Elizabethan Era* in the line that begins *Elizabeth I,* which appears about halfway down page 1.
2. Press and hold the CTRL key. Select the phrase *Elizabethan Era* in the following line.
3. Scroll to view page 2. Select the phrase *Elizabethan Era* in line 2 near the top of the page. Release the CTRL key.
4. Click the **Bold** button. **B**
5. Press the CTRL + HOME keys to move the insertion point to the top of the document. Select the side heading *William Shakespeare.* Press and hold the CTRL key. Select the side heading *The Original Globe Theater* at the bottom of page 1 and the side heading *The New Globe Theater* near the middle of page 2. Release the CTRL key.
6. Click the **Underline** button. **U** Press the CTRL + HOME keys.
7. Use the I-beam to select the play names *Julius Caesar, Hamlet, Henry V,* and *Macbeth* near the bottom of page 1. Click the **Italic** button. *I* Press the CTRL + HOME keys. Save the document.

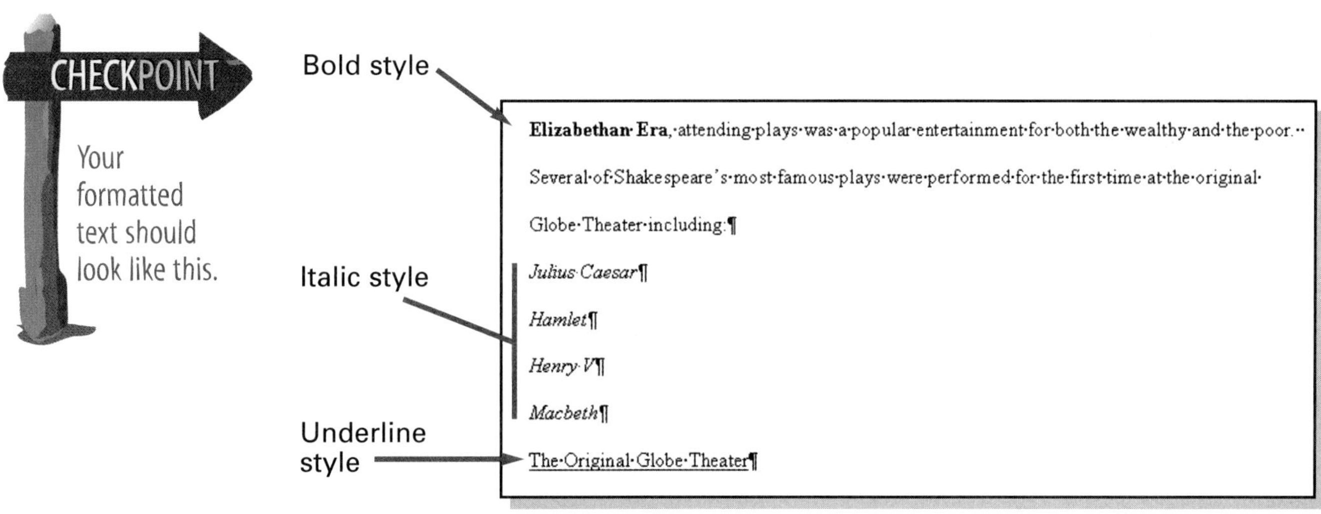

Super! Now, replace a word with another word using the thesaurus.

Project | *Skills Review*

You learned a lot in this project! We are very impressed with your progress. Let's take a few minutes to review the skills that you learned.

Paste *Excel* worksheet data as a table, embedded workbook object, or a picture object	In *Excel:* choose **Edit** on the menu bar and choose **Copy**. In *PowerPoint:* choose **Edit** on the menu bar and choose **Paste**. Click the **Paste Options** icon drop-down arrow and click an option.
Edit an embedded *Excel* workbook object or picture object	Double-click the object.
Insert a Summary Slide	Switch to Slide Sorter view, select the slides, and click the **Summary Slide** button.
Create hyperlinks	Select text or a slide object and then choose **Insert** on the menu bar and choose **Hyperlink**.
Create action buttons	Choose **Slide Show** on the menu bar, point to **Action Buttons**, and click an icon on the grid.
Create speaker notes	Type the notes in the notes pane below the slide pane. Then preview and print them on separate notes pages.

TRAIL 2 MARKER

Using the Thesaurus

antonym
synonym
thesaurus

Use *Word*'s built-in thesaurus to replace a selected word with a synonym or antonym. A synonym is a word with the same or similar meaning. An antonym is a word that has the opposite meaning.

You can find synonyms and antonyms for a word very easily. When you right-click the word and point to **Synonyms** on the shortcut menu, a list of synonyms and antonyms appears. Simply click a synonym or antonym from the list to replace the current word. To open the **Research** task pane and search for more synonyms or antonyms, choose **Thesaurus** on the shortcut menu.

You can also open the **Research** task pane by choosing **Tools** on the menu bar, pointing to **Language**, and then choosing **Thesaurus**.

Let's replace the words *copy* and *exactly* in the *Globe Theater3* document with synonyms.

1. Right-click the word *copy* in the first sentence of the second body paragraph on page 1. Point to **Synonyms** on the shortcut menu.

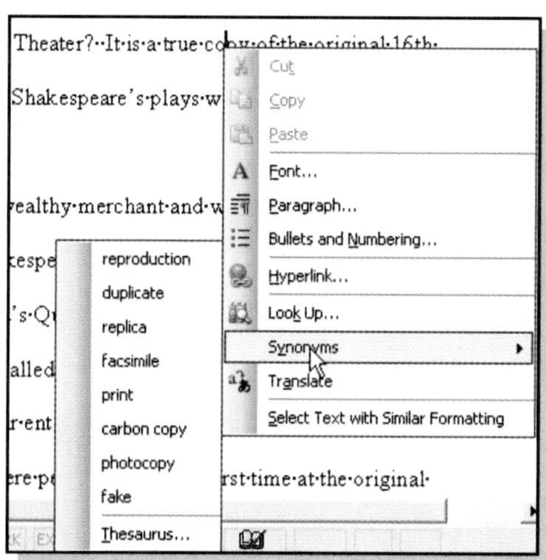

2. Click **replica**.
3. Scroll to view the top of page 2. Right-click the word *exactly* in the first sentence on page 2. Point to **Synonyms** and click **just**. Press the CTRL + HOME keys. Save the document.

Apply It!

Let's add speaker notes to slide 2 and preview the notes page.

1. View **slide 2** and click inside the *notes pane* below the slide pane to position the insertion point. Type the following text and italicize the phrase *Renaissance man.*

   Leonardo da Vinci is called a *Renaissance man* because of the multiple interests he explored during the Italian Renaissance of the fifteenth and sixteenth centuries. He made important discoveries in science, imagined inventions before it was possible to create them, and was an accomplished artist.

2. Click the **Print Preview** button.
3. Click the **Print What** button drop-down arrow and click **Notes Pages**. Scroll to view the notes page for **slide 2**.

CHECKPOINT
Your slide 2 notes page should look similar to this.

Slide 2 notes page with speaker notes

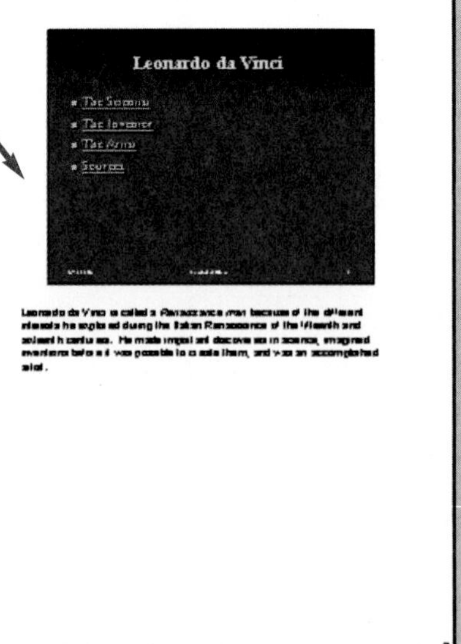
Leonardo da Vinci

4. Close Print Preview. Good work! Now have some fun by adding the slide transitions *of your choice* to all the slides and the custom animation *of your choice* to the Title Slide. Run the slide show; then save and close the presentation.

CHECKPOINT

Your replaced words should look like this.

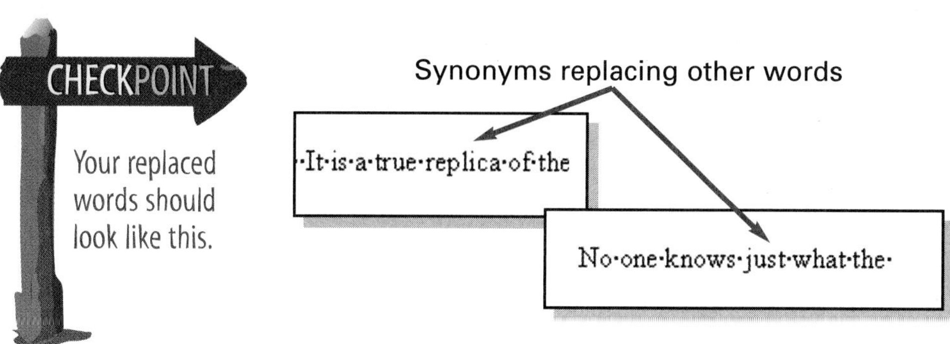
Synonyms replacing other words
·It·is·a·true·replica·of·the
No·one·knows·just·what·the·

Well done! Next, you will create a bulleted list.

TRAIL 3 MARKER

Creating a Bulleted List

bulleted list
list
numbered list
ordered list
unordered list

A list is two or more short paragraphs that itemize information in a document. To make a list easier to read and more attractive, you can format it as a bulleted list or as a numbered list.

A bulleted list, sometimes called an unordered list, begins each paragraph with a bullet graphic. A numbered list, sometimes called an ordered list, begins each paragraph with a number in sequence, such as 1, 2, 3. To create a bulleted list or a numbered list from existing paragraphs, select the paragraphs and click the **Bullets** button or the **Numbering** button on the Formatting toolbar.

Another way to create bulleted and numbered lists is by choosing **Format** on the menu bar and choosing **Bullets** and **Numbering**. The **Bullets** and **Numbering** dialog box has several options for styles of bullets and numbers.

Let's select the list of the names of four plays first performed at the original Globe and then format the list as a bulleted list. A bulleted list should be preceded and followed by a double space; however, the list itself is single-spaced.

Apply It!

Let's format the play names as a single-spaced bulleted list.

1. Scroll to view the list of play names near the bottom of page 1.
2. Use the I-beam to select the play names *Julius Caesar, Hamlet, Henry V,* and *Macbeth.*
3. Click the **Bullets** button. Deselect the paragraphs.
4. Select the bulleted paragraphs *Julius Caesar, Hamlet,* and *Henry V. Do not select the Macbeth paragraph.* Click the **Line Spacing** button drop-down arrow and click **1.0.** Deselect the bulleted paragraphs. Save the document.

Let's run the slide show and navigate using hyperlinks and action buttons.

1. View **slide 1** and run the slide show. Click the mouse button to advance to slide 2.
2. Click the **The Scientist** hyperlink to jump to slide 3. Point to the **action button** in the upper-right corner of slide 3. The mouse pointer becomes a pointing hand. Click the **action button** to jump back to slide 2. **The Scientist** hyperlink changes color to indicate that you have already clicked it.
3. Continue by clicking the hyperlinks on slide 2 to jump to a specific slide and then clicking the action button to jump back to slide 2. Tap the ESC key when you have finished with the slide show. Save the presentation.

Well done! Your last task is to add speaker notes to slide 2 and add slide transitions, slide timings, and custom animation.

TRAIL 6 MARKER

Adding Speaker Notes

notes pages
speaker notes

You can add additional information you want to tell your audience as you advance your slides during a slide show as speaker notes. Speaker notes are typed in the notes pane below the slide pane and printed as separate notes pages. Each notes page contains both a miniature of the slide and the note text.

Speaker notes are also typed in the text placeholder on notes pages. To view the notes pages, choose **View** on the menu bar and choose **Notes Pages**.

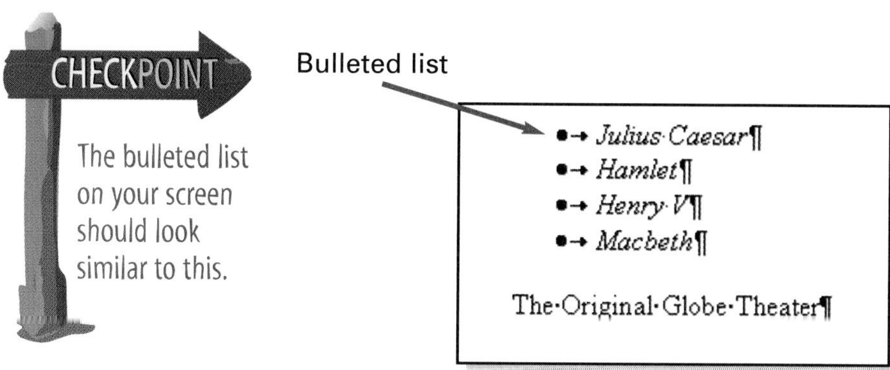
CHECKPOINT
The bulleted list on your screen should look similar to this.
Bulleted list
•→ Julius·Caesar¶
•→ Hamlet¶
•→ Henry·V¶
•→ Macbeth¶
The·Original·Globe·Theater¶

Nice job! Next, let's rearrange two paragraphs by cutting and pasting existing text and then copying and pasting existing text.

You can quickly convert a bulleted list to a numbered list and vice versa. Just select the list and click either the **Bullets** or the **Numbering** button. Try it!

TRAIL 4 MARKER

Cutting, Copying, and Pasting Text

copying and pasting
cutting and pasting
Office Clipboard

Moving text from one place to another in a document is called cutting and pasting the text. To cut and paste text, first select it; then click the **Cut** button on the Standard toolbar to remove the selected text. Move the insertion point to where you want the cut text to appear and click the **Paste** button on the Standard toolbar.

Duplicating text is called copying and pasting the text. To copy and paste selected text, click the **Copy** button; move the insertion point to where you want the duplicate text to appear; and click the **Paste** button.

Text that you cut or copy is temporarily stored in a special place in your computer's memory called the Office Clipboard. You can store up to 24 cut or copied items on the Office Clipboard and paste them one at a time or all at once using features in the **Clipboard** task pane. Items remain on the Office Clipboard until you clear them.

The **Clipboard** task pane usually opens automatically when more than one cut or copied item is stored on the Office Clipboard. To manually open the **Clipboard** task pane, choose **Edit** on the menu bar and choose **Office Clipboard**.

3. Click the **Hyperlink to** drop-down arrow. Click **Slide** to open the **Hyperlink to Slide** dialog box. Click **2. Leonardo da Vinci** in the **Slide title** list.

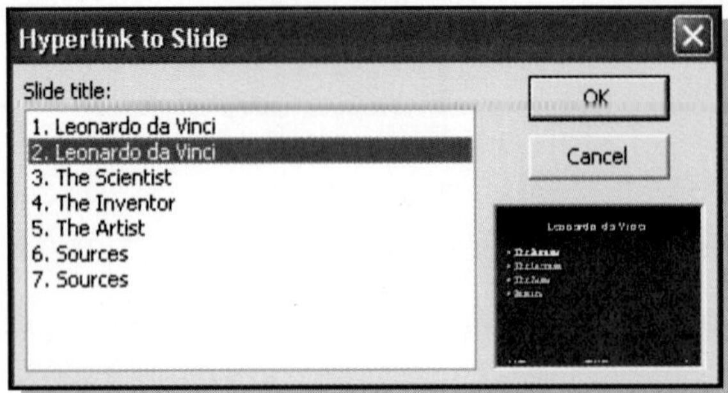

4. Click the **OK** button. Click the **OK** button in the **Action Settings** dialog box. The selected action button is now linked to slide 2. Drag the bright yellow adjustment handle in the upper-left corner of the action button to the right to give the button a more dramatic 3-dimensional look.

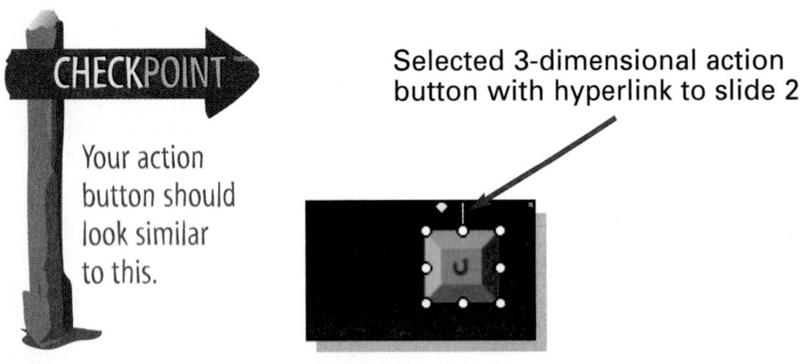

CHECKPOINT
Your action button should look similar to this.
Selected 3-dimensional action button with hyperlink to slide 2

5. Copy the selected action button. Then deselect it. Paste the copied action button in the upper-right corners of slides 4 and 5. Deselect the pasted buttons. Save the presentation.

Excellent! Each time you click an action button, you will jump back to slide 2. Now you are ready to run the slide show and test all the hyperlinks.

Let's move a paragraph to a new location and then duplicate text.

1. Scroll to view page 2.
2. Move the insertion point immediately in front of the word *Before* in the paragraph that begins *Before 1576.* Press and hold the SHIFT key. Click at the end of the paragraph to select the entire paragraph.

Before·1576,·plays·were·performed·by·traveling·actors·in·the·private·homes·of·the·wealthy,·town·halls,·and·inn·courtyards.··By·1599,·when·the·original·Globe·Theater·was·built,·open-air·theaters·were·very·popular.··Two·other·open-air·theaters,·the·Rose·and·the·Swan,·were·also·located·on·the·south·bank·of·the·Thames·near·the·Globe·Theater.¶

The·New·Globe·Theater¶

3. Click the **Cut** button.
4. Move the insertion point in front of the word *No* in the paragraph that begins *No one knows* on page 1. Click the **Paste** button.
5. Select the phrase *Globe Theater* and the following space in the first sentence of the second paragraph on page 2. Click the **Copy** button. Move the insertion point immediately in front of the word *accidentally* in the next to last sentence of the second paragraph.

Clipboard task pane

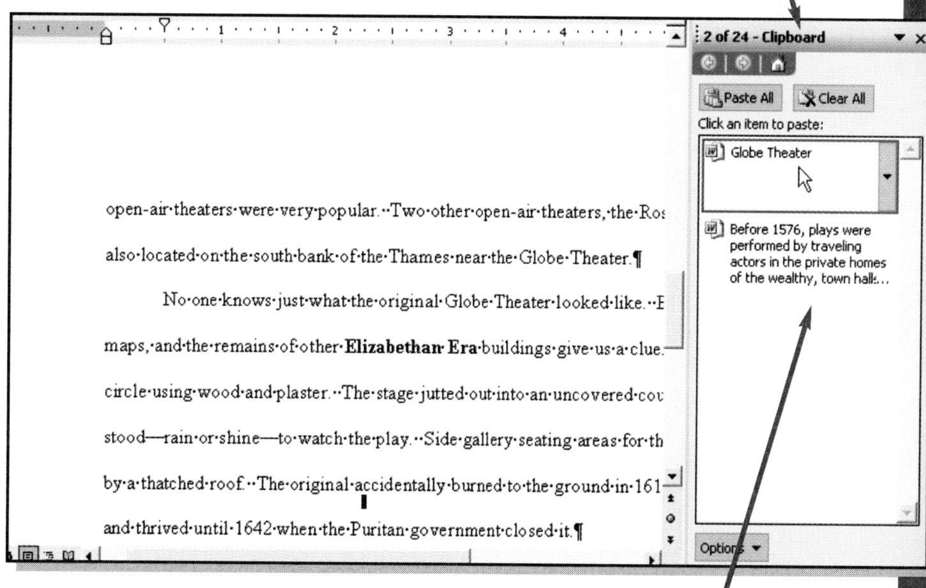

Cut or copied text on the Office Clipboard

The **Clipboard** task pane should open and contain the last two cut and copied items. If it does not automatically open, choose **Edit** on the menu bar and choose **Office Clipboard**.

6. Click the **Globe Theater** item in the task pane to insert it at the position of the insertion point.
7. Click the **Clear All** button in the task pane. Click the **Close** button on the task pane title bar. Save the document.

Well done! Now let's set the correct margins for a two-page unbound report and insert page numbers.

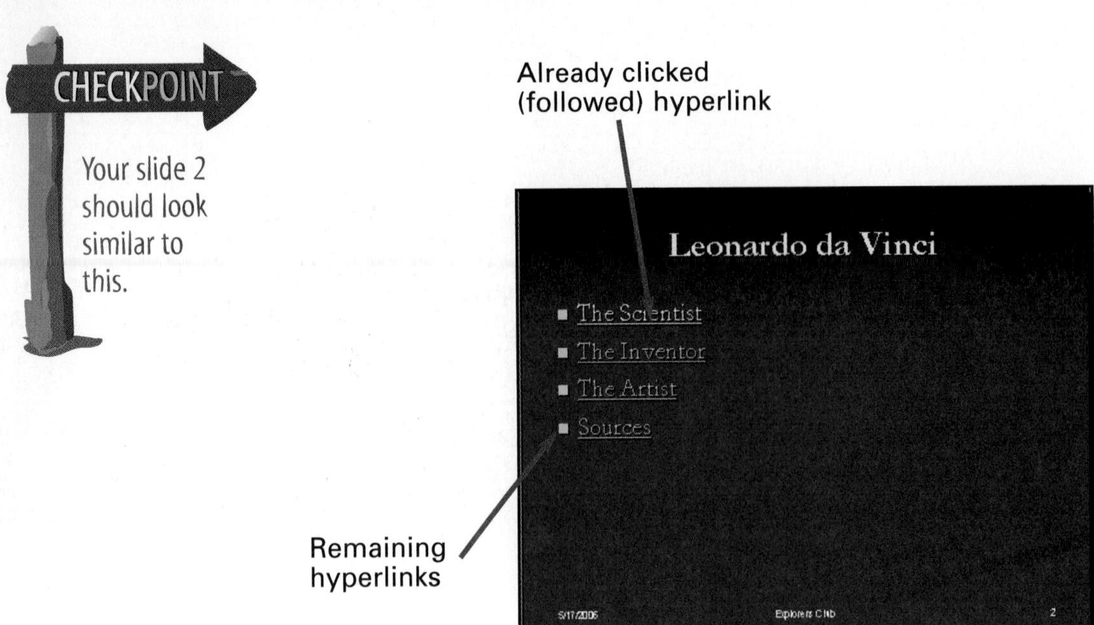

Fantastic! Next, create action button hyperlinks that jump back to slide 2 on slides 3–5.

Action Button Hyperlinks

action button

Another way to create a hyperlink is with an action button. An action button is a predesigned button icon you draw with the mouse pointer. Create action buttons by choosing **Slide Show** on the menu bar, pointing to **Action Buttons**, and clicking an action button style on the grid. Then draw the button and assign a hyperlink to it.

Let's create action button hyperlinks on slides 3–5 that jump back to slide 2. To save time, create the first action button on slide 3 and then copy and paste it on slides 4 and 5.

1. View **slide 3**. Choose **Slide Show** on the menu bar and point to **Action Buttons**. Use ScreenTips to locate the **Action Button: Return** icon in the grid. Click the **Action Button: Return** icon. The mouse pointer becomes a crosshair drawing pointer.
2. Move the drawing pointer to the upper-right corner of the slide. Drag down and to the right approximately 1/2 inch to draw the button. Release the mouse button. The **Action Settings** dialog box opens.

Inserting Page Breaks, Section Breaks, and Page Numbers

When you create multi-page documents, such as the *Globe Theater3* report, you must be sure that the text breaks correctly between pages. You must also number the pages.

Page Breaks

A page break is where one page ends and another page begins. There are two kinds of page breaks: a soft page break and a hard page break. When a page is full, *Word* automatically inserts a soft page break and moves the remaining text to the next page.

hard page break
soft page break

In **Normal** view, a soft page break is shown with a single dotted line across the page and a hard page break is shown with a single dotted line and the words **Page Break** in the line.

If you delete text, change the margins, or apply formatting that changes the amount of text that fits on a page, *Word* automatically adjusts the position of the soft page breaks.

A hard page break is one that you insert manually. You can insert page breaks anywhere you want in a document. To insert a hard page break, choose **Insert** on the menu bar and then choose **Break** to open the **Break** dialog box. You can also press the CTRL + ENTER keys to insert a hard page break. *Warning! Word* cannot reposition or delete a hard page break. If you add or delete text or change the formatting so that the amount of text on a page changes, you must manually move or delete your hard page breaks.

Section Breaks

Next page section break
section break

A section break is a special type of break that allows you to change the layout of text, such as margins and columns, for a single page within a multi-page document. To insert a section break, choose **Insert** on the menu bar and choose **Break** to open the **Break** dialog box. Then click the break option you want.

The *first page* of an unbound report has a 2-inch top margin. The *second page* of a two-page unbound report, such as the *Globe Theater3* document, should have a 1-inch top margin.

To change the top margin for the second page, you must replace the existing soft page break on page 1 with a Next page section break. This will both break the page and start a new section on the next page. Then you can set a new top margin for the new section.

Let's use the bulleted list text on slide 2 to create hyperlinks to the related slides in the same presentation.

1. View slide 2, if necessary, and select **The Scientist** text. Use ScreenTips to locate the **Insert Hyperlink** button on the Standard toolbar. Then click the **Insert Hyperlink** button to open the **Insert Hyperlink** dialog box.
2. Click the **Place in This Document** button in the **Link to** pane. Click **3. The Scientist** in the **Select a place in this document** pane.

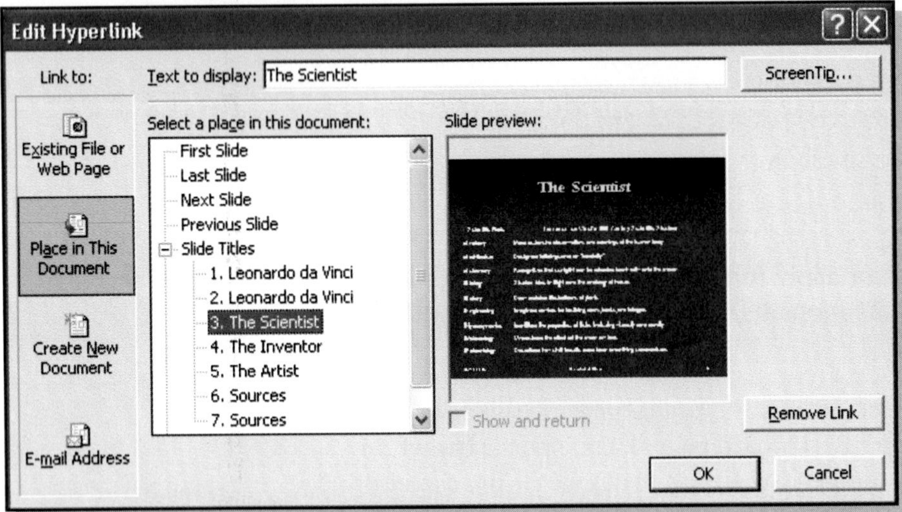

3. Click the **OK** button and deselect the placeholder. **The Scientist** bulleted list text is now a different color and underlined, indicating a hyperlink to slide 3.
4. Run the slide show for slide 2 to test the hyperlink. Move the mouse pointer to **The Scientist** hyperlink. The mouse pointer becomes a pointing hand. Click **The Scientist** hyperlink to view slide 3. Tap the ESC key to stop the slide show.
5. View **slide 2**. **The Scientist** hyperlink is now a different color, which shows that you have already clicked it. Using the previous steps as your guide, create the following hyperlinks on slide 2: **The Inventor** text to slide 4; **The Artist** text to slide 5; and **Sources** to slide 6. Deselect the placeholder and save the presentation.

In **Normal** and **Print Layout** views, a section break is shown by a double-dotted line with the words **Section Break** and the type of section break in parentheses.

Let's insert a Next page section break and change the top margin for the second page of the *Globe Theater3* document.

1. Move the insertion point immediately in front of <u>The Original Globe Theater</u> side heading near the bottom of page 1.
2. Choose **Insert** on the menu bar and choose **Break** to open the **Break** dialog box. Click the **Next Page** option.

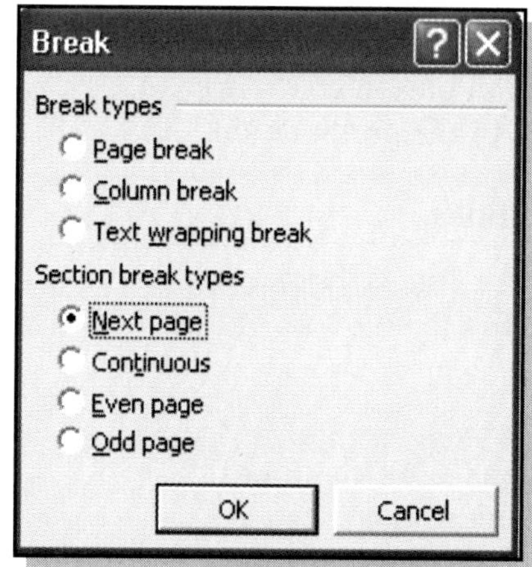

3. Click the **OK** button. Scroll to view pages 1 and 2. A **Next page** section break is inserted on page 1 and the insertion point and remaining text are moved to the top of page 2.
4. Choose **File** on the menu bar and choose **Page Setup**. Set the top margin to 1 inch. Make certain that the **Apply to** list shows *This section.* Click the **OK** button.
5. Scroll the document to view the section break on page 1 and the new 1-inch top margin on page 2. Press the CTRL + HOME keys. Save the document.

Page Numbers

header
footer

Page numbers are inserted at the top of the page in a header or at the bottom of a page in a footer. To insert a page number, choose **Insert** on the menu bar and choose **Page Numbers** to open the **Page Number** dialog box. Then choose whether you want the page number to be positioned at the top or bottom of the page; aligned at the right, left, or center position; and whether or not the page number should appear on the first page of the document. A multi-page report, such as the *Globe Theater3* document, should have page numbers in the top-right corner of each page *except* the first page.

Creating Hyperlinks

You have learned how to advance slides *sequentially* during a slide show—from slide 1 to slide 2 to slide 3 and so forth. You can also advance slides or return to previous slides *in any order* you choose by using hyperlinks. You can also use hyperlinks in a slide show to:

- Jump to a slide in a different presentation
- Open another file type such as an *Excel* workbook
- Start your Web browser and load a Web page

Hyperlinks can be created using text, clip art, pictures, AutoShapes, WordArt, and special shapes called action buttons. Text hyperlink and action button colors are controlled by the design template and color scheme applied to the presentation.

Text, Clip Art, Picture, AutoShape, or WordArt Hyperlinks

To create hyperlinks, select text or a slide object and click the **Insert Hyperlink** button on the Standard toolbar to open the **Insert Hyperlink** dialog box. In the Insert Hyperlink dialog box:

To link to another slide in the same presentation	Click the **Place in This Document** button in the **Link to** list — click a slide in the **Select a place in this document** list
To link to another file or Web page	Click the **Existing File or Web Page** button in the **Link to** list — use the **Look in** drop-down arrow to locate and select the file, or — type the Web page URL in the Address text box

You can also create hyperlinks by choosing **Insert** on the menu bar and choosing **Hyperlink**.

Let's insert a right-aligned page number in a header on all pages except the first page.

1. Choose **Insert** on the menu bar and choose **Page Numbers**.
2. Click the **Position** drop-down arrow and click **Top of page (Header)**.
3. Click the **Alignment** drop-down arrow and click **Right**, if necessary.
4. Click the **Show number on first page** checkbox to remove the check mark.

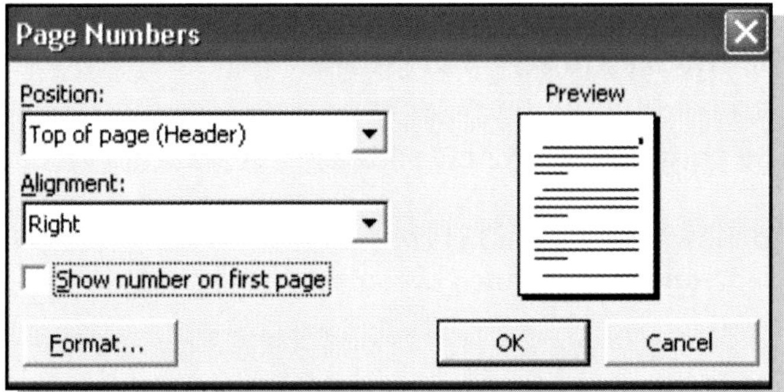

5. Click the **OK** button. Save the document.
6. Scroll to view the page number 2 in the top-right corner of the second page header. Then press the CTRL + HOME keys, if necessary.

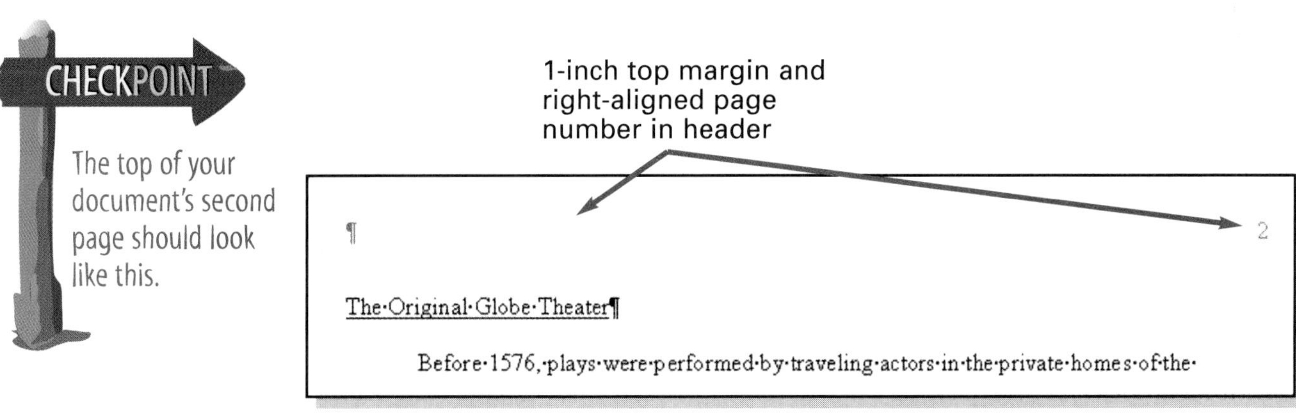

The report is looking better and better! To wrap up the report, you need to cite Ray's sources using footnotes.

Warning! Slides to be included on a Summary Slide must have a slide layout that includes a title placeholder.

Let's create a summary slide.

1. Switch to **Slide Sorter View** and use the SHIFT key to select **slides 2–5**. Use ScreenTips to locate the **Summary Slide** button on the Slide Sorter toolbar. Click the **Summary Slide** button. A new slide 2, titled Summary Slide, is inserted.
2. Double-click **slide 2** (Summary Slide) to view it in Normal view. Select the Summary Slide title and type **Leonardo da Vinci**. Deselect the placeholder and save the presentation.

Automatically created Summary Slide

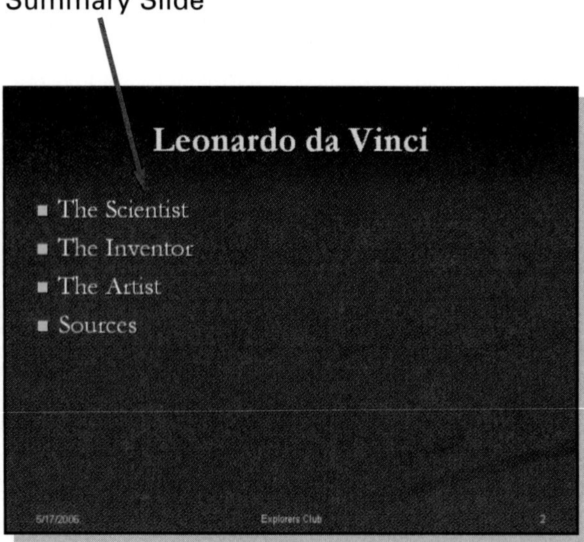

Terrific! Next, you will create hyperlinks you can click to navigate during a slide show.

TRAIL 6 MARKER

Adding Footnotes

endnote
footnote
note reference mark
note separator line
source

You must always cite, or give credit for, the facts and ideas you use in a report. You do this by providing the name and date of the source and the author's name, if possible. You can cite your sources in either footnotes or endnotes. Footnotes appear at the bottom of the same page as the referenced text. Endnotes appear on a separate page at the end of a report. Check out Appendix A to see the citation formats for different types of sources: books, magazines, journals, and Web pages.

The content of books, magazines, journals, and Web pages is protected by copyright law. If you copy information directly from another source, you must enclose the information in quotation marks and cite the source.

Ray used both book and Web page sources to find information for his report on the Globe. Use footnotes to cite Ray's sources in the *Globe Theater3* document.

To insert a footnote, move the insertion point to the end of the text to be cited. Then choose **Insert** on the menu bar, point to **Reference**, and choose **Footnote** to open the **Footnote and Endnote** dialog box. You set the type of citation and numbering options in this dialog box.

A footnote has two parts: the note reference mark and the footnote text. When you insert a footnote, *Word* automatically inserts a note reference mark at the insertion point, a short line called the note separator line near the bottom of the page, and the same note reference mark below the note separator line. The note separator line separates the document text from the footnote text. When you insert multiple footnotes, *Word* automatically numbers the footnotes sequentially as 1, 2, 3, and so forth.

In Normal view, footnotes and endnotes are typed in the notes pane. In this Trail Marker, the footnotes are created in Print Layout view.

CHECKPOINT
Your slide 4 should look similar to this.

Excel worksheet data pasted and formatted as a picture object

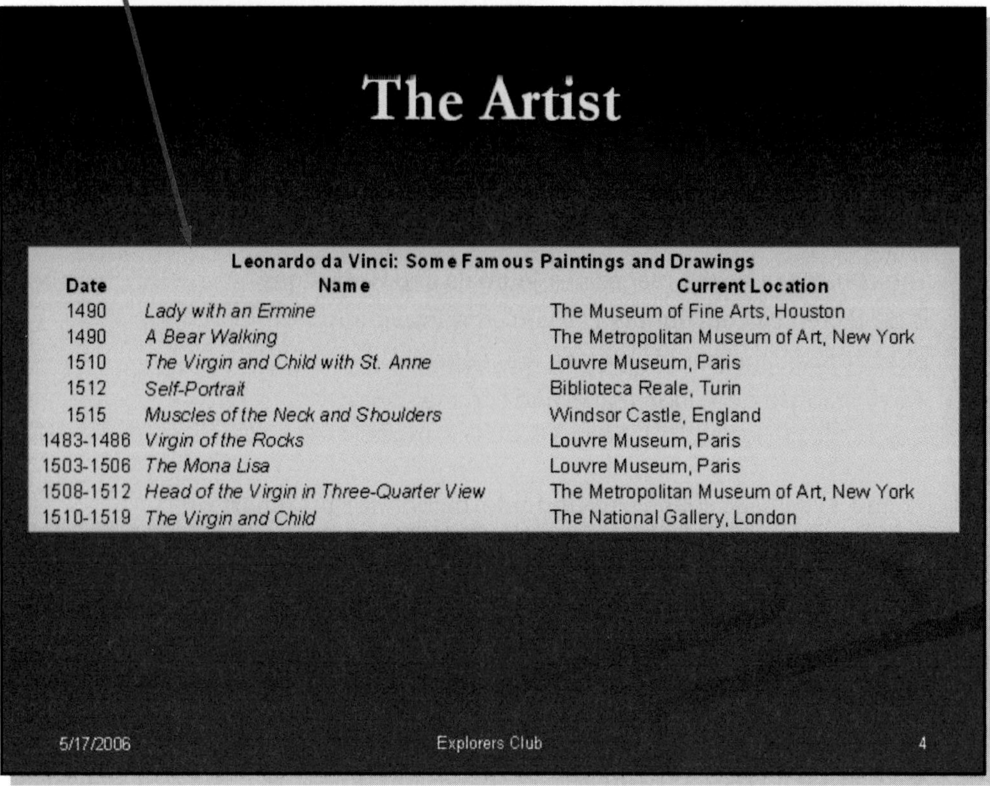

Leonardo da Vinci: Some Famous Paintings and Drawings

Date	Name	Current Location
1490	*Lady with an Ermine*	The Museum of Fine Arts, Houston
1490	*A Bear Walking*	The Metropolitan Museum of Art, New York
1510	*The Virgin and Child with St. Anne*	Louvre Museum, Paris
1512	*Self-Portrait*	Biblioteca Reale, Turin
1515	*Muscles of the Neck and Shoulders*	Windsor Castle, England
1483-1486	*Virgin of the Rocks*	Louvre Museum, Paris
1503-1506	*The Mona Lisa*	Louvre Museum, Paris
1508-1512	*Head of the Virgin in Three-Quarter View*	The Metropolitan Museum of Art, New York
1510-1519	*The Virgin and Child*	The National Gallery, London

Super! You have learned three great ways to paste *Excel* worksheet data on a slide! Now let's add a summary slide.

TRAIL 4 MARKER

Inserting a Summary Slide

Summary Slide

The second slide in a presentation—called a Summary Slide— is often used to list the topics to be covered in the remaining slides. Like a book's table of contents that lists the titles of each chapter, a Summary Slide lists the titles of each slide. Instead of manually creating a Summary Slide, you can let *PowerPoint* do it for you!

Just switch to Slide Sorter view and select the slides whose titles you want to appear on the Summary Slide. Then click the **Summary Slide** button on the Slide Sorter toolbar.

Let's insert the footnotes.

1. Move the insertion point to the end of the first paragraph on page 1.
2. Choose **Insert** on the menu bar, point to **Reference**, and choose **Footnote**. The **Footnotes** option button should be selected. Be certain that all the other options in your dialog box look like this.

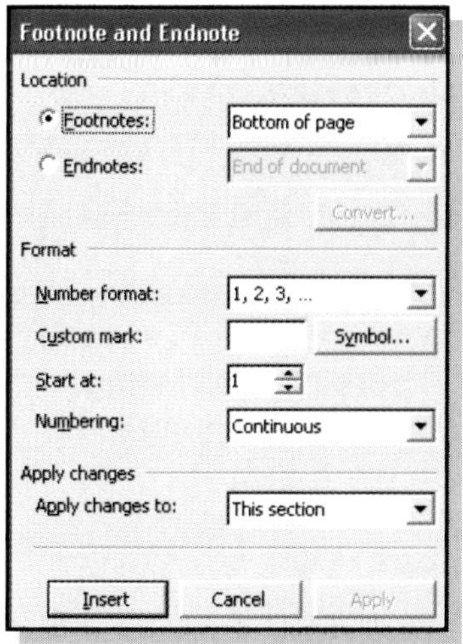

3. Click the **Insert** button. The superscript note reference mark [1] appears at the end of the paragraph, and the note separator line and the same note reference mark appear at the bottom of the page.
4. Type the first footnote text exactly as follows. Apply the Italic style to the Web page name and allow *Word* to format the URL. Then tap the ENTER key.
   "Rebuilding the Globe: Architecture and Construction," *Shakespeare's Globe Online,* http://www.shakespeares-globe.org/ **(accessed September 23, 2006).**

   The next three sources are books. Apply the Italic style to the book names.

5. Move the insertion immediately following the sentence that ends *and the poor.* in the third line *above* the bulleted list on page 1.
6. Choose **Insert** on the menu bar, point to **Reference**, and choose **Footnote**. Click the **Insert** button. Type the second footnote as follows. Do not tap the ENTER key when finished.
   Diane Yancey, *Life in the Elizabethan Theater* (San Diego: Lucent Books, 1997), p. 11.
7. Move the insertion point immediately following the sentence that ends *and inn courtyards.* in the first body paragraph on page 2. Insert footnote 3 and tap the ENTER key when finished.
   Christopher Martin, *Shakespeare* (Vero Beach: Rourke Enterprises, Inc., 1988), p. 35.

Let's copy the data on the *Artist* worksheet, paste it on slide 4 as a picture object, and then edit the picture object to change its fill and line colors.

1. Switch to the *Leonardo research* workbook. Tap the ESC key and press the CTRL + HOME keys to activate cell A1.
2. Click the **Artist** sheet tab. Select the range **A1:C11** and click the **Copy** button.
3. Switch to the *Leonardo15* presentation, view **slide 4**, and click the **Paste** button.
4. Click the **Paste Options** button drop-down arrow and click **Picture of Table (smaller file)**. The data is pasted as a picture object. Sizing handles appear on the object's boundary and the mouse pointer becomes a move pointer when you place it on the object.

Double-clicking a picture object opens the **Format Picture** dialog box. You can change the object's fill and line color, size, and position in this dialog box. Let's change the fill and line colors using design template and color scheme colors.

5. Double-click the picture object to open the **Format Picture** dialog box. Then click the **Colors and Lines** tab, if necessary.
6. Click the **Color** list drop-down arrow in the Fill section and click the light orange color or other light color in the color scheme section of the grid. Click the **Color** list drop-down arrow in the Line section and click the light purple color or other light color in the color scheme section of the grid.
7. Click the **OK** button, then deselect the object, and save the presentation. Run the slide show for slide 4.

8. Move the insertion point immediately following the sentence that ends *government closed it.* at the end of the second body paragraph on page 2. Insert footnote 4. Do not tap the ENTER key when finished. **Peter Chrisp, *Shakespeare* (New York: Dorling Kindersley Eyewitness Books, 2002), p. 35.**

To delete a footnote, you must select and delete the note reference mark in the paragraph.

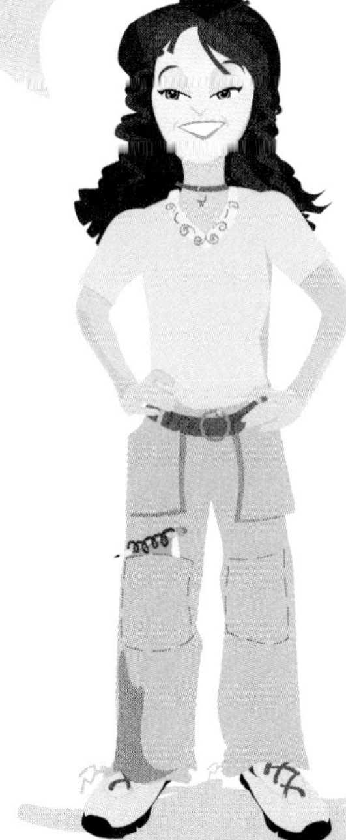

You can format footnote text just like you format body text. The footnotes should be indented 0.5 inch from the left margin and the font size should be 12 point.

Apply It!

Let's format the footnotes.

1. Scroll to view the footnotes at the bottom of page 1. Use the I-beam to select the footnote numbers and text at the bottom of page 1. Press and hold the CTRL key.
2. Scroll to view the footnotes at the bottom of page 2. Use the I-beam to select the footnote numbers and text at the bottom of page 2. Release the CTRL key.
3. Drag the **First Line Indent** marker to the 0.5-inch position on the horizontal ruler.
4. Change the **Font Size** to 12 point. Deselect the footnotes.

Your formatted footnotes should look like this.

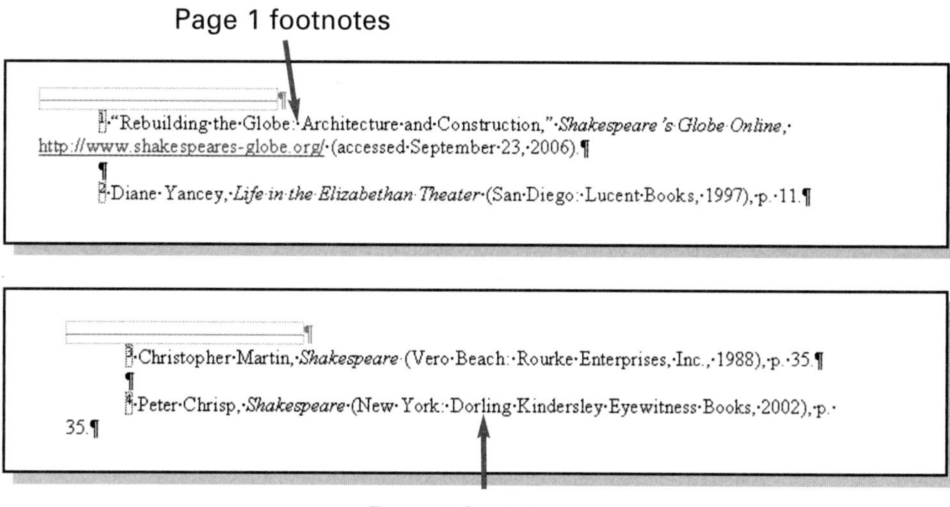
Page 1 footnotes

[1]·"Rebuilding·the·Globe:·Architecture·and·Construction,"·*Shakespeare's·Globe·Online,*·http://www.shakespeares-globe.org/·(accessed·September·23,·2006).¶
¶
[2]·Diane·Yancey,·*Life·in·the·Elizabethan·Theater*·(San·Diego:·Lucent·Books,·1997),·p.·11.¶

[3]·Christopher·Martin,·*Shakespeare*·(Vero·Beach:·Rourke·Enterprises,·Inc.,·1988),·p.·35.¶
¶
[4]·Peter·Chrisp,·*Shakespeare*·(New·York:·Dorling·Kindersley·Eyewitness·Books,·2002),·p.·35.¶

Page 2 footnotes

5. Save the document. Close the document.

Congratulations! Ray's *Globe Theater3* document is ready to go!

4. Click twice (two single clicks, not a double-click) in the gray work area outside the slide to deactivate and deselect the embedded workbook object. Run the slide show for slide 3 to better see the object. Then save the presentation.

CHECKPOINT
Your slide 3 should now look similar to this.

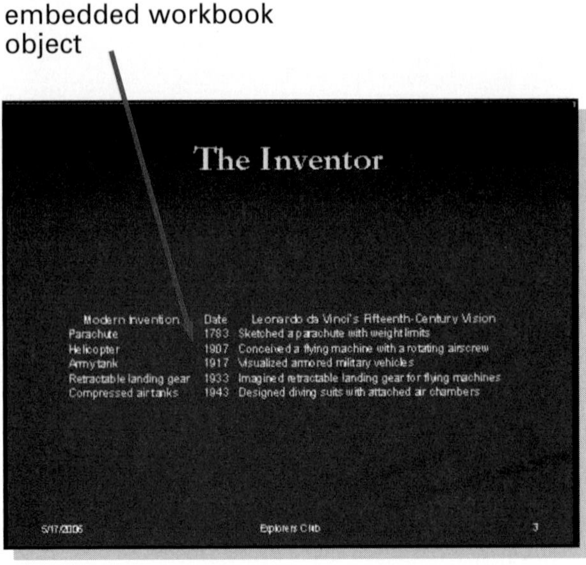

Edited *Excel* embedded workbook object
The Inventor
Modern Invention
Date
Leonardo da Vinci's Fifteenth-Century Vision
Parachute
1783
Sketched a parachute with weight limits
Helicopter
1907
Conceived a flying machine with a rotating airscrew
Army tank
1917
Visualized armored military vehicles
Retractable landing gear
1933
Imagined retractable landing gear for flying machines
Compressed air tanks
1943
Designed diving suits with attached air chambers
5/17/2006
Explorers Club
3

Terrific! Next, let's copy and paste the data from the *Artist* worksheet.

Pasting *Excel* Worksheet Data as a Picture Object

Pasting worksheet data as a *table* or as an *embedded workbook object* allows you to edit the data on the slide. The third paste option is **Picture of Table (smaller file size)**. If you do not need to edit the data, use this option to paste the data as a picture object.

A picture object can be resized, repositioned, and edited just like clip art or an AutoShape, but the data itself *cannot* be changed.

Project | *Skills Review*

You learned a lot in this project! We are very impressed with your progress. Let's take a few minutes to review the skills that you learned.

Apply font styles	Choose **File** on the menu bar and choose **Font**.
Replace a word with a synonym or antonym	Choose **Tools** on the menu bar, point to **Language**, and choose **Thesaurus**. Right-click a word, point to **Synonyms**, and click a synonym or antonym.
Create a bulleted or numbered list	Choose **Format** on the menu bar and choose **Bullets and Numbering**.
Cut, copy, and paste text	Choose **Edit** on the menu bar and choose **Cut**, **Copy**, or **Paste**.
Insert a hard page break or a section break	Choose **Insert** on the menu bar and choose **Break**. Press the CTRL + ENTER keys (hard page break).
Insert page numbers	Choose **Insert** on the menu bar and choose **Page Numbers**.
Insert footnotes	Choose **Insert** on the menu bar, point to **Reference**, and choose **Footnotes**.

Let's double-click the workbook object and edit it to change the font color and remove the gridlines that are visible when the font color is changed.

1. Double-click the embedded workbook object. It now looks like a miniature workbook and is active and ready for editing. Look carefully at the menu bar, the Standard toolbar, and the Formatting toolbar. The menu bar commands and the toolbar buttons are now *Excel*'s commands and buttons! Look carefully at the title bar. You are still working in *PowerPoint*!

Excel menu bar and toolbars

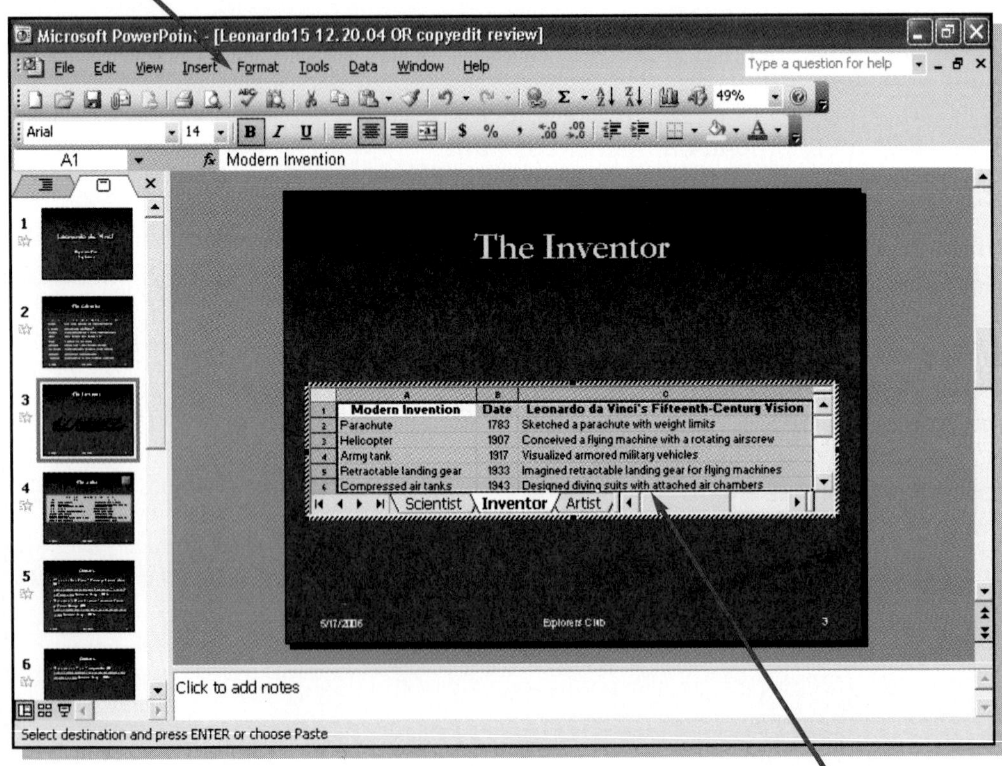

Active embedded workbook object

2. Select the range **A1:C6** in the embedded object on the *Inventor* worksheet, if necessary. Click the **Font Color** button drop-down arrow and click the white color on the grid.
3. Choose **Tools** on the menu bar and choose **Options**. Click the **View** tab and click the **Gridlines** checkbox to remove the check mark. Click the **OK** button.

Exploring on Your Own

Blaze your own trail by practicing your new skills! Use classroom, library, CD-ROM, or online resources to learn about Sam Wanamaker and the building of the new Globe in London. Take notes about what you learn. Then create a new document and save it as *Wanamaker3*. Set a 2-inch top margin and 1-inch left and right margins. Type the centered, uppercase main heading ***SAM WANAMAKER AND THE GLOBE*** followed by a quadruple space (QS). Then, using your research notes, type several paragraphs about Wanamaker and his dream of creating a replica of the original Globe. Use cut, copy, and paste as necessary to arrange the paragraphs or duplicate text. Type at least two side headings. Double-space the body text paragraphs and side headings. Indent the body text paragraphs (but not the side headings) 0.5 inch from the left margin. *After formatting, your document should be no more than two pages long.*

Underline the side headings. Use the Bold or Italic font styles to add emphasis to important words. Create a single-spaced, bulleted or numbered list within the document. Use the thesaurus to replace a word with a synonym. Cite your sources using footnotes. Use a **Next Page** section break to create both a page and section break between the first and second page. Set a 1-inch top margin for the second page. Insert page numbers on all pages *except* the first page. Spell-check, save, and close the document.

Reading in Action

Using a Timeline

A timeline helps you organize facts into chronological order so that you can see events at a glance. Read the data file *Globe Theater3.* Create a timeline that shows important events in the history of this theater.

Math in Action

Finding the Area

The Globe had a circular yard with a stage and standing room for the audience. The circular yard was 70 feet in diameter, and the stage was 50 feet × 25 feet. To find out how much area was available for the standing audience, subtract the area of the stage from the area of the yard. The area of a circle is equal to pi (π) times the radius (r) of the circle squared. The radius of a circle is half of the diameter. Pi is approximately equal to 3.14.

area of the Globe $= \pi \times (70 \text{ ft} \div 2)^2 = 3.14 \times 1225 \text{ ft}^2 = 3846.5 \text{ ft}^2$

area of the stage $= 50 \text{ ft} \times 25 \text{ ft} = 1250 \text{ ft}^2$

$3846.5 \text{ ft}^2 - 1250 \text{ ft}^2 = 2596.5 \text{ ft}^2$ standing room in the yard

Now you try it!

- How much standing room would there be if the Globe was 50 feet in diameter?
- How much standing room would there be if the stage was 40 feet long and 30 feet wide?

4. Point to the **Paste Options** button in the lower-right corner of the slide.

5. Click the **Paste Options** drop-down arrow and click **Excel Table (entire workbook)**. The data is pasted as an embedded workbook object. Sizing handles appear on its boundary and the mouse pointer becomes a move pointer when you place it on the object. Deselect the object and save the presentation. *Don't worry if you can't clearly read the text in the embedded object. You will edit the object in the next section.*

CHECKPOINT
Your slide 3 should look similar to this.

Excel worksheet data pasted as an embedded workbook object

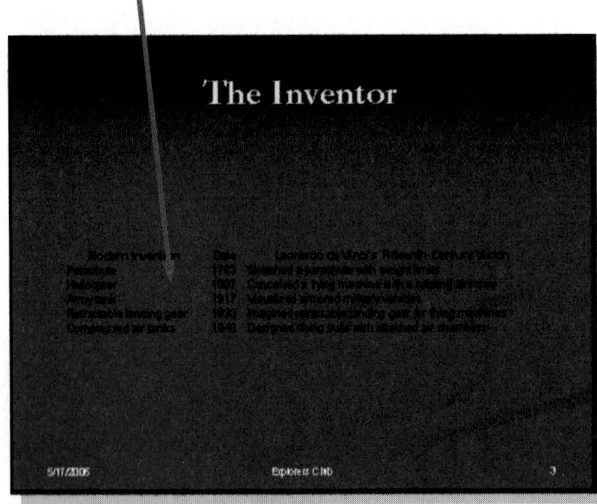

Like pasted *Excel* data in a table, changes you make to the embedded workbook object *do not* affect the original *Excel* workbook.

Now you need to edit the embedded workbook object. To edit an embedded workbook object, double-click the object. This allows you to use *Excel* features while working in *PowerPoint*!

Exploring Across the Curriculum

Internet/Web

Open your Web browser and use a favorite to view the Learning with Computers Web page (www.lwcgreen.keyboarding.com). Click the **Links** option. Click **Project 3**. Click the links to research the life of William Shakespeare. Take notes about what you learn.

The Web

Create a new document and save it as *Shakespeare3.* Set a 2-inch top margin and 1-inch left and right margins. Type the centered, uppercase main heading **WILLIAM SHAKESPEARE** followed by a quadruple space (QS). Then, using your research notes, type several paragraphs about Shakespeare. Use cut, copy, and paste as necessary to arrange the paragraphs. Type at least two side headings. Double-space the body text paragraphs and side headings. Indent the body text paragraphs (but not the side headings) 0.5 inch from the left margin.

Underline the side headings. Use the Bold and Italic font styles to add emphasis to specific words. Create a single-spaced, bulleted or numbered list within the document. Use the thesaurus to replace a word with a synonym. Cite your sources using footnotes.

Use a **Next Page** section break to create both a page and section break between the first and second page. Set a 1-inch top margin for the second page. Insert page numbers on all pages *except* the first page. Spell-check, save, and close the document.

Language Arts: Words to Know

Look up the meaning of the following words, terms, or phrases in a classroom dictionary, CD-ROM dictionary or encyclopedia, or online dictionary.

amphitheater	Elizabethan Era	groundling	playwright
stage	thatched roof	tiring-room	trap door

Create a new document. Save the document as *definitions3* followed by your initials. Type each term on one line and its definition on the following line. Insert a blank line between each definition and the next term. Select all the terms using the CTRL key and apply the Bold font style. Select all the definitions using the CTRL key and apply the Italic font style. Check the spelling. Then save and close the document.

Explore More

Your slide 2 should look similar to this.

Excel worksheet data pasted as a table

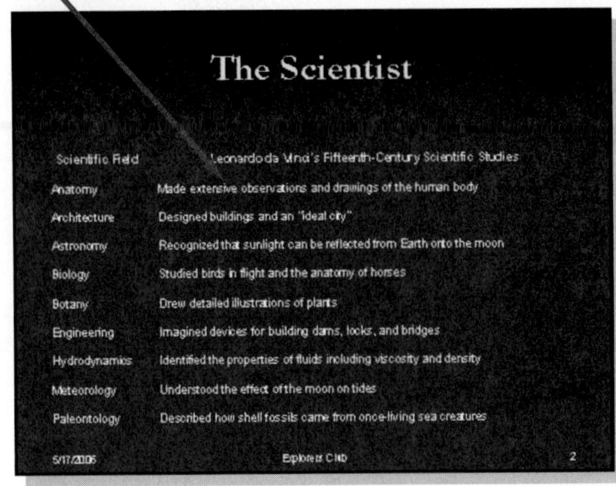

Nice work! Now let's copy and paste the data from the *Inventor* worksheet.

Pasting *Excel* Worksheet Data as an Embedded Object

embedded workbook object

The second paste option is **Excel Table (entire workbook)**. This option lets you paste *Excel* worksheet data onto a *PowerPoint* slide as an embedded workbook object. An embedded workbook object *must* be edited using the *Excel* toolbars and menus instead of the *PowerPoint* toolbars and menus.

Let's copy the data on the *Inventor* worksheet and paste it on slide 3 as an embedded workbook object.

1. Click the *Excel - Leonardo research* button on the taskbar to switch to the workbook. Tap the ESC key to clear the copied data from the Clipboard and then press the CTRL + HOME keys to activate cell A1.
2. Click the **Inventor** sheet tab, select the range **A1:C6**, and click the **Copy** button.
3. Switch to the *Leonardo15* presentation and view **slide 3**. Click the **Paste** button.

Exploring Across the Curriculum

Social Studies: Research and Write

Work with a classmate to use library, classroom, or online resources to research life in London, England, during the Elizabethan Era. What was daily life like? How were actors and playwrights treated? Take notes.

Create a new document and save it as *Elizabethan London3.* Set a 2-inch top margin and 1-inch left and right margins. Type the centered, uppercase main heading **AN ACTOR IN ELIZABETHAN LONDON** followed by a quadruple space (QS). Then, using your research notes, imagine that you are a young actor living in London during the Elizabethan Era. Type several paragraphs describing what you see, smell, hear, and do during a typical day.

Type at least two side headings. Double-space the body text paragraphs and side headings. Indent only the body text paragraphs 0.5 inch from the left margin. Underline the side headings. Use the Bold and Italic font styles to add emphasis to specific words. Create a single-spaced, bulleted or numbered list within the document. Use the thesaurus to replace a word with a synonym. Cite your sources using at least two footnotes.

Insert a **Next Page** section break and set a 1-inch top margin for the second page. Insert page numbers to appear only on the second page. Spell-check, save, and close the document.

Getting Help

Getting Help

Choose **Tools** on the menu bar and choose **Options** to open the **Options** dialog box. Then click the **Help** button on the title bar. Your mouse pointer changes into a Help pointer (a mouse pointer with a question mark). Clicking a dialog box option with the Help pointer displays a ScreenTip that briefly describes the option. Use the Help pointer to learn more about some of the options in this dialog box.

Your Personal Journal

Open your personal journal document. Insert today's date. Would you like to travel back in time to be a London actor in Elizabethan England? Why or why not? Write one or two short paragraphs to answer these questions. Spell-check, save, and close your journal document.

Online Enrichment Games (Fun Stuff)  www.lwcgreen.keyboarding.com

Pasting *Excel* Worksheet Data as a Table

When you paste *Excel* worksheet data as a table, the data is pasted in a *PowerPoint* table in columns and rows without borders. As you learned in Project 14, you can resize a *PowerPoint* table by dragging a sizing handle; you can reposition it by dragging the table's placeholder boundary. Don't forget! You can edit the text in a *PowerPoint* table just as you do in a *Word* table. Any changes you make to the table *do not* affect the original *Excel* worksheet!

Look at your taskbar to find the application buttons for *Excel* and *PowerPoint*. You will use these buttons to switch between the workbook and the presentation as you complete the Apply It! steps.

Let's copy *Excel* worksheet data and paste it as a table on a slide.

1. Make sure that *Excel* is the active application and that the *Scientist* worksheet in the *Leonardo research* workbook is active. Then select the range **A1:B10** using the SHIFT + click method and click the **Copy** button.
2. Click the *PowerPoint - Leonardo15* button on the taskbar to switch to the *Leonardo15* presentation. Then view **slide 2** and click the **Paste** button. By default, the data is automatically pasted as a borderless table.
3. Deselect the placeholder and run the slide show for slide 2 to more clearly see the pasted data. Then save the presentation.

3a Review o, t, n, g

Key each line twice. Double-space between 2-line groups.

o

1 l o l o|olo olo|loj loj|olko olko|dojo dojo|os os;

2 do do|so so|for for|look look|sold sold|hole hole;

t

3 f t f t|tft tft|thft thft|tjft tjft|trft trft|tft;

4 the the|tree tree|seat seat|jolt jolt|there there;

n

5 j n j n|njn njn|hjn hjn|nhk nhk|knjs knjs;|jnj jn;

6 on on|note note|nook nook|north north|inner; inner

g

7 f g f g|gfg gfg|gtg gtg|tgfg tgfg|ghfg ghfg|dg df;

8 go go|gas; gas|dog dog|gaggle gaggle|gadget gadget

3b Technique: ENTER

Key each line twice single-spaced; double-space between 2-line groups.

1 I did too.

2 Did he take it?

3 We went to the game.

4 James took their picture.

5 Juan will leave next Thursday.

6 We don't meet again for five weeks.

7 They bought a new computer for Jennifer.

8 Her school has basketball tryouts next month.

9 Both of the girls may go to the docks by the lake.

Starting Out!

Begin by opening Ray's presentation and saving it with a new name, applying a design template, and changing the color scheme. Then open Ray's workbook.

1. Open the *Leonardo* presentation and save it as *Leonardo15*. Apply the design template of your choice with a color scheme that has a dark blue background. Then start *Excel* and open the *Leonardo research* workbook.

Ergonomics *TIP*

Do not forget to rest your eyes by focusing on an object 20 to 40 feet away for 10 to 30 seconds.

The *Leonardo research* workbook has three worksheets: *Scientist*, *Inventor*, and *Artist*. Each worksheet contains facts about Leonardo da Vinci. Ray wants you to put this data on three separate slides in the *Leonardo15* presentation.

Just copy the data from the worksheet, view the *PowerPoint* slide where you want to place the data, and paste the data on the slide. By default the data is pasted as a table. To select a different paste option, click the **Paste Options** button drop-down arrow. The table below shows three paste options you will use.

Paste Option	Description
Table	Pastes the data as a table without borders. The table can be edited using *PowerPoint* tools.
Excel Table (entire workbook)	Pastes the data as an embedded *Excel* object. The data must be edited using *Excel* tools.
Picture of Table (smaller file size)	Pastes the data as a picture object. The data cannot be edited.

First, let's copy and paste the data on the *Scientist* worksheet.

Another way to paste copied worksheet data onto a slide is to choose **Edit** on the *PowerPoint* menu bar and choose **Paste Special**. In the **Paste Special** dialog box, click the **Paste** option and type of object.

Project 4
Word Processing

Exploring Greek Mythology

Explorers' Guide

Data file: *Greek Mythology*

Objectives:

In this project, you will:

- use the **Format Painter**
- find and replace text
- create tabbed and newspaper columns
- use Click and Type
- set margins and insert page numbers in multiple document sections
- insert endnotes

Exploring on Your Own

additional practice in:

- using the **Format Painter**
- finding and replacing text
- creating tabbed and newspaper columns
- using Click and Type
- setting margins and inserting page numbers in multiple document sections
- inserting endnotes

Exploring Across the Curriculum

Internet/Web
Language Arts
Social Studies
Getting Help
Your Personal Journal

Our Exploration Assignment:

Formatting sections in a multi-page bound report

Did you know that some of your favorite movies, television shows, or books may be based on stories from ancient Greece? Luis has written a report about ancient Greek myths, and he needs your help to turn it into a first-rate, correctly formatted report. Follow the Trail Markers to use the **Format Painter** to format text, find and replace text, create tabbed and newspaper columns, add a title page, set margins and insert page numbers in multiple document sections, and cite sources with endnotes.

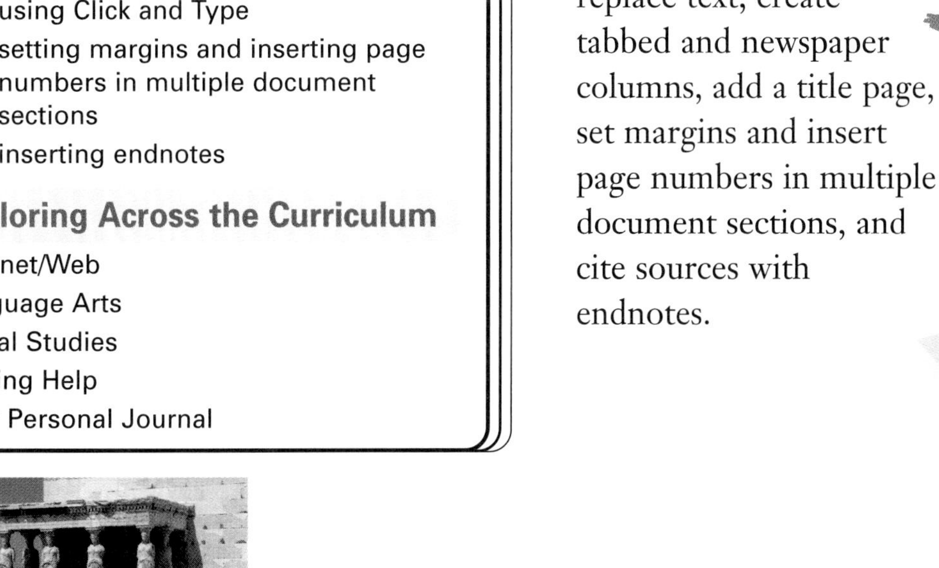

Project 15

Application Integration

Exploring the Mind of Leonardo

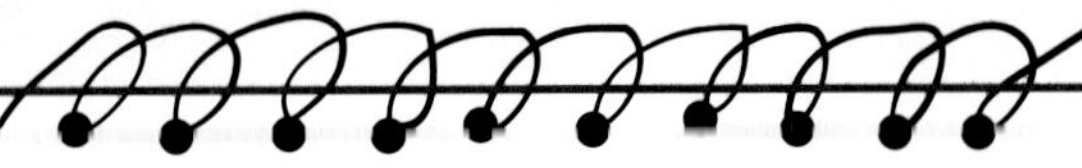

Explorers' Guide

Data files: *Leonardo research.xls*
artists.xls
Leonardo.ppt
High Renaissance.ppt

Objectives:

In this project, you will:

- paste *Excel* worksheet data as a table
- paste *Excel* worksheet data as an embedded object
- paste *Excel* worksheet data as a picture object
- insert a Summary Slide
- create hyperlinks
- add speaker notes

Exploring on Your Own

additional practice in:

- copying *Excel* worksheet data and pasting it on a slide
- inserting a Summary Slide
- creating hyperlinks
- adding speaker notes

Exploring Across the Curriculum

Internet/Web
Language Arts
Art
Getting Help
Your Personal Journal

Our Exploration Assignment:

Add *Excel* worksheet data, a Summary Slide, and hyperlinks to a slide show

At the next meeting, the Explorers Club members will learn about Leonardo da Vinci and his work. Ray entered his research data about Leonardo in an *Excel* workbook and created his *PowerPoint* presentation. Can you help him put his *Excel* data into his *PowerPoint* presentation? Thanks! Just follow the Trail Markers to copy and paste *Excel* worksheet data on slides, create a Summary Slide, create hyperlinks to navigate during a slide show, and add speaker notes.

Starting Out!

Begin by opening Luis's document and saving it with a new name.

1. Open the *Greek Mythology* document and save it as *Greek Mythology4.*

You are ready to go! Let's start by applying the Bold and Underline font styles using a new tool called the **Format Painter**.

Ergonomics TIP

After working at the computer for a while, you need a break! Stand up, stretch, roll your shoulders, and flex your fingers and wrists. Good job! Now you are ready to get back to work.

TRAIL 1 MARKER

Using the Format Painter

Format Painter paragraph heading

The Format Painter is a great tool for copying, or *painting*, formats from formatted text to unformatted text. To use the **Format Painter**, first move the insertion point into the text that is already formatted. Then click the **Format Painter** button on the Standard toolbar. When the **Format Painter** is turned on, the I-beam has a paintbrush icon. Drag the I-beam across the text or click a single word that you want to format.

A paragraph heading, which is used to introduce a paragraph, is a short, underlined phrase followed by a period. The *Greek Mythology4* document uses paragraph headings instead of side headings.

To use the **Format Painter** on more than one text selection, double-click the **Format Painter** button. To turn off the **Format Painter** after you are finished, click it again.

Apply It!

Let's use the Format Painter to apply the Bold font style to important words and apply the Underline font style to the paragraph headings.

1. Double-click the word *myth* in the first sentence of the first body paragraph on the first page to select it. Apply the Bold font style.
2. Click the **Format Painter** button.

14a Review 7 & 3

Key each line twice. Double-space between 2-line groups.

1 j 7 j 7 | j u 7 j u 7 | ju7 ju7 | 78 78 | 71 71 | 79 79 | 747;

2 Add the numbers 7, 77, and 747. Only 77 finished.

3 d 3 d 3 | d e 3 d e 3 | de3 de3 | 37 37 | 30 30 | 35 35 | 433;

4 On May 30 Dr. Baxter worked from 1:30 to 4:30 p.m.

5 Only 37 out of 103 finished the course by July 14.

6 Did Jacob add 801, 940, 375, and 307 to the total?

7 I hit .308 in June, .347 in July, and .195 in May.

8 They have lived at 3047 Summit since May 15, 1987.

Do not rest your palms on the keyboard or desk as you key.

14b Technique: Double Letters

Key each line twice single-spaced; double-space between 2-line groups.

1 summer guessed committee called attend week assign

2 current appears written comma books committee will

3 Massachusetts Mississippi Illinois Missouri Hawaii

4 Fillmore Kennedy Fillmore Coolidge Hoover Harrison

5 Allison Roosevelt will keep your books three days.

6 Sally will keep books for a business in Tennessee.

7 Allan and Kellee are from Apple Valley, Minnesota.

8 William Jeffers has excellent proofreading skills.

9 Phyllis Woods and Debbie Babbitt keep calling you.

10 The spelling bee committee chair looked befuddled.

3. Scroll to view the last sentence of the third body text paragraph on the first page. Drag the I-beam with the paintbrush icon across the words *epic poems* in the sentence to paint the Bold font style.
4. Select the *Nature Myth: Persephone.* paragraph heading in the first single-spaced paragraph. *Do not select the period.* Apply the Underline font style.
5. Click the **Format Painter** button.
6. Drag to select the *Trickster Myth: Eris.* paragraph heading in the second single-spaced paragraph. (Use your scroll bar to find it.) *Do not drag across the period.* Deselect the text and save the document.

Outstanding! The phrase *Epic poems* has been painted with the Bold font style and *Trickster Myth: Eris* has been painted with the Underline font style.

TRAIL 2 MARKER

Finding and Replacing Text

To find a word in a document to format or replace, choose **Edit** on the menu bar and then choose **Find** or **Replace**. Use options on the **Find** tab in the **Find and Replace** dialog box to locate specific text. Use options on the **Replace** tab to find specific text and then replace it with other text. Use the **More** button to set additional search criteria, such as matching case.

Use the **Go To** tab options in the **Find and Replace** dialog box to move the insertion point to a specific element in your document, such as the top of a specific page.

Let's replace the word *time-honored* with the word *traditional* in the *Greek Mythology4* document.

1. Press the CTRL + HOME keys to move the insertion point to the top of the document. Then choose **Edit** on the menu bar and choose **Replace**. In the **Find what** text box, type **time-honored** and tap the TAB key.
2. Type **traditional** in the **Replace with** text box.

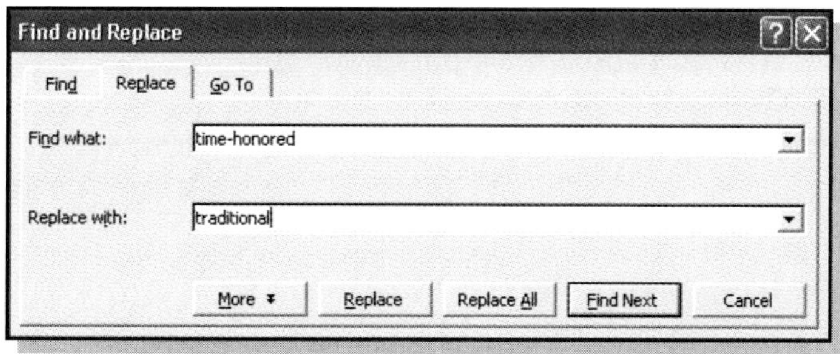

Exploring Across the Curriculum

Science: Research, Write, and Present

Work with a classmate to use library, CD-ROM, or online resources to learn about the chemical process that takes place in a sourdough starter. Then create a new presentation. Apply the slide design and color scheme of your choice. Add an appropriate title and subtitle to the Title Slide. Insert Title and Text, Content or Text and Content, and Blank slides as necessary to describe the chemical process. Cite your sources on a Title and Text slide at the end of the presentation. Add slide transitions and timings as desired. Apply custom animation to at least one slide. Insert a picture or clip art of your choice as the background on one slide and remove the design template background graphics from the slide.

Insert today's date as an automatically updating date, your name as footer text, and slide numbers on all the slides *except* the Title Slide. Run the slide show, and then save the presentation. Finally, preview and save the presentation as a Web page.

Getting Help

Type **add a chart** in the **Ask A Question** box and tap the ENTER key. Research how to add a chart to a slide. Then create a new presentation and add a chart to a slide using the sample data in the chart's Datasheet. Format the chart as you would an *Excel* chart. Then close the presentation without saving it.

Your Personal Journal

Open your personal journal document. Insert today's date and two blank lines. Think about popular sayings that mention bread. For example, when we sit down to eat, we say that we "break bread." People often refer to their jobs as their "bread and butter." Other well-known sayings include "Man does not live by bread alone." "Half a loaf is better than no bread." "If's and but's butter no bread." Choose a saying and write a paragraph that explains what the saying means. Spell-check, save, and close your journal.

Online Enrichment Games (Fun Stuff)  www.lwcgreen.keyboarding.com

3. Click the **Find Next** button. The first instance of the word *time-honored* is selected.
4. Click the **Replace** button. The word is replaced. No more instances of the word are found. Click the **OK** button in the confirmation dialog box. Click the **Close** button in the **Find and Replace** dialog box. Save the document.

Your replaced word should look like this.

Replaced word

The·traditional·stories·that·make·up·Greek·mythology·include·Creation,·Sacred,·Nature,·Trickster,·and·Heroic·myths,·such·as:¶

Warning! Clicking the **Replace All** button in the **Find and Replace** dialog box without first carefully setting the **More** button search options can return some surprising results!

Great! Next, let's arrange text in columns.

Creating Tabbed and Newspaper Columns

There are two ways to place text in columns: tabbed columns or newspaper columns.

Center tab
Decimal tab
Left tab
Right tab
tab formatting mark
tab indicator
tab stop
tabbed column

Tabbed Columns

Tabbed columns are created with tab stops and tab formatting marks. A tab stop is an icon on the Horizontal Ruler that indicates a specific typing position on a line. To align text at a tab stop, you tap the TAB key to move the insertion point to the tab stop position and then type the text. Each time you tap the TAB key, *Word* inserts a tab formatting mark.

Tab stops are also used to align text at the right margin and to move the first line of a paragraph inward from the left margin.

Exploring Across the Curriculum

Internet/Web

You can learn more about the history of bread by using the Web.

Open your Web browser and use a favorite to view the Learning with Computers Web page (www.lwcgreen.keyboarding.com). Click the **Links** option. Click **Project 14**. Click the links to research the history of bread. Take notes about what you learn.

Then create a new presentation and save it as *history of bread14*. Apply the design template and color scheme of your choice. Add an appropriate title and subtitle to the Title Slide. Insert slides with different layouts, such as Title and Text, Content or Text and Content, and Blank slides, to present the history of bread. Cite your sources on Title and Text slides at the end of your presentation. Add the slide transitions and timings of your choice. Apply the custom animation of your choice to at least one slide. Insert a picture or clip art of your choice as the slide background on one slide and remove the design template background graphics from the slide.

Add today's date as an automatically updating date, slide and page numbers, and your name as footer text to the slides. Include the same information on an audience handout. Run the slide show and save the presentation. Then preview and save the presentation as a Web page.

Language Arts: Words to Know

Look up the meaning of the following terms using a classroom, library, CD-ROM, or online encyclopedia or dictionary.

barm	ethanol	fermentation	fungus
lactobacilli	leaven	sourdough	yeast

Create a new presentation. Save it as *definitions14*. Type **Sourdough** as the title and **Definitions** as the subtitle on the Title Slide. Apply the slide design with the color scheme of your choice. Insert four slides using the Title and Content slide layout. Type **Terms** as the title. Create a table with 2 columns and 2 rows on each slide. Type two terms and two definitions in the table on each slide. Size, position, and format each table as desired. Add slide transitions and timings of your choice. Run the slide show and then save and close the presentation.

Explore More

By default, Left tab stops are set at every 0.5 inch on the Horizontal Ruler. However, Left, Right, Center, or Decimal custom tab stops can be set at any position on the Horizontal Ruler. Here are four main types of tab stops and their icons:

Left tab	Indents text from the left margin or left-aligns text columns	∟
Right tab	Right-aligns text columns or aligns dates and other text at the right margin	┘
Center tab	Centers headings over text columns	┴
Decimal tab	Aligns numbers on the decimal point	┴.

To set a tab stop, click the tab indicator button to the left of the Horizontal Ruler to select the type of tab stop you want. Then click the Horizontal Ruler where you want to position the tab stop. When a custom tab stop is set on the Horizontal Ruler, all the default Left tab stops to the left of the custom tab stop are automatically removed.

Here's a neat trick! Point to a tab stop on the Horizontal Ruler and then press *both* the left and right mouse buttons at the same time to see the tab stop position in inches. Try it!

Luis wants you to list examples of different types of Greek myths in single-spaced tabbed columns following the second paragraph on the first report page. First, you will set Center tab stops for the column headings and type the headings.

Let's set Center tab stops and type the column headings.

1. Move the insertion point to the blank line below the second body text paragraph on the first report page. Then click the tab indicator button to the left of the Horizontal Ruler until the Center tab stop icon appears.
2. Move the mouse pointer to the .75-inch position on the Horizontal Ruler and click to insert a Center tab stop. Set Center tab stops at the 1.75-inch and 3.5-inch positions.

Exploring on Your Own

Reading in Action

Standardized Test Prep Practice

A standardized test may require you to read a passage and answer multiple-choice questions. Here is an example. Read the passage and use context clues to answer the questions.

Adding yeast, which is the process of leavening bread, gives bread its lightness. Some leavened breads are called quick breads because baking powder is used instead of yeast to make the bread rise. Instead of using dried or cultivated baker's yeast as a leavening agent, sourdough bread is leavened with a starter. The starter is made of flour, water, and wild or cultivated yeasts. The starter is kept in an active state. Only part of the starter is used each time the bread is made. Fresh flour and water are added to the starter to keep it active for future use. Because the starter has fermented for a very long time, it adds a slightly sour flavor to the dough.

1. Based on the passage, you can infer that leavened bread

   A. is flat.

   B. needs yeast.

   C. requires a starter.

   D. is lighter than unleavened bread.

2. Sourdough bread is different from other types of leavened bread because

   A. it is only made with wild yeast.

   B. it is made from an active starter.

   C. it is made with baking powder.

   D. it does not rise.

Math in Action

Using Ratios and Proportions

A recipe for bread calls for 2 teaspoons of olive oil and 12 ounces of dough. If you want to use 1.5 pounds of dough, how many teaspoons of olive oil will you need?

First, convert the pounds of dough into ounces.
1 lb = 16 oz   1.5 lb × 16 oz = 24 oz

Next, determine the ratio of olive oil to dough.
2 tsp : 12 oz = 1 tsp : 6 oz

Use the ratio to determine how much olive oil is needed for 24 ounces of dough. Let x = the amount of olive oil needed for 24 ounces of dough. Cross-multiply.

$$\frac{24\text{ oz}}{x\text{ tsp}} = \frac{6\text{ oz}}{1\text{ tsp}}$$

$$24 = 6x$$

$$x = 4$$

You will need 4 tsp of olive oil if you have 1.5 lb of bread.

Now you try it!
How much olive oil will you need if you have 3 pounds of dough?
How much dough will you need if you have 6 teaspoons of olive oil?

3. Tap the TAB key and type **Myth**. Tap the TAB key and type **Type**. Tap the TAB key and type **Description**. Tap the ENTER key. The column heading text is centered at each tab stop.

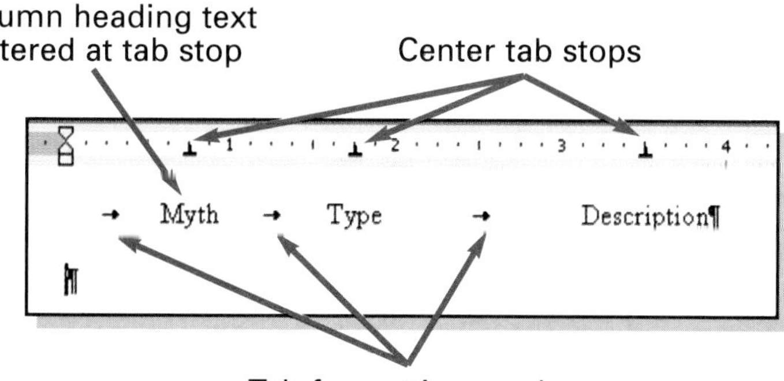

Word remembers the Center tab stops you set for the previous paragraph (the column headings) and includes them in the formatting for the new paragraph. You must remove these tab stops by dragging them off the Horizontal Ruler. Then set the new Left tab stops for the paragraph.

Let's remove unwanted Center tab stops, set new Left tab stops, and type the text.

1. Point to the first Center tab stop on the Horizontal Ruler. Press and hold the mouse button and drag the tab stop downward off the ruler. Drag the remaining two Center tab stops off the ruler.
2. Click the **tab indicator** button until the Left tab icon appears. Move the mouse pointer to the Horizontal Ruler and set Left tab stops at the 0.5-inch, the 1.5-inch, and the 2.38-inch positions on the Horizontal Ruler.
3. Tap the TAB key and type **Titans**. Tap the TAB key and type **Creation**. Tap the TAB key and type **Giant beings that created gods and humans**. Tap the ENTER key.
4. Continue to use the TAB key and type the remaining four tabbed paragraphs as follows.

Olympians	**Sacred**	**Gods and goddesses interacting with humans**
Persephone	**Nature**	**Changing of the seasons**
Eris	**Trickster**	**Creating discord and strife**
Achilles	**Heroic**	**Great warrior with a tragic flaw**

5. Apply the Bold font style to the column headings. Select the column headings and all the tabbed paragraphs *except* the last one (the Achilles paragraph) and single-space them. Deselect the text and save the document.

Exploring on Your Own

You have learned several new skills in this project. Now blaze your own trail by practicing these skills on your own! Use library or online resources to locate a recipe for sourdough bread. Then create a new presentation and save it as *bread14*. Apply the design template and color scheme of your choice.

Type **Making Sourdough Bread** and **your name** as the title and subtitle text on the Title Slide. Then insert slide 2 from the *sourdough14* presentation. Insert two slide layouts from Content or Text and Content group; use the first one to type the sourdough bread ingredients and the second one to type the recipe's instructions. Next, cite your sources on a Title and Text slide. Insert a Blank slide at the end of the presentation. Insert a picture or clip art of your choice as the slide's background and remove any design template graphics from the slide.

Add the slide transitions and timings of your choice to all the slides. Apply the custom animation of your choice to the two recipe slides. Create audience handouts; include in the header your name, page numbers, and today's date as an automatically updating date. Add today's date as an automatically updating date, your name as a footer, and slide numbers to all the slides except the Title Slide. Run the slide show and save the presentation.

Then preview and save the presentation as a Web page. Close the presentation.

Explore More

Your tabbed columns should look similar to this.

Single-spaced tabbed columns

Nature, Trickster, and Heroic myths, such as:¶

Myth	Type	Description¶
Titans	Creation	Giant beings that created gods and humans¶
Olympians	Sacred	Gods and goddesses interacting with humans¶
Persephone	Nature	Changing of the seasons¶
Eris	Trickster	Creating discord and strife¶
Achilles	Heroic	Great warrior with a tragic flaw¶

Greek myths were originally part of an oral tradition or history told by one

Fantastic! Now, let's place the two single-spaced paragraphs in newspaper columns.

You can also set and delete tab stops in the **Tabs** dialog box. Choose **Format** on the menu bar and choose **Tabs**.

Newspaper Columns

newspaper column

Another type of text column is a newspaper column. In newspaper columns, text flows from one narrow column to another, like columns in your local newspaper. To format text in newspaper columns, first select the text. Then click the **Columns** button on the Standard toolbar and choose the number of columns from the grid. *Word* automatically inserts **Continuous** section breaks before and after the text and places the text in the columns.

You can also create newspaper columns by choosing **Format** on the menu bar and choosing **Columns**. Then set the options you want in the **Columns** dialog box.

Let's place the single-spaced paragraphs in two newspaper columns.

1. Use the SHIFT + click method to select all the single-spaced text beginning with the <u>*Nature Myth: Persephone*</u>. paragraph heading on the first report page and ending with the text *thus launching the Trojan War* on the second report page.
2. Click the **Columns** button.
3. Point to the second column in the grid. The bottom of the grid shows **2 Columns**.
4. Click the second column in the grid. Deselect the text. Scroll to view the text in two newspaper columns.

Project | *Skills Review*

You learned a lot in this project! We are very impressed with your progress. Let's take a few minutes to review the skills that you learned.

Add a Title and Content slide	Choose **Format** on the menu bar and choose **Slide Layout**. New Slide
Insert a picture as a slide background	Choose **Format** on the menu bar and choose **Background**.
Add slide transitions and timings	Choose **Slide Show** on the menu bar and choose **Slide Transition**.
Apply custom animation	Choose **Slide Show** on the menu bar and choose **Custom Animation**.
Add header and footer text, a date, and page numbers to audience handouts	Choose **View** on the menu bar and choose **Header and Footer**.
Preview a presentation as a Web page and save it as a Web page	Choose **File** on the menu bar and choose **Web Page Preview** or **Save as Web Page**.

CHECKPOINT
Your newspaper columns should look like this.

Continuous section break inserted to place text in newspaper columns

played·in·their·daily·lives.¶ .... Section Break (Continuous) ....

Nature·Myth:·Persephone.··Persephone·was·the·daughter·of·Demeter,·the·sister·of·Zeus·and·goddess·of·the·harvest.··One·day·Persephone·was·kidnapped·by·Hades,·god·of·the·Underworld.··In·her·anger·and·sadness,·Demeter·caused·a·great·winter·to·fall·on·the·Earth·and·no·fruit,·grain,·or·grass·grew.··Because·the·

Zeus·granted·Demeter·her·wish·that·Hades·return·Persephone·to·the·Earth's·surface just as long as Persephone had not·eaten·anything·in·the·Underworld.··But·Hades·gave·Persephone·a·few·red·pomegranate·seeds·before·her·return·and·she·ate·them.··In·a·compromise,·Zeus·allowed·Persephone·to·return·to·her·

Text in two newspaper columns

Nice work! Now let's create a separate title page at the top of the document.

TRAIL 4 MARKER

Using Click and Type

Click and Type
Click and Type pointer

Reports often have a title page with the name of the report, the writer's name, a school or organization name, and the current date. To create a title page, first insert a new blank page at the top of the document. Then make sure you are working in Print Layout view so that you can use *Word*'s **Click and Type** feature and the Vertical Ruler to quickly position text on the page.

When you move the I-beam over the blank page in Print Layout view, the mouse pointer changes shape and becomes the **Click and Type pointer** with a paragraph formatting icon. The paragraph formatting icon indicates the type of paragraph formatting—horizontal alignment, tab stop, or indentation—that will automatically be applied to the text. For example, if you point to the center of the page, the Click and Type pointer includes a Center align icon. When you type your text, *Word* automatically centers it horizontally on the page.

Warning! The Click and Type feature does not work in Normal view, and the Vertical Ruler is not visible in Normal view.

Let's preview the *sourdough14* presentation as a Web page and then save it as a Web page.

1. View **slide 1**, if necessary. Then choose **File** on the menu bar and choose **Web Page Preview**. In a few seconds, the presentation will open in your Web browser. Look carefully at the navigation pane containing a list of slide titles and numbers. Locate the **Next Slide** arrow, **Previous** slide arrow, and **Slide Show** button below the slide.

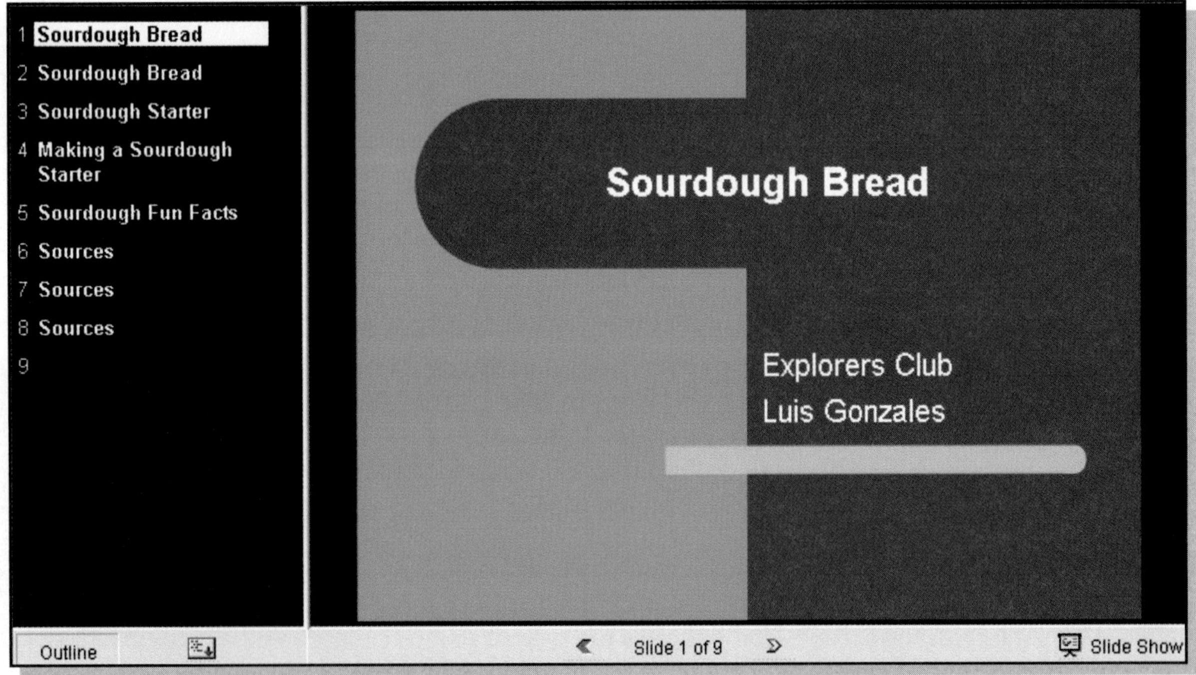

2. Click several slide titles in the navigation pane to view the slides. Then close the browser.
3. Choose **File** on the menu bar and choose **Save as Web Page**. Switch to the folder that contains your solution files and click the **Save** button in the **Save As** dialog box. The presentation is saved as a single-file Web page named *sourdough14.htm*. Close the presentation.

Congratulations! Luis's presentation is ready to go!

Apply It!

Let's create a title page and add the text using Click and Type.

1. Press the CTRL + HOME keys to move the insertion point to the top of the document and then press the CTRL + ENTER keys to insert a hard page break. Press the CTRL + HOME keys again to move the insertion point to the top of the new blank title page.
2. Type the title **GREEK MYTHOLOGY** in ALL CAPS and tap the ENTER key.
3. Scroll to view the 3-inch position on the Vertical Ruler. Move the Click and Type pointer to the center of the page at about the 3-inch vertical position. Notice that the pointer has a Center align icon.

4. Double-click to center the insertion point. *Word* automatically inserts paragraph formatting marks from the last paragraph you typed (the title) to the insertion point.
5. Type **Luis Gonzales** and tap the ENTER key twice. Type **Explorers Club** and tap the ENTER key.
6. Use Click and Type to center the insertion point at approximately the 7-inch vertical position and type or insert today's date. Save the document.

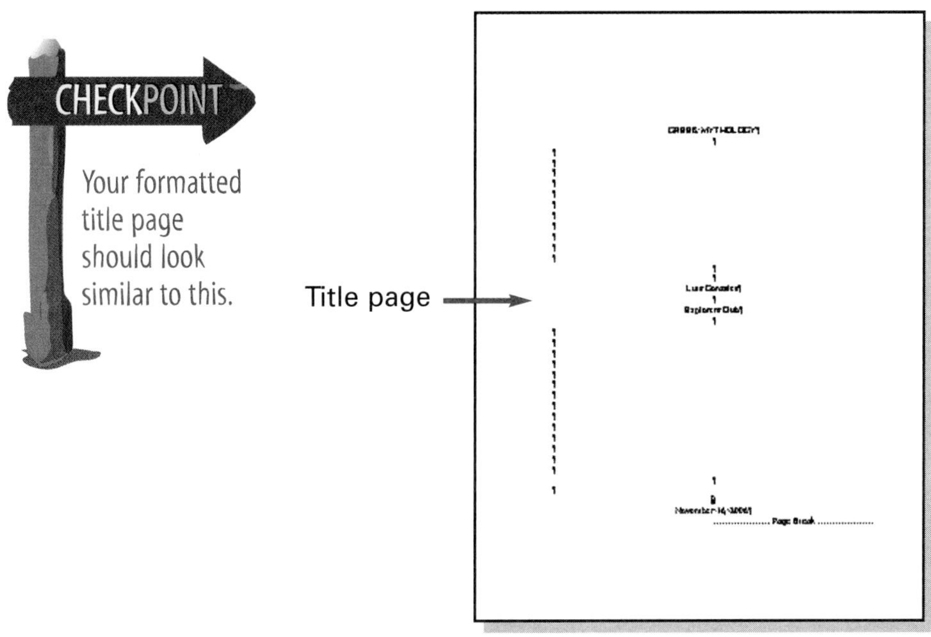
CHECKPOINT
Your formatted title page should look similar to this.
Title page

Super! Now, let's set the correct margins for the multipage bound report and add page numbers.

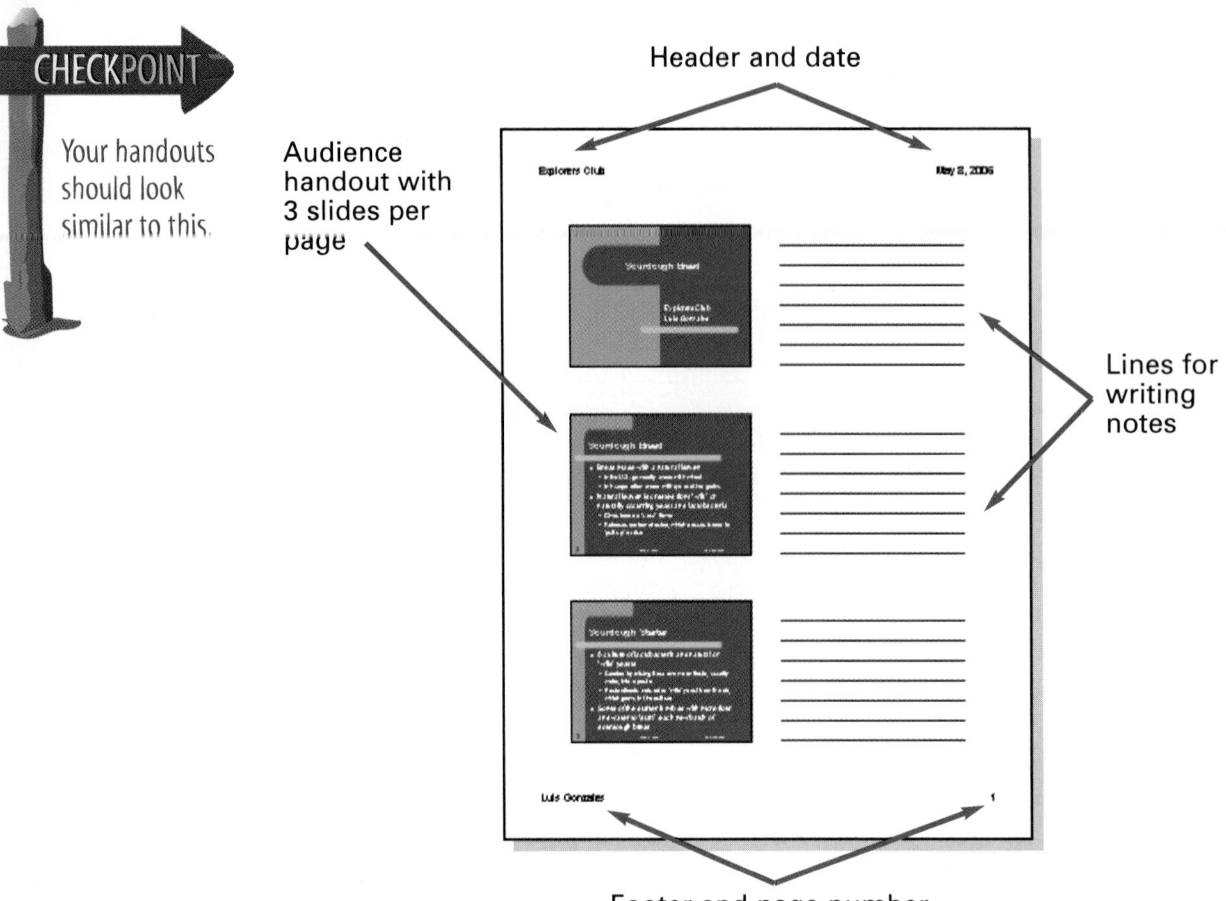

Terrific! Finally, Luis wants to save the presentation as a Web page to post on the school's website.

Saving a Presentation as a Web Page

TRAIL 6 MARKER

You can preview a *PowerPoint* presentation as a Web page and then save it as a Web page by choosing **File** on the menu bar and choosing **Web Page Preview** and **Save as Web Page**.

You navigate between slides when previewing a presentation in your Web browser by clicking a slide title in the navigation pane to the left of the slide or by clicking the slide navigation arrows below the slide. Click the **Slide Show** button below the slide to run a full-screen slide show.

Another way to align all the text on a page vertically at the top, center, or bottom of the page is by setting the **Vertical alignment** option in the **Layout** tab in the **Page Setup** dialog box. Check it out!

The **Sec** indicator on the status bar tells you which document section contains the insertion point. **Sec 1** means the insertion point is in Section 1. Check it out!

Setting Margins and Inserting Page Numbers in Multiple Document Sections

The *Greek Mythology4* document now has four document sections—a title page, two report pages, and text in columns. Now you need to add one more page for your endnotes. After a page for the endnotes is created, your document will have five sections including the section that has newspaper columns set apart with **Continuous** section breaks and the paragraph that follows the newspaper columns. You will set margins for each section and then insert page numbers in two of the sections.

Setting Margins for a Multipage Bound Report

bound report
gutter

Reports with three pages or more, such as the *Greek Mythology4* document, are usually bound at the left or right margin with a plastic clip or other binding. A bound report must have additional white space, called a gutter, added to the margin for the binding. To add a gutter to the *Greek Mythology4* document, set the **Left Gutter** option in the **Margins** tab in the **Page Setup** dialog box to 0.5 inch. Here are the margin, gutter, and page number settings for each section in the *Greek Mythology4* document.

Section 1	Title page and first report page	2-inch top margin and 1-inch left, right, and bottom margins; 0.5-inch gutter; no page numbers
Section 2	Second report page	1-inch top margin and 1-inch left, right, and bottom margins; 0.5-inch gutter; page number
Section 3	Newspaper columns	1-inch top margin and 1-inch left, right, and bottom margins; 0.5-inch gutter; no page number
Section 4	Second report page text following the newspaper columns	1-inch top margin and 1-inch left, right, and bottom margins; 0.5-inch gutter; no page number
Section 5	ENDNOTES page	2-inch top margin and 1-inch left, right, and bottom margins; 0.5-inch gutter; page number

Let's insert *Explorers Club* as header text, *Luis Gonzales* as footer text, today's date as an automatically updating date, and page numbers on the audience handouts.

1. Choose **View** on the menu bar and choose **Header and Footer** to open the **Header and Footer** dialog box. Click the **Notes and Handouts** tab, if necessary.
2. Click the **Update automatically** option button in the Date and time area, if necessary. Click the text box drop-down arrow and click the fourth date format (month spelled out/day/year).
3. Click the **Header** checkbox to insert a check mark, if necessary, and type **Explorers Club** in the text box. Click the **Page number** checkbox to insert a check mark, if necessary. Click the **Footer** checkbox to insert a check mark, if necessary, and type **Luis Gonzales** in the text box.

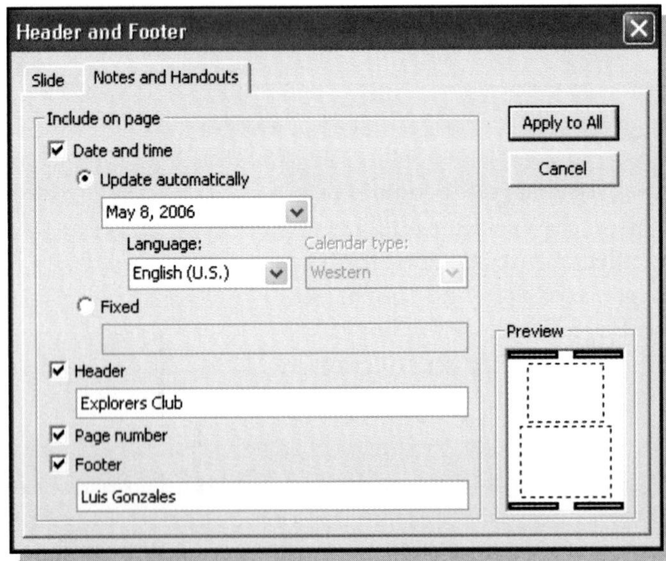

While the Header and Footer dialog box is open, let's add a date, footer, and slide numbers to all the slides except the Title Slide.

4. Click the **Slide tab**. Add **Luis Gonzales** as footer text, today's date as an automatically updating date, and slide numbers to all the slides *except* the title slide. Then click the **Apply to All** button.
5. Click the **Print Preview** button to view the audience handouts.

   Click the **Print What** drop-down arrow and click **Handouts (3 slide per page)**. Observe the header, footer, date, and page numbers on the handout and the footer, date, and slide numbers on the individual slides. Close **Print Preview** and save the presentation.

Let's set the margins and gutter beginning with Section 1.

1. Press the CTRL + HOME keys. Open the **Page Setup** dialog box and set a 2-inch top margin and 1-inch left and right margins. Type **.5** in the **Gutter** text box. *Don't forget to type the period.*
2. Click the **Gutter position** drop-down arrow and click **Left**. Look at the margin preview in the lower-right corner of the dialog box to see a preview of the 0.5-inch gutter added to the left margin. Make certain that the **Apply to** list is *This section.*

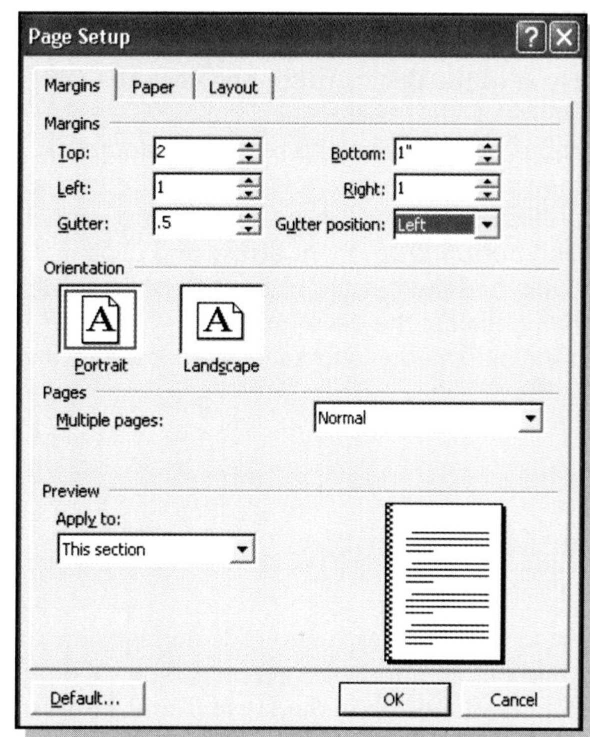

3. Click the **OK** button. The margins and gutter are set for Section 1, which includes the title page and the first page of the report.

   Next, let's insert a **Next page** section break to create a new Section 2 and then set a different top margin.

4. Move the insertion point to the end of the last double-spaced paragraph on the first report page. (The insertion point should be immediately in front of the **Continuous** section break indicator and the paragraph mark.)

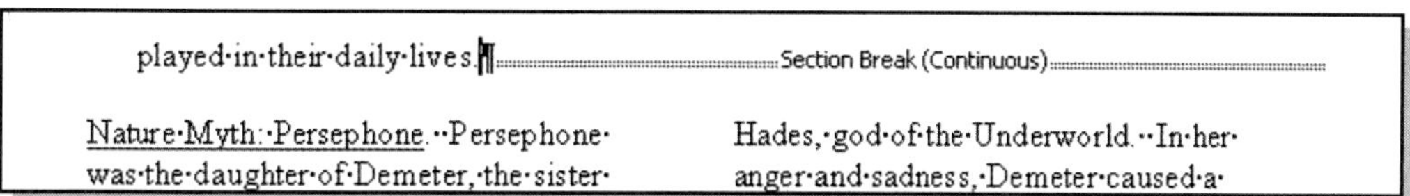
played·in·their·daily·lives.¶ ::::::::::Section Break (Continuous)::::::::::

Nature·Myth:·Persephone.··Persephone·was·the·daughter·of·Demeter,·the·sister·

Hades,·god·of·the·Underworld.··In·her·anger·and·sadness,·Demeter·caused·a·

5. Insert a **Next page** section break to move the text in newspaper columns to the next page and create a new Section 2. Look at the status bar to verify that the section indicator is **Sec 2**.

Let's set the animation effect to have it occur automatically and with the Medium speed.

5. Click the **Start** button drop-down arrow in the task pane and click **With previous** to have the animation occur automatically. Click the **Speed** button drop-down arrow and click **Medium**, if necessary. Click the **Play** button in the task pane to view the animation effect. Deselect the title placeholder.
6. Select the bulleted list placeholder. Click the **Add Effect** button in the task pane, point to **Entrance**, and click **Fly in**. If **Fly in** does not appear in the short list, click **More Effects** to open the **Add Entrance Effect** dialog box, click **Fly in** in the Basic group, and click the **OK** button.
7. Click the **Start** button drop-down arrow in the task pane and click **After previous** to have the animation occur automatically after the title animation. Click the **Direction** button drop-down arrow and click **From Left**. Click the **Speed** button drop-down arrow and click **Medium**, if necessary. Click the **Play** button in the task pane to view the animation effect. Then deselect the placeholder.
8. Close the task pane, run the slide show, and save the presentation.

Terrific! Now, you are ready to create Luis's audience handouts.

TRAIL 5 MARKER

Creating Audience Handouts

handout master

You learned how to insert footer text, a date, and slide numbers on slides. You can also insert this kind of information on audience handouts by using options on the **Notes and Handouts** tab in the **Header and Footer** dialog box. Placeholders for footer, page number, and date information are controlled by the **handout master**.

View the handout master by choosing **View** on the menu bar, pointing to **Master**, and choosing **Handout Master**.

6. Open the **Page Setup** dialog box and change the top margin to 1 inch.

   Now, let's change the margins for Section 3 (the newspaper columns), Section 4 (the text following the newspaper columns on the second report page), and Section 5 (the ENDNOTES page).

7. Move the insertion point into the first newspaper column on the second report page. Open the **Page Setup** dialog box and set the left and right margins to 1 inch and the left gutter to 0.5 inch.
8. Move the insertion point in front of the paragraph that follows the newspaper columns near the bottom of the second report page. Look at the status bar to verify that the insertion point is in Section 4. Open the **Page Setup** dialog box and set the left and right margins to 1 inch and the left gutter to 0.5 inch.
9. Move the insertion point in front of the text ENDNOTES near the bottom of the second report page. Insert a **Next page** section break. Open the **Page Setup** dialog box and set a 2-inch top margin, 1-inch left and right margins, and a 0.5-inch left gutter. Scroll the document to view the new margins for each section, and then save the document.

Now that you have set the correct margins for the five document sections, you need to add page numbers to Sections 2 and 5 (the report pages and the Endnotes page). Adding page numbers is not applicable for Section 3 (the newspaper columns) and Section 4 (the paragraph following the newspaper columns).

Adding Page Numbers

To insert page numbers in different sections of a document, you must view the header area for each section and insert a page number using buttons on the Header and Footer toolbar. To view the header and footer areas and the Header and Footer toolbar, choose **View** on the menu bar and choose **Header and Footer**.

Warning! *Word* automatically links or duplicates headers across sections; when you type text in a header for one section, the header then automatically appears for all sections. To prevent the unwanted duplication of headers you must unlink a header from the previous section's header. To do this, click the **Link to Previous** button on the Header and Footer toolbar.

Let's animate the title and bulleted list on slide 5 by applying custom animation effects "on entrance" or when slide 5 appears during a slide show. Use a different animation effect for the title and the bulleted list.

1. View **slide 5**. Click the **Other Task Panes** arrow on the task pane title bar and click **Custom Animation** to open the **Custom Animation** task pane.
2. Press and hold the SHIFT key and click the title placeholder to select the placeholder and its contents. Look carefully at the options in the **Custom Animation** task pane. You can add an effect, modify it, or remove it with options in the task pane.
3. Click the **Add Effect** button in the task pane, point to **Entrance**, and click **More Effects** to open the **Add Entrance Effect** dialog box. Scroll to view the different animation effects organized by group: Basic, Subtle, Moderate, and Exciting.
4. Click **Faded Swivel** in the Subtle group and click the **OK** button. The task pane options now indicate that the animation effect will occur on a mouse click.

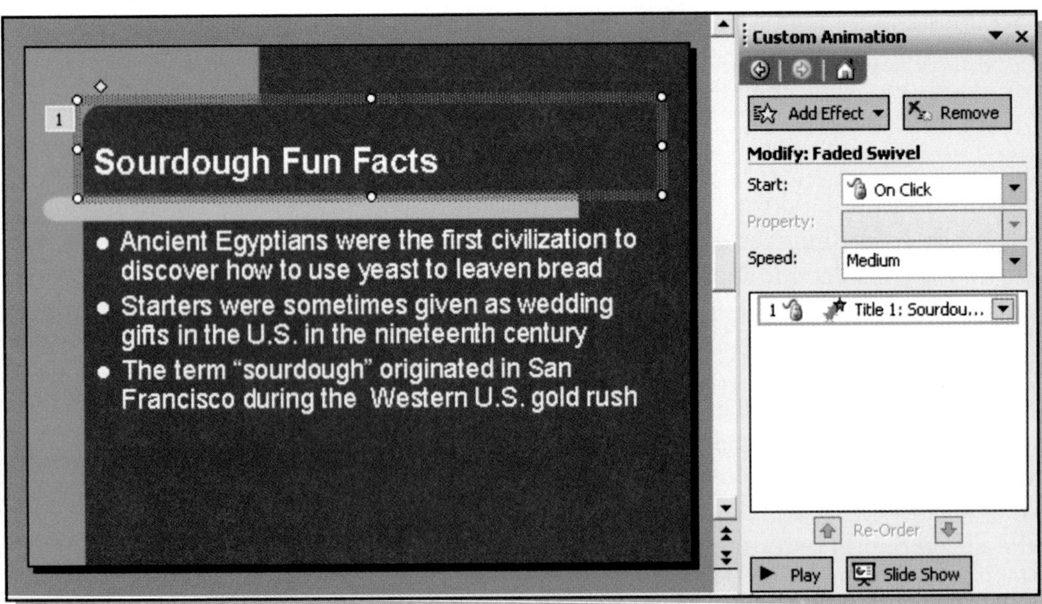

Let's display the Section 2 header area, unlink it from the Section 1 header, and insert page numbers for Sections 2 and 5.

1. Move the insertion point to the top of the second report page (Section 2). Choose **View** on the menu bar and choose **Header and Footer**. The Section 2 header area opens, and it contains the insertion point at the left margin. See that the header area has its own Center and Right tab stops.

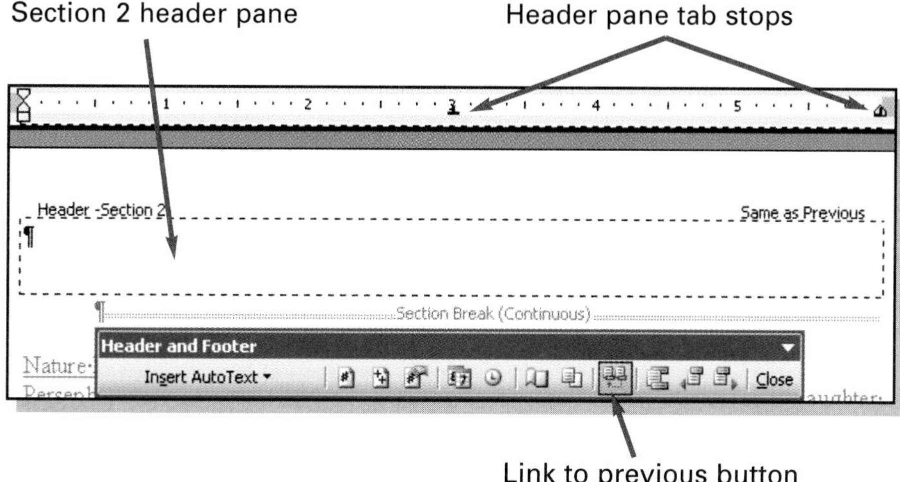

2. Click the **Link to Previous** button on the Header and Footer toolbar to unlink the Section 2 header from the Section 1 header.
3. Drag the header area's Center tab stop off the Horizontal Ruler. Tap the TAB key to move the insertion point to the Right tab stop position in the header area.
4. Click the **Insert Page Number** button on the Header and Footer toolbar to insert a page number.
5. Click the **Format Page Number** button on the Header and Footer toolbar to open the **Page Number Format** dialog box.

   Because the title page is not included in the pagination of the report, the first page of the report is actually page 2 of your document. So, you must set the **Start at option** to 2.

Let's explore different slide transition effects and then apply a slide transition effect and slide timings to all the slides.

1. View **slide 1**. Choose **Slide Show** on the menu bar and choose **Slide Transition** to open the **Slide Transition** task pane. Click **Blinds Vertical** in the **Apply to selected slides** list. The transition effect is applied to **slide 1**. Click the **Speed** drop-down arrow and click **Medium**.
2. Click the **Play** button at the bottom of the task pane to view the transition effect again. Continue to explore the slide transitions by applying them to **slide 1** and observing the slide transition effect. Change the speed from Fast, to Medium, to Slow as desired.
3. Select your favorite slide transition with the speed of your choice and then set eight-second slide timings. Click the **Automatically after** checkbox to insert a check mark, if necessary, and leave the check mark in the **On mouse click** checkbox for the most flexibility. Click the **Apply to All Slides** button.
4. Run the slide show to observe the slide transition effects and slide timings applied to all the slides. Save the presentation. Leave the task pane open for the next Trail Marker.

Outstanding! Next, Luis wants to add fun to a slide with custom animation.

TRAIL 4 MARKER

Applying Custom Animation

custom animation

In the previous project, you learned how to apply an animation scheme to slides. Instead of applying one animation scheme to all the slides and their contents, you can use custom animation to apply different motion and sound effects to individual parts of a slide. For example, the title on a slide can fly in from the top, bottom, left, or right. Or each line in a bulleted list under the title can appear and leave with a screech. Clip art can arrive with the sound of a camera clicking.

You can set timings for the effects and specify whether they should occur on a mouse click or automatically. When multiple effects are added to the same slide, you can also specify the order of the effects. When the effects are no longer wanted, you can remove them.

You can open the **Custom Animation** task pane by choosing **Slide Show** on the menu bar and choosing **Custom Animation**.

6. Click the **Start at option** button and type **2** in the text box.
7. Click the **OK** button. Click the **Close** button on the Header and Footer toolbar to close the header area.
8. Scroll the document to verify that the title page and the first report page do not have page numbers and that the second report page and the Endnotes page do have page numbers. You did not have to insert page numbers for Section 5 because its header is automatically linked to the Section 2 header. Save the document.

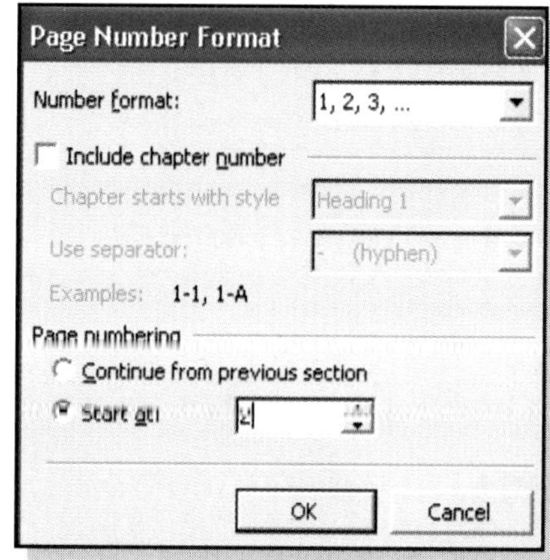

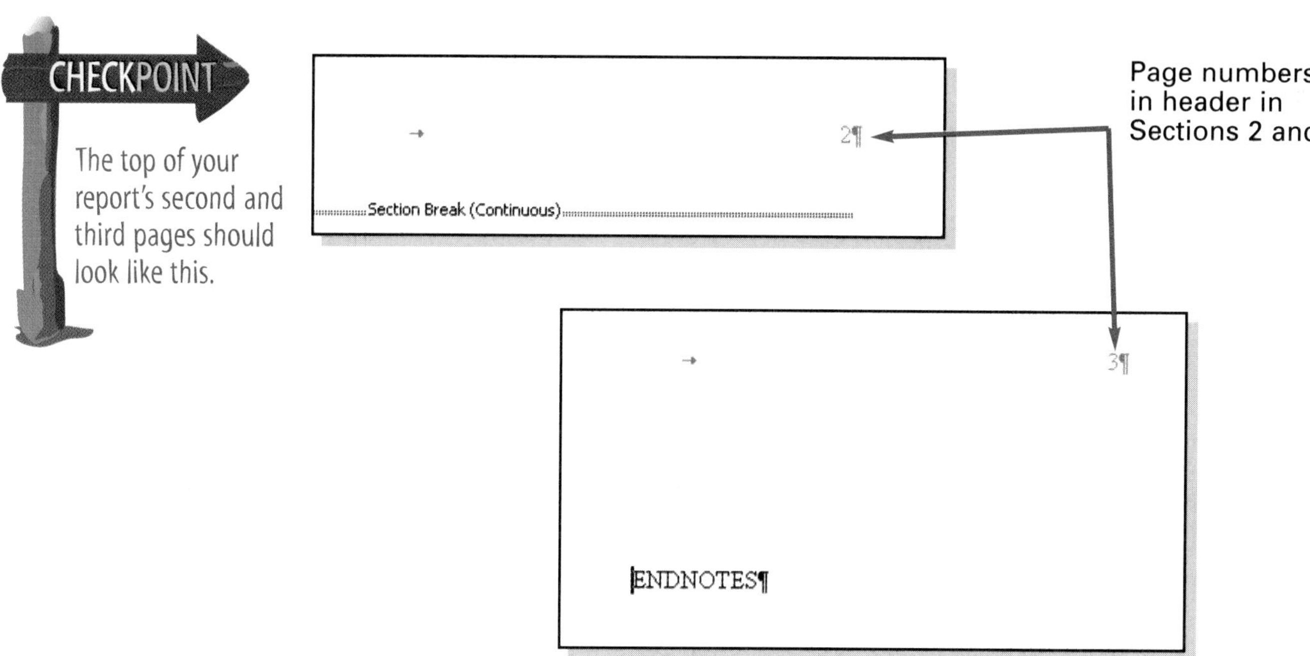

What a great job! To wrap up the document, you must cite Luis's sources in endnotes.

CHECKPOINT

Your slide 9 should look like this.

Slide with picture background

Super! Now, let's add some slide transitions.

TRAIL 3 MARKER

Adding Slide Transitions

In Project 13, you learned about slide transitions—motion you see as slides advance during a slide show. You can manually add slide transitions to one or more slides by selecting a transition option in the **Slide Transition** task pane. You can also choose a transition's speed and add sound effects. When you apply a slide transition effect to a slide in Normal view, you immediately see the effect in action!

Remember! Too much motion and sound can annoy your audience. Don't overdo it!

Inserting Endnotes

In the previous project, you learned that endnotes are source citations that appear at the end of a document. When you create an endnote, *Word* automatically inserts a note reference mark at the insertion point and on the last page of the document. It also inserts an endnote separator line on last page above the endnotes. Because you have already created a separate page for endnotes, you will delete the endnote separator line.

Let's insert the endnotes and delete the endnote separator line.

1. Move the insertion point to the end of the second *Nature Myth: Persephone.* paragraph near the top of the second newspaper column on report page 2. Choose **Insert** on the menu bar, point to **Reference**, and choose **Footnote**. Click the **Endnotes** option button. Make certain all the other options in your dialog box look like this. Then click the **Insert** button.

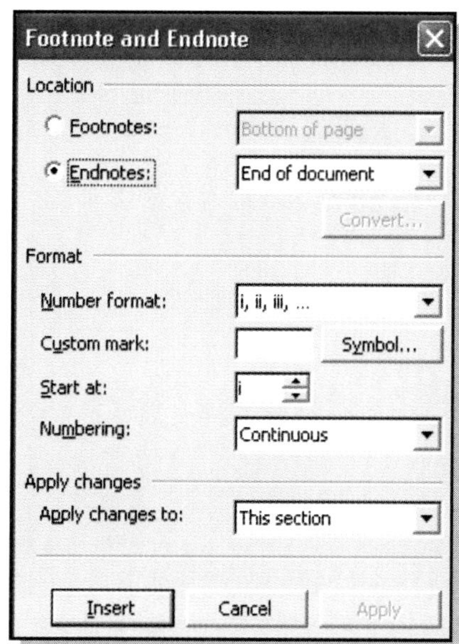

TRAIL 2 MARKER

Inserting a Picture as the Slide Background

In Project 12, you learned how to remove a slide's background graphics or change its background colors. You can also use special fill effects—like a picture—for a slide's background.

Let's insert a picture of sourdough bread as the background on slide 9 and remove the design template's background graphics from the slide.

1. View **slide 9**. Choose **Format** on the menu bar and choose **Background** to open the **Background** dialog box.
2. Click the **Background fill** drop-down arrow and choose **Fill Effects** on the color grid to open the **Fill Effects** dialog box. Click the **Picture** tab.
3. Click the **Select Picture** button to open the **Select Picture** dialog box. Switch to the folder that contains your data files and double-click the picture named **sourdough bread**.
4. Click the **Lock picture aspect ratio** checkbox to insert a check mark. This option maintains the picture's proportions when it is resized to cover the entire slide.
5. Click the **OK** button to return to the **Background** dialog box. Click the **Omit background graphics from master** checkbox to insert a check mark, and click the **Apply** button. The design template's background graphics are removed and the sourdough bread picture covers the entire slide.

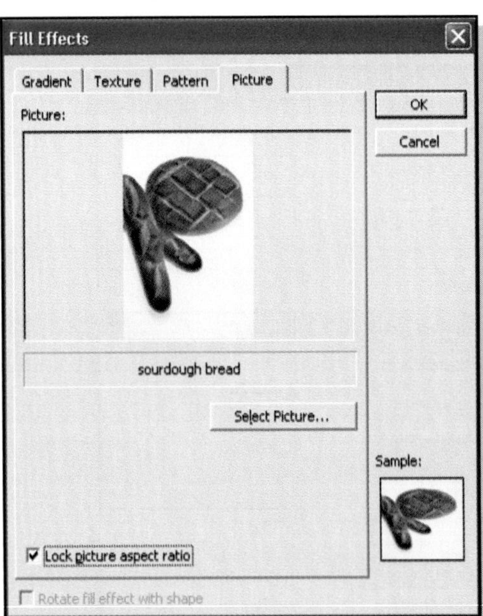

A superscript note reference mark *i* appears at the end of the paragraph and the insertion point moves to the ENDNOTES page. Next, type the endnote text. Be sure to apply the Italic font style to book and website names. Allow *Word* to automatically format Web page URLs.

2. Type endnote *i* as follows and then tap the ENTER key.
   Alice Low, *The Macmillan Book of Greek Gods and Heroes* (New York: Macmillan, 1985), pp. 38-44.
3. Move the insertion point to the end of the *Trickster Myth: Eris.* paragraphs at the bottom of the second newspaper column on report page 2. Insert endnote *ii* as follows:
   "Eris," *Wikipedia,* May 10, 2004, http://en.wikipedia.org/wiki/Eris (accessed November 16, 2006).

You should format the endnotes just like you formatted the footnotes in the previous project.

4. Scroll to view the Endnotes page and select the endnote reference marks and text. Indent the first line of each footnote 0.5 inch from the left margin and change the font size to 12 point. Deselect the endnotes.

Let's remove the endnote separator line in the note pane.

5. Switch to **Normal** view. Choose **View** on the menu bar and choose **Footnotes** to open the note pane. Click the **Endnote** list drop-down arrow and click **Endnote Separator**. Select the **Endnote Separator** line and tap the DELETE key. Click the **Close** button on the note pane.
6. Switch to **Print Layout** view and scroll to view the ENDNOTES page.

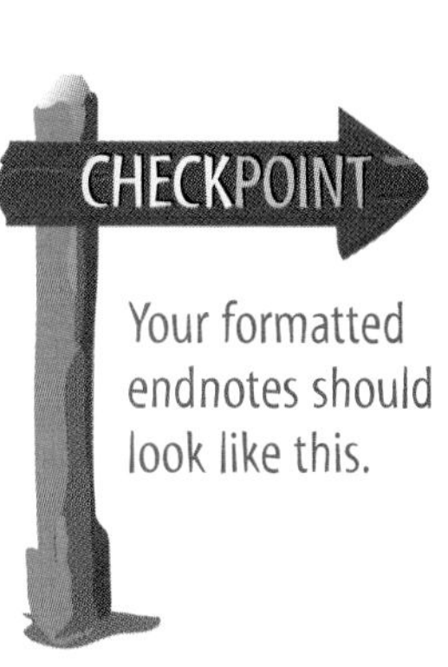

CHECKPOINT
Your formatted endnotes should look like this.

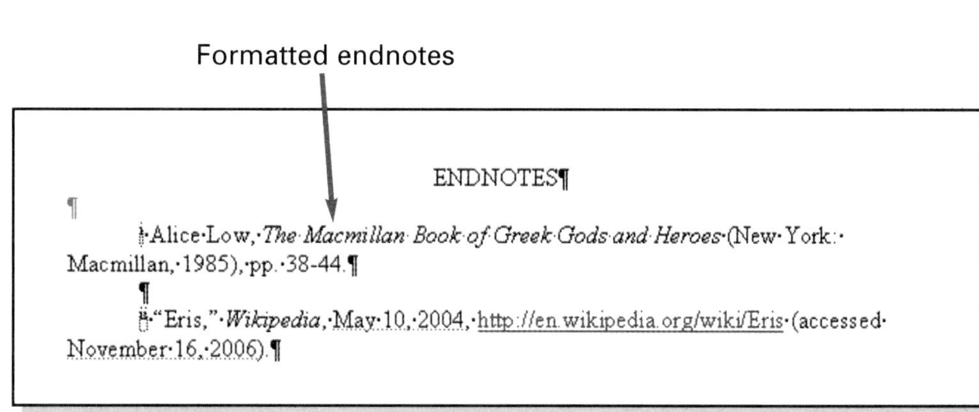

ENDNOTES¶

¶

i·Alice·Low,·*The·Macmillan·Book·of·Greek·Gods·and·Heroes*·(New·York:·Macmillan,·1985),·pp.·38-44.¶

¶

ii·"Eris,"·*Wikipedia*,·May·10,·2004,·http://en.wikipedia.org/wiki/Eris·(accessed·November·16,·2006).¶

7. Save and close the document.

Very well done! Luis's *Greek Mythology* report document looks fantastic!

9. Click in the bulleted list placeholder and type the following list. Let *PowerPoint* automatically resize the font to fit all the text in the placeholder. *Don't worry if the text gets very small; you will resize the placeholder and the text in the next step.*

   - **Mix flour and water in a bowl or ceramic crock and store uncovered in a warm place (80-85 degrees)**
   - **Stir once or twice every 24 hours and look for bubbles**
   - **Remove 1/2 cup of starter and stir in 1/2 cup warm water and 2/3 cup flour every 48 hours**
   - **Continue 48-hour cycle for 7 to 8 days**
   - **Lightly cover and refrigerate until needed**

10. Drag the bulleted list placeholder's bottom sizing handle downward approximately 1/4 inch to make the placeholder and font size larger. Deselect the placeholder.

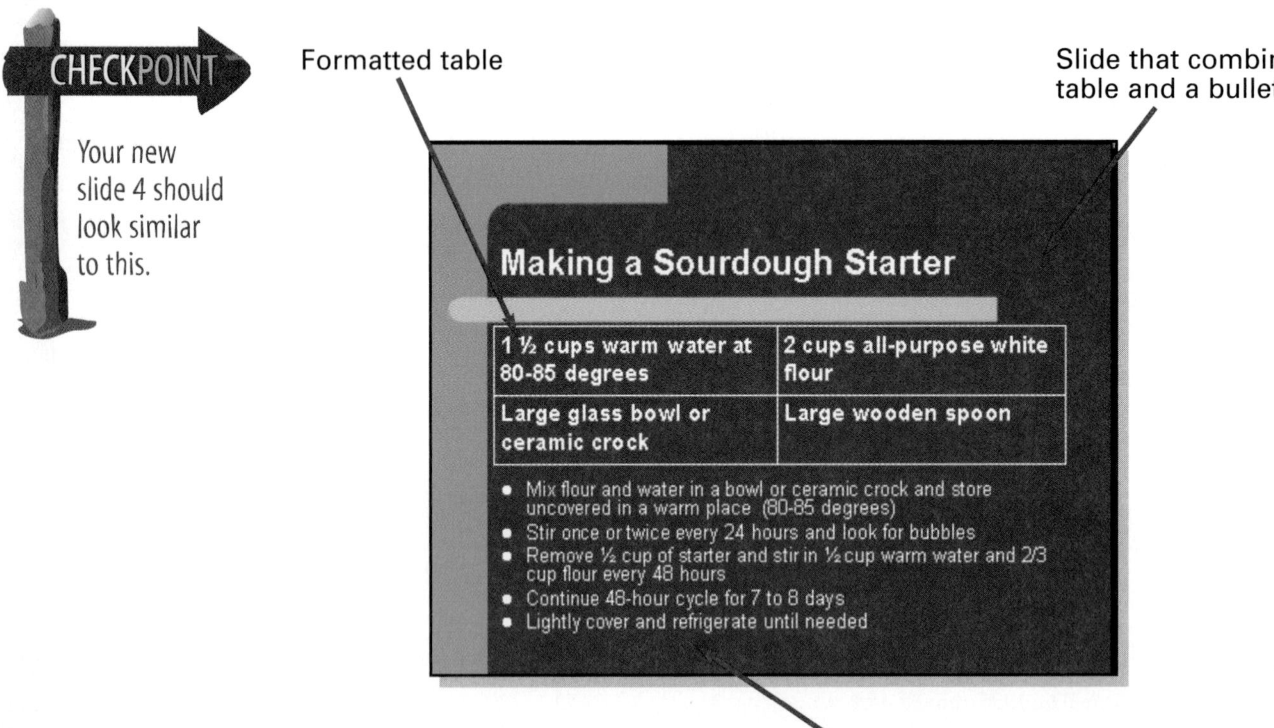

Fantastic! Now let's use a picture of sourdough bread as the background for slide 9.

Did you know? You can use buttons on the Tables and Borders toolbar to format a table and its contents in both *Word* and *PowerPoint*. Check it out!

Project | *Skills Review*

You learned a lot in this project! We are very impressed with your progress. Let's take a few minutes to review the skills that you learned.

Skill	How to
Paint formats from formatted text to unformatted text	
Find and replace text	Choose **Edit** on the menu bar and choose **Find** or **Replace**.
Set tab stops on the horizontal ruler	Choose **Format** on the menu bar and choose **Tabs**. Click the tab indicator to select the tab stop type and then click at the desired position on the Horizontal Ruler.
Create newspaper columns	Choose **Format** on the menu bar and choose **Columns**.
Place the insertion point anywhere on the page in Print Layout view	Double-click with the Click and Type pointer.
Create document sections	Choose **Insert** on the menu bar and choose **Break**. Then choose **Next Page** to insert a new page and a new section. Choose **Continuous** to set text in columns.
Insert page numbers in the header	Choose **View** on the menu bar and choose **Header and Footer**. Use the buttons on the Header and Footer toolbar.
Insert endnotes	Choose **Insert** on the menu bar, point to **Reference**, and choose **Footnote**. Click **Endnotes** and set options.

3. Click the **Title and Content over Text** slide layout. Then close the **Slide Layout** task pane. The new slide has a title placeholder and a content placeholder above a bulleted list placeholder.

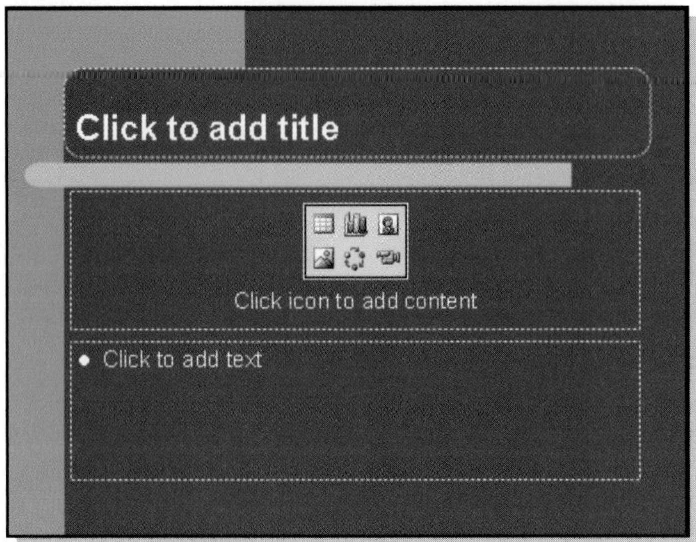

4. Type **Making a Sourdough Starter** in the title placeholder. Then deselect it.
5. Use ScreenTips to view the name of each icon in the content placeholder. Click the **Insert Table** icon. The content placeholder is selected and the **Insert Table** dialog box opens. You can specify the number of columns and rows in your table in this dialog box.
6. Click the **OK** button to insert a table with two columns and two rows in the content placeholder. The insertion point appears in the first table cell.

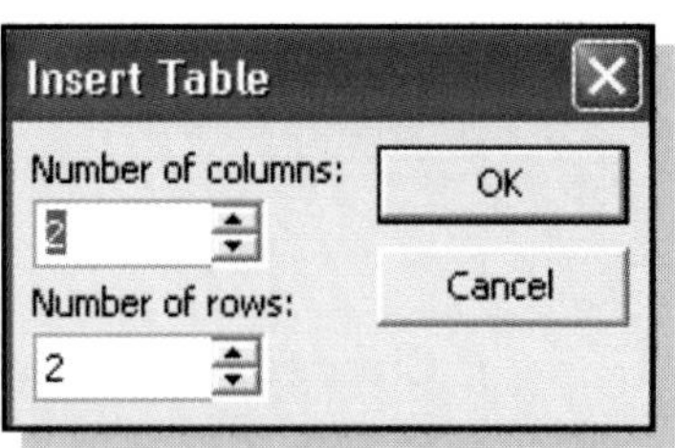

You work with a *PowerPoint* table just like you do with a *Word* table—navigate with the TAB and SHIFT + TAB keys and format the cell contents with buttons on the Formatting toolbar. To resize a *PowerPoint* table, drag a sizing handle on the table's boundary.

7. Type **1 1/2 cups warm water at 80-85 degrees** in the first cell in the first row and tap the TAB key. Type **2 cups all-purpose white flour** in the second cell in the first row and tap the TAB key. Type **Large glass bowl or ceramic crock** in the first cell in the second row and tap the TAB key. Type **Large wooden spoon** in the second cell in the second row. Deselect the placeholder.
8. Press and hold the SHIFT key and click the table placeholder's boundary to select the placeholder and its contents. Click the **Bold** button on the Formatting toolbar. **B** Deselect the placeholder.

Exploring on Your Own

Blaze your own trail by practicing your new skills! Use classroom, library, or online resources to research one of the following ancient Greek Heroic myths: *Theseus and the Minotaur, Achilles and the Trojan War, Herakles and the Twelve Labors*, or *Perseus and the Gorgon Medusa*. Take notes about what you learn.

Then create a multipage bound report that has a title page, at least two double-spaced report pages based on your notes, and an ENDNOTES page. Use Click and Type to add text to the title page. Include *either* single-spaced tabbed columns or newspaper columns as part of the report text. Use the **Format Painter** to paint keyword and paragraph heading formats.

Use **Find and Replace** to find a word and replace it with another word. Set the appropriate margins for each section of the report including a 0.5-inch gutter. Insert page numbers for the sections that contain the report pages and the ENDNOTES page. Cite your sources with endnotes. Spell-check, save, and close the document.

Reading in Action

Sequence of Events

When you read a story, put the events in order to help you remember what you have read. Read the data file *Greek Mythology4.* Choose one of the myths. Use a graphic organizer to list the events of the myth in order.

Persephone is kidnapped by Hades.
↓
Demeter turns the world into winter.
↓
Zeus grants Demeter her wish.

Math in Action

Pythagorean Theorem

Pythagoras was an ancient Greek mathematician, famous for his theorem about right triangles. A right triangle has a 90° angle at the point where two of the sides meet. The Pythagorean Theorem states that the sum of the squares of the smaller sides of a right triangle is equal to the square of the largest side, which is called the hypotenuse.
$A^2 + B^2 = C^2$

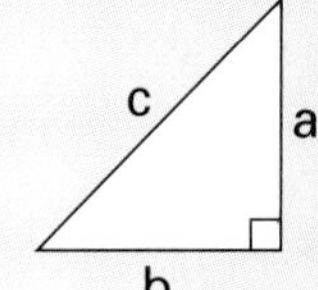

If the length of A is 3 inches and the length of B is 4 inches, how long is C?

$3^2 + 4^2 = C^2$ $9 + 16 = C^2$

$25 = C^2$ $C = 5$

Now you try it!

If A = 5 and B = 12, how long is C, the hypotenuse?

If B = 12 and C = 15, how long is A, the shortest side?

Starting *Out*!

Begin by opening Luis's presentation, applying a design template, changing the color scheme, and saving the presentation with a new name.

1. Open the *sourdough* presentation. Apply the **Capsules** design template with the dark green background color scheme. Save the presentation as *sourdough14*.

Great! Now let's add a recipe for a sourdough starter using a Text and Content slide layout.

Ergonomics *TIP*

Don't forget to sit up straight. Your knees should be no more than 3 or 4 finger-lengths away from the end of your chair!

TRAIL 1 MARKER

Using a Text and Content Slide Layout

You have already learned how to select different slide layouts in the **Slide Layout** task pane. Two groups of slide layouts—Content group and Text and Content group—in the **Slide Layout** task pane are useful when you have several kinds of content that you want to put on one slide. Layouts in these two groups combine title and bulleted list placeholders together with a content placeholder. A content placeholder has icons you click to insert different types of slide content: a table, a chart, clip art, a picture from file, a diagram, or a media clip.

Content group
content placeholder
Text and Content group

First, let's look at the Content and Text and Content slide layout groups. Then we will insert a new Title and Content over Text slide.

1. View **slide 3** in the slide pane and then click the **New Slide** button. New Slide
2. Scroll the **Slide Layout** task pane to view the slide layouts. Look for the *Content Layouts* and *Text and Content Layouts* groups of layouts. Then use ScreenTips to locate the **Title and Content over Text** slide layout in the *Text and Content Layouts* group.

Exploring Across the Curriculum

Internet/Web

Open your Web browser and use a favorite to view the Learning with Computers Web page (www.lwcgreen.keyboarding.com). Click the **Links** option. Click **Project 4**. Click the links to research the ancient Greek pantheon of major gods and goddesses, who lived on Mount Olympus, called the Olympians. Take notes about five of the Olympians you find most interesting.

Then create a multipage bound report that has a title page, at least two double-spaced report pages based on your notes, and an ENDNOTES page. Use Click and Type to add text to the title page. Include *either* single-spaced tabbed columns or newspaper columns as part of the report text. Use paragraph headings. Use the **Format Painter** to paint keyword and paragraph heading formats.

Set the appropriate margins for each section of the report including a 0.5-inch gutter. Insert page numbers for the sections that contain the report pages and the ENDNOTES page. Cite your sources with endnotes. Spell-check, save, and close the document.

The Web

Language Arts: Words to Know

Look up the meaning of the following words, terms, or phrases in a classroom dictionary, CD-ROM dictionary or encyclopedia, or online dictionary.

heroic	Homer	*Iliad*	mythic
mythology	*Odyssey*	pantheon	trickster

Create a new document. Save the document as *definitions4* followed by your initials. Change the margins to a 2-inch top margin and 1-inch left, right, and bottom margins. Type **TERMS AND DEFINITIONS** as a centered, uppercase main heading at the top of the document; then insert two blank lines. Starting on the second blank line below the main heading, type each term on one line and its definition on the following line. Insert a blank line between each definition and the next term. Select all the text *below the main heading* using the CTRL + SHIFT + END keys and create two newspaper-style columns. Use the **Format Painter** to apply the Bold font style to the terms. Spell-check, save, and close the document.

Explore More

Project 14

Presentations and Multimedia

Making Sourdough Bread

Explorers' Guide

Data files: *sourdough*
sourdough bread.jpg

Objectives:

In this project, you will:

- use a Text and Content slide layout
- insert a picture as the slide background
- add slide transitions
- apply custom animation
- create audience handouts
- save a presentation as a Web page

Exploring on Your Own
additional practice in:

- using a Text and Content slide layout
- insert a picture as the slide background
- adding slide transitions
- applying custom animation
- creating audience handouts
- saving a presentation as a Web page

Exploring Across the Curriculum

Internet/Web
Language Arts
Science
Getting Help
Your Personal Journal

Our Exploration Assignment:

Create a slide show with a table, transitions, and custom animation. Then save it as a Web page.

Yum! Hot, delicious sourdough bread! Explorers Club members are learning how to bake sourdough bread. Luis has started a presentation containing fun facts about sourdough bread and needs your help to finish it. Just follow the Trail Markers to insert a new Text and Content slide, insert a picture as a slide background, add slide transitions, apply custom animation, preview and save the presentation as a Web page, and then create audience handouts.

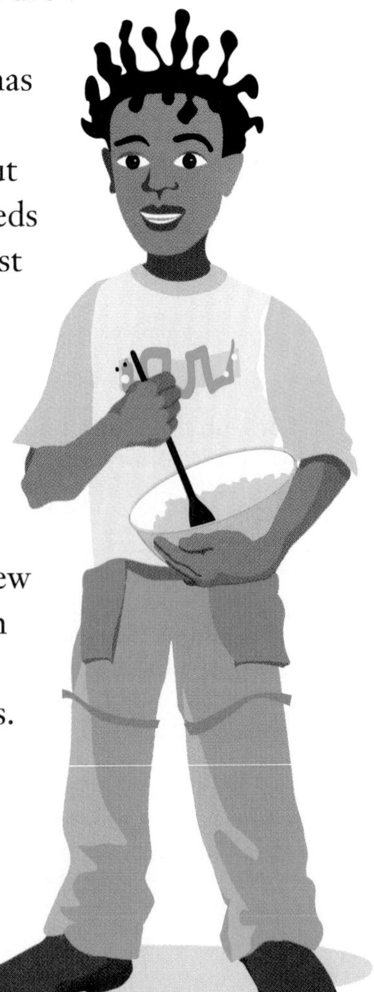

Exploring Across the Curriculum

Social Studies: Research and Write

Ancient myths from different cultures around the world share common themes. Working with a classmate, use library, classroom, or online resources to research ancient Asian, African, North and South American, Norse, and Celtic myths. Look for Creation, Sacred, Heroic, Trickster, and Nature myths. Then create a properly formatted multipage bound report that briefly describes at least three myths that share common themes with ancient Greek myths. Cite your sources with appropriately formatted endnotes on a separate page at the end of the report. Spell-check, save, and close the document.

Getting Help

Type **tab stops** in the **Ask A Question** box on the menu bar. Use the **Help** links to research how to set Right and Decimal tab stops and tab stops with leaders. Then create a new blank document. Set Center tab stops at the 1-inch and 3-inch positions for the column headings; type **Snack** and **Cost** as the column heading text. Tap the ENTER key. Set a Left stop at the 0.5-inch position for the snack name and set a Decimal tab stop at the 3-inch position for the snack cost. Use the TAB key and type the names of five of your favorite snacks and their cost in dollars and cents in two tabbed columns. Close the document without saving it.

Create another new document. Set Center tab stops at the 0.75-inch position and 2-inch position. Using the TAB key to position the insertion point, type **Name** and **Phone Number** as the column headings. Tap the ENTER key. Set a Left tab stop at the 0.25-inch position for a name and a Right tab stop *with a dotted tab leader* at the 2.5-inch position for a phone number. Using the TAB key to position the insertion point, type fictitious names and telephone numbers for five people in two tabbed columns. Close the document without saving it.

Your Personal Journal

Open your personal journal document. Insert today's date. Choose one of the myths that you learned about in this project. What does the myth explain? What can you learn about life from this myth? Update your journal with two or three paragraphs that answer these questions. Spell-check, save, and close your journal document.

Online Enrichment Games (Fun Stuff) @ www.lwcgreen.keyboarding.com

13a Review 4, 0, & 5

Key each line twice. Double-space between 2-line groups.

1 f 4 f 4 | f r 4 f r 4 | fr4 fr4 | vfr4 vfr4 | v4 f4 r4 v4;

2 a4b c4d e4f g4h i4j k4l m4n o4p q4r s4t u4v w4x yz

3 ; 0 ; 0 | ; p 0 ; p 0 | 0 p ; 0 p ; | 40 40 | 100 100 | 400

4 0a 0b 0c 0d 0e 0f 0j 0k 0l 0m 0n 0o 0p 0q 0r 0s 0t

5 f 5 f 5 | f r 5 f r 5 | f t 5 f t 5 | f5tr f5tr | f5rt f5r

6 5u 5v 5w 5x 5y 5z; 5a1 5b4 5c0 5d5 5e9 fg5 hi5 jk5

7 Tim said 4 plus 5 equals 9; Jason agreed with him.

8 Jan averaged 90 with scores of 81, 90, 94, and 95.

9 Bev was born on May 15, 1981, Jay on May 14, 1980.

10 Lance said the train left at 10:45 p.m. on June 9.

Reach up to the number keys without moving your hands away from your body.

13b Technique: ENTER

Key each line once single-spaced. Key the lines a second time trying to go faster.

1 Rick

2 Rick said

3 Rick said that

4 Rick said that they

5 Rick said that they have

6 Rick said that they have only

7 Rick said that they have only four

8 Rick said that they have only four days

9 Rick said that they have only four days, not

10 Rick said that they have only four days, not five.

Keyboarding Project 4

4a Review Left Shift, Period, u, c

Key each line twice. Double-space between 2-line groups.

left shift

1 j J j J | l L l L | n N n N | k K k K | h H h H | i I i I | oO

2 John John | Jake Jake | Kate Kate | Lane Lane | Hank Hank;

period

3 l . l . | .l. .l. | lo. lo. | .o. .o. | .li. .li. | .l. .l.;

4 Nos. Nos. | e.g. e.g. | Ltd. Ltd. | ft. ft. | Kans. Kans.;

u

5 j u j u | ujn ujn | uhn uhn | juh juh | uns uns | kun kun | ju

6 sun sun | use use | dust dust | just just | fuse fuse | suit

c

7 d c d c | edc edc | fec fec | rcd rcd | ecga ecga | ctc ctc;

8 cut cut | duck duck | card card | clue clue | dance dance;

Technique Tip

To key capital letters with the right hand:

1. Hold down the Left Shift with the little finger on the left hand.
2. Tap the letter with the right hand.
3. Return finger(s) to home-key positions.

4b Build Skill

Key each line twice single-spaced; double-space between 2-line groups.

balanced-hand words

1 me or it nap rub key the and bus air big rid; jam;

2 auto city girl dock down goal name risk hair shelf

3 rich maps sick kept paid owns town when envy flame

4 sign work rich maid iris form dusk held both dial;

5 elbow cycle fight audit chair aisle civic; bushels

6 worms widow their whale right girls; gowns; blame;

7 Jan and Jay may go to the city hall for the title.

8 Jake lent the auditor a hand with the work for us.

Exploring Across the Curriculum

Language Arts: Words to Know

Look up the meaning of the following terms using a classroom, library, CD-ROM, or online encyclopedia or dictionary.

conclusion	evaluation	experiment	hypothesis
objectivity	observation	theory	scientist

Create a new presentation. Save it as *definitions13.* Type **Scientific Method** as the title and **Definitions** as the subtitle on the Title Slide. Apply the slide design and color scheme of your choice. Modify the slide master to change the horizontal alignment and font color of the title text. Add slide numbers to all the slides *except* the Title Slide. Insert four Title and Text slides. Type **Terms** as the title on each slide. Type *two terms and their definitions on each slide* creating a two-item bulleted list. Then convert the bulleted list on each slide to a numbered list using the **Bullets and Numbering** dialog box. Change the starting number on each slide using the **Start at** option in the dialog box. The numbered list on slide 2 starts with number 1; slide 3 starts with number 3; slide 4 starts with number 5; and slide 5 starts with number 7. Run the slide show and save and close the presentation.

Getting Help

Type **custom show** in the **Ask A Question** box and tap the ENTER key. Research how to create and run multiple customs shows based on a single presentation. Then open the presentation of your choice and set up at least two custom shows. Run the shows and then close the presentation without saving it.

Your Personal Journal

Open your personal journal document. Insert today's date and two blank lines. Write about an experiment that you have conducted. What was the purpose of your experiment? Did you get the results you expected? Did you have to repeat the experiment because you missed a step? Explain what you learned about the importance of the scientific method. Spell-check, save, and close your journal.

Online Enrichment Games (Fun Stuff)  www.lwcgreen.keyboarding.com

Project 5
Word Processing

Battling Antarctica with Shackleton

Explorers' Guide

Data file: *letter text*
museum text

Objectives:

In this project, you will:

- create a personal-business letter
- insert a file
- follow proofreaders' marks
- use drag and drop
- create and format a table
- add an envelope

Exploring on Your Own
additional practice in:

- creating a personal-business letter
- inserting a file
- following proofreaders' marks
- using drag and drop
- creating and formatting a table
- adding an envelope

Exploring Across the Curriculum

Internet/Web
Language Arts
Social Studies
Getting Help
Your Personal Journal

Our Exploration Assignment:

Creating a personal-business letter and envelope

Crunch! Snap! The men on board the *Endurance* heard these frightening sounds of their icebound ship being crushed by pack ice! Ray is researching the dramatic tales of Sir Ernest Shackleton's Antarctic expeditions. He wants to view a special collection of Shackleton expedition photographs in the archives of a museum, and he needs your help to write a letter to the curator to arrange a visit. Follow the Trail Markers to learn how to create and format a personal-business letter, insert a file into an existing document, edit a document using proofreaders' marks, use drag and drop to move or copy text, create and format a table, and add an envelope to the letter.

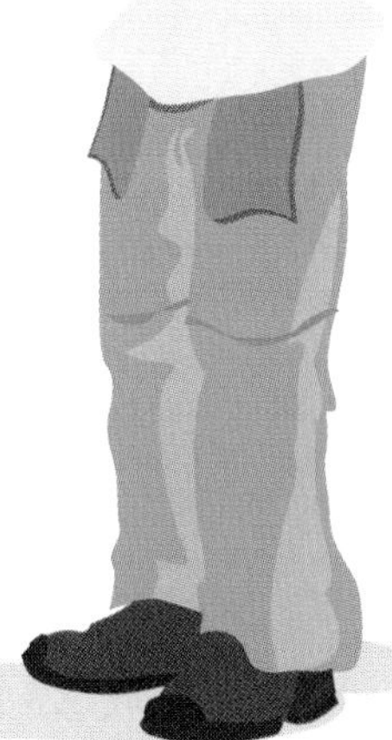

Exploring Across the Curriculum

Internet/Web

You can learn more about how famous scientists developed the scientific method by using the Web. Open your Web browser and use a favorite to view the Learning with Computers Web page (www.lcwgreen.keyboarding.com). Click the **Links** option. Click **Project 13**. Click the links to learn more about Roger Bacon, Francis Bacon, Aristotle, Galileo Galilei, and Isaac Newton. Take notes about what you learn.

Create a new presentation and save it as *scientists13*. Apply the design template and color scheme of your choice. Add an appropriate title and subtitle on the Title Slide. Insert slide 1 from the *scientific method* presentation as slide 2 in the *scientists13* presentation. Manually insert additional Title and Text, Content, and Blank slides as necessary to present facts about these five scientists and their role in the development of the scientific method. Convert one of the bulleted lists into a numbered list. Cite your sources on Title and Text slides at the end of your presentation.

Modify the slide master to change the horizontal alignment and font color of the slide title text. Insert the motion clip of your choice on the slide master so that it appears on all the slides except the Title Slide. Add today's date, slide numbers, and your name as the footer on all the slides in the presentation *except* the Title Slide. Insert sound effects as desired. Set slide timings and apply the animation scheme of your choice. Set up the slide show to run unattended in a continuous loop. Save and close the presentation.

Science: Research, Write, and Present

Work with a classmate to use the scientific method in planning each step of a science experiment of your choice. Then create a new presentation that describes each step of the experiment as it follows the scientific method. Apply the slide design and color scheme of your choice. Modify the slide master to change the title text font color and horizontal alignment. Insert the motion clip of your choice on the slide master so that it appears on all the slides except the Title Slide. Insert today's date, slide numbers, and your and your classmate's names in a footer on all the slides in the presentation *except* the Title Slide.

Insert Title and Text, Content, and Blank slides as necessary to describe your experiment. Add slide timings, apply the animation scheme of your choice, and then set up the slide show to run unattended in a continuous loop. Save and close the presentation.

Explore More

Starting Out!

Begin by creating and saving a new document for your personal-business letter.

1. Create a new blank document and save it as *Shackleton letter5*.

Great! Now let's start Ray's letter.

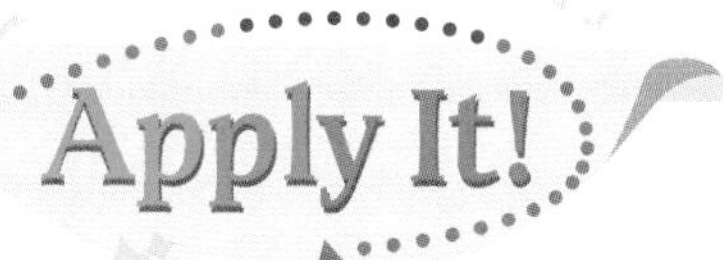

Creating a Personal-Business Letter

Ray's letter arranging to view photos taken during Shackleton's four Antarctic expeditions is a formal letter written about a personal topic. This type of letter is called a personal-business letter.

A personal-business letter has the following seven basic parts: the return address (sender's address), the date, the letter address (the receiver's name and address), the salutation (greeting), the body (message), the complimentary close, and the writer's name. Appendix A in the back of this book has an example of the parts of a personal-business letter.

Personal-business letters are generally typed in block format, which means all the parts of the letter begin at the left margin, the salutation is followed by a colon (:), and the complimentary close is followed by a comma (,). Set the top margin for a personal-business letter at 2 inches, the bottom margin at 1 inch, and the left and right margins at either 1 inch or the default 1.25 inches.

block format
body
complimentary close
date
letter address
personal-business letter
return address
salutation
writer's name

Apply It!

Let's start Ray's personal-business letter by setting the margins and then typing all the letter parts *except* the body.

1. Set a 2-inch top margin and 1-inch left, right, and bottom margins. Then type the following return address at the top of the page at the left margin and tap the ENTER key.

   1135 Evergreen Avenue
   Madison, WI 53707-1135

2. Insert today's date with the month spelled out and tap the ENTER key four times (QS).

Exploring on Your Own

Create a new presentation and save it as *experiment13*. Type **Following the Scientific Method** as the title and **your name** as the subtitle on the Title Slide. Insert all the slides from the *experiment* presentation data file following the Title Slide. Apply the Profile design template with the default gray/red color scheme.

Modify the slide master to: center the title text; change the font color to the dark red color in the color scheme; apply the Bold font style, and change the point size to 32. Then select and delete the bottom red line graphic on the slide master. View the title master and insert the motion clip or clip art of your choice so that it appears only on the Title Slide. Resize and reposition the clip and insert sound effects on the title master as desired. Add today's date and the slide number on all the slides in the presentation *except* the Title Slide. Set five-second slide timings and apply the animation scheme of your choice. Set up the slide show to run unattended in a continuous loop. Run the presentation, letting it loop at least twice, and then save and close it.

Reading in Action

Reading a Science Investigation

Read this summary of an experiment. Which sentence states the hypothesis? Which sentences analyze the result and state the conclusion?

To grow, plants need light. Does the color of light affect a plant's growth? Light is made up of different colors, and objects absorb and reflect light depending on their color. If plants are grown under green light, they should not grow as well as plants grown under red and blue lights because they will reflect, not absorb, the green light. I put pieces of blue, red, and green cellophane on a window. Then I put a seedling in front of each color. I measured the growth of each seedling every two days for two weeks. The seedlings in front of the red and blue cellophane grew more than the seedling in front of the green cellophane. Because of their green chlorophyll, plants absorb red and blue wavelengths and reflect green wavelengths.

Math in Action

The Speed of Light

The speed of light is 186,000 miles per second. The average distance between the Sun and Earth is 93,000,000 miles. How many minutes does it take light to travel from the Sun to Earth?

Formula: distance ÷ the speed of light = time

$$\frac{93000000 \text{ miles}}{186000 \text{ miles/second}} = 500 \text{ seconds}$$

500 seconds ÷ 60 seconds/minute = 8.33 minutes

Now you try it!

How long does it take light to travel from the Sun to Mars? Mars is 142,000,000 miles from the Sun.

How long does it take light to travel from the sun to Neptune? Neptune is 2,795,000,000 miles from the Sun.

3. Type the following letter address and tap the ENTER key twice (DS).

Dr. Mark Appleby
Photographic Archivist
Museum of Science and Industry
1400 South Lakeshore Drive
Chicago, IL 60605-6001

4. Type **Dear Dr. Appleby:** as the salutation, and tap the ENTER key twice (DS). Type **Sincerely yours,** as the complimentary close. *Don't forget to type the comma.* Tap the ENTER key four times (QS). Type **Ray Jackson** as the writer's name. Save the document.

CHECKPOINT

Your partially completed letter should look like this.

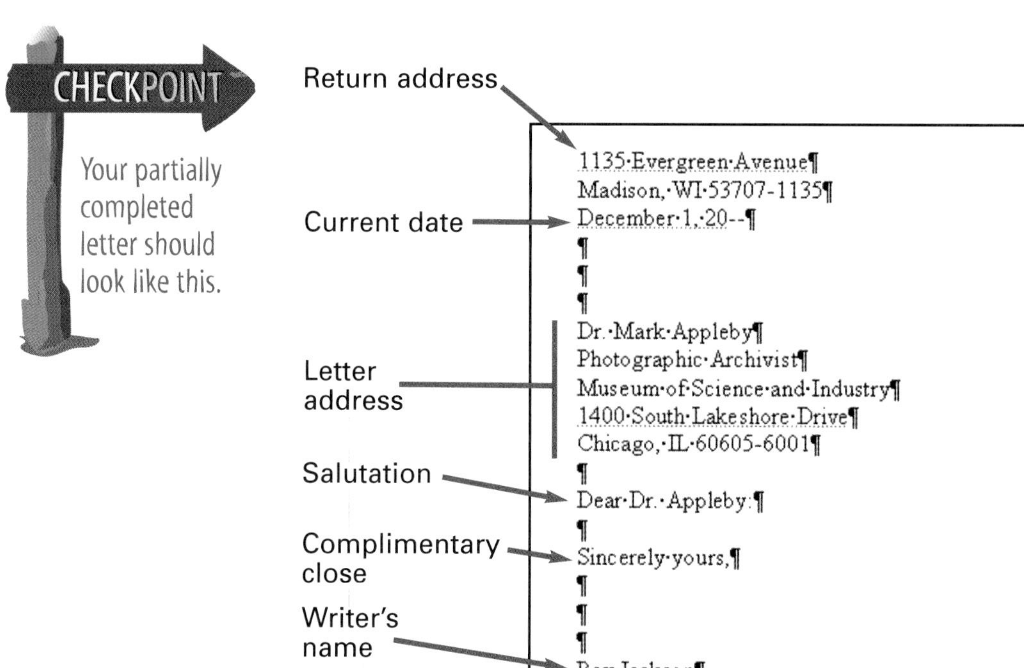

Super! Instead of typing the letter's body, you can insert it from a saved document.

Ergonomics *TIP*

Click! Click! Click! Remember, just rest your finger lightly on the mouse button in between clicks; do not hold your finger above the button.

Project | *Skills Review*

You learned a lot in this project! We are very impressed with your progress. Let's take a few minutes to review the skills that you learned.

Insert slides from files	Choose **Insert** on the menu bar and choose **Slides from Files....**
Convert a bulleted list to a numbered list and vice versa	Choose **Format** on the menu bar and choose **Bullets and Numbering.**
View the title and slide masters	Choose **View** on the menu bar, point to **Master,** and choose **Slide Master.**
Insert footer text, slide numbers, or a date on slides	Choose **View** on the menu bar and choose **Header and Footer.**
Insert motion clips, sound effects, or video	Choose **Insert** on the menu bar, point to **Movies and Sounds,** choose either **Movie from Clip Organizer, Movie from File, Sound from Clip Organizer,** or **Sound from File.**
Set slide timings	Choose **Slide Show** on the menu bar and choose **Slide Transition.** Click the **Other task panes** button in the open task pane and click **Slide Transition.**
Apply an animation scheme	Choose **Slide Show** on the menu bar and choose **Animation Schemes.**
Set up a slide show	Choose **Slide Show** on the menu bar and choose **Set Up Show.**

Inserting a File

Sometimes it is useful to take text from one document and place it in another document. One way to do this is to open both documents, copy selected text from one document, and paste it into the other document.

But when you want to place *all* the text from a saved document into your currently open document, it is faster to simply insert the complete saved document by choosing **Insert** on the menu bar and choosing **File**. The saved document is inserted at the insertion point in the open document.

Ray drafted a few paragraphs for the body of his letter to Dr. Appleby and saved the document as *letter text.* Let's insert the complete letter text document into the *Shackleton letter5* document.

Don't worry if you accidentally insert a saved document in the wrong place. Just click the **Undo** button, reposition the insertion point, and try again!

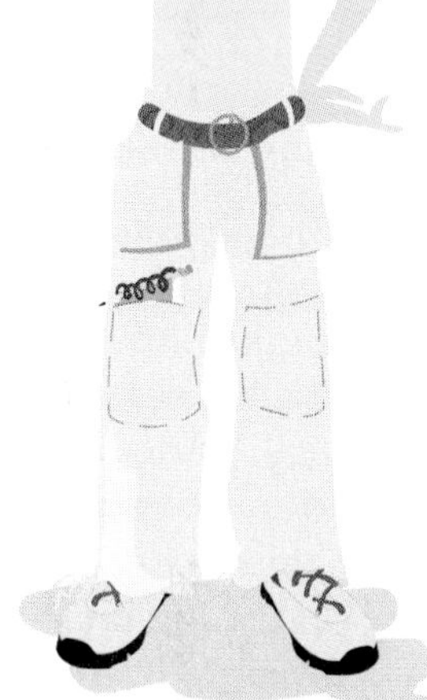

Let's insert the *letter text* document into the *Shackleton letter5* document.

1. Move the insertion point immediately in front of the complimentary close *Sincerely yours.*
2. Choose **Insert** on the menu bar and choose **File** to open the **Insert File** dialog box. Switch to the folder that contains your data files. Double-click the *letter text* filename. Tap the ENTER key. Save the document.

Your letter's inserted body text should look like this.

Inserted body text

¶
I·am·very·interested·in·viewing·the·following·of·photographs:¶
¶
As·I·mentioned·during·our·telephone·conversation,·my·Explorers·Club·is·learning·about·Antarctica·and·i·am·preparing·a·report·about·the·Antarctic·expeditions·of·Sir·Ernest·Shackleton.··I·would·permission·to·view·the·museum's·special·collection·of·expedition·photographs.··I·will·bein·Chicago·on·Saturday,·December·9,·and·would·like·to·view·the·photographs·in·the·afternoon·between·1·and·3·p.m.··Please·contact·me·by·e-mail·at·Ray.Jackson@xeon.net·to·confirm·this·date·and·time¶
¶

Well done! The next step is to edit the letter's body text.

Running an Unattended Slide Show in a Continuous Loop

loop

Julie wants the *method13* slide show to run unattended—without someone manually advancing the slides—on a computer at the science fair. She wants the slide show to run over and over from beginning to end in a continuous loop while the Explorers Club members take care of their individual science projects.

To set up a slide show to run unattended in a continuous loop based on previously set slide timings, set options in the **Set Up Show** dialog box. Open the dialog box by choosing **Slide Show** on the menu bar and choosing **Set Up Show**.

Let's set up the *method13* slide show to run unattended in a continuous loop.

1. Choose **Slide Show** on the menu bar and choose **Set Up Show** to open the **Set Up Show** dialog box.
2. Under **Show** Type, click the **Browsed at a kiosk (full screen)** option button. Under **Show Options**, note that the **Loop Continuously Until 'Esc'** checkbox contains a check mark and, under **Advance slides**, the **Using timings, if present** option is selected.
3. Click the **OK** button. Run the slide show from slide 1. Tap the ESC key after the slide show has looped two or three times. Then save and close the presentation.

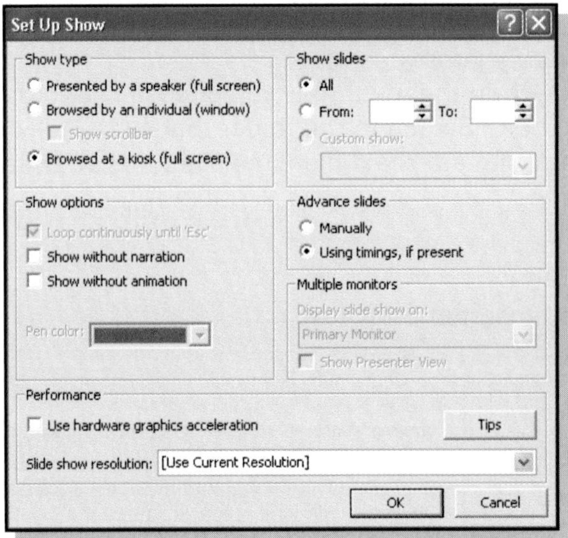

Congratulations! Julie's slide show is ready for the science fair!

Following Proofreaders' Marks

proofreaders' marks
proofreading

It is important to look for errors or formatting changes by proofreading each document you create very carefully. Ray proofread the *letter text* document and used special symbols called proofreaders' marks to mark six changes you must make. Here are Ray's marked changes.

I am very interested in viewing the following of photographs:

As I mentioned during our telephone conversation, my Explorers Club is learning about Antarctica and i am preparing a report about the Antarctic expeditions of Sir Ernest Shackleton. I would like permission to view the museum's special collection of expedition photographs. I will bein Chicago on Saturday, December 9, and would like to view the photographs in the afternoon between 1 and 3 p.m. ¶ Please contact me by e-mail at Ray.Jackson@xeon.net to confirm the date and time

Appendix A in the back of this book has a list of common proofreaders' marks. Check it out!

Now, using the proofreaders' marks as your guide, make all the changes to the *Shackleton letter5* document. You may need to select and change just a few characters. Here's a quick way to select one or more characters using the keyboard. Move the insertion point in front of the characters, press and hold the SHIFT key, and tap the Right arrow key.

TRAIL 5 MARKER

Applying an Animation Scheme

animation scheme
slide transitions

To make your presentation more fun and exciting, you can add special animation effects, called an animation scheme. Some animation schemes also contain a slide transition effect. Slide transitions are special motion effects that appear during a slide show as one slide leaves the screen and another one takes its place.

You can apply an animation scheme to individual slides or to all the slides in a presentation. To apply an animation scheme, choose **Slide Show** on the menu bar and choose **Animation Schemes...** to open the **Slide Design-Animation Schemes** task pane. To remove an animation scheme, click **No Animation** in the **Slide Design-Animation Schemes** task pane.

Another way to open the **Slide Design-Animation Schemes** task pane is to click the **Other Task Panes** button at the top of any open task pane. Then choose **Slide Design-Animation Schemes**.

Animation schemes are grouped into three categories: Subtle, Moderate, and Exciting. The simplest animation schemes are in the Subtle group. The most complex animation schemes are in the Exciting group.

Let's explore several animation schemes using slide 2 and then apply an animation scheme to all the slides.

1. View **slide 2** and then choose **Slide Show** on the menu bar; choose **Animation Schemes....** Scroll to view the list of animation schemes in the **Slide Design-Animation Schemes** task pane.
2. Point to the **Elegant** animation scheme in the Moderate group. This animation scheme has a slide transition effect and applies the same animation effect to both title and body text.
3. Click the **Elegant** animation scheme and observe the animation on slide 2. Click the **Play** button in the task pane to see the animation a second time.
4. Using steps 1–3 as your guide, explore several other animation schemes by applying them to slide 2. Then apply the **Bounce** animation scheme (in the Exciting group) to all the slides. View slide 1, run the slide show, and save the presentation. Close the task pane.

Let's use proofreaders' marks to edit the letter's body text.

1. Follow the proofreaders' marks to insert and delete words, insert a space, create a new paragraph, change text case, and insert missing punctuation. Delete any extra spaces at the end of a paragraph, if necessary. Then save the document.

Your letter's body should look like this.

Edited body text

¶
I·am·very·interested·in·viewing·the·following·photographs:¶
¶
As·I·mentioned·during·our·telephone·conversation,·my·Explorers·Club·is·learning·about·Antarctica·and·I·am·preparing·a·report·about·the·Antarctic·expeditions·of·Sir·Ernest·Shackleton.··I·would·like·permission·to·view·the·museum's·special·collection·of·expedition·photographs.··I·will·be·in·Chicago·on·Saturday,·December·9,·and·would·like·to·view·the·photographs·in·the·afternoon·between·1·and·3·p.m.¶
¶
Please·contact·me·by·e-mail·at·Ray.Jackson@xeon.net·to·confirm·this·date·and·time.¶
¶

Nice work! Now, let's move one of the body paragraphs and copy a word.

TRAIL 4 MARKER

Using Drag and Drop

dotted line insertion point
drag and drop

In a previous project you learned how to move or duplicate text using the **Cut**, **Copy**, and **Paste** commands or buttons. You can also move or duplicate text using the mouse pointer in an action called drag and drop.

To move text using drag and drop, first select the text. Then place the mouse pointer on the selected text, press and hold down the left mouse button, and drag the text to a new location. You will see a dotted line insertion point that moves with the mouse pointer as you drag the text to a new location.

If a paragraph is followed by a blank line, you can select both the text and the blank line; then use drag and drop to move or copy both at one time.

Let's move the second paragraph so that it becomes the first paragraph.

Large sound and video files are *linked* to a presentation, not inserted in it. If you move your presentation to a different computer, be sure to also move copies of any linked video or sound files.

TRAIL 4 MARKER

Setting Slide Timings

slide timings

Setting slide timings allows you to move away from the computer as you speak to your audience or set the slide show up to run unattended. Slide timings specify the amount of time, usually in seconds, between slides. Slide timings can be set for one slide, selected slides, or all the slides with the **Advance slide** options in the **Slide Transition** task pane.

Remember to set your timings so that the audience has plenty of time to read each slide.

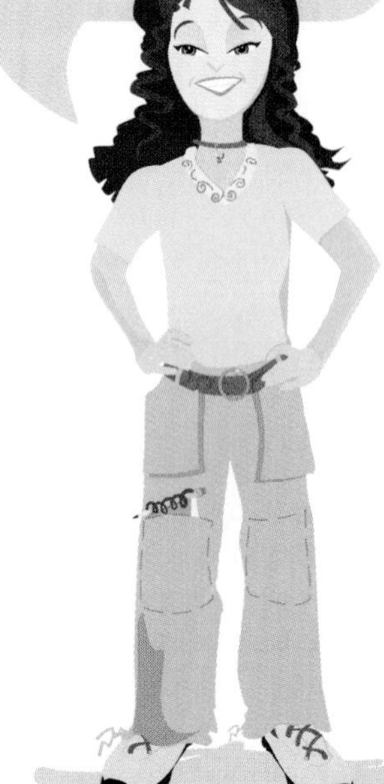

Apply It!

Let's set ten-second slide timings for all the slides.

1. Choose **Slide Show** on the menu bar and choose **Slide Transition** to open the task pane. Click the **On mouse click** checkbox in the **Advance slide** options to *remove* the check mark, if necessary. Click the **Automatically after** checkbox in the **Advance slide** options to *insert* a check mark, if necessary.
2. Select the contents of the **Automatically after** text box and type **10**. Click the **Apply to All Slides** button in the task pane to add the slide timings to each slide.
3. Click the **Slide Show** button in the task pane to run the slide show. Do not try to advance the slides manually. Just sit back and watch the show! Tap the ESC key at the end of the slide show to return to Normal view and close the task pane.

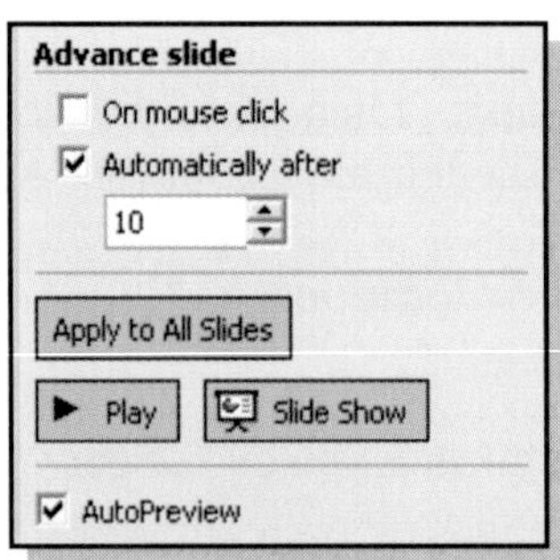

Let's use drag and drop to move a paragraph.

1. Use the I-beam to select the second body paragraph and the following blank line.
2. Move the mouse pointer into the selected paragraph. Press and hold down the left mouse button. Notice the dotted line insertion point to the left of the mouse pointer tip and the square box at the base of the mouse pointer. These symbols tell you that you can now move the selected text by dragging it to a new location. Your mouse pointer should look like this.

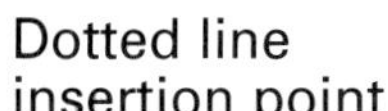

Dotted line insertion point

Drag and drop mouse pointer

¶
As·I·mentioned·during·our·telephone·conversation,·my·Explorers·Club·is·learning·about·Antarctica·and·I·am·preparing·a·report·about·the·Antarctic·expeditions·of·Sir·Ernest·Shackleton.··I·would·like·permission·to·view·the·museum's·special·collection·of·expedition·photographs.··I·will·be·in·Chicago·on·Saturday,·December·9,·and·would·like·to·view·the·photographs·in·the·afternoon·between·1·and·3·p.m.¶
¶
Please·contact·me·by·e-mail·at·Ray.Jackson@xeon.net·to·confirm·this·date·and·time.¶

Selected paragraph and following blank line

3. Slowly drag upward until the dotted line mouse pointer is positioned immediately in front of the word *I* at the left margin of the first body paragraph. Your mouse pointer should look like this.

Dotted insertion point and drag and drop mouse pointer in a new location

¶
I·am·very·interested·in·viewing·the·following·photographs:¶

As·I·mentioned·during·our·telephone·conversation,·my·Explorers·Club·is·learning·about·Antarctica·and·I·am·preparing·a·report·about·the·Antarctic·expeditions·of·Sir·Ernest·Shackleton.··I·would·like·permission·to·view·the·museum's·special·collection·of·expedition·photographs.··I·will·be·in·Chicago·on·Saturday,·December·9,·and·would·like·to·view·the·photographs·in·the·afternoon·between·1·and·3·p.m.¶
¶

Let's insert a motion clip on all the slides *except* the Title Slide and insert sound effects that play automatically when the Title Slide is viewed.

1. View the slide master. Choose **Insert** on the menu bar, point to **Movies and Sounds**, and choose **Movie from Clip Organizer**. The **Clip Art** task pane opens, and it contains video files or motion clips available in the Clip Organizer.
2. Scroll the list and click an appropriate motion clip or the clip's shortcut to insert the clip on the title slide. Resize the clip, if desired, and position it in the lower-right corner of the bulleted list placeholder. Then deselect it.
3. Scroll to view the title master. Choose **Insert** on the menu bar, point to **Movies and Sounds**, and choose **Sound from Clip Organizer**. The **Clip Art** task pane opens with a list of the sound files available in the Clip Organizer.
4. Scroll the list and click any sound file to insert a sound icon on the slide master. Click the **Automatically** button in the confirmation dialog box to allow the sound to play automatically when the Title Slide is viewed. Drag the sound icon to the lower-right corner of the subtitle placeholder and deselect it. Close the task pane.
5. View **slide 1** in Normal view and then run the slide show to hear the sound and see the motion clip in action. Save the presentation.

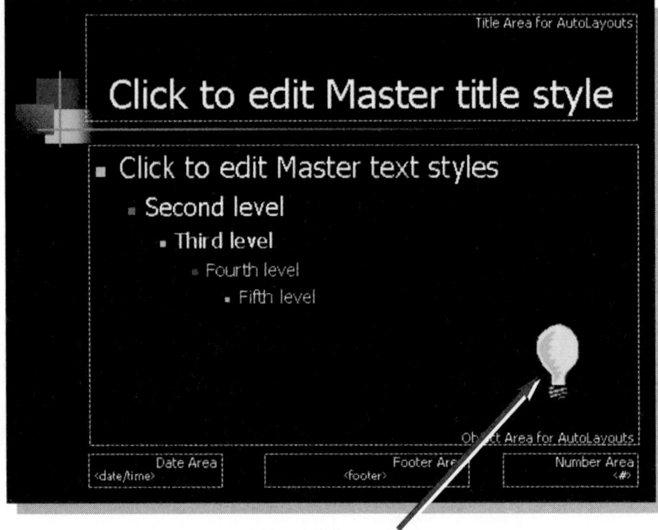

Clip art on slide master

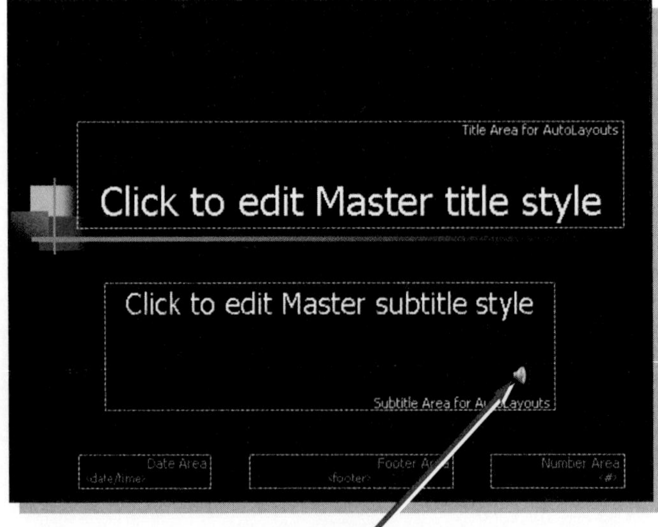

Sound icon on title master

Very nice! Next, you will add slide timings.

4. Release the mouse button. The second body paragraph is moved to the first body paragraph position. Deselect the text.

To copy text using drag and drop, press and hold the CTRL key as you drag the selected text to a new location. *Warning!* After you drag the selected text to a new location, be careful to release the mouse button *before* you release the CTRL key. *If you release the CTRL key first, the text is moved instead of copied.*

5. Select the text *Shackleton* in the first sentence of the first body paragraph. Move the mouse pointer to the selected text. Press and hold down the left mouse button. Press and hold down the CTRL key. Notice the plus sign symbol near the bottom of the mouse pointer. This tells you that you are copying the selected text.
6. Drag the selected text immediately in front of the word *expedition* in the next sentence. Release the mouse button. Release the CTRL key. The word *Shackleton* is copied to the new location and a space is inserted between it and the word *expedition.* Deselect the text and save the document.

CHECKPOINT
Your letter's body should look like this.

Repositioned paragraph

Copied text

¶
As·I·mentioned·during·our·telephone·conversation,·my·Explorers·Club·is·learning·about·Antarctica·and·I·am·preparing·a·report·about·the·Antarctic·expeditions·of·Sir·Ernest·Shackleton.··I·would·like·permission·to·view·the·museum's·special·collection·of·Shackleton·expedition·photographs.··I·will·be·in·Chicago·on·Saturday,·December·9,·and·would·like·to·view·the·photographs·in·the·afternoon·between·1·and·3·p.m.¶
¶
I·am·very·interested·in·viewing·the·following·photographs:¶
¶
Please·contact·me·by·e-mail·at·Ray.Jackson@xeon.net·to·confirm·this·date·and·time.¶
¶

Unlike using the **Cut**, **Copy**, and **Paste** commands, using drag and drop to move or copy text *does not* temporarily store the text on the Office Clipboard.

The letter looks fantastic! But we need to add a little more information to it.

Your slide 2 should look similar to this.

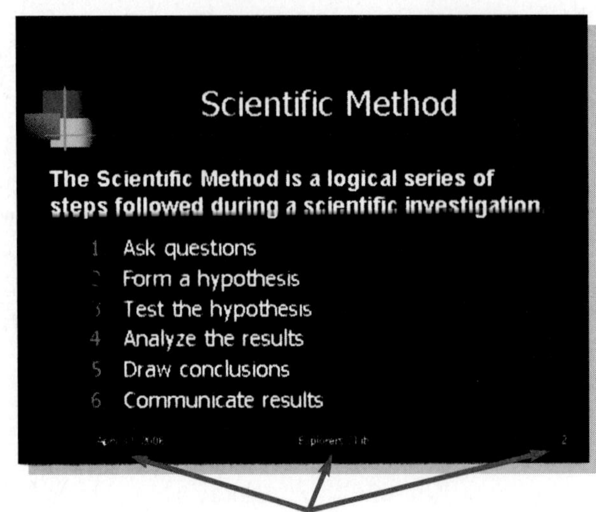

Scientific Method
The Scientific Method is a logical series of steps followed during a scientific investigation
1 Ask questions
Form a hypothesis
Test the hypothesis
4 Analyze the results
5 Draw conclusions
6 Communicate results

Date, footer, and slide number

Outstanding! Let's add some sound and animated clip art to the slides.

TRAIL 3 MARKER

Inserting Motion Clips and Sound Effects

motion clip
movie file
sound file

Sound files, movies, and motion clips can add fun to a slide show. Sound files play music or other sound effects, while movie files include video files and motion clips, which are animated clip art.

Sound and video files can be set to play automatically when a slide is viewed during a slide show, or they can be set to play manually when the person running the slide show clicks an icon on the slide. Motion clip animation plays automatically.

To insert sound or movie files, choose **Insert** on the menu bar and point to **Movies and Sounds**. The **Movies and Sounds** submenu has commands you can use to find movie or sound files in the Office Clip Organizer or in other folders.

Did you know? A quick way to insert the same motion clip or clip art on all the slides in a presentation (except the Title Slide) is to insert it on the slide master!

Ergonomics *TIP*

Remember to hold your wrists in a neutral position as you are typing. Do not bend them up or down!

TRAIL 5 MARKER

Creating and Formatting a Table

cell
column
row
table

You have learned how to organize text in tabbed columns. Another way to organize text in columns is to type it in a table. A table is a grid of vertical columns and horizontal rows. You type your text in the cell at the intersection of a column and row.

To create a table, click the **Insert Table** button on the Formatting toolbar and then drag down and across the column and row grid to select the number of columns and rows you want in the table. By default, *Word* adds a dark border to the table and its cells. You can remove the border with options in the **Borders and Shading** dialog box. Open the dialog box by choosing **Format** on the menu bar and choosing **Borders and Shading**.

Another way to create a table is by choosing **Table** on the menu bar, pointing to **Insert**, and choosing **Table**.

You will insert a table with two columns and four rows in the *Shackleton letter5* document. The table will contain a description of the Shackleton expedition photographs you would like to see.

Let's create the table.

1. Move the insertion point to the blank line below the second body paragraph that ends *following photographs:* and tap the ENTER key. Click the **Insert Table** button to view a grid of columns and rows.
2. Drag down to select four rows and then across to select two columns. The bottom of the grid shows **4 x 2 Table**.

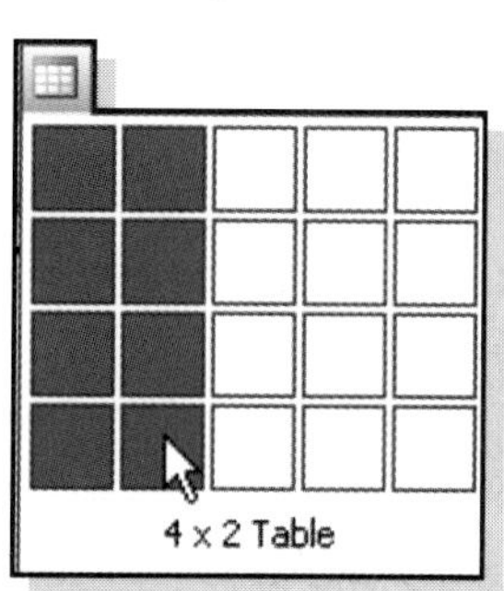

Inserting Footers, Slide Numbers, and Dates

You can insert footer text, slide numbers, or a date on selected slides, on all the slides, or on all slides *except* the Title Slide. A date can be inserted as a fixed date or as a date that automatically changes to the current date each time the presentation is opened.

As you saw in the previous steps, the position of the footer text, slide numbers, or a date is controlled by placeholders on the slide and title masters. To insert a footer, slide numbers, or a date, choose **View** on the menu bar and choose **Header and Footer** to open the **Header and Footer** dialog box.

Let's insert today's date, slide numbers, and footer text on all slides except the Title Slide. Before you begin, be sure you are viewing slide 1 in Normal view.

1. Choose **View** on the menu bar and choose **Header and Footer** to open the **Header and Footer** dialog box. Click the **Slide** tab, if necessary.
2. Click the **Fixed** option button in the **Date and time** area, if necessary. Type today's date with the month spelled out in the text box. Click the **Slide number** checkbox to insert a check mark. Click the **Footer** checkbox to insert a check mark, if necessary. Type **Explorers Club** in the text box. Click the **Don't show on title slide** checkbox to insert a check mark.

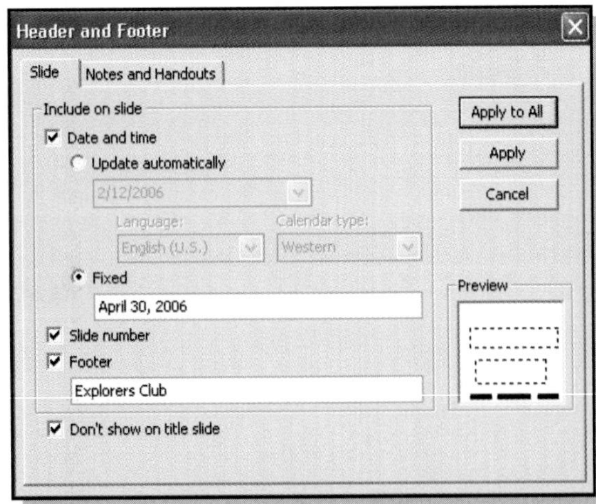

3. Click the **Apply to All** button. Scroll the slides to see that the Title Slide does not have the footer text, slide number, or date but all the remaining slides do. View **slide 2** and save the presentation.

3. Release the mouse button to create the table. Save the document.

CHECKPOINT
Your empty table should look like this.

Table with two columns and four rows

I·am·very·interested·in·viewing·the·following·photographs:¶
¶

¤	¤
¤	¤
¤	¤
¤	¤

¶

Outstanding! Now you can size and center the table.

Keep your eye on the **Insert Table** button when you select rows, columns, or cells. It changes purpose to become the **Insert Rows** or **Insert Columns** or **Insert Cells** button. Check it out!

Sizing and Centering the Table

You can change the width of the columns or the table's horizontal position on the page in the **Table Properties** dialog box. Open the dialog box by choosing **Table** on the menu bar and choosing **Table Properties** while the insertion point is inside the table.

Another way to align a table horizontally is to select the entire table and then click the **Align Left**, **Center**, or **Align Right** buttons on the Formatting toolbar. Try it!

The new table's columns should be 2.5 inches wide and the table should be centered horizontally between the left and right margins. Before you change a table's properties, make sure that the insertion point is inside the table.

Let's view the slide and title masters and then change the horizontal alignment and font color for the title text.

1. View **slide 1**. Choose **View** on the menu bar, point to **Master**, and choose **Slide Master**. The title master slide appears. Look carefully at the placeholders on the title master, including the Date Area, Footer Area, and Number Area placeholders. These placeholders control the position and appearance of text on the Title Slide. Notice that the font color of the title text is gray and has a left horizontal alignment.

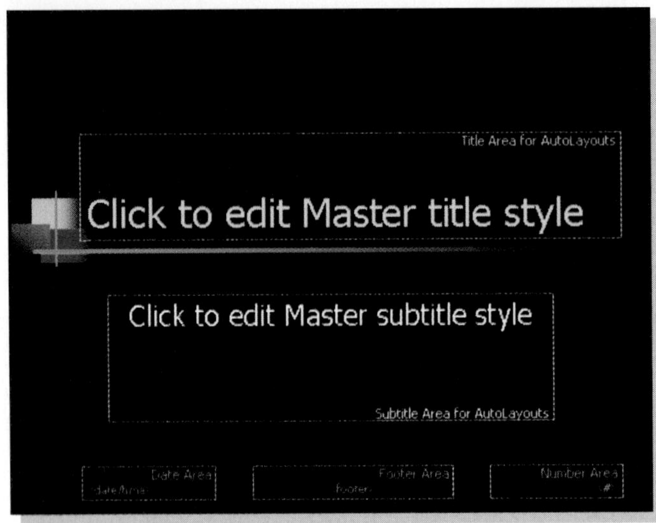

2. Click the **Previous Slide** button to view the slide master. Look carefully at the placeholders and the title text color and alignment.
3. Click in the **Click to edit Master title style** text in the title placeholder to select it. Then click the **Center** button. Click the **Font Color** button drop-down arrow and click the white color on the grid. This action will change the horizontal alignment and font color for the title text on all the slides including the Title Slide.
4. Deselect the placeholder and view the changes to the title text on the slide and title master. Then click the **Normal View** button to return to **slide 1** in Normal view. Scroll the slides to see that the title text on each slide is now white and centered inside its placeholder. Then view **slide 1**.

Let's size and center the table.

1. Click in the first cell in the first column, if necessary, to position the insertion point.
2. Choose **Table** on the menu bar and choose **Table Properties** to open the **Table Properties** dialog box. Click the **Table** tab, if necessary, and click the Center option.
3. Click the **Column** tab and type **2.5** in the **Preferred width** text box. Click the **Next Column** button. Type **2.5** in the **Preferred width** text box. Click the **OK** button. Click in the first table cell, if necessary. Save the document.

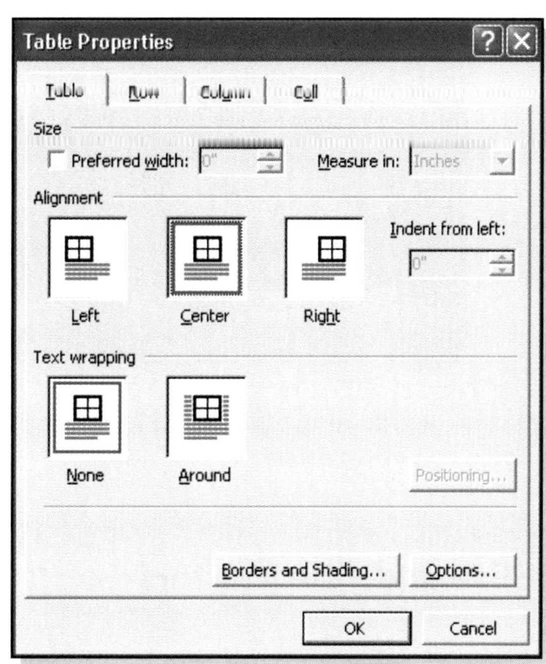

Resized and centered table

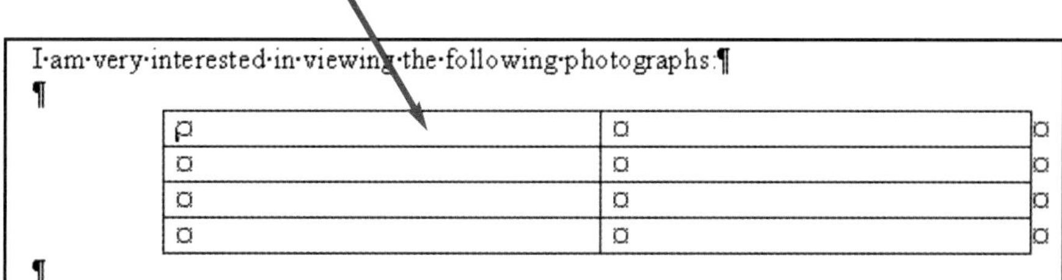

Great job! Now you are ready to type text in the table cells.

Bulleted list converted into a numbered list

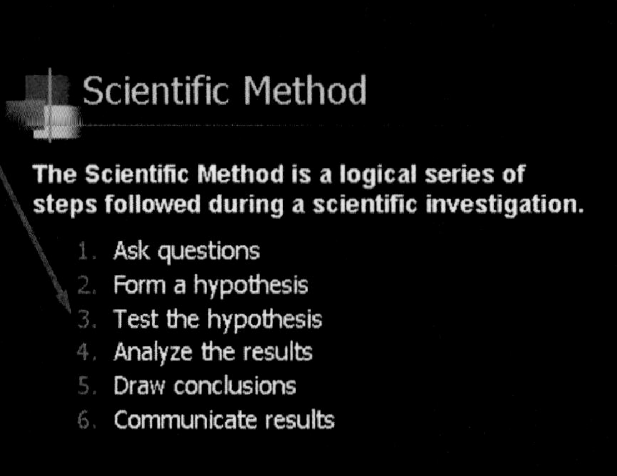

Scientific Method
The Scientific Method is a logical series of steps followed during a scientific investigation.
1. Ask questions
2. Form a hypothesis
3. Test the hypothesis
4. Analyze the results
5. Draw conclusions
6. Communicate results

Super! Now, let's see how to control slide formatting and add footer information and slide numbers using the slide and title masters.

TRAIL 2 MARKER

Using the Slide and Title Masters

slide master
title master

The title master and slide master are special, hidden slides—included in each presentation—that control the appearance of the Title Slide (title master) and all other slides (slide master). All of the formatting of a design template is stored in the title and slide masters. Just as you can change a design template used in a presentation, you can also modify the title and slide masters to change font sizes, font styles, font colors, and horizontal alignment and to change placeholder size and position.

The Slide Master View toolbar automatically appears when you are viewing the slide or title masters. Check it out!

To see the *slide master*, view any slide *except* the Title Slide and choose **View** on the menu bar, point to **Master**, and choose **Slide Master**. The *slide master* has placeholders for the slide title, a bulleted list, a footer, a date, and a slide number. To view the *title master*, view the Title Slide first. The *title master* has placeholders for the title and subtitle, a footer, a date, and a slide number. No matter which master you view first, you can then scroll or click the **Next Slide** or **Previous Slide** buttons to see the other master.

Modifying the Slide Master

When you make a formatting change to an element on the slide master, all the slides that contain that element change. For example, each slide in the *method13* presentation has a title. If you want to change the format of the title—such as the font's size, style, color, or alignment—on *all* the slides, make the change *just once* on the slide master. The title on all the existing slides will have the new formatting. Any new slides that you insert will also have the new formatting.

Typing Text in Table Cells

Before you begin typing in the table, make sure that the insertion point is in the first cell in the first row. You move the insertion point from cell to cell by using the TAB key, the SHIFT + TAB keys, the arrow keys, or by clicking a cell with the I-beam.

- Tap the TAB key to move the insertion point to the next cell to the right.
- Tap the TAB key when the insertion point is in the last cell of a row to move the insertion point down to the first cell in the next row. Tapping the TAB key when the insertion point is in last table cell adds another row to the bottom of the table. If you add another row by mistake, click the **Undo** button.
- Press the SHIFT + TAB keys to move the insertion point to the previous cell to the left.
- Tap the Up and Down arrow keys to move the insertion point into a cell in the same column.
- Tap the Left or Right arrow keys to move the insertion point to the next cell to the left or right. If there is text in the cell, tapping these arrow keys only moves the insertion point left or right in the same cell.

Warning! Tapping the ENTER key in a cell inserts a new paragraph in the cell.

Let's type text in the table cells.

1. Type **Description** and tap the TAB key. Type **Expedition** and tap the TAB key. The insertion point moves to the first cell in the second row.
2. Type **Shackleton, Scott, and Wilson** and tap the TAB key. Type **1901 National Antarctic** and tap the TAB key. Type **Shackleton, Wild, and Adams** and tap the TAB key. Type **1909 Nimrod** and tap the TAB key.
3. Type **Endurance and pack ice** and tap the TAB key. Type **1914 Endurance** and tap the TAB key. A new blank row is added to the bottom of the table.
4. Continue by typing the following text in the table. *After you type the last expedition name, do not tap the TAB key to add another row to the bottom of the table.*

Endurance crew on icebound ship	1914 Endurance
Icebound Endurance at night	1914 Endurance
Shackleton and pet dog	1921 Shackleton-Rowett

2. Drag the horizontal scroll box to see all the slides in the **Select slides** pane. Then click the **Insert All** button to insert all the slides into the *method13* presentation. The slides are inserted after the Title Slide. Close the dialog box, save the presentation, and switch to Slide Sorter view.

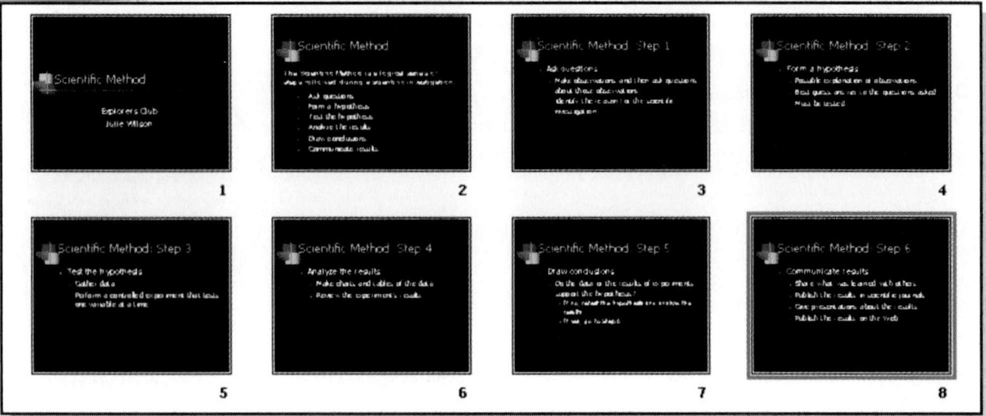

You can insert a new slide, change the design template or color scheme, or apply slide transitions to slides in Slide Sorter view by clicking buttons on the Slide Sorter toolbar. Check it out!

Good job! Now, let's modify slide 2 by changing its bulleted list to a numbered list.

Working with bulleted and numbered lists on a slide is very similar to working with them in *Word*. For example, you can convert a bulleted list to a numbered list or vice versa by selecting the list and clicking the **Bullets** or the **Numbering** buttons on the Formatting toolbar. You can also format slide text as a bulleted or numbered list with options in the **Bullets and Numbering** dialog box. Open the dialog box by choosing **Format** on the menu bar and choosing **Bullets and Numbering**.

Let's convert the bulleted list on slide 2 to a numbered list and resize the numbers.

1. Double-click the **slide 2** miniature to view the slide in Normal view. Then use the I-beam to select the six items in the bulleted list.
2. Choose **Format** on the menu bar, choose **Bullets and Numbering**, and click the **Numbered** tab in the **Bullets and Numbering** dialog box.
3. Click the second box numbering option (1, 2, 3) and select the contents of the **Size** text box. Type **100** and click the **OK** button. Deselect the placeholder.

CHECKPOINT
Your table should look like this.

I am very interested in viewing the following photographs:

Description	Expedition
Shackleton, Scott, and Wilson	1901 National Antarctic
Shackleton, Wild, and Adams	1909 Nimrod
Endurance and pack ice	1914 Endurance
Endurance crew on icebound ship	1914 Endurance
Icebound Endurance at night	1914 Endurance
Shackleton and pet dog	1921 Shackleton-Rowett

Excellent work! Now you are ready to format the table's text. But first, let's take a look at ways to select in a table using the mouse pointer.

Selecting Cells, Rows, and Columns

Here's how to select a single cell, a row, a column, multiple rows or columns, or the entire table using the mouse pointer.

Select a single cell	Move the small black arrow mouse pointer just inside the cell at the left boundary and click.
Select a row	Move the large white arrow mouse pointer just outside the left boundary of the row and click.
Select a column	Move the small black arrow mouse pointer to the top of the column and click.
Select multiple cells, rows, or columns	Drag the correct mouse pointer shape across the cells, rows, or columns.
Select the entire table	Use the mouse pointer to select all the rows or all the columns. In Print Layout view, move the mouse pointer over the table until the table's move handle appears in the upper-left corner. Click the move handle.

You can also select a cell, row, column, or the entire table by choosing **Table** on the menu bar, pointing to **Select**, and choosing **Table**, **Column**, **Row**, or **Cell**.

Starting *Out*!

Begin by creating a new presentation, applying a design template and color scheme, and then saving the presentation.

1. Create a new blank presentation. Type **Scientific Method** as the title and **Explorers Club** and **Julie Wilson** as the subtitles on the Title Slide.
2. Apply the **Blends** design template and color scheme with the black background. Save the presentation as *method13* and close the task pane.

Great! Now, let's add additional slides by inserting them from another presentation.

Inserting Slides From Files

Julie has already created some slides that she wants to use in the new presentation. It is easy to insert slides from one presentation into another. Choose **Insert** on the menu bar and choose **Slides from Files** to open the **Slide Finder** dialog box. In the **Slide Finder** dialog box, first find the presentation that contains the slides you want. If you want to insert all the slides into your new presentation, just click the **Insert All** button. If you want to insert only specific slides, select individual slides in the **Select slides** pane and click the **Insert** button. The slides are inserted after the slide you are viewing and, by default, are reformatted with the new presentation's design template and color scheme.

Let's insert slides from the *scientific method* data file into the *method13* presentation.

1. Choose **Insert** on the menu bar and choose **Slides from Files** to open the **Slide Finder** dialog box. Click the **Find Presentation** tab, if necessary. Click the **Browse** button, switch to the folder that contains your data files, and double-click the *scientific method* filename. The slides from the *scientific method* presentation appear in the dialog box's **Select slides** pane.

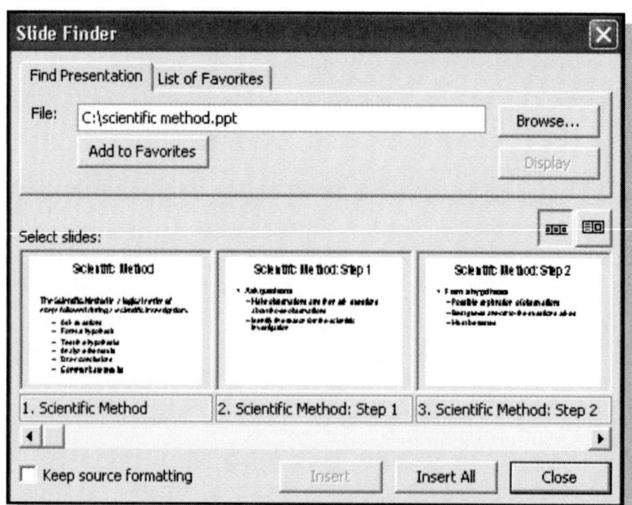

Let's practice selecting cells, rows, columns, and the entire table.

1. Move the small black mouse pointer just *inside* the left boundary of the first cell and click the mouse button to select the cell. Move the large white mouse pointer just *outside* the left boundary of the first row. Click the mouse button to select the row.
2. Move the small black mouse pointer just to the top of the second column. Click the mouse button to select the column. Move the large white mouse pointer to just *outside* the left boundary of the first row. Press and hold the button and drag down until all five rows are selected. *Do not select the line of text below the table!* Click anywhere in the table to deselect the rows.

Now you are ready to format the table text.

Formatting Table Text

You can format table text by selecting cells, rows, or columns and applying font, font size, font styles, and horizontal alignment formatting with toolbar buttons and menu commands.

Let's format the table text.

1. Select the first table row and then apply the Bold font style and Center align the text. Deselect the row.
2. Apply the Italic font style to the names of the ships, *Endurance* and *Nimrod.* Save the document.

Your formatted table should look like this.

Formatted table

I·am·very·interested·in·viewing·the·following·photographs:¶

¶

Description	**Expedition**
Shackleton,·Scott,·and·Wilson	1901·National·Antarctic
Shackleton,·Wild,·and·Adams	1909·*Nimrod*
Endurance·and·pack·ice	1914·*Endurance*
Endurance·crew·on·icebound·ship	1914·*Endurance*
Icebound·*Endurance*·at·night	1914·*Endurance*
Shackleton·and·pet·dog	1921·Shackleton-Rowett

¶

Project 13

Presentations and Multimedia

Describing the Scientific Method

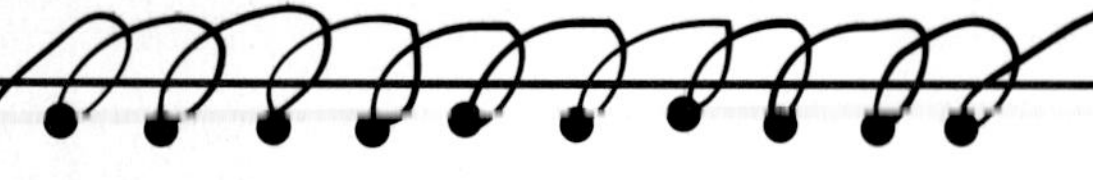

Explorers' Guide

Data files: *scientific method experiment*

Objectives:

In this project, you will:

- insert slides from files
- use the slide and title masters
- insert motion clips and sound effects
- set slide timings
- apply an animation scheme
- run an unattended slide show in a continuous loop

Exploring on Your Own
additional practice in:

- inserting slides from files
- using the slide and title master
- inserting motion clips and sound effects
- setting slide timings
- applying an animation scheme
- running an unattended slide show in a continuous loop

Exploring Across the Curriculum

Internet/Web
Science
Language Arts
Getting Help
Your Personal Journal

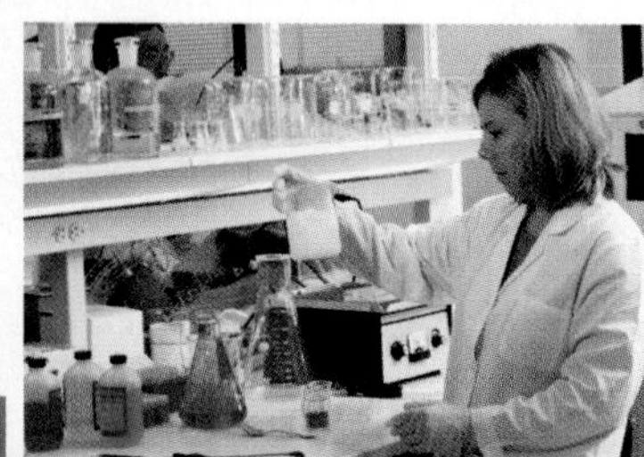

Our Exploration Assignment:

Create a slide show that runs unattended in a continuous loop

The Explorers Club is getting ready for the science fair! Julie wants to create a slide show for the fair that will run over and over again so that everyone who stops by the Explorers Club booth can see it. She has already created some slides to insert in this new presentation. Can you help Julie finish the slide show? Fantastic! Just follow the Trail Markers to insert slides from another presentation, use the slide and title masters, insert motion clips and sound effects, set slide timings, apply an animation scheme, and then set up the slide show to run unattended in a continuous loop.

Your table looks great! Now, you will wrap up the *Shackleton letter5* document by adding an envelope.

TRAIL 6 MARKER

Adding an Envelope

delivery address

Word can automatically use the letter address in a personal-business letter as an envelope's delivery address. Just identify the letter address by moving the insertion point into it. Then create the envelope by choosing **Tools** on the menu bar, pointing to **Letters and Mailings**, and choosing **Envelopes and Labels** to open the **Envelopes and Labels** dialog box.

According to the U.S. Postal Service guidelines, an envelope's delivery address should be typed in all UPPERCASE letters *without* punctuation. This format allows an envelope to be processed more efficiently by the Postal Service's equipment.

You must also specify which size envelope to use. For a personal-business letter, use a Size 10 envelope. Finally, you can print just the envelope or you can add it to the letter document and print them both together.

Let's add an envelope to the *Shackleton letter5* document.

1. Move the insertion point to the first line of the letter address. Choose **Tools** on the menu bar, point to **Letters and Mailings**, and choose **Envelopes and Labels**. Click the **Envelopes** tab, if necessary. *Word* automatically selects the letter address for the envelope's delivery address.

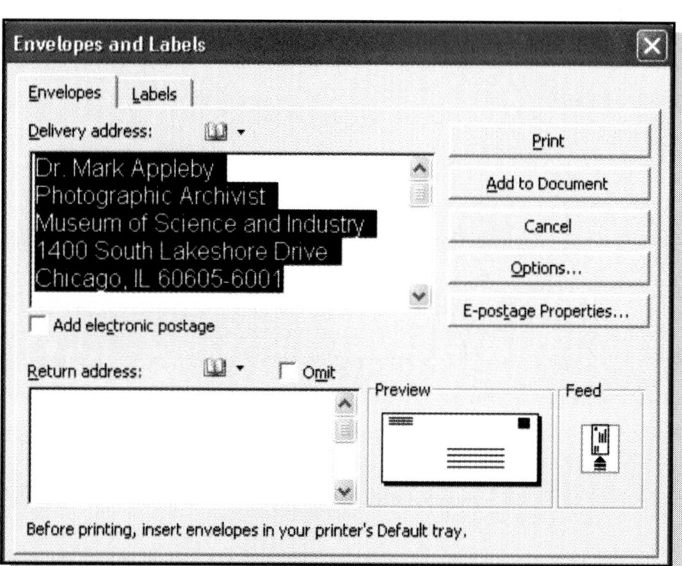

12a Review 8, 1, & 9

Key each line twice. Double-space between 2-line groups.

Technique Tip

Reach up to the number keys without moving your hands away from your body.

1 k 8 k 8|k i 8 k i 8|ki8 ki8|8k8 8k8|8i8 8i8|8, 8,;

2 k8a k8b k8c k8d k8e k8f k8g k8h k8i k8j k8l k8m k8

number 1 3 a 1 a 1|a q 1 a q 1|aq1 aq1|zaq1 zaq1|z1 z1|q1 q1;

number 1 4 a1n a1o a1p a1q a1r a1s a1t a1u a1v a1w a1x a1y 1z

letter l 5 l 9 l 9|l o 9 l o 9|lo9 lo9|9l9 9l9|.9. .9.|9l. 9l

6 a9b c9d e9f g9h i9j k9l m9n o9p q9r s9t u9v w9x yz

7 Jane bowled 189; Tim bowled 119; Jesse bowled 118.

8 Out of 1,898 students, only 819 finished the exam.

12b Speed Check

1. Key each paragraph once.
2. Take two 2' timings on paragraphs 1–2 combined.
3. Determine the number of words you keyed.

all letters used | *gwam* 2'

Laura Ingalls Wilder is a beloved writer of books for children. 7
Most of her books are based on her own experiences as a youth. Her 13
first book was about her life in Wisconsin. From just reading such a 20
book, children are able to fantasize about what it would have been 27
like to live with the pioneers during this time period of our nation. 34

Besides writing about her own life and the life of her family, she 41
also wrote about the life of her husband, Almanzo, and his family. Her 48
second book was about the early years of his life growing up on a farm 55
near the Canadian border in the state of New York. Through these 62
exquisite books, this period of time in our history is preserved forever. 69

gwam 2' | 1 | 2 | 3 | 4 | 5 | 6 |

2. Click in the **Return address** text box and type the following return address:

   Ray Jackson
   1135 Evergreen Avenue
   Madison, WI 53707-1135

3. Click the **Options** button. Click the **Envelope Options** tab, if necessary. Click the **Envelope size** drop-down arrow and click **Size 10 (4 1/8 x 9 1/2 in)**, if necessary. Click the **Delivery address Font** button. Click the **Font** tab, if necessary. Click the **All caps** checkbox in the **Envelope Address** dialog box and click the **OK** button. Click the **OK** button in the **Envelope Options** dialog box.
4. Delete the period after *DR* and the comma after *CHICAGO* in the delivery address. Click the **Add to Document** button. Click **No** if asked to save the new return address as the default return address. Click the **Zoom** button drop-down arrow. 100% Click **Two Pages** to see both the envelope and letter.

CHECKPOINT
Nice work!
Your letter and envelope should look like this.

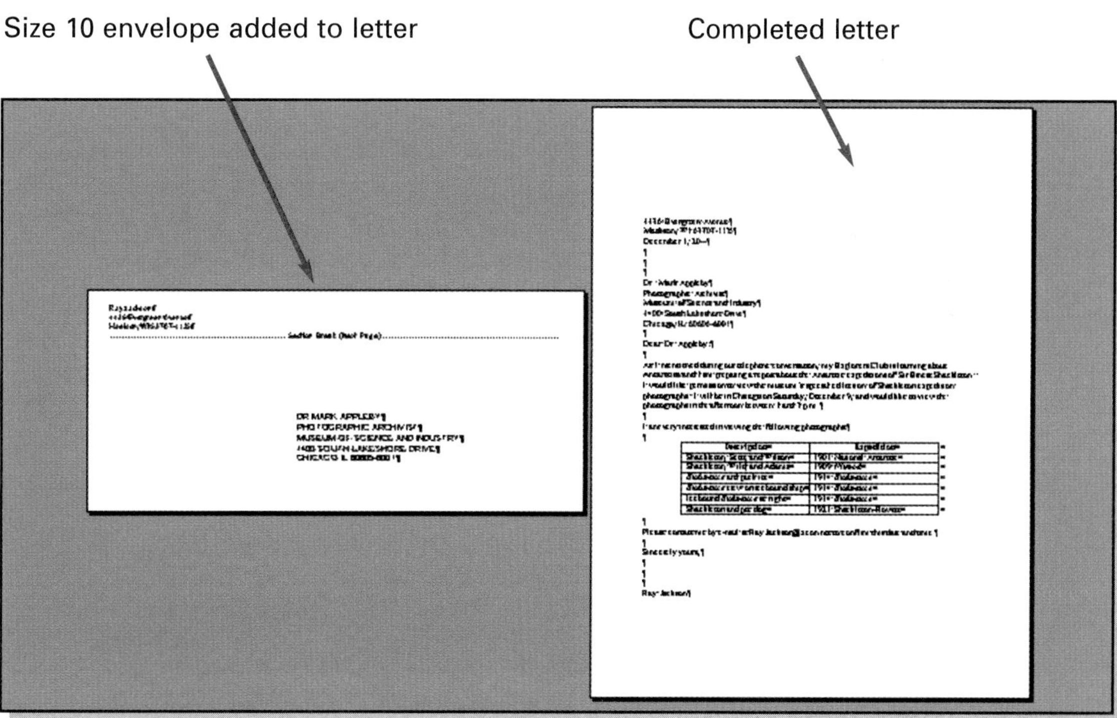

5. Click the **Zoom** button drop-down arrow and click **100%** to zoom back. Spell-check, save, and close the document.

Exploring Across the Curriculum

Language Arts: Words to Know

Look up the meaning of the following terms using a classroom, library, CD-ROM, or online encyclopedia or dictionary.

caldera	eruption	lava	magma
plate tectonics	pyroclastic	tsunami	volcanology

Create a new presentation. Save it as *definitions12.* Type **Volcanoes** as the title and **Definitions** as the subtitle on the Title slide. Apply the slide design and color scheme of your choice. Insert a Title and Text slide for each term and change its layout to Title Only. Type the name or term as the title. Then draw a text box and type the definition. Resize, format, and position each text box as desired. Run the slide show, and then save and close the presentation.

Getting Help

Type **add diagram** in the **Ask A Question** box and tap the ENTER key. Research how to draw and edit a diagram or organization chart. Then create a new presentation. Change the title slide's layout to a Blank slide and practice drawing, editing, and deleting different types of diagrams. Close the presentation without saving it.

Your Personal Journal

Open your personal journal document. Insert today's date and two blank lines. Imagine that you are a Dutch trader on the Indonesian island of Sumatra on August 27, 1883, the day the volcano Krakatau erupted four times. What would you hear? What would you see? What would you smell? What happened to people on the coastline of Sumatra and other nearby islands on that day? Update your journal with one or two paragraphs that answer these questions. Spell-check, save, and close your journal.

Online Enrichment Games (Fun Stuff)  www.lwcgreen.keyboarding.com

Project | *Skills Review*

You learned a lot in this project! We are very impressed with your progress. Let's take a few minutes to review the skills that you learned.

Insert a file	Choose **Insert** on the menu bar and choose **File**.
Move and copy text using drag and drop	To move selected text, drag it to a new location with the mouse pointer. To copy selected text, press and hold the CTRL key, then drag the text to a new location. Release the mouse button before you release the CTRL key.
Create a table	Choose **Table** on the menu bar, point to **Insert**, and choose **Table**. Click the **Insert Table** button on the Formatting toolbar and select the number of rows and columns on the grid.
Create an envelope	Choose **Tools** on the menu bar, point to **Letters and Mailings**, and choose **Envelopes and Labels**.

Exploring Across the Curriculum

Internet/Web

The Web

You can learn more about volcanoes by searching the Web. Open your Web browser and use a favorite to view the Learning with Computers Web page (www.lcwgreen.keyboarding.com). Click the **Links** option. Click **Project 12**. You will use the Google search engine to perform a Boolean search for government websites that have information about U.S. volcanoes.

A Boolean search uses the word *and* or the *plus sign* (+) to include keywords in a search. For example, if you type the keywords *+volcanoes+ U.S.+.gov* in the Search text box, the search engine will find the URLs for *only* those Web pages that contain the word *volcanoes*, the abbreviation *U.S.*, and the domain *.gov* (*government*) in the page's URL. Type **+volcanoes+U.S.+.gov** in the Google Search text box. Be sure to type a space following the word *volcanoes* and the *U.S.* abbreviation.

Click the **Google Search** button. Click the links in the search results list. Click the Web page links to learn more about U.S. volcanoes. Find answers to these questions: How many active volcanoes are there in the United States? What are their names? When was the last eruption for the most active U.S. volcanoes? What damage did these eruptions do? Take notes about what you learn.

Then, create a new presentation and save it as *U.S. volcanoes12.* Apply the design template of your choice and change the color scheme. Add a title and subtitle on the Title Slide. Use bulleted lists, clip art, and AutoShapes to present what you learned about U.S. volcanoes. Cite your sources on a Title and Text slide at the end of your presentation. Insert Title and Text slides and Blank slides as needed. Remove any background graphics from the Blank slides. Align and distribute pictures, AutoShapes, and text boxes as necessary. Run the slide show. Then save and close the presentation.

Science: Research, Write, and Present

Work with a classmate on this activity. Use classroom, library, CD-ROM, or online resources to learn about volcanology. What is volcanology? What does a volcanologist do? Then create a new presentation to present what you learn. Apply the slide design and color scheme of your choice. Include a Title slide and insert at least three other slides and change their layout, as necessary. Use bulleted lists, clip art, pictures, and AutoShapes to present your information. Cite your sources on a Title and Text slide. Run the slide show, and then save and close the presentation.

Explore More

Exploring on Your Own

Use classroom, library, or online resources to locate the name and address of a museum in your area. Then create a new document, save it as *museum5*, and use it to write a personal-business letter to Ms. Olivia Jefferson, Educational Programs Director at the museum. For Ms. Jefferson's address, use the name and address of the local museum you found in your research.

> The Explorers Club members are very excited about the the museum's Science and Careers program sponsored by the Women in Antarctica Association. many of our Explorer's Club members enjoy working on scienceprojects and are thinking about a scientific career We are very eager meet the women scientists who live and work in Antarctica and to learn more about different scientific career opportunities.
>
> Please enroll the following members in the Science and Careers program:

Set a 2-inch top margin and 1-inch left and right margins and include all the correct letter parts. Use your return address and your name. Insert the contents of the *museum text* data file as the body text of your letter. Edit the text as shown.

Use drag and drop to move the third paragraph and following blank line so that it becomes the second paragraph. Use drag and drop to copy the *Explorers Club* text in the first paragraph and paste it in front of the word *members* in the second paragraph. Insert a table with 4 rows and 2 columns on a *second* blank line following the second paragraph. Size the table's columns to 1.5 inches and center the table. Type the following text in the table, and then bold and center the column headings. Create a Size 10 envelope and add it to the letter. Spell-check, save, and close the document.

Member	Career Interest
Julie Wilson	Nature Photography
Ray Jackson	Computer Science
Semeka Watson	Climatology
Liz Yuen	Marine Biology
Luis Gonzales	Glaciology
Your Name	Your Interest

Reading in Action

Using Suffixes

The Greek suffix *-logy* means "the science, theory, or study of." When combined with the word root *geo-*, which means "earth," the word *geology* is formed. Geology is the study of earth. Write a definition for the words *biology, climatology,* and *glaciology.*

Math in Action

Converting Celsius to Fahrenheit

Convert 1°F into degrees Celcius.

Formula: $C = \frac{5}{9}(F - 32)$

$C = \frac{5}{9}(1 - 32) = \frac{5}{9}(-31) = 17.22 = 17°$ Celsius

Now you try it! Convert −21°F to Celsius. Convert 34°F to Celsius.

Exploring on Your Own

Blaze your own trail! Open the *hazards* presentation and save it as *hazards12*. On the Title Slide, replace *Student Name* with your name. Apply a different slide design template and change its color scheme.

Insert a new slide following slide 3, change its layout to Blank slide, and remove the background graphics. On the Blank slide 4, draw and format AutoShapes and text boxes as desired to illustrate the six hazards of volcano eruptions listed on slides 2 and 3. Distribute and align the slide objects neatly on the slide and then group them into one object.

Insert the *lava.jpg* picture on slide 9 and resize it proportionally from its center point so that it is approximately the same size as the pictures on slides 5–8. On slides 5–9, distribute the text boxes and pictures vertically and align them vertically at their center points. Then group the objects. Delete slide 11 and run the slide show. Then save and close the presentation.

Reading in Action

Using Exact Words

Use a thesaurus to find synonyms—or words that have the same or nearly the same meaning as another word—to replace weak or inexact words.

The lava that erupted from the volcano was <u>hot</u>.

The lava that erupted from the volcano was <u>searing</u>.

The word *searing* is a more exact word that describes the intense heat of lava.

Now you try it! Rewrite the following sentences, replacing the underlined words with more exact words.

The <u>loud</u> explosion was heard 3,000 miles away!

The eruption caused <u>a lot of</u> damage.

When pressure builds up, magma and gases <u>come</u> out of the volcano.

Math in Action

Finding the Volume of a Cone

A cone has a circle at its base and sides that meet at one point, called the vertex. If a volcanic cone has a height of 1,000 feet and the area of its base is 502,400 square feet, what is the volume of the cone? Volume is three-dimensional, so it is measured in cubic feet.

Formula:

$\frac{1}{3} \times$ (area of base) $\times$ (height of cone) = volume of cone

$\frac{1}{3} \times 502{,}400 \text{ feet}^2 \times 1{,}000 \text{ feet} =$

$\frac{1}{3} \times 502{,}400{,}000 \text{ feet}^3 = 167{,}466{,}666.66$ cubic feet

Now you try it! Find the volume of a cone that has:

- a height of 300 feet and a base with an area of 31,400 feet^2
- a height of 200 feet and a base with an area of 785,000 feet^2

Exploring Across the Curriculum

Internet/Web

Sir Ernest Shackleton did not achieve his goals of reaching the South Pole or circumnavigating Antarctica. But he is still remembered today for the leadership, endurance, and perseverance he exhibited during his 1914 Antarctic expedition to reach the South Pole.

To learn more about Shackleton and his 1914 Antarctic expedition, you can use the Web. Open your Web browser and use a favorite to view the Learning with Computers Web page (www.lwcgreen.keyboarding.com). Click the **Links** option. Click **Project 5**. Click the links to research Shackleton's disastrous 1914 expedition and to learn what Shackleton did to ensure that all the expedition's members survived. Take notes about what you learned.

Create a new document and save it as *expedition5.* Imagine that you are a surviving member of Shackleton's 1914 expedition. Use the new document to create a personal-business letter addressed to the editor of a local newspaper. Use your address as the return address and your name as the writer's name. The letter's body should include at least three paragraphs describing how Shackleton got all his 1914 expedition members to safety. Use drag and drop as necessary to move or copy text. Use a table to organize information. Create a properly formatted Size 10 envelope and add it to the letter. Spell-check, save, and close the document.

Language Arts: Words to Know

Look up the meaning of the following terms using a classroom, CD-ROM, or online encyclopedia or dictionary.

circumnavigate	floe	frostbite	pack ice
scurvy	sextant	snow blindness	South Pole

Create a new document. Save the document as *definitions5.* Type your name at the top of the document. Tap the ENTER key twice. Create a two-column table with nine rows. Type **Term** and **Definition** as the column headings in row 1. Apply the Bold font style to the column headings and center them.

In the remaining rows, type the term in the first column and its definition in the second column. Select and center the table horizontally. Size the columns attractively. Spell-check, save, and close the document.

Explore More

Project | *Skills Review*

You learned a lot in this project! We are very impressed with your progress. Let's take a few minutes to review the skills that you learned.

Change the slide design template and color scheme	Choose **Format** on the menu bar and choose **Slide Design.** Design
Draw and format AutoShapes and text boxes	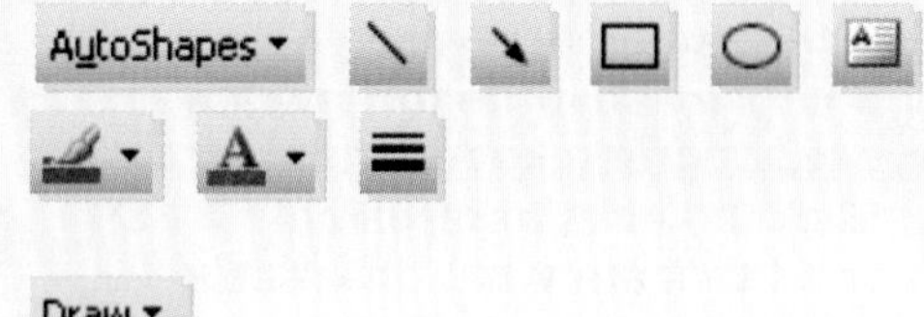
Group, align, and distribute objects on a slide	Draw
Align objects horizontally or vertically on a slide	Click the **Draw** button on the Drawing toolbar, point to **Align or Distribute**, and choose a horizontal or vertical alignment command.
Insert a new slide	New Slide
Change a slide's layout	Choose **Format** on the menu bar and choose **Slide Layout.** New Slide
Modify a slide's background	Choose **Format** on the menu bar and choose **Background.**
Insert clip art or a picture	Choose **Insert** on the menu bar, point to **Picture**, and choose **Clip Art** or **From File.**
Delete a slide	Choose **Edit** on the menu bar and choose **Delete Slide.** In Slide Sorter view or on the **Slides tab**, select the slide miniature and tap the DELETE key.

Exploring Across the Curriculum

Social Studies: Research and Write

Use classroom, library, or online resources including maps to learn more about the climate and geography of the continent of Antarctica. Take notes about what you learn. Then, review the format for a *modified-block* style letter, which can be viewed in Appendix A in the back of this book.

Create a new document and use it to write a modified-block style personal letter to a friend or classmate inviting him or her to a special Explorers Club presentation on Antarctica. Include at least three brief paragraphs describing Antarctica and the topics to be discussed at the meeting. Create a Size 10 envelope with your return address and add it to the letter. Spell-check, save, and close the document.

Getting Help

Type **create and print a label** in the **Ask A Question** box on the menu bar and tap the ENTER key. Click the **Create and print labels for a single item or address** link to learn how to create and print a sheet of labels with the same information. Then create a sheet of Avery 5660 labels containing your name and address. With your teacher's permission, print the first sheet of labels on plain paper.

Your Personal Journal

Open your personal journal document. Insert today's date and two blank lines. A name poem, also called an acrostic poem, uses the letters of a name to begin each line in the poem. Type the word *Endurance* vertically in your journal. Then write a sentence or phrase, starting with each letter, that describes or tells something about Sir Ernest Shackleton. What kind of a person was he? What did he accomplish? Spell-check, save, and close your journal.

Online Enrichment Games (Fun Stuff)  @ www.lwcgreen.keyboarding.com

Vertically distributed and aligned clip art and text boxes grouped into one object

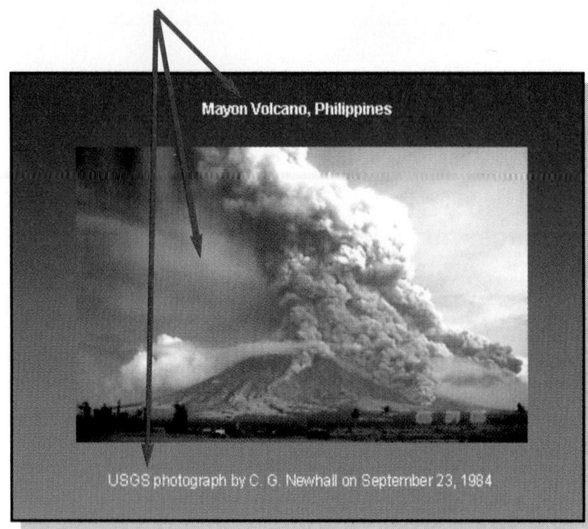

Nice work! Now you are ready to delete an unwanted slide and run the slide show.

TRAIL 6 MARKER

Deleting Slides

Because slide 3 doesn't have much information, Ray wants to delete it. You can delete slides in Normal view by choosing **Edit** on the menu bar and choosing **Delete Slide**. You can also switch to Slide Sorter view, select a slide, and tap the DELETE key, or select a slide miniature on the **Slides tab** and tap the DELETE key.

Instead of deleting a slide, you can temporarily hide it. Switch to Slide Sorter view, select the slide, and click the **Hide Slide** button on the Slide Sorter toolbar. To unhide the slide, click the **Hide Slide** button again. Try it!

Let's delete slide 3.

1. Click the **slide 3** miniature on the **Slides tab** and tap the DELETE key. Slide 3 is deleted and the remaining slides are renumbered.
2. Click the **slide 1** miniature on the **Slides tab** and run the slide show. Then save and close the presentation.

5a Review w, Right Shift, b, y

Key each line twice. Double-space between 2-line groups.

w

1 sw sw | sws sws | swj swj | wks wks | lws lws | hsw hsw | s;w;

2 saw saw | won won | wash wash | work work | willow willow;

right shift

3 aA aA | sS sS | dD dD | fF fF | gG gG | eE eE | rR rR | tT tT | wW

4 Chase Chase | Dick Dick | Ruth Ruth | Greg Greg | Ron Ron;

b

5 fb fb | bfb bfb | rbf rbf | fbrb fbrb | fbjb fbjb | fbo fbob

6 bow bow | Bob Bob | cabs cabs | rabbit rabbit | debt debt;

y

7 jy jy | yjy yjy | jyn jyn | y; y; | fy fy | jujy jujy | fy fy;

8 yet yet | year year | July July | eyes eyes | nylon nylon;

To key capital letters with the left hand:

1. Hold down the Right Shift with the right little finger.
2. Tap the letter with the left hand.
3. Return finger(s) to home-key positions.

5b Build Skill

Key each line twice single-spaced; double-space between 2-line groups.

balanced-hand sentences

1 Jake paid for the six men to fix the big oak door.

2 Keith may work with the city auditor on the forms.

3 Pamela may make a formal sign to hang by the dock.

4 Six of the eight firms bid to do the work for Jan.

5 Hal and Nan may go to the island to dig for clams.

6 The man did the work for the girls on their gowns.

7 I may pay the auto firm for the bodywork they did.

8 Janel and I may bicycle to the big lake with them.

gwam 20" | 3 | 6 | 9 | 12 | 15 | 18 | 21 | 24 | 27 | 30 |

Inserting and Resizing Clip Art or Pictures

TRAIL 5 MARKER

You can insert clip art or a picture on a slide just like you do in *Word* and *Excel*. Click the **Insert Clip Art** or **Insert Picture From File** buttons on the Drawing toolbar or choose **Insert** on the menu bar, point to **Picture**, and choose **Clip Art** or **From File**.

Some slide layouts have a special placeholder for clip art or pictures. But clip art or pictures can be inserted on any slide, including a Blank slide. If there is no placeholder, *PowerPoint* inserts the clip art or picture in the middle of the slide. You can resize clip art or a picture by dragging a sizing handle just like you do in *Word* or *Excel*.

Let's insert the picture and resize it. Then add and resize text boxes and align and distribute the objects.

1. Make sure that you are looking at the Blank slide, slide 10. Click the **Insert Picture** button on the Drawing toolbar, switch to the data files, and double-click the **pyroclastic flow** filename to insert the picture of a volcano. The picture is inserted in the middle of the slide.
2. Move the mouse pointer to the lower-right-corner sizing handle and press and hold the CTRL key. Drag down and to the right until the picture is approximately three times its original size. Be sure to leave room at the top and bottom of the slide for some text. Deselect the picture.

Now let's add two text boxes that describe the photograph and give credit to the photographer. Then align the text boxes and the picture on the slide.

3. Draw a text box approximately 2 inches wide above the picture. Type **Mayon Volcano, Philippines**. Use the I-beam to select the text and bold it. Draw another text box below the picture. Type **USGS photograph by C. G. Newhall on September 23, 1984**. Resize both text boxes to fit the text. Make the text boxes wide enough so that the text *does not* wrap.
4. Select all three objects, distribute them vertically, and align them vertically at their center points. Group the three objects. Deselect the grouped object and save the presentation.

Project 6
Word Processing

Balancing the Three Branches of Government

Explorers' Guide

Data files: *infographic*
us-flag.gif

Objectives:

In this project, you will:

- change page orientation
- add a page border
- format text with styles and font effects
- insert symbols
- use the Drawing tools
- add a footer

Exploring on Your Own
additional practice in:

- changing page orientation
- adding a page border
- formatting text with styles and font effects
- inserting symbols
- using the Drawing tools
- adding a footer

Exploring Across the Curriculum

Internet/Web
Language Arts
Social Studies
Getting Help
Your Personal Journal

Our Exploration Assignment:

Creating an infographic

The Explorers Club is learning about the three branches of the U.S. government. Can you help Luis create an infographic that illustrates how the system of checks and balances keeps each branch from misusing its powers? Great! Just follow the Trail Markers to change page orientation, add a page border, format text with styles and font effects, insert symbols, use the Drawing tools, and add a footer.

Let's insert a new slide at the end of the presentation, change its layout to Blank, and remove its background graphics.

1. Press the CTRL + END keys to view the last slide and click the **New Slide** button to open the **Slide Layout** task pane. New Slide
2. Click the **Blank** slide layout. The new slide is blank, with no title and bulleted list placeholders. The background color and graphics remain. Close the task pane.
3. Choose **Format** on the menu bar and choose **Background**. Click the **Omit background graphics from master** checkbox to insert a check mark.

4. Click the **Apply** button. The background graphic at the bottom of the slide is removed.
5. Check to make sure that the other slides have not changed. Click the **slide 2** and then the **slide 1** thumbnail in the **Slides tab** to view the slides in the slide pane. The slides still have the background graphic. Click the last thumbnail in the **Slides tab**—the Blank slide thumbnail—to view it in the slide pane. Save the presentation.

Excellent! Now you are ready to insert the picture of a volcano on the slide.

Starting Out!

Begin by opening a document and saving it with a new name.

1. Open the *infographic* document and save it as *infographic6.*

An infographic combines text, pictures, and drawings to convey a message. Let's create Luis's infographic.

Ergonomics *TIP*

Can you see dust and fingerprints on your monitor's screen? If you can, it is time to clean it! A clean screen prevents eye strain. Do you wear glasses? If you do, do not forget to clean them too!

TRAIL 1 MARKER

Changing Page Orientation

Landscape orientation
page orientation
Portrait orientation

You can specify how you want *Word* to print text on a page—horizontally or vertically—by setting the page orientation in the **Page Setup** dialog box. If you want to print the text in a wide, horizontal format, set up the page in Landscape orientation. If you want the text on the page to be printed vertically, set up the page in Portrait orientation.

Let's change the page orientation of the *infographic6* document to Landscape. Then, to see the Landscape page more easily, let's zoom it to Page Width.

Did you know that you can mix Portrait and Landscape orientation in a multi-page document? Just use a **Next page** section break to separate Portrait and Landscape pages!

Selecting all the objects and then grouping them into one object helps keep them neatly aligned and allows you to reposition all of the objects at one time. You can group and ungroup objects by choosing **Group** or **Ungroup** on the **Draw** menu.

5. Use the SHIFT key to select the three explosion objects and the three text boxes. Click the **Draw** button and choose **Group**. All of the selected objects are now grouped together in one object. Note the single object's sizing handles. Deselect the object and save the presentation.

CHECKPOINT

Your slide should look similar to this.

AutoShapes and text boxes aligned and distributed neatly on the slide

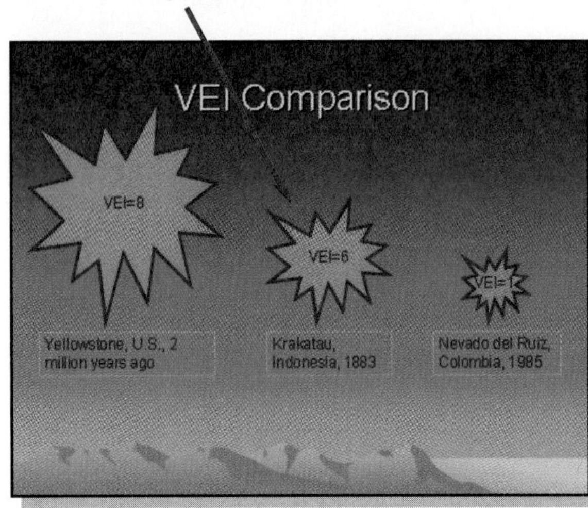

Fantastic! What a neat looking slide! Now let's insert a new slide and change its layout and background.

TRAIL 4 MARKER

Changing Slide Layout and Background

Ray wants to add a slide with a picture of a volcano to the end of the presentation. He needs to insert a new slide with a Blank layout, which does not have placeholders. He also wants to use a plain background, without the graphics that are part of the design template.

To remove the slide background, choose **Format** on the menu bar and choose **Background** to open the **Background** dialog box. Then click the option to remove the background graphics and apply the changes to the individual slide.

Warning! Be sure to click the **Apply** button when making dialog box changes to a *single slide*. Clicking the **Apply to All** button changes all the slides!

Let's change the page orientation to Landscape.

1. Switch to Print Layout view, if necessary. Open the **Page Setup** dialog box and click the **Margins** tab, if necessary. Click the **Landscape** option and change the top and bottom margins to 1 inch.
2. Click the **OK** button.
3. Click the **Zoom** button drop-down arrow and click **Page Width**. 100% You can now see the left and right edges of the page without scrolling. Save the document.

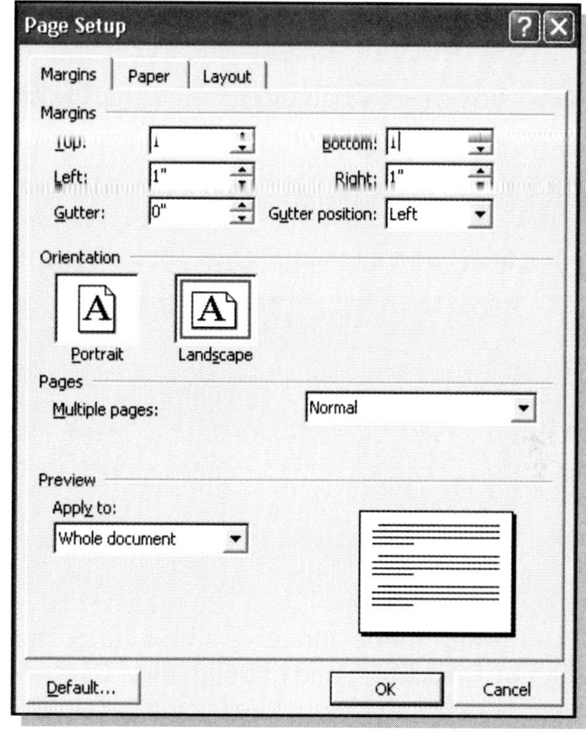

Your *infographic6* document should now look like this.

Landscape document zoomed to Page Width

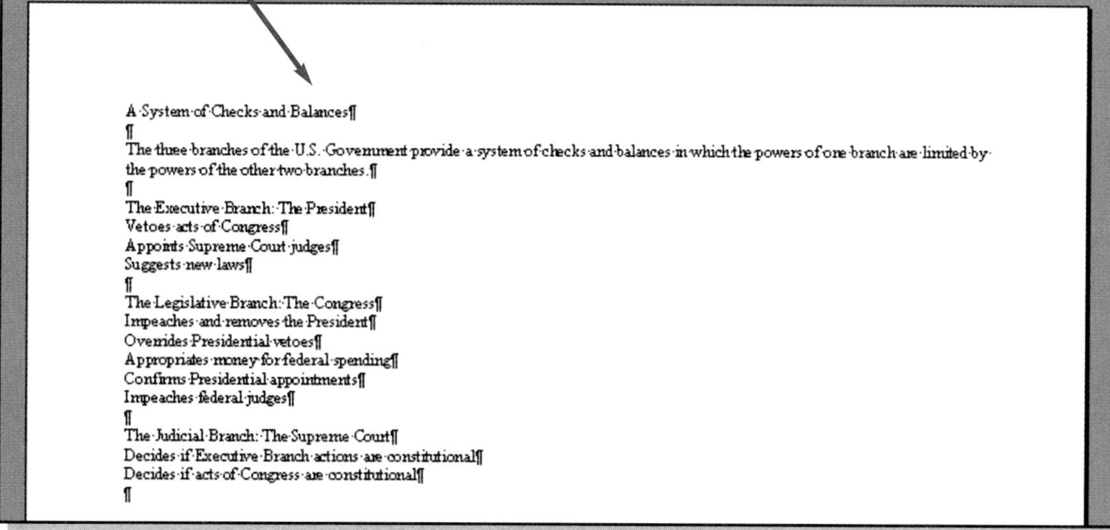
A·System·of·Checks·and·Balances¶
¶
The·three·branches·of·the·U.S.·Government·provide·a·system·of·checks·and·balances·in·which·the·powers·of·one·branch·are·limited·by·the·powers·of·the·other·two·branches.¶
¶
The·Executive·Branch:·The·President¶
Vetoes·acts·of·Congress¶
Appoints·Supreme·Court·judges¶
Suggests·new·laws¶
¶
The·Legislative·Branch:·The·Congress¶
Impeaches·and·removes·the·President¶
Overrides·Presidential·vetoes¶
Appropriates·money·for·federal·spending¶
Confirms·Presidential·appointments¶
Impeaches·federal·judges¶
¶
The·Judicial·Branch:·The·Supreme·Court¶
Decides·if·Executive·Branch·actions·are·constitutional¶
Decides·if·acts·of·Congress·are·constitutional¶
¶

Well done! Now let's add a colored border around the entire document.

Let's distribute and align the AutoShapes and text boxes on slide 6.

1. View **slide 6**, if necessary. Press and hold the SHIFT key and click each text box to select all three. Click the **Draw** button, point to **Align or Distribute**, and choose **Distribute Horizontally**. Draw ▾

   Click the **Draw** button, point to **Align or Distribute**, and choose **Align Bottom**. The text boxes are spaced horizontally an equal distance apart and aligned at their bottom points.

2. Deselect the text boxes. Then use the SHIFT key to select the first Explosion AutoShape and its text box. Click the **Draw** button, point to **Align or Distribute**, and choose **Align Center**. The two objects are aligned vertically at their center points.

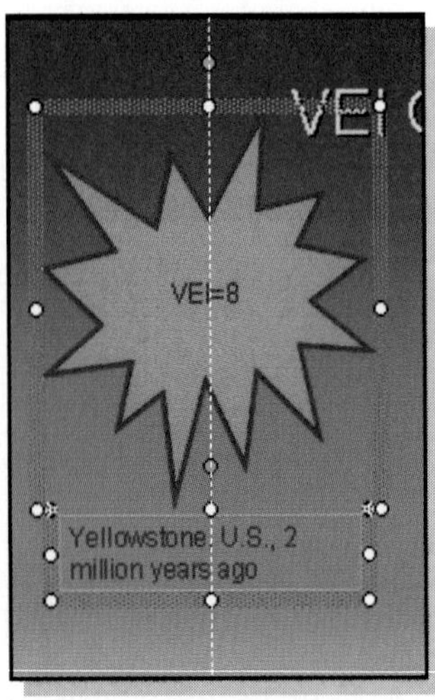

3. Deselect the objects. Using step 2 as your guide, align the other two Explosion AutoShapes with their matching text boxes at their center points.
4. Select all three AutoShapes. Click the **Draw** button, point to **Align or Distribute**, and choose **Align Bottom** to align them horizontally at their bottom points. Deselect them.

TRAIL 2 MARKER

Adding a Page Border

borders
shading

Borders (dark lines) and shading (background fill) can be added to selected paragraphs or to a complete page by selecting options in the **Borders and Shading** dialog box. Open the **Borders and Shading** dialog box by choosing **Format** on the menu bar and choosing **Borders and Shading**.

Let's add a 2¼-point blue page border to the *infographic6* document.

1. Choose **Format** on the menu bar and choose **Borders and Shading**. Click the **Page Border** tab, if necessary.
2. Click the **Box** setting option. Click the **Color** drop-down arrow and click **Blue** on the grid. Click the **Width** drop-down arrow and click **2¼ pt**.
3. Look at the Preview section on the right side of the dialog box. Click the **top**, **bottom**, **left**, and **right** buttons, as necessary, to show the page border on all sides of the document. Verify that the **Apply to** list is **Whole document**.

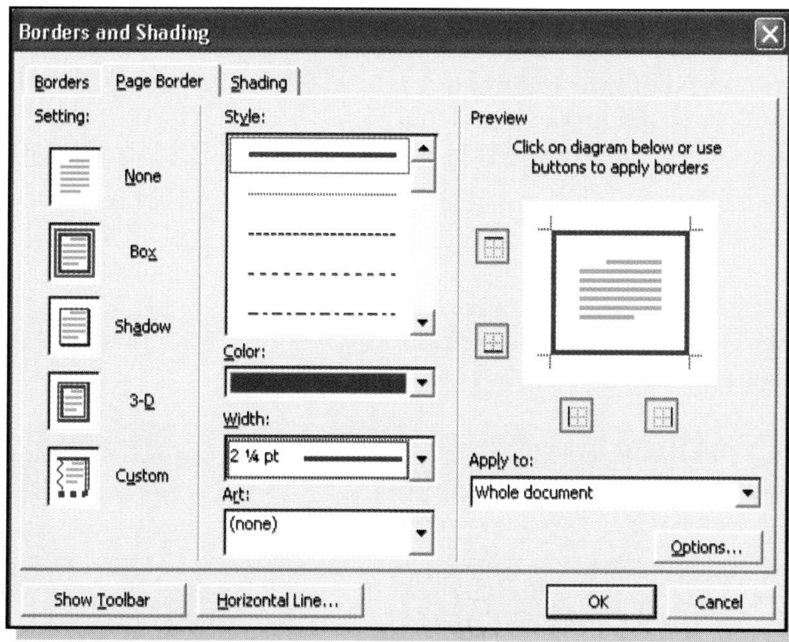

4. Click the **OK** button. A 2¼-point blue border appears on the top, bottom, left, and right edges of the page. Save the document.

CHECKPOINT

Your slide should look similar to this.

Formatted AutoShapes

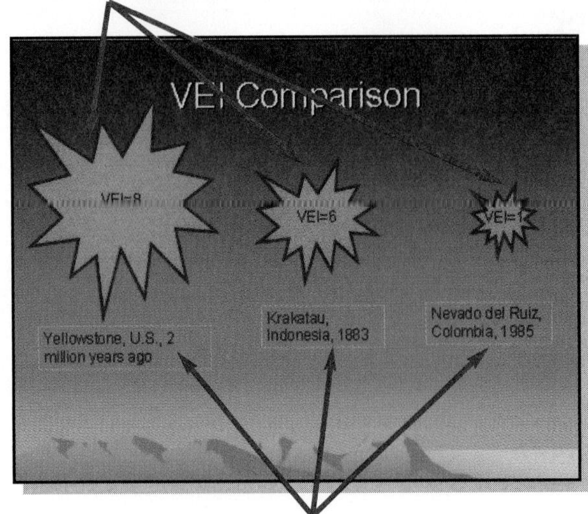

Formatted text boxes

Super! Now you are ready to arrange the explosion and text box objects more neatly on the slide.

TRAIL 3 MARKER

Distributing and Aligning Slide Objects

align
distribute

Now it's time to neatly position the AutoShapes and text boxes. You can distribute the text boxes so that there is an even amount of space between them and then align the AutoShapes and text boxes both vertically and horizontally. Instead of positioning them using drag and drop, you can let *PowerPoint* do it for you. Just select the objects, click the **Draw** button, and click a command on the **Align or Distribute** submenu.

- Choose **Distribute Horizontally** or **Distribute Vertically** to position three or more objects with an equal amount of space between each object.
- Choose **Align Top**, **Align Middle**, or **Align Bottom** to align *horizontal* objects across the slide through their top or bottom edges or middle position. *Be careful! Using these commands to align selected vertical objects stacks them on top of each other.*
- Choose **Align Left**, **Align Center**, or **Align Right** to align *vertical* objects down the slide through their left or right edges or center position. *Warning! Using these commands to align selected horizontal objects stacks them on top of each other.*

If you align objects incorrectly, just click the **Undo** button on the Standard toolbar or choose **Edit** on the menu bar and choose **Undo**.

Let's distribute the text boxes horizontally to add equal space between them. Then, let's align them so that the bottom of each box is on the same line. Then we will align each AutoShape vertically with its matching text box at their center points and horizontally at their bottom points.

Your *infographic6* document should now look like this.

Blue, 2¼ pt page border

A·System·of·Checks·and·Balances¶
¶
The·three·branches·of·the·U.S.·Government·provide·a·system·of·checks·and·balances·in·which·the·powers·of·one·branch·are·limited·by·the·powers·of·the·other·two·branches.¶
¶
The·Executive·Branch:·The·President¶
Vetoes·acts·of·Congress¶
Appoints·Supreme·Court·judges¶
Suggests·new·laws¶
¶
The·Legislative·Branch:·The·Congress¶
Impeaches·and·removes·the·President¶
Overrides·Presidential·vetoes¶
Appropriates·money·for·federal·spending¶
Confirms·Presidential·appointments¶
Impeaches·federal·judges¶
¶
The·Judicial·Branch:·The·Supreme·Court¶
Decides·if·Executive·Branch·actions·are·constitutional¶
Decides·if·acts·of·Congress·are·constitutional¶
¶

Fantastic! Now let's format the document's text using preset styles and special font effects.

TRAIL 3 MARKER

Formatting Text with Styles and Font Effects

drop cap

You already know how to choose fonts, font sizes, and font colors and how to apply the three basic font styles: Bold, Italic, and Underline. But *Word* also has some preset styles that you can apply to headings and other text. In addition, *Word* has some special font effects that can make your text stand out.

Chapters in some books begin with a large capital letter, called a drop cap. To turn the first letter of the first word in a paragraph into a capital letter that "drops down" two or three lines, select the letter, choose **Format** on the menu bar, and choose **Drop Cap**. Try it!

Styles

style

The **Style** box to the left of the **Font** box on the Formatting toolbar lists the four basic preset styles included in each new *Word* document. Each style contains formatting such as the font, font size, and line spacing.

Let's change the font and line color and line size.

1. Press and hold the SHIFT key and click each of the Explosion AutoShapes to select all three.
2. Click the **Line Style** button and click **3 pt** on the list. Click the **Line Color** button drop-down arrow and click **More Line Colors** to open the **Colors** dialog box. Click the **Standard** tab, if necessary, and click the **sixth color** in the **first row** (dark blue).

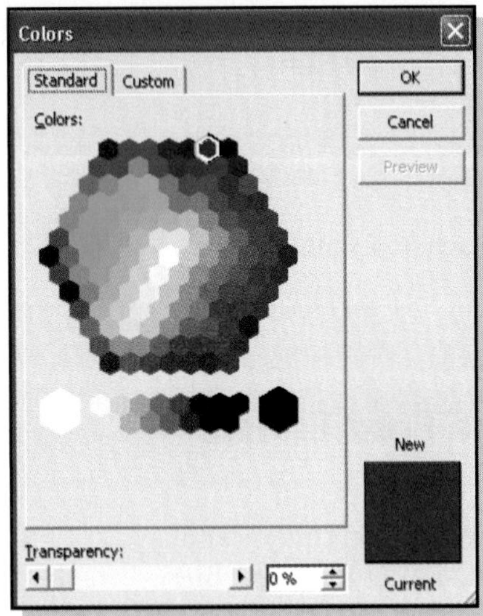

3. Click the **OK** button. The AutoShapes now have thick dark blue lines. The dark blue color is added to the color scheme.
4. Click the **Font Color** button drop-down arrow and click the dark blue color in the grid. Deselect the explosion objects.
5. Use the SHIFT key to select all the text boxes. Click the **Font Color** button to change the text to dark blue. Click the **Line Color** drop-down arrow and click the bright orange color on the grid. Deselect the text boxes and save the presentation.

Style Name	Formatting Contained in the Style
Heading 1	Arial 16 point; Bold; 12 points of spacing before and 3 points of spacing after text
Heading 2	Arial 14 point; Bold and Italic; 12 points of spacing before and 3 points of spacing after the text
Heading 3	Arial 13 point; Bold; 12 points of spacing before and 3 points of spacing after the text
Normal	Times New Roman 12 point; Left alignment; single spacing

You can also apply styles by clicking the **Styles and Formatting** button on the Formatting toolbar to open the **Styles and Formatting** task pane. Then click the name of the style.

To apply a style, select the text, click the **Style** box drop-down arrow on the Formatting toolbar, and click the name of the style. Even after you apply a preset style, you can continue to format the text—for example, by making it bold or indenting it—just as you have already learned.

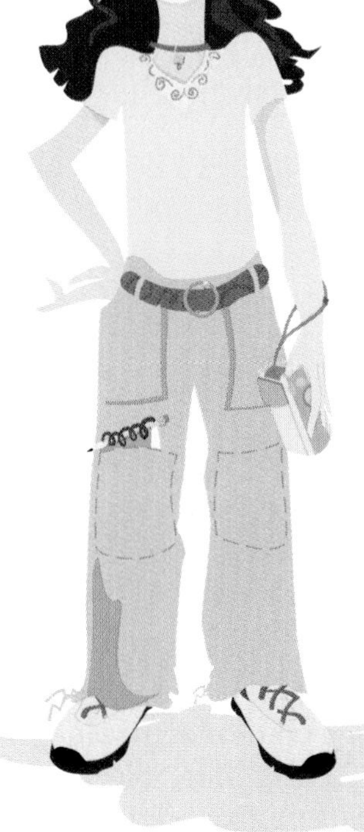

Let's format a paragraph with the Heading 1 style, change its font color, and indent it from the left and right margins.

1. Select the paragraph beginning *The three branches* below the title. Click the **Style** box drop-down arrow and click the **Heading 1** style. Normal Click the **Font Color** button drop-down arrow and click **Blue** on the grid. A
2. Drag the Left indent marker to the 1-inch position and the Right indent marker to the 8-inch position on the Horizontal Ruler. Deselect the text and save the document.

CHECKPOINT

Your formatted paragraph should now look like this.

Paragraph formatted with the Heading 1 style and blue font color and indented from the left and right margins

A·System·of·Checks·and·Balances¶
¶

The·three·branches·of·the·U.S.·Government·provide·a·system·of·checks·and·balances·in·which·the·powers·of·one·branch·are·limited·by·the·powers·of·the·other·two·branches.¶

7. Click the **Text Box** button. Draw a text box immediately below the first Explosion AutoShape, and type **Yellowstone, U.S., 2 million years ago**. Resize the text box, if necessary, so that the text wraps on two lines. Deselect the text box.
8. Draw a text box below the second AutoShape and type **Krakatau, Indonesia, 1883**. Draw a text box below the third AutoShape and type **Nevado del Ruiz, Colombia, 1985**. Resize both text boxes so that the text wraps on two lines. *Don't worry about the exact position of the text boxes. You will position them neatly on the slide in the next Trail Marker.*

Your slide should look similar to this.

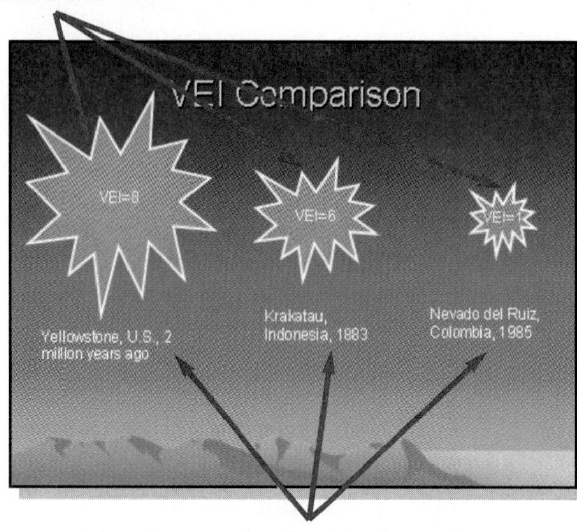

Now, let's make the three AutoShapes stand out more by changing the line color and font color to dark blue and making the line size 3 points. To change the line color to dark blue, select the AutoShape and click the **Line Color** button on the Drawing toolbar. The colors you will see on the color grid belong to the color scheme you applied. Dark blue is not part of this color scheme, so you need to click **More Line Colors**. *PowerPoint* automatically adds the new color you choose to the color scheme *for this presentation only*.

Ergonomics *TIP*

Is your monitor's screen at eye level? If not, adjust your chair height or tilt your monitor so that you can look straight ahead at the screen.

Special Font Effects

Word's font effects allow you to change the look of text in a number of ways including Superscript or Subscript, ALL CAPS, Shadow, and SMALL CAPS. Apply a font effect by choosing **Format** on the menu bar and choosing **Font** to open the **Font** dialog box. Then click an **Effects** checkbox.

font effect

Here's a great way to clear all the formatting from selected text. Click the **Style** box drop-down arrow on the formatting toolbar and click **Clear Formatting**. Try it! Then click the **Undo** button to reapply the styles.

Let's apply the Small caps font effect.

1. Use the CTRL key to select the following short paragraphs:
   The Executive Branch: The President
   The Legislative Branch: The Congress
   The Judicial Branch: The Supreme Court
2. Choose **Format** on the menu bar and choose **Font** to open the **Font** dialog box. Click the **Small caps** checkbox to insert a check mark.

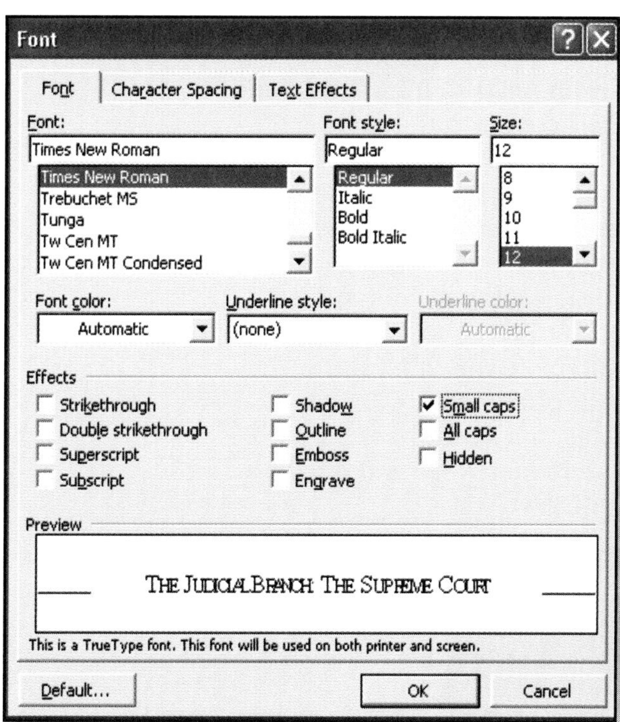

3. Click the **OK** button. Deselect the text and save the document.

Let's draw, size, position, and format AutoShapes and text boxes.

1. View slide 5 and read the description of the VEI. Then view slide 6. You will use AutoShapes and text boxes to illustrate the VEI.
2. Click the **AutoShapes** button, point to **Stars and Banners**, and click the **Explosion 1** AutoShape. AutoShapes ▾ Draw an Explosion 1 AutoShape that is approximately 2.5 inches wide. Then drag it to the left side of the slide, below the title.
3. Right-click the Explosion AutoShape and choose **Add Text**. Type **VEI=8** and deselect the AutoShape.

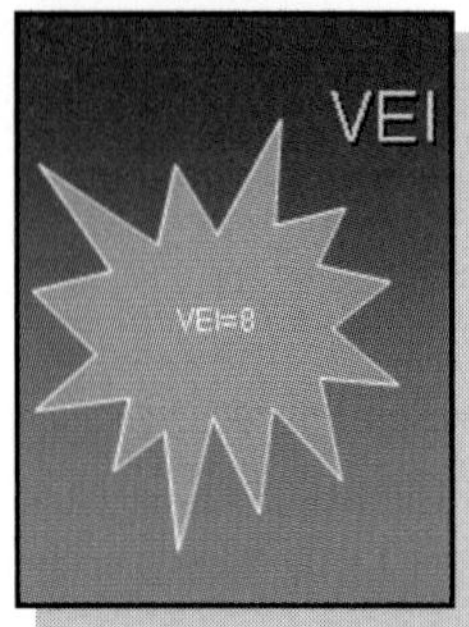

4. Copy the AutoShape by moving the mouse pointer to it, pressing and holding the CTRL key, and dragging and dropping it to the right. Release the mouse button and then the CTRL key.
5. Now resize that AutoShape. Move the mouse pointer to its lower-right corner sizing handle, press the CTRL key, and drag upward and to left to size it approximately 1 inch wide *from the object's center point.* Click in the text and change **VEI=8** to **VEI=6**. Deselect the AutoShape.
6. Use drag and drop to create a third Explosion AutoShape by copying the second one. Position the third AutoShape to the right of the other two. Resize the new AutoShape to approximately 0.5 inch wide. Edit the text to be **VEI=1** and deselect the AutoShape. *Do not worry about the exact position of the AutoShapes. You will position them neatly on the slide in the next Trail Marker.*

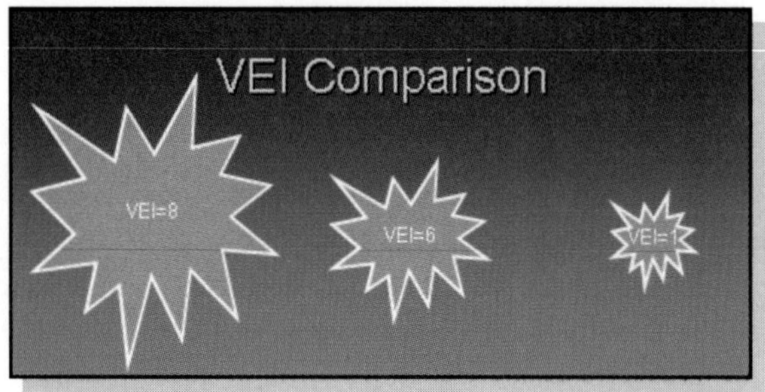

Your formatted text should now look like this.

Text formatted with Small caps font effect

¶
THE EXECUTIVE BRANCH: THE PRESIDENT¶
Vetoes acts of Congress¶
Appoints Supreme Court judges¶
Suggests new laws¶
¶
THE LEGISLATIVE BRANCH: THE CONGRESS¶
Impeaches and removes the President¶
Overrides Presidential vetoes¶
Appropriates money for federal spending¶
Confirms Presidential appointments¶
Impeaches federal judges¶
¶
THE JUDICIAL BRANCH: THE SUPREME COURT¶
Decides if Executive Branch actions are constitutional¶
Decides if acts of Congress are constitutional¶

Very nice! Now let's create bulleted lists using the *checkmark in a box* symbol.

TRAIL 4 MARKER

Inserting Symbols

symbol

Have you used this symbol in letters or e-mails: ☺? A symbol is a special font character, such as the copyright symbol (©), a computer symbol (💻), directional arrows (🡔➔🡑🡓), or letters with accent marks (á).

To insert a symbol at the insertion point, open the **Symbol** dialog box by choosing **Insert** on the menu bar and choosing **Symbol**. Select a font to view the symbols available in the font. Then click a symbol and click the **Insert** button. Click the **Close** button to close the dialog box.

You can also use a symbol as the graphic for a bulleted list. To create a bulleted list, choose **Format** on the menu bar and choose **Bullets and Numbering**. Instead of choosing one of the default bullet options, you can choose a bullet from the **Symbol** options. Let's select the *checkmark in a box* symbol (☑) and then create bulleted lists to point out the powers of each branch of the government.

The **Special Characters** tab in the **Symbol** dialog box has a short list of the most commonly used symbols. Check it out!

Your slide 1 should look similar to this.

Mountain Top design template with alternate color scheme

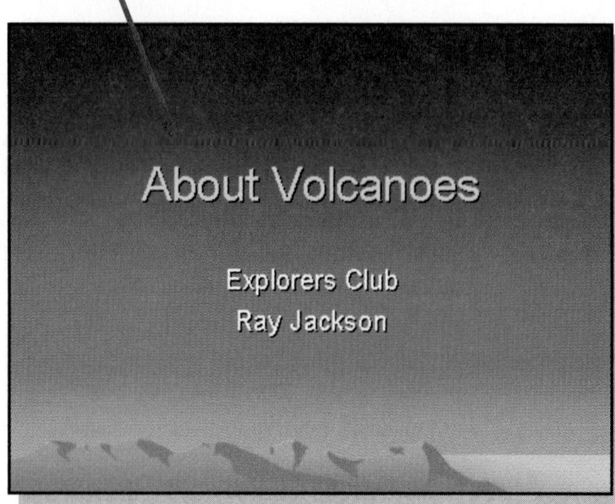

What a big improvement! Next, let's use AutoShapes and text boxes to enhance a slide.

TRAIL 2 MARKER

Using the Drawing Tools

You can draw rectangles, lines, ovals, arrows, or other AutoShapes or text boxes in *PowerPoint* just like you do in *Word* and *Excel*. Just click the appropriate button on the Drawing toolbar, move the mouse pointer to the slide, and drag down and across to draw the shape or text box. Then you can position the shape or box on the slide using drag and drop, or you can copy it using the CTRL key and drag and drop.

The colors of the text box or AutoShape, as well as the fill color and font color, are automatically determined by the design template and color scheme. However, you can change the colors with buttons on the Formatting or Drawing toolbars.

Slide 5 describes the Volcanic Explosivity Index (VEI) that is used to measure the explosive power of volcanic eruptions. Let's use AutoShapes to create an illustration of this index on slide 6.

Do you know how to draw a square or a circle? Just click the **Rectangle** or **Oval** button on the Drawing toolbar, press and hold the SHIFT key, and drag down and across. Try it!

Remember to drag a corner sizing handle to resize a text box or AutoShape proportionally. Press and hold the CTRL key and drag a corner sizing handle to resize a text box or shape proportionally from the center outward. Try it!

Apply It!

Let's select the text, select a symbol graphic for a bulleted list, and then create the lists.

1. Use the CTRL key to select the list of powers for the Executive Branch, Legislative Branch, and Judicial Branch.

¶
THE EXECUTIVE BRANCH: THE PRESIDENT¶
Vetoes acts of Congress¶
Appoints Supreme Court judges¶
Suggests new laws¶
¶
THE LEGISLATIVE BRANCH: THE CONGRESS¶
Impeaches and removes the President¶
Overrides Presidential vetoes¶
Appropriates money for federal spending¶
Confirms Presidential appointments¶
Impeaches federal judges¶
¶
THE JUDICIAL BRANCH: THE SUPREME COURT¶
Decides if Executive Branch actions are constitutional¶
Decides if acts of Congress are constitutional¶

2. Choose **Format** on the menu bar and choose **Bullets and Numbering**. Click the **Bulleted** tab if necessary. Click the first bullet option and click the **Customize** button to open the **Customize Bulleted List** dialog box. Click the **Character** button to open the **Symbol** dialog box.
3. Change the font to Wingdings. Scroll to view the bottom row of the Wingding symbols and then click ☑ (*checkmark in a box*). Click the **OK** button. Click the **OK** button in the **Customize Bulleted List** dialog box. Deselect the text and save the document.

Warning! When you customize a bullet option, it remains customized until you reset it to its default setting. Click the customized bullet option in the **Bulleted** tab in the **Bullets and Numbering** dialog box; click the **Reset** button to reset the option.

CHECKPOINT
Your bulleted lists should look like this.

Bulleted list with custom symbol graphic

¶
THE EXECUTIVE BRANCH: THE PRESIDENT¶
☑ Vetoes acts of Congress¶
☑ Appoints Supreme Court judges¶
☑ Suggests new laws¶
¶
THE LEGISLATIVE BRANCH: THE CONGRESS¶
☑ Impeaches and removes the President¶
☑ Overrides Presidential vetoes¶
☑ Appropriates money for federal spending¶
☑ Confirms Presidential appointments¶
☑ Impeaches federal judges¶
¶
THE JUDICIAL BRANCH: THE SUPREME COURT¶
☑ Decides if Executive Branch actions are constitutional¶
☑ Decides if acts of Congress are constitutional¶

Terrific! Next, you will use the Drawing tools to add text boxes, clip art, and an AutoShape to the *infographic6* document.

Starting Out!

Begin by opening Ray's presentation and saving it with a new name.

1. Start the *PowerPoint* application, if necessary.
2. Click the **Open** button on the Formatting toolbar, switch to the folder that contains your data files, and open the *volcanoes* presentation. Save it as *volcanoes12*.

Great! Now let's change the slide design and color scheme of Ray's presentation.

TRAIL 1 MARKER

Changing the Slide Design and Color Scheme

color scheme

Ray picked a plain design template for his *volcanoes12* presentation. He also chose a very plain pre-defined color scheme—the background color and color of fonts and bullets that comes with a design template. You can see the color scheme that Ray chose in the **Slide Design** task pane. To see the other color schemes available for this design template, click the **Slide Design-Color Schemes** link in the **Slide Design** task pane to open the **Color Schemes** task pane. Let's apply a different design template and change the color scheme to improve the appearance of the *volcanoes12* presentation.

Apply It!

Let's change the design template and color scheme.

1. Click the **Slide Design** button to open the **Slide Design** task pane. Design
2. Scroll the task pane to see the available design templates. Click a design template of your choice to see how the slides change. Then apply a couple more design templates, just to see the variety of templates available.
3. Locate and click the **Mountain Top** design template. Click the **Color Schemes** link at the top of the task pane to open the **Slide Design-Color Schemes** task pane. The default color scheme for the Mountain Top design template should be selected in the task pane.
4. Click a few more color schemes to see how the slides look with different color schemes. Then apply the third color scheme in the second column (light blue background).
5. View **slide 1**, save the presentation, and close the task pane.

Using the Drawing Tools

By using buttons on the Drawing toolbar, you can place typed text in a box and move it, create and format special text objects, insert pictures, and draw and format shapes. To view the Drawing toolbar, choose **View** on the menu bar, point to **Toolbars**, and click **Drawing**; or click the **Drawing** button on the Standard toolbar.

Don't forget to use ScreenTips to learn the names of the buttons on the new toolbars you use in this section! Use the **View** menu, if necessary, to display the toolbars that do not automatically appear.

Inserting, Repositioning, and Formatting Text Boxes

floating object
nudging
sizing handle
text box

A text box is a moveable container for text or pictures. You can reposition text boxes anywhere on the page using drag and drop. Text boxes, pictures, and shapes that you can move or copy using drag and drop are called floating objects. You can also move a selected floating object to position it a short space up, down, left, or right by tapping one of the arrow keys in a process called nudging.

Another way to create a text box is to choose **Insert** on the menu bar and choose **Text Box**.

You can create a text box by clicking the **Text Box** button on the Drawing toolbar. You can type and format text in a text box just like you do in the body of a document. If the text is already typed, just select it and then click the **Text Box** button to place the text in a text box.

Use the **Fill Color**, **Line Color**, and **Font Color** buttons on the Drawing toolbar to format a selected text box and the text inside it. To resize a text box, drag a sizing handle—one of the white circles on the text box border.

Let's insert the text that describes the separation of powers for the three branches of government into three text boxes; then format the text boxes to change the font and line color. After you create and format each text box, you will drag it out of the way near the bottom of the page.

Project 12

Presentations and Multimedia

Investigating Volcanoes

Explorers' Guide

Data files: *volcanoes, pyroclastic flow.jpg, hazards, lava.jpg*

Objectives:

In this project, you will:

- change the slide design and color scheme
- use the drawing tools
- distribute and align slide objects
- change slide layout and background
- insert and resize clip art or pictures
- delete slides

Exploring on Your Own
additional practice in:

- changing the slide design and color scheme
- using the drawing tools
- distributing and aligning slide objects
- changing the slide layout and background
- inserting and resizing clip art or pictures
- deleting a slide

Exploring Across the Curriculum

Internet/Web
Science
Language Arts
Getting Help
Your Personal Journal

Our Exploration Assignment:

Create a slide show presentation about volcanoes

Imagine an explosion so loud that it was heard 3,000 miles away! That's what happened in 1883 when a volcano named Krakatau erupted in Indonesia. Ray is working on a presentation about volcanoes for the Explorers Club. His presentation has some great facts about volcanoes, but it needs to be much more visually appealing. Follow the Trail Markers to change the slide design and color scheme, use the drawing tools, align objects on a slide, change a slide's layout, modify a slide's background, insert and resize clip art, and delete a slide.

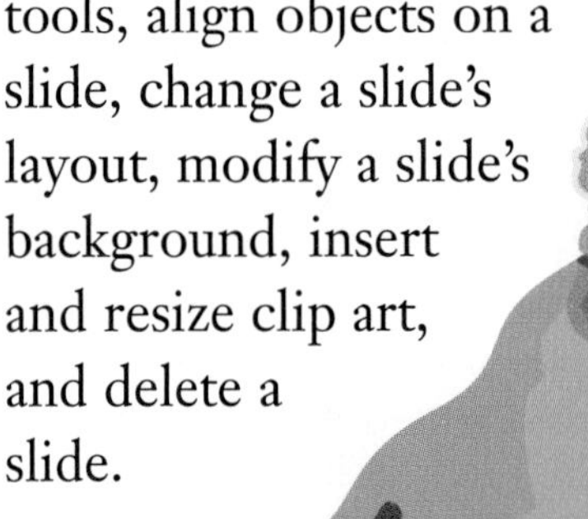

Let's create text boxes, starting with the last three short paragraphs on the page.

1. Click the **Drawing** button to show the Drawing toolbar at the bottom of the *Word* window above the status bar.
2. Select the three short paragraphs that describe the Judicial Branch. Click the **Text Box** button to create the text box containing the selected text.
3. Click the **Line Color** button drop-down arrow and click **Blue** on the grid. Click the **Font Color** button drop-down arrow and click **Blue** on the grid.

THE JUDICIAL BRANCH: THE SUPREME COURT¶
☑ Decides if Executive Branch actions are constitutional¶
☑ Decides if acts of Congress are constitutional¶

4. Move the mouse pointer to the text box boundary. The mouse pointer becomes a move pointer with four black arrows. Drag the text box out of the way and drop it near the bottom of the page. Do not worry about exactly where you drop the text box. You will reposition it later in this Trail Marker.
5. Using steps 2–4 as your guide, insert and format two more text boxes: one box for the text about the Legislative Branch and one box for the text about the Executive Branch. Drag the text boxes out of the way for now. Save the document.

Your text boxes should look similar to this.

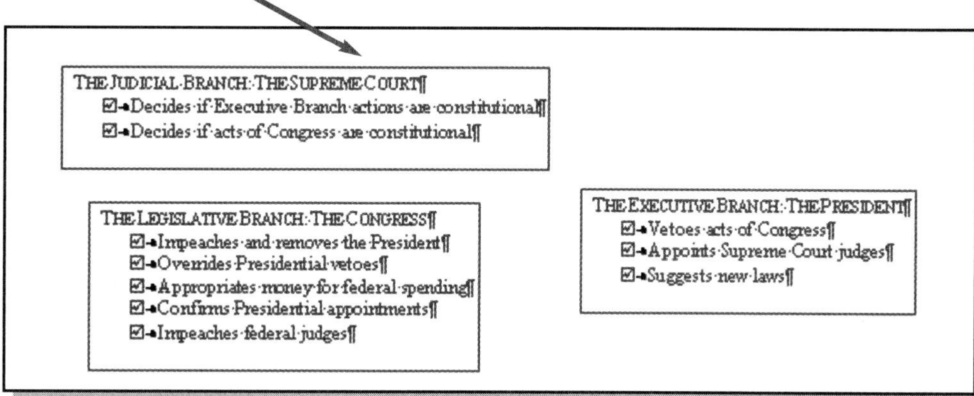

Text boxes repositioned near the bottom of the page
THE JUDICIAL BRANCH: THE SUPREME COURT¶
☑ Decides if Executive Branch actions are constitutional¶
☑ Decides if acts of Congress are constitutional¶
THE LEGISLATIVE BRANCH: THE CONGRESS¶
☑ Impeaches and removes the President¶
☑ Overrides Presidential vetoes¶
☑ Appropriates money for federal spending¶
☑ Confirms Presidential appointments¶
☑ Impeaches federal judges¶
THE EXECUTIVE BRANCH: THE PRESIDENT¶
☑ Vetoes acts of Congress¶
☑ Appoints Supreme Court judges¶
☑ Suggests new laws¶

11a Build Skill

Key each line twice. Double-space between 2-line groups.

balanced-hand sentences

1 She may or may not do the handiwork for the panel.
2 Diane bid on the land by the field for the chapel.
3 Helen laid it by the mantle by the end of the rug.
4 Burn wood and a small bit of coal for a big flame.
5 Jane and Alan may fix the problem with the signal.
6 Pamela and Glen may visit the ancient city chapel.
7 The toxic odor by the lake may make the girl sick.
8 Six official tutors may work with the eight girls.

11b Speed Check

1. Key a 1' timing on paragraph 1.
2. Determine the number of words you keyed.
3. Key another 1' timing on paragraph 1. Try to go two words a minute faster.
4. Repeat steps 1–3 for paragraph 2.
5. Key a 2' timing on paragraphs 1–2 combined.
6. Determine the number of words you keyed.

all letters used *gwam* 2'

Government is the structure by which public laws are made 6
for a group of people. One type of structure is where the populace 13
has the right to elect citizens to govern for them and make the laws. 20
A representative government would be an example of this way of 26
making the laws and policies. 29

The democracy or the republic form of government are two 35
names that are quite often used to refer to this type of governance 42
by the people. This type of a structure is in direct contrast to a 48
dictatorship where all the decisions are made by just one person. 55

gwam 2' | 1 | 2 | 3 | 4 | 5 | 6 |

Inserting and Formatting WordArt

inline WordArt

You can format text as WordArt by clicking the **Insert WordArt** button on the Drawing toolbar. WordArt text can be sized, colored, and shaped with buttons on the WordArt toolbar to create an interesting, colorful, and fun text effect.

By default, a WordArt object is positioned inline with the text. When a WordArt object is inline with the text, it can be repositioned horizontally on the line only by clicking the **Align Left**, **Center**, or **Align Right** buttons on the Formatting toolbar.

To convert an inline WordArt object to a floating object, click the **Text wrapping** button on the WordArt toolbar, which appears automatically when you select a WordArt object.

Let's use the title text to create a WordArt object.

1. Select the title text. Click the **Insert WordArt** button on the Drawing toolbar to open the **WordArt Gallery** dialog box. Click the fifth WordArt style in the second row.

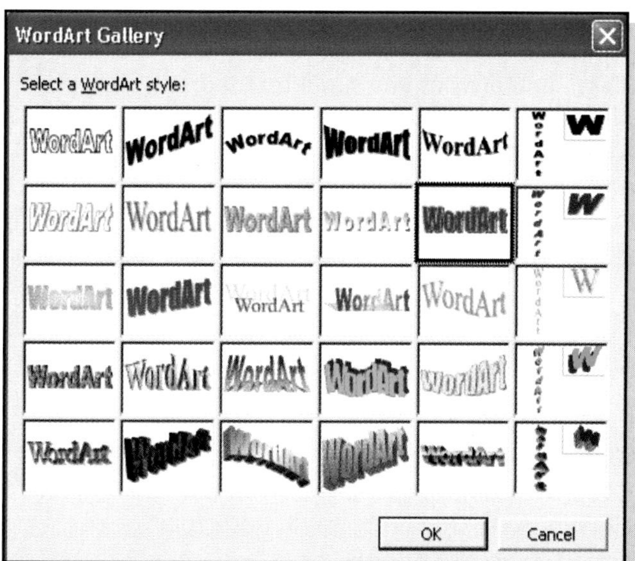

2. Click the **OK** button to open the **Edit WordArt Text** dialog box. Click the **OK** button to accept the default font and font size. Click the WordArt object to select it, if necessary. Center the WordArt title object on the line and then deselect it.

Exploring Across the Curriculum

Science: Research, Write, and Present

Use classroom, library, CD-ROM, or online resources to learn about the fantastic glowing algae that appears in the North Atlantic Ocean each spring and that can be seen from space. Take notes about what you learn. Then create a new presentation with a Title Slide and three Title and Text slides. Organize the facts you learn about the glowing algae on two of the Title and Text slides and cite your sources on the last slide. Apply the slide design of your choice. Use the Slide Sorter view to rearrange slides, if necessary. Run the slide show. With permission, preview and print the slides. Save and close the presentation.

Getting Help

Type **AutoContent Wizard** in the **Ask A Question** box and tap the ENTER key. Research how to create a new presentation using the AutoContent Wizard and the **New Presentation** task pane. Then, using what you have learned, create a new presentation using the AutoContent Wizard and the Generic presentation type. Close the presentation without saving it.

Your Personal Journal

Open your personal journal document. Insert today's date and two blank lines. Think about what you have learned about photosynthesis and the carbon cycle. What role do plants and oceans play in the carbon cycle? What is the human role in the carbon cycle? What effects do photosynthesis and the carbon cycle have on the global climate? Update your journal with one or two paragraphs that answer these questions. Spell-check, save, and close your journal.

Online Enrichment Games (Fun Stuff)  www.lwcgreen.keyboarding.com

CHECKPOINT
Your WordArt title object should look similar to this.

Title text converted to a WordArt object

A System of Checks and Balances

The·three·branches·of·the·U.S.·Government·provide·a·system·of·checks·and·balances·in·which·the·powers·of·one·branch·are·limited·by·the·powers·of·the·other·two·branches.¶

Inserting, Resizing, and Repositioning Clip Art

clip art

Pictures and drawings that come with applications like *Word* are called clip art. You can insert clip art stored on your hard drive, network drive, or a CD by choosing **Insert** on the menu bar, pointing to **Picture**, and clicking **From File**; or by clicking the **Insert Picture** button on the Drawing toolbar to open the **Insert Picture** dialog box. Then switch to the folder that contains the clip art you want and insert it.

To search for clip art, click the **Insert Clip Art** button on the Drawing toolbar, type your search keywords in the **Insert Clip Art** task pane, and click the **Go** button.

By default, *Word* inserts clip art inline with the text. To drag clip art to a new location or to wrap text around it, you must first convert it to a floating object by clicking **Text Wrapping** button on the Picture toolbar and clicking a wrapping style. The Picture toolbar should automatically appear when you select clip art.

You resize clip art just like you resize a text box—by dragging a sizing handle. To resize a text box or clip art proportionally, drag a corner sizing handle. To resize a text box or clip art from the center while maintaining its proportions, press and hold down the CTRL key while dragging a corner sizing handle.

Here is a great way to tell if clip art or a WordArt object is inline or floating. If it has square black sizing handles, it is inline. If it has white circle sizing handles, it is floating. Check it out!

Exploring Across the Curriculum

Internet/Web

You can learn more about photosynthesis and the carbon cycle by using the Web. Open your Web browser and use a favorite to view the Learning with Computers Web page (www.lwcgreen.keyboarding.com). Click the **Links** option. Click **Project 11**. Click the links to research the carbon cycle and take notes about what you learn.

Then create a new, blank presentation and save it as *carbon cycle11*. On the Title Slide, type **About the Carbon Cycle** as the title and **Explorers Club** as the subtitle. Edit the subtitle to add your name. Insert at least three Title and Text slides with facts about the carbon cycle. Be sure to include facts about how carbon cycles through land, ocean, and the atmosphere. Add facts to explain the role plant photosynthesis and human respiration play in the carbon cycle.

Apply the design template of your choice. Cite your sources on a Title and Text slide at the end of the presentation. Use Slide Sorter view to rearrange your slides. Run the slide show. Then, with your teacher's permission, preview and print your slides using the Handouts (3 slides per page) layout. Save and close the presentation.

Language Arts: Words to Know

Look up the meaning of the following terms using a classroom, library, CD-ROM, or online encyclopedia or dictionary.

oxygen	chlorophyll	chloroplast	stomata
heterotroph	carbohydrate	carbon dioxide	autotroph

Create a new presentation. Save it as *definitions11*. On the Title Slide, type **Photosynthesis** as the title and **Definitions** as the subtitle. Insert a Title and Text slide for each term. Type the name or term as the title and the definition as the bulleted text. Apply the slide design of your choice. Use Slide Sorter view to rearrange the slides so that the terms and definitions are in ascending alphabetical order. Run the slide show. With permission, preview and print the slides as handouts, 6 per page. Save and close the presentation.

Explore More

Let's insert a picture of the U.S. flag from the data files, resize it, convert it to a floating object, and reposition it.

1. Move the insertion point to the left margin of the paragraph below the WordArt title. Click the **Insert Picture** button to open the **Insert Picture** dialog box. Switch to the data files folder and double-click *us-flag.gif* to insert the picture.
2. Click the flag picture to select it, if necessary. Move the mouse pointer to the sizing handle in the lower-right corner of the picture. The mouse pointer changes shape to a double-headed arrow sizing pointer.
3. Press and hold the CTRL key and drag the sizing handle downward and to the right until the flag picture is about 1.5 times its original size. Release the CTRL key.
4. Locate the Picture toolbar. It may be floating on top of the *Word* document or anchored with the other toolbars at the top of the window. Click the **Text Wrapping** button. Choose **Tight** on the drop-down menu. The flag picture now has small white circle sizing handles—it is now a floating object and you can reposition it by using drag and drop or by nudging it using the arrow keys.
5. Move the mouse pointer to the selected flag. It changes shape to a move pointer with four black arrows. Drag the flag picture and drop it on the right side of the paragraph.
6. Nudge the flag picture up, down, left, or right by tapping the arrow keys until it is positioned attractively to the right of the text. Deselect the flag picture and save the document.

Resized and repositioned clip art object

Exploring on Your Own

Use classroom, library, CD-ROM, or online resources to learn why leaves change color in the fall season. Then, create a slide show presentation you can use to lead a classroom discussion on the topic. Save the presentation as *fall leaves11*. Your presentation should have a Title Slide and at least three Title and Text slides: two for your facts and one for your source citations. Check out Appendix A, if necessary, for examples of how to cite your sources.

On the Title Slide, type **Why Leaves Change Color** as the title and **Explorers Club** as the subtitle. Edit the subtitle to add your name. Apply the design template of your choice to the presentation. Use Slide Sorter view to rearrange your slides, if necessary. Use Slide Show view to see how your presentation will look to an audience. With your teacher's permission, preview and print your slides as a handout to accompany the class discussion. Save and close the presentation.

Reading in Action

Using a Graphic Organizer

Read the paragraph about photosynthesis. Then fill out the graphic organizer to help you understand what you have read.

Plants make their own food through a process called photosynthesis. Photosynthesis occurs in chloroplasts, located in cells of leaves. Chloroplasts contain the green pigment chlorophyll. During photosynthesis, chlorophyll absorbs light energy from the sun. Carbon dioxide enters the leaves through tiny holes called stomata, and water absorbed by the roots travels to the leaves through veins. The chloroplasts use light energy to convert carbon dioxide and water into glucose and oxygen. The plant uses glucose as food and oxygen exits through the stomata.

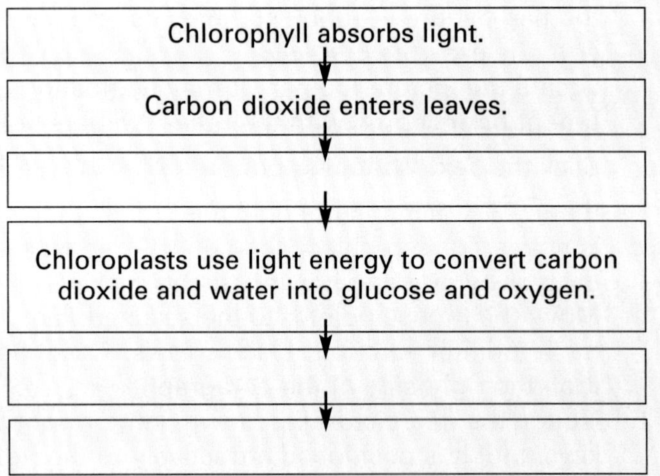

Chlorophyll absorbs light.
Carbon dioxide enters leaves.
Chloroplasts use light energy to convert carbon dioxide and water into glucose and oxygen.

Math in Action

Interpreting Graphs

The rate of photosynthesis is affected by the intensity of light shining on a plant. Look at the graph. When a plant is in the dark, the light intensity = 0, and photosynthesis stops (rate = 0). How does the rate of photosynthesis change as light intensity increases from 0 to 2? What happens when the light intensity is greater than 3?

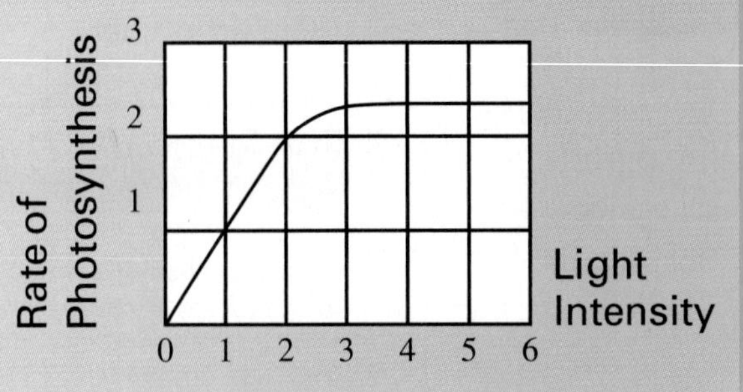

Rate of Photosynthesis
3
2
1
0
1
2
3
4
5
6
Light Intensity

Drawing and Formatting AutoShapes

You can also use buttons on the Drawing toolbar and the mouse pointer to draw shapes called drawing objects—block arrows, rectangles, circles, and so forth—in the *infographic6* document. Drawing objects are also called AutoShapes. By default, AutoShapes are created as floating objects.

When you draw an AutoShape, the Drawing Canvas may appear. The Drawing Canvas is used to keep multiple drawing objects together. In this project, we do not need the Drawing Canvas; if it appears, close it by tapping the ESC key.

You can change an AutoShape's fill color or line color, add a shadow, and flip or rotate it using buttons on the Drawing toolbar or commands on the **Draw** button menu. You can also rotate an AutoShape with the mouse pointer by dragging its rotate handle clockwise or counterclockwise to a new position. AutoShapes are resized just like text boxes and clip art.

AutoShape
Drawing Canvas
drawing object
rotate handle

Another way to format an AutoShape or a text box is to right-click it and choose **Format AutoShape** or **Format Text Box** on the shortcut menu. Try it!

Let's draw, format, and rotate an AutoShape.

1. Click the **AutoShapes** button, point to **Block Arrows**, and click the **Left-Right-Up Arrow** icon (last icon in the second row) on the grid. AutoShapes ▾ Tap the ESC key to close the Drawing Canvas, if necessary. The mouse pointer becomes a black cross-hair drawing pointer. Move the drawing pointer to about the center of the page at least 1 inch below the WordArt title and paragraph.
2. Click and hold down the mouse button and drag down and to the right to approximately 1.5 inches to draw the AutoShape. Click the **Fill Color** button drop-down arrow and click **Blue** on the grid. Click the **Line Color** button drop-down arrow and click **Red** on the grid.
3. Move the mouse pointer to the green rotate handle at the top of the AutoShape. The mouse pointer becomes a circular rotate pointer. Drag the rotate handle to the right to rotate the AutoShape about 45 degrees.

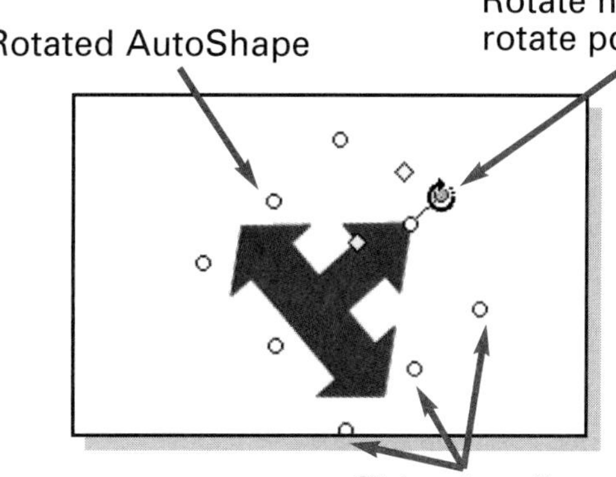

Project | *Skills Review*

You learned a lot in this project! We are very impressed with your progress. Let's take a few minutes to review the skills that you learned.

Create a new presentation	Choose **File** on the menu bar and choose **New.**
Open the Slide Layout task pane	Choose **Format** on the menu bar and choose **Slide Layout.** New Slide
Insert a new slide	Choose **Insert** on the menu bar and choose **New Slide.** New Slide
Move the insertion point up or down a level in a bulleted list	Tap the TAB key or press the SHIFT + TAB keys.
Apply a design template	Choose **Format** on the menu bar and choose **Slide Design.** Design
Navigate slides	Drag the scroll box on the vertical scroll bar. Press the CTRL + HOME or CTRL + END keys. Click the **Previous Slide** or **Next Slide** buttons.
Switch to Slide Sorter or Slide Show view	Choose **View** on the menu bar and choose **Slide Sorter** or **Slide Show.**
Navigate between slides in a slide show	Click the mouse button, tap the Right or Down arrow key, or tap the Spacebar to advance to the next slide. Tap the Left or Up arrow key to return to the previous slide. Right-click the screen or click the icon in the lower-left corner of the slide show screen and click a shortcut menu command.
Preview and print presentation	Choose **Print Preview** or **Print** on the **File** menu. Print...

4. Click the Executive Branch text box boundary to select the text box. Drag the text box to the right of the top-pointing arrow on the AutoShape. Select and drag the Legislative Branch text box to the left of the left-pointing arrow; then select and drag the Judicial Branch text box to the right of the right-pointing arrow.
5. Use the arrow keys to nudge the AutoShape and text boxes until they are grouped attractively on the page below the paragraph. Save the document

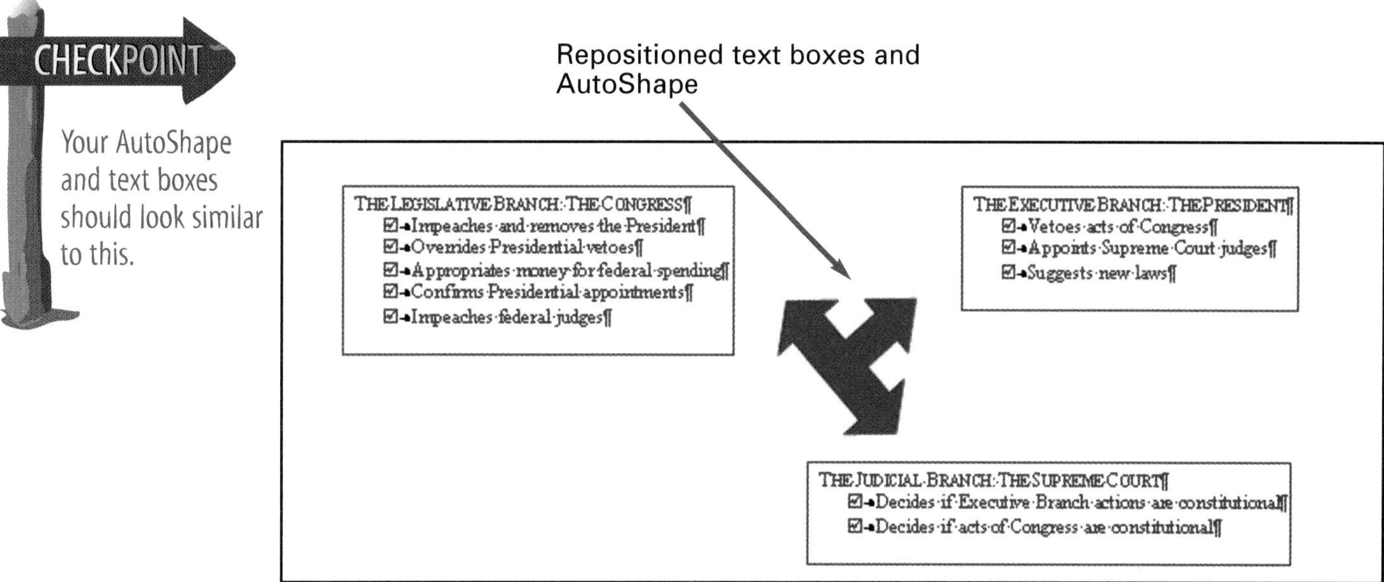

Your AutoShape and text boxes should look similar to this.

The infographic is almost finished. The last thing to do is to add a footer with Luis's name, the *Explorers Club* name, and the date.

TRAIL 6 MARKER

Adding a Footer

You use a footer to add Luis's name, the *Explorers Club* name, and today's date at the bottom of the infographic. Display the header and footer areas by choosing **View** on the menu bar and choosing **Header and Footer**. Then click the **Switch Between Header and Footer** button on the Header and Footer toolbar to move the insertion point into the footer area.

As you learned in Project 4, the header and footer areas have preset Center and Right tab stops set for the default Portrait page orientation. But because we are working in Landscape page orientation, you will need to change the tab stop positions.

Let's preview the presentation and then print it using the three slides per page layout.

1. Click the **Print Preview** button. Then click the **Print What** button drop-down arrow on the Print Preview toolbar, and click **Handouts (3 slides per page).** Print What: Slides

CHECKPOINT

Your Handouts (3 slides per page) preview should look like this.

Print preview of handouts in Handouts (3 slides per page) layout

About Photosynthesis

Photosynthesis

How Photosynthesis Works

1

2. With permission, click the **Print** button and then click the **OK** button in the **Print** dialog box. Print...
3. Click the **Close Preview** button on the Print Preview toolbar, and then save and close the presentation. Close *PowerPoint*.

Just as in *Word* or *Excel*, you can preview and print by choosing **File** on the menu bar and then choosing **Print Preview** or **Print**.

Let's view the header and footer areas and type the footer text.

1. Choose **View** on the menu bar and choose **Header and Footer**. Click the **Switch Between Header and Footer** button to move the insertion point into the footer area.
2. Drag the **Center** tab stop to the 4.5-inch position and the **Right** tab stop to the right margin on the Horizontal Ruler.
3. Type **Luis Gonzales** at the left margin and tap the TAB key. Type **Explorers Club** and tap the TAB key. Click the **Insert Date** button.
4. Select the footer line and change the font color to blue. Click the **Close Header and Footer** button. Close

Congratulations! Your completed *infographic6* document should look similar to this.

Completed Landscape infographic with page border, formatted text, WordArt, text boxes, AutoShape, and footnote

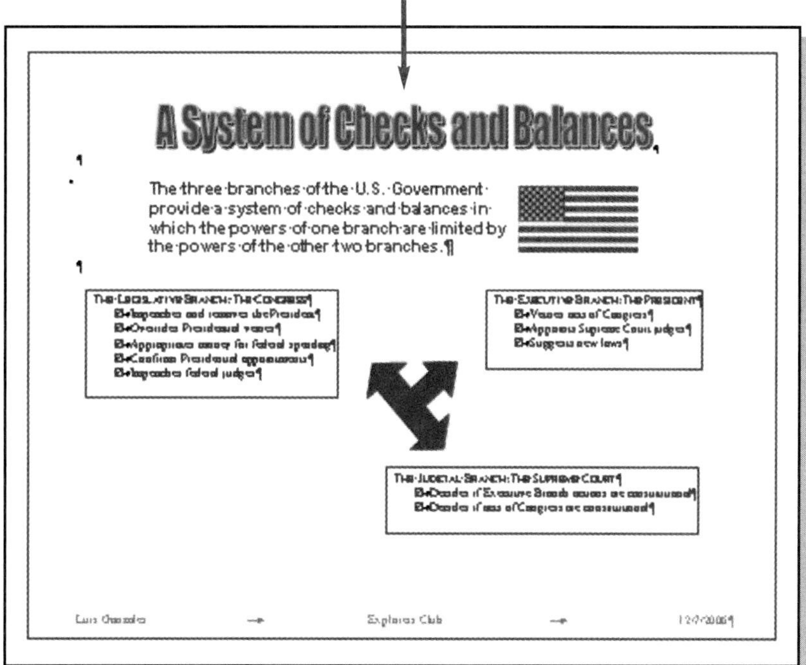

5. Zoom the document back to 100%. Close the Drawing toolbar. Save and close the document.

Here are ways you can navigate through slides during a slide show using the mouse or the keyboard.

- Click the mouse button to advance to the next slide.
- Tap the Right or Down arrow key to advance to the next slide.
- Tap the Left or Up arrow key to return to the previous slide.
- Tap the Spacebar to advance to the next slide.
- Right-click the screen or click the menu icon in the lower-left corner of the screen and then click **Next**, **Previous**, or point to **Go** and click a slide title.

The slide show ends when you advance one screen beyond your final slide. To stop a slide show at any time, tap the ESC key.

To project a *PowerPoint* slide show on a wall or projection screen, the computer must be connected to a special type of projector.

Let's run the slide show.

1. Double-click **slide 1** to view it in Normal view. Then use ScreenTips to locate the **Slide Show** button in the lower-left corner of the screen. Click the **Slide Show** button. The slide show begins with slide 1.
2. Click the mouse button to advance to **slide 2**. Tap the Right arrow key to advance to **slide 3**. Use either method to advance to **slide 4** and to the end of the slide show. Click the mouse button when you see the black exit screen to return to slide 1 in Normal view.

Terrific! You did it! Let's finish the presentation by previewing and printing our audience handouts.

TRAIL 6 MARKER

Previewing and Printing a Presentation

handouts

Printed slides are often used as handouts for a slide show audience. You can print each slide on its own page or print multiple slides on a single page. Use Print Preview to view different print layouts and then select the one you want to use and print the slides. The **Handouts (6 slides per page)** print layout is useful for proofreading your slides. The **Handouts (3 slides per page)** print layout is *very* useful for an audience because it has preprinted lines for writing notes!

Remember to ask your teacher before you print any slides in this unit.

Project | *Skills Review*

You learned a lot in this project! We are very impressed with your progress. Let's take a few minutes to review the skills that you learned.

Change page orientation	Choose **File** on the menu bar and choose **Page Setup**.
Zoom the view of a document	100%
Add a page border	Choose **Format** on the menu bar and choose **Borders and Shading**.
Apply a style	Normal
Apply font effects	Choose **Format** on the menu bar and choose **Font**.
Insert symbols	Choose **Insert** on the menu bar and choose **Symbol**.
Customize a bullet option with a symbol	Choose **Format** on the menu bar and choose **Bullets and Numbering**. Click a bullet option and click **Customize**. Click the **Character** button to open the **Symbol** dialog box.
Insert a text box	Choose **Insert** on the menu bar and choose **Text Box**.
Insert a WordArt object	Choose **Insert** on the menu bar, point to **Picture**, and choose **WordArt**.
Insert clip art	Choose **Insert** on the menu bar, point to **Picture**, and choose **Clip Art** or **From File**.
Insert AutoShapes	Click the **AutoShapes** button on the Drawing toolbar and choose any AutoShape.
Change an AutoShape or text box fill color, line color, or font color	Right-click the AutoShape or text box and click **Format AutoShape** or **Format Text Box**.

2. Click **slide 3** to select it. Notice that slide 3 now has a narrow dark border indicating it is selected. Move the mouse pointer to **slide 3**. Drag **slide 3** immediately to the left of **slide 2**. A vertical line appears indicating where the slide will be placed when the mouse button is released.

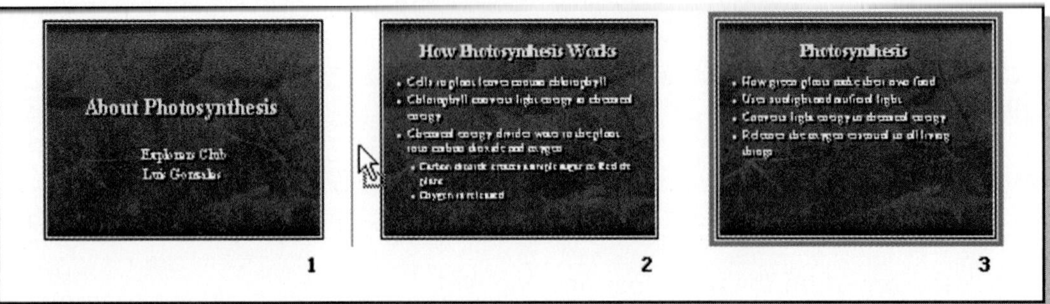

3. Release the mouse button to move the slide.

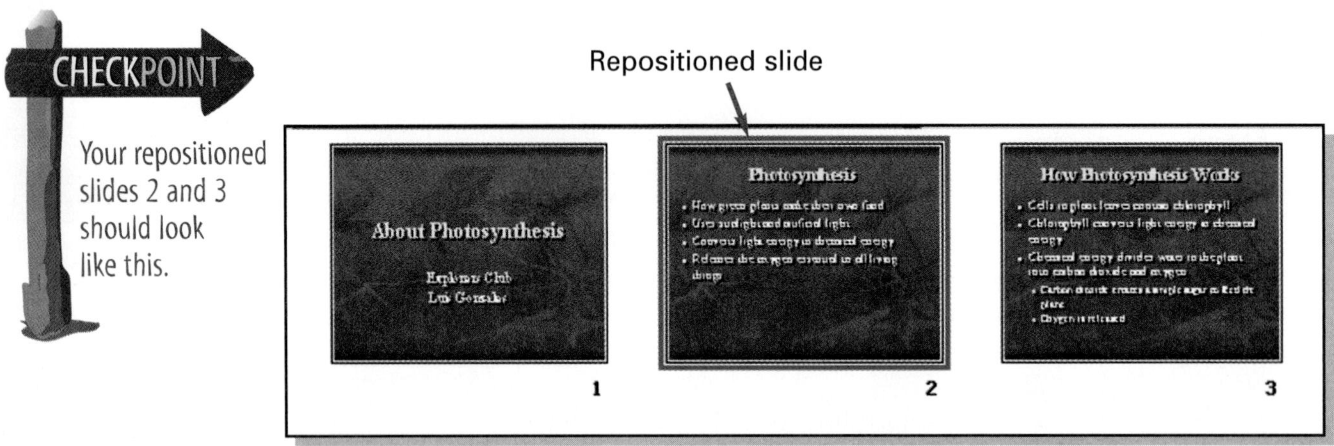

Great! Now you are ready to see how your slides will look to an audience.

Running a Slide Show

slide show

Displaying each slide so that it covers the entire screen is called *running the slide show*. You run a slide show to project the slides on a wall or projector screen. You can also use your computer monitor to run the slide show anytime without being connected to a projector so you can see how your presentation will look to an audience. Run the slide show starting with the current slide by clicking the **Slide Show** button or by choosing **Slide Show** on the menu bar and choosing **View Show**.

Exploring on Your Own

You have learned several new skills in this project. Now blaze your own trail by practicing these skills on your own!

In the United States, state governments have certain powers and the federal government has certain powers. Some powers, such as setting taxes, are shared by both governments. Use classroom, library, CD-ROM, or online resources to research powers of the state and federal governments; and then create three lists: powers allocated to the federal government, powers allocated to state governments, and powers that are shared by both.

Next, create a new *Word* document and save it as *powers6*. Change the page orientation to Landscape and set 1-inch top and bottom margins. Add a colored page border. Insert your name, school name, and current date in a footer using the font color of your choice.

Type the title **Federal and State Powers** and then type the headings **Federal**, **State**, and **Shared** followed by lists of powers under each heading. Then format the information to create an infographic:

- Convert the title to a WordArt object using the style of your choice.
- Search for and insert clip art of your choice below the WordArt title.
- Format the list headings as Small caps.
- Select each list and insert it in a text box. Format each text box with the line and font colors of your choice.
- Format the text inside the text boxes as bulleted lists, customizing a bullet option with a symbol.
- Insert and format an AutoShape of your choice.

Resize and reposition the WordArt, clip art, text boxes, and AutoShape as desired to create an attractive and useful infographic. Save and close the document.

Explore More

Using Slide Sorter View and Running a Slide Show

Slide show view
Slide Sorter view

You have been using Normal view to add and edit your slides. You can use **Slide Sorter view** to see all the slides at one time and **Slide Show view** to see how the slides look when projected on a wall or projection screen.

Slide Sorter View

In Slide Sorter view, you can select slides, move slides, and delete slides. Look at the lower-left corner of the *PowerPoint* window above the Drawing toolbar. Do you see the three view buttons: **Normal View**, **Slide Sorter View**, and **Slide Show**? Switch between *PowerPoint* views by clicking one of these view buttons or by choosing **View** on the menu bar.

After switching to Slide Sorter view, use drag and drop to move a slide to a new position.

Here's a quick way to reposition a slide in Normal view. Drag a slide miniature in the Slides tab up or down. Try it!

Let's reposition slide 3.

1. Use ScreenTips to locate the **Slide Sorter View** button in the lower-left corner of the screen. Click the **Slide Sorter View** button to see all four slides as miniatures.

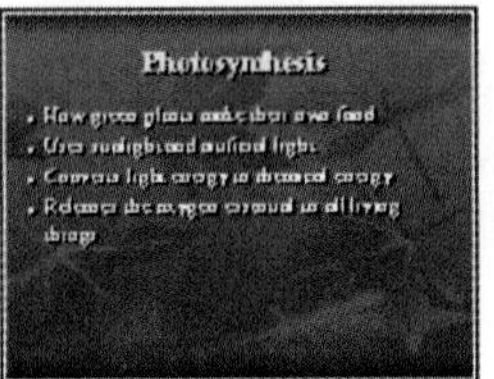

Exploring on Your Own

Reading in Action

Understanding What You Read

When you take a standardized test, you may be asked to read an infographic and use it to answer questions. Here is an example of such a question:

Read *infographic6.* Give one example of the principle of checks and balances.

First, make sure you understand the term "checks and balances." Use the context to find the meaning—"the powers of one branch are limited by the powers of the other two branches." Apply what you know about the meaning of the word *check*—"something that holds back or controls." Each branch has some power to "check" the power of the other two branches. These checks keep the three branches in balance; each branch watches the others.

Then look for one way that the Executive Branch checks the power of the Legislative Branch. The President can veto, or reject, a bill or law that Congress proposes.

Now you try it!

Give one example of how the Judicial Branch checks the power of the Legislative Branch.

Give one example of how the Legislative Branch checks the power of the Executive Branch.

Math in Action

Using Percents

Congress determines how much money is spent on federal services such as Medicare, Social Security, and the military. The following pie chart shows what percentage of the federal budget is spent on government services.

United States Budget 2005

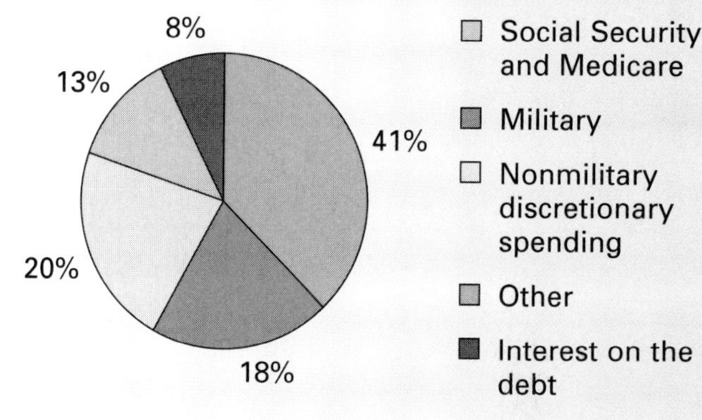

The budget for the United States in 2005 was approximately \$2 trillion (\$2,000,000,000,000). Use the pie chart to find how much money was spent in 2005 on Social Security and Medicare.

$\$2,000,000,000,000 \times 41\% = \$2,000,000,000,000 \times 0.41 = \$820,000,000,000$ spent on Social Security and Medicare

Now you try it!

How much money was spent in 2005 on the military? on nonmilitary discretionary spending in 2005?

Let's apply a design template.

1. Click the **Slide Design** button to open the **Slide Design** task pane. Design
2. Scroll the task pane to view the templates. Move the mouse pointer to a template to see a ScreenTip with the template's name and then locate the Maple template. If you do not have the Maple design template installed, choose a different template.
3. Click the **Maple** template. In a few seconds, the Maple template with maple leaves in the background and a fall color scheme is applied to all the slides. Close the **Slide Design** task pane.
4. Click the **Next Slide** button three times to view **slides 2**, **3**, and **4**, and then drag the scroll box on the vertical scroll bar up to view **slide 1**. Save the presentation.

CHECKPOINT

If you used the Maple design template, your Title Slide should look like this.

Title slide with Maple design template

Another way to open the **Slide Design** task pane is to choose **Format** on the menu bar and choose **Slide Design**.

Excellent! Now let's rearrange two of the slides and then run the slide show to see how the presentation will look to an audience.

Exploring Across the Curriculum

Internet/Web

You can learn more about the government on the Web. Open your Web browser and use a favorite to view the Learning with Computers Web page (www.lwcgreen.keyboarding.com). Click the **Links** option. Click **Project 7**. Click the links and review the resources available at these websites. For example, take a virtual tour of the White House; locate the names, addresses, and e-mail addresses of your state's representatives or senators; or view photographs of the Supreme Court Building. Next, complete parts 1 and 2 as assigned by your teacher.

Part 1: Create a new *Word* document and save it as *government6*. Create a Landscape-oriented infographic about information you learned from one of the websites you visited. Dress up your infographic with clip art, WordArt, text boxes, and AutoShapes. Customize a bullet option with a symbol and create bulleted lists inside the text boxes. Save and close the document.

Part 2: You can send an open document to a classmate or friend via e-mail by clicking the **E-mail** button on the Standard toolbar. With your teacher's permission, open the *infographic6* or *government6* document, click the **E-mail** button, and send the document to a classmate.

Language Arts: Words to Know

Look up the meaning of the following terms using a classroom, library, CD-ROM, or online encyclopedia or dictionary.

appropriate	Cabinet	confirm	impeachment
legislation	ratify	U.S. Constitution	veto

Create a new document and save it as *definitions6.* Change the orientation to Landscape and the top and bottom margins to 1 inch. Type the title **Project 6 Definitions**. Select the title text and apply the Heading 1 style; center it horizontally on the page. Beginning on the second line below the title, type each term on one line and the term's definition on the next line or lines. Insert a double space between the definition and the next term. Apply the Small caps font effect to all the terms. After selecting all the terms and definitions, place them in three newspaper columns. Add a page border with the color and line width and style of your choice. Save and close the document.

Explore More

Your completed slide 4 citations with hyperlinks should look similar to this.

Online citations with hyperlinks

> **Sources**
>
> - "Photosynthesis: How Do Plants Make Food," *PBS*, http://www.ktca.org/newtons/9/phytosy.html (accessed April 4, 2006).
> - "The Carbon Cycle," *NASA Earth Observatory*, http://earthobservatory.nasa.gov/Library/CarbonCycle/ (accessed April 4, 2006).

4. Press the CTRL + HOME keys and save the presentation.

Nice job! Now let's apply a design template to make the presentation more interesting and fun.

TRAIL 4 MARKER

Applying a Design Template

design template

You can change the look of a presentation by applying a **design template**—a color-coordinated format that defines fonts, colors, and background color or clip art. To apply a design template, click the **Slide Design** button on the Formatting toolbar to open the **Slide Design** task pane and click the design template you want. It is a good idea to use the same design template on all the slides in a presentation to give it a unified look.

To view a specific slide, drag the scroll box on the vertical scroll bar up or down. To see the previous or next slides, click the **Previous Slide** or **Next Slide** buttons below the scroll bar.

Exploring Across the Curriculum

Social Studies: Research, Write, and Draw

Social Studies

Work with a classmate to use classroom, library, CD-ROM, or online resources to research the relationship between the two houses of the U.S. Congress: the House of Representatives and the Senate. Then, create a new *Word* document and save it as *Congress6.* Use the document to create a Landscape-oriented infographic that illustrates what you learned in your research. Dress up your infographic with WordArt, clip art, text boxes, and AutoShapes. Add a colored page border. Insert your name, your school's name, and the current date as a footer. Save and close the document.

Getting Help

Getting Help

Type **previewing as a Web page** in the **Ask A Question** box on the menu bar and tap the ENTER key. Research how to preview a document as a Web page. Type **create a Web page** in the **Ask A Question** box and tap the ENTER key. Research how to save an existing *Word* document as a Web page. Then open the *infographic6* document you just created and, using what you learned, preview it as a Web page. Close the browser. Then save the *infographic6* document as a Web page using the filename *Web page6.*

Your Personal Journal

Open your personal journal document. Insert today's date and two blank lines. You have learned many new word processing skills in the past six projects. What word processing skills do you think will be most helpful in your school work? Why? Update your journal with one or two paragraphs that answer these questions. Spell-check, save, and close your journal.

Online Enrichment Games (Fun Stuff) @ www.lwcgreen.keyboarding.com

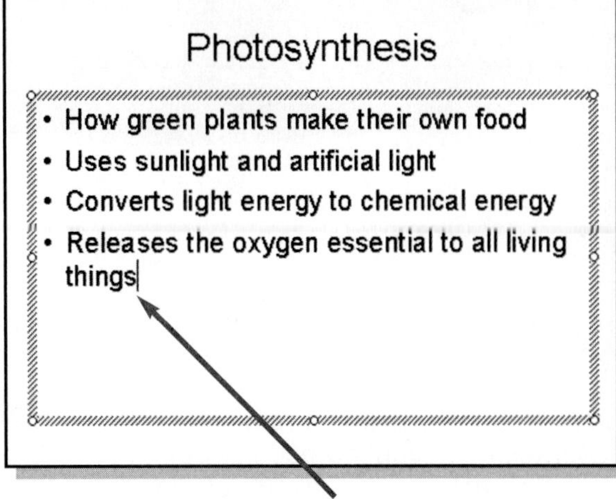

Photosynthesis
• How green plants make their own food
• Uses sunlight and artificial light
• Converts light energy to chemical energy
• Releases the oxygen essential to all living things

Completed slide with insertion point in the placeholder

Remember to spell-check your presentation! *PowerPoint* has a spelling checker, just like *Word*. When you see a wavy red line below your text, you can correct the spelling by using a shortcut menu or you can spell-check the entire presentation by clicking the **Spelling** button on the Standard toolbar.

Next, let's insert a slide and cite Luis's online sources for the facts about photosynthesis. Like *Word*, when you type a Web source's URL, *PowerPoint* converts it to a hyperlink. Leave the automatic hyperlink formatting as part of your citation.

Other keyboard shortcut keys you learned for *Word* and *Excel*—such as SHIFT + click, CTRL + HOME, and CTRL + END—work in the same or similar ways in *PowerPoint*. Let's insert a Title and Text slide and move the insertion point from placeholder to placeholder using the CTRL + ENTER keys. Then use the CTRL + HOME keys to move to slide 1.

Let's create a third Title and Text slide, and view slide 1.

1. Press the CTRL + ENTER keys to insert a new Title and Text slide as slide 4. Then press the CTRL + ENTER keys again to move the insertion point into the title placeholder.
2. Type **Sources** and press the CTRL + ENTER keys to move the insertion point into the bulleted list placeholder.
   Type **"Photosynthesis: How Do Plants Make Food,"** ***PBS,*** http://www.ktca.org/newtons/9/phytosy.html **(accessed today's date)**. and tap the ENTER key. *Remember to italicize the website name; type today's date with the month spelled out, the day, and the year in four- digits format; and type the period following the parenthesis.*
3. Type **"The Carbon Cycle,"** ***NASA Earth Observatory,*** http://earthobservatory.nasa.gov/Library/CarbonCycle/ **(accessed today's date)**. and deactivate the placeholder.

Keyboarding Project 6

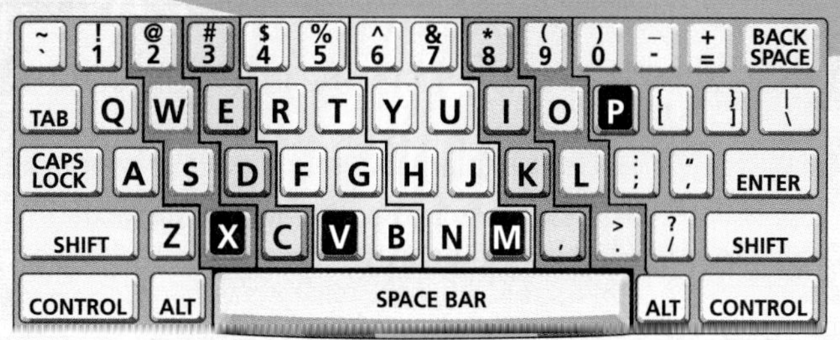

6a Review m, x, p, v

Key each line twice. Double-space between 2-line groups.

m

1 jm jm | mjm mjm | jmu jmu | jmn jmn | muj muj | mj nj mj nj;

2 math math | game game | came came | team team | mail mail;

x

3 sx sx | xs xs | swx swx | jsx jsx | jxk jxk | lwx lwx | cx cx;

4 tax tax | next next | wax wax | hoax hoax; | Baxter Baxter

p

5 ; p; ; p; | p;p p;p | op; op; | p.p p.p | pojp pojp; | ;p ;p

6 up up | pup pup | pin pin | camp camp | wrap wrap | cap cap;

v

7 fv fv; | vf vf | fbv fbf | bfv bfv | rvf rvf | jfv jfv | vf vf

8 save save | river river | vote vote | pave pave | van van;

Quickly tap the ENTER key at the end of a line and immediately begin keying the next line.

6b Speed Check

1. Key a 1' timing on paragraph 1.
2. Determine the number of words you keyed.
3. Key another 1' timing on paragraph 1. Try to go two words a minute faster.
4. Repeat steps 1–3 for paragraph 2.
5. Key a 2' timing on paragraphs 1–2 combined.
6. Determine the number of words you keyed.

all letters used — *gwam* 2'

Do you think someone is going to wait around just for a 6
chance to key your term paper? Do you believe when you get out 12
into the world of work that there will be someone to key your work 19
for you? Think again. It does not work that way. 24

Even the head of a business now uses a keyboard to send 29
and retrieve data as well as other information. Be quick to realize 36
that you will not go far in the world of work if you do not learn how 43
to key. Excel at it and move to the top. 47

gwam 2' | 1 | 2 | 3 | 4 | 5 | 6 |

Your completed slide should look like this.

Multilevel bulleted list

How Photosynthesis Works

- Cells in plant leaves contain chlorophyll
- Chlorophyll converts light energy to chemical energy
- Chemical energy divides water in the plant into carbon dioxide and oxygen
  - Carbon dioxide creates a simple sugar to feed the plant
  - Oxygen is released

Nice work! Now let's insert a slide that summarizes the photosynthesis process.

A quick way to move the insertion point into the next placeholder is to press the CTRL + ENTER keyboard shortcut keys.

Let's insert a second Title and Text slide.

1. Click the **New Slide** button. A new Title and Text slide is inserted as slide 3. Close the Slide Layout task pane. New Slide
2. Press the CTRL + ENTER keys and type **Photosynthesis** in the **Click to add title** placeholder.
3. Press the CTRL + ENTER keys, type **How green plants make their own food**, and tap the ENTER key. Type **Uses sunlight and artificial light** and tap the ENTER key. Type **Converts light energy to chemical energy** and tap the ENTER key. Type **Releases the oxygen essential to all living things**. Leave the insertion point *in the placeholder* for now.

Worksheets

Unit 2

Geography shapes the way we live. Julie, Luis, and I are beginning our study of the natural world and invite you to join us as we:

- **Discover the World's Five Great Oceans**
- **Identify Biosphere Reserves**
- **Budget for a Wildlife Preserve**
- **Journey to Oceania**

While exploring the world's geography and learning interesting facts about protecting our environment, you will organize and analyze data using an application called *Excel*. You will learn how to create and open workbooks and how to enter data in worksheets. *Excel* has some great tools for performing calculations, and we will show you how to create formulas that let you add, subtract, and multiply numbers with a few clicks of your mouse. You will even learn how to perform a *what-if analysis* on the data. You will also learn how to use *Excel* to turn worksheet data into attractive and useful pie, column, and line charts. Ready! Set! Go!

Let's insert a new Title and Text slide.

1. Click the **New Slide** button to insert a new Title and Text slide as slide 2. New Slide Click the **Close** button on the task pane title bar to close the **Slide Layout** task pane.
2. Click in the **Click to add title** placeholder and type **How Photosynthesis Works**. Click in the **Click to add text** placeholder to position the insertion point at the first bullet in the bulleted list. Type **Cells in plant leaves contain chlorophyll** and tap the ENTER key to move the insertion point to the next bullet.
3. Type **Chlorophyll converts light energy to chemical energy** and tap the ENTER key. Type **Chemical energy divides water in the plant into carbon dioxide and oxygen** and tap the ENTER key. Tap the TAB key to demote the bullet, type **Carbon dioxide creates a simple sugar to feed the plant** and tap the ENTER key.
4. Type **Oxygen is released**. Click in the gray slide work area outside the slide to deactivate the placeholder and save the presentation.

How Photosynthesis Works

- Cells in plant leaves contain chlorophyll

How Photosynthesis Works

- Cells in plant leaves contain chlorophyll
- Chlorophyll converts light energy to chemical energy
- Chemical energy divides water in the plant into carbon dioxide and oxygen
  - Carbon dioxide creates a simple sugar to feed the plant

Project 7
Worksheets

Discovering the World's Five Great Oceans

Data file: *none*

Objectives:

In this project, you will:

- name and save a new workbook
- navigate and select in a worksheet
- enter text and numbers
- format a worksheet
- sort data
- preview and print a worksheet

Exploring on Your Own

additional practice in:

- naming and saving a new workbook
- navigating and selecting in a worksheet
- entering text and numbers
- formatting a worksheet
- sorting data
- previewing and printing a worksheet

Exploring Across the Curriculum

Internet/Web
Language Arts
Science
Getting Help
Your Personal Journal

Our Exploration Assignment:

Organize data about the world's oceans in a worksheet

It's amazing! The world's five great oceans—Southern, Atlantic, Pacific, Arctic, and Indian—cover more than 70 percent of Earth's surface! The Explorers Club is learning about oceans, and Julie needs your help to organize her notes in an *Excel* workbook. Follow the Trail Markers to learn how to name and save a workbook; navigate and select in a worksheet; enter, format, and sort data; and preview and print a worksheet.

Your edited Title Slide should look like this.

Edited titles and subtitles

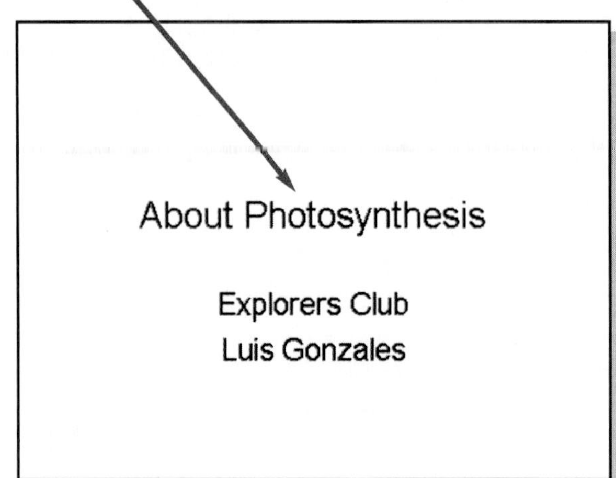

Super! Now let's insert a new slide with a different slide layout.

Here are two other ways to demote or promote bulleted text: click the **Increase Indent** or **Decrease Indent** buttons on the Formatting toolbar, or display the Outlining toolbar and click the **Promote** or **Demote** buttons. Try both!

TRAIL 3 MARKER

Inserting New Slides

To insert a new slide, click the **New Slide** button on the Formatting toolbar or choose **Insert** on the menu bar and choose **New Slide**. All new slides are automatically formatted with the Title and Text slide layout. Because the **Slide Layout** task pane automatically opens each time you insert a new slide, you can use it to easily change the slide layout, if necessary. You will use the Title and Text layout for slide 2.

The bulleted list on a Title and Text slide can have multiple levels of bulleted text, and each level has a different bullet graphic. As you type the bullet text, tap the TAB key to *demote* the text to the next level or press the SHIFT + TAB keys to *promote* it to a previous level.

You want your audience to be able to quickly scan a slide and pick out the important points. So keep the text brief and limit the number of bullets on each Title and Text slide to no more than four or five first-level bullets.

Ergonomics *TIP*

Improve your posture! Sit straight at your computer and keyboard so that the B key lines up with your navel.

Starting Out!

Begin by starting the *Excel* application and opening a new, blank workbook.

1. Click the **Start** button on the task bar. start Point to **All Programs**. Point to ***Microsoft Office*** and click ***Microsoft Excel***.

If you have an icon on your desktop for *Excel*, just double-click it to open the application.

Terrific! The *Excel* application has great tools to help you solve problems and analyze data. You can calculate totals, find the smallest or largest value, sort the data into a specific order, or analyze it in a number of other ways using *Excel* tools. Let's get started!

TRAIL 1 MARKER

Naming and Saving a New Workbook

The *Excel* window looks a lot like the *Word* window with similar title bar, menu bar, Standard and Formatting toolbars, and scroll bars. But because the *Excel* application is used to solve problems and analyze data, it also has some important new features.

active cell
cell
cell reference
column
column heading
Formula Bar
Name Box
range
row
row heading
sheet tab
workbook
worksheet

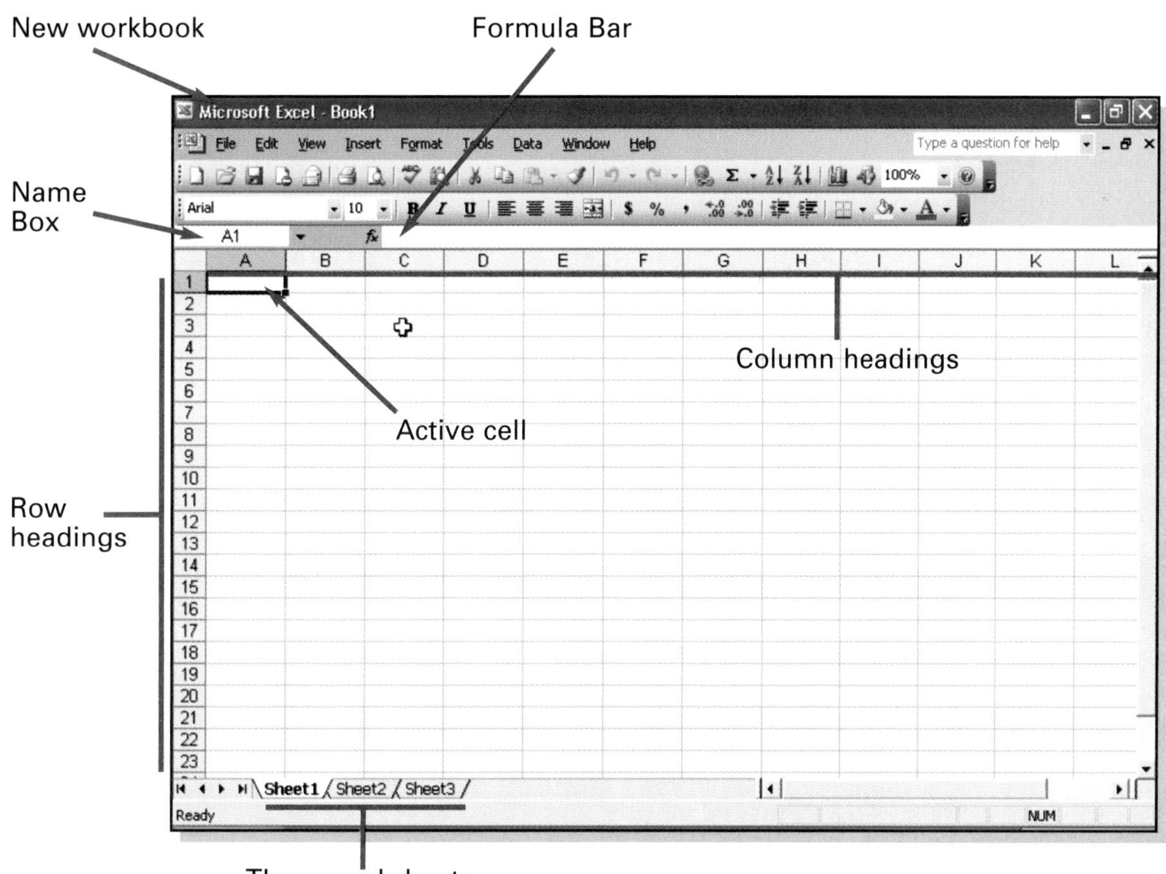

CHECKPOINT

Your Title Slide should look like this.

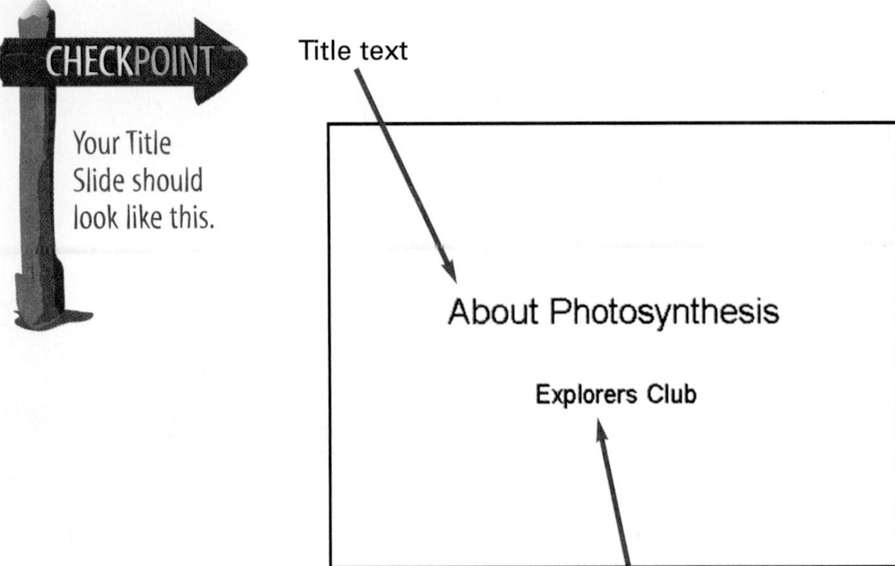

The default slide font is Arial and the default font sizes are very large. Fonts with clean lines, such as Arial, and fonts in a large size make it easier for an audience to read slides projected on a wall or projection screen.

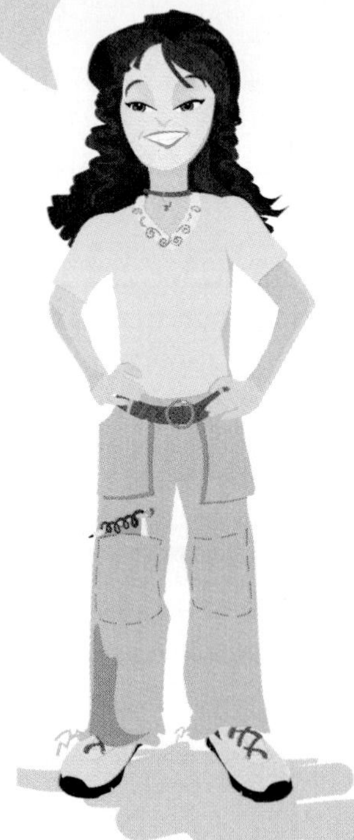

Editing and formatting placeholder text is just like editing text in a *Word* document: click in the text or use the I-beam to select it; then change the font, font size, font color, font style, and horizontal alignment using buttons on the Formatting toolbar.

Let's edit the subtitle text by adding Luis's name and changing the font size.

1. Move the I-beam pointer to the end of the *Explorers Club* text and click to position the insertion point. Tap the ENTER key to move the insertion point to the center position on the next line. Type **Luis Gonzales**.
2. Use the I-beam to select both subtitle text lines. Click the **Font Size** button drop-down arrow and click **36.** 12
3. Click in the gray slide work area outside the slide to deactivate the placeholder. Save the presentation.

Ergonomics *TIP*

Stop! Look at something at least 20 feet away from your monitor's screen for 20 seconds. Can you remember to do this every 20 minutes or so to avoid eyestrain? Great!

An *Excel* file is called a workbook, and a new blank workbook with the temporary name *Book1* opens each time you start *Excel.* A workbook is a single file, but it contains multiple pages called worksheets. By default, a new *Excel* workbook contains three worksheets named *Sheet1*, *Sheet2*, and *Sheet3*. However, a workbook can contain up to 255 worksheets! When you save a workbook, you save all the worksheets in the workbook.

A worksheet is similar to a *Word* table because it has a grid of columns and rows. Each worksheet grid is very large with 65,536 rows and 256 columns. Row headings are numbered from 1 through 65536 and they run down the left side of the worksheet. Column headings are lettered from A through IV and they run across the top of the worksheet.

The term *spreadsheet* is sometimes used interchangeably with *worksheet*; however, when you work in the *Excel* application, use the correct term—*worksheet.*

The Name Box, which shows the cell reference of the active cell, and the Formula Bar, which shows the contents of the active cell, appear immediately below the Formatting toolbar.

The intersection of a column and row is called a cell. The active cell—the cell in which you can enter text or numbers—has a dark border around it. The cell's column heading and row heading is called a cell reference. For example, the cell reference for the first cell in column A and row 1 is **A1**.

A group of adjacent cells is called a range. For example, the group of cells beginning with cell A1 and ending with cell B3 is the range **A1:B3**. You will use individual cell references or range references to enter data, select data, apply formatting, or create formulas to perform calculations on the data.

To activate a worksheet, click its sheet tab, the tab at the bottom of the screen above the status bar. The default sheet tab names for the three worksheets in a new workbook are Sheet1, Sheet2, and Sheet3. It is useful to rename each worksheet you use instead of leaving the default sheet tab name. A sheet tab name should be 32 or fewer characters (including spaces). To rename a sheet tab, double-click the sheet tab and type the new name.

To make the first or last cell in a column or row the active cell, just activate any cell in the row or column, press and hold the CTRL key, and tap an arrow key. Try it!

Adding and Editing Slide Text

Blank
placeholder
slide layout
Title and Text
Title Slide

Each slide has a specific **slide layout** with boxes, called **placeholders**, which can contain text or clip art, tables, and charts. *PowerPoint* has many different slide layouts including the **Title Slide** (title and subtitle text placeholders), **Title and Text** (title text and bulleted list placeholders), and **Blank** (no placeholders) layouts. You can view these and other slide layouts on the **Slide Layout** task pane. Open the task pane by choosing **Format** on the menu bar and choosing **Slide Layout**.

Because the first slide in a presentation usually contains the title and other introductory information such as your name, *PowerPoint* automatically applies the **Title Slide** layout to slide 1 in a new presentation.

To add the title and subtitle to slide 1, simply click inside a placeholder to position the insertion point!

Like *Word* and *Excel*, the mouse pointer becomes an I-beam pointer when placed in a text placeholder.

Apply It!

Let's add a title and subtitle to slide 1.

1. Click inside the **Click to add title** placeholder. A slanted-line border appears around the placeholder indicating the placeholder contains the insertion point. Type **About Photosynthesis**.

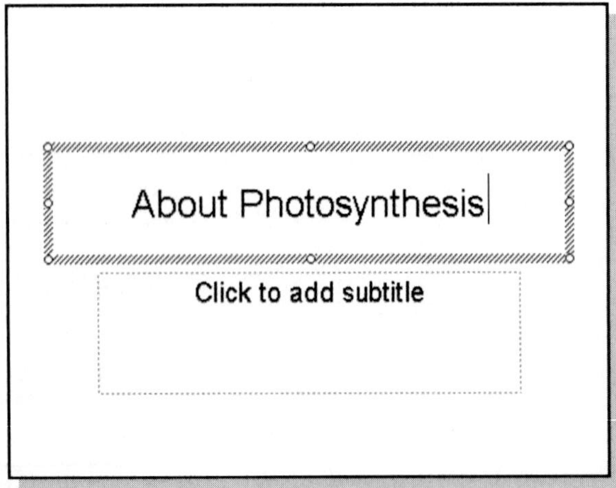
About Photosynthesis
Click to add subtitle

2. Click in the **Click to add subtitle** placeholder to make it the active placeholder and to position the insertion point. Type **Explorers Club**.
3. Click in the gray slide work area outside the slide to deactivate the placeholder. Save the presentation.

You can name and save a workbook exactly like you would a *Word* document by choosing **File** on the menu bar and choosing **Save As** or **Save** or by clicking the **Save** button on the Standard toolbar. Remember to give the workbook a file-name that is relevant to its contents.

Let's rename the *Sheet1* worksheet and save the *Book1* workbook.

1. Double-click the *Sheet1* sheet tab. Type **Five Great Oceans** and tap the ENTER key.

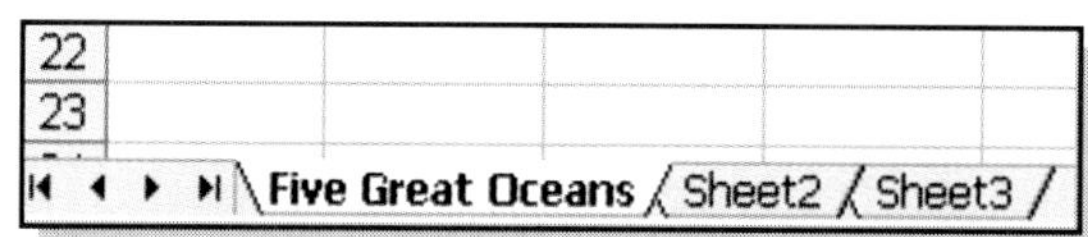

2. Click the **Save** button.
3. Switch to the folder that contains your solution files. Type *oceans7* in the **File name** text box and click the **Save** button.

Well done! You have just named a *worksheet* within a *workbook* and saved the entire workbook. Now let's look at different ways to navigate and select in a worksheet.

TRAIL 2 MARKER

Navigating and Selecting in a Worksheet

home cell

Before you can enter data in a cell, you must make it the active cell. Clicking a cell activates it. Then you can tap the TAB key or Right arrow key to activate the next cell to the right. If you want to activate the previous cell to the left, press the SHIFT + TAB keys or tap the Left arrow key. Tapping the ENTER key usually activates the next cell in the same column. Tapping the Up arrow key activates the previous cell in the same column. Pressing the CTRL + HOME keys in *Excel* makes the first cell at the top of the worksheet—A1, often called the home cell—the active cell.

Clicking a single cell, row heading, or column heading selects the contents of the cell, row, or column. To select the contents of one or more ranges, multiple rows, or multiple columns, drag across the cells, row headings, or column headings with the mouse pointer.

Just as you start with a new *Word* document and a new *Excel* workbook, each time you start *PowerPoint*, you begin with a new blank file called a **presentation**. To create a new presentation when *PowerPoint* is already open, click the **New** button on the Standard toolbar or choose **File** on the menu bar and choose **New** to open the **New Presentation** task pane.

Don't forget to use ScreenTips to identify new toolbar buttons or other *PowerPoint* screen elements!

A new, blank presentation contains one individual page, called a **slide**. You can add text, graphics, video, and even sound to a slide. You can also insert additional slides as you need them. Slides are numbered sequentially beginning with slide 1. When you save the presentation, all the slides are saved together in one file.

By default, *PowerPoint* opens in **Normal view**—the view in which you create and edit your slides. Normal view features include:

Slide pane	Add text, drawings, clip art, video, and sound to a slide
Outline tab	Create and view slides in an outline format
Slides tab	See a tiny version of each slide, called a **thumbnail**
Notes pane	Type additional comments or speaker notes about the slide
Drawing toolbar	Tools for drawing automatically displayed at the bottom of the window above the status bar
Status bar	Shows the number of the slide in the slide pane and the total number of slides in the presentation

Let's save the blank presentation with a new name. You save a *PowerPoint* presentation just like you save your *Word* documents and *Excel* workbooks.

Let's name and save the presentation.

1. Click the **Save** button. Switch to the folder that contains your solution files, type *photosynthesis11* in the **File name** text box, and click the dialog box **Save** button.

Great! Now let's add title and subtitle text to slide 1.

Apply It!

Use the SHIFT + click and CTRL + click selection methods to select adjacent and nonadjacent rows and columns. Try it!

Let's practice selecting in a worksheet.

1. Click cell **C2**, hold down the mouse button, drag across the row to cell **F2**, and then release the mouse button to select the range C2:F2.
2. Click cell **A4**, hold down the mouse button, drag down and across to cell **G13**, and then release the mouse button to select the range A4:G13.
3. Press the CTRL + HOME keys to activate cell **A1**. Press and hold the SHIFT key and click cell **F5** to select the adjacent cells in the range A1:F5.
4. Press the CTRL + HOME keys. Select the range **A1:A4**. Press and hold the CTRL key and select the range **C1:C4** to select two *nonadjacent* ranges.
5. Click the row **3** heading to select the entire row; then click the column **D** heading to select the entire column.
6. Drag across the column headings **B:D** to select multiple columns. Drag across the row headings **3:6** to select multiple rows. Tap an arrow key or click a cell to deselect the rows.

Super! Now you are ready to enter Julie's data on the world's five great oceans.

TRAIL 3 MARKER

Entering Text and Numbers

enter data
numeric keypad

You will follow a three-step process to enter data in a cell: (1) activate the cell; (2) type the text or numbers; and (3) enter the data by activating a different cell. The most common ways to enter data in a cell are by tapping the ENTER key, the TAB key, or an arrow key.

Text automatically aligns at the left side of a cell. Numbers automatically align at the right side of a cell. You can change this alignment using the alignment buttons on the Formatting toolbar.

Starting Out!

Begin by starting the *PowerPoint* application and opening a new, blank presentation.

1. Click the **Start** button on the task bar, point to **All Programs**, point to ***Microsoft Office***, and click ***Microsoft PowerPoint***.

Good job! The *PowerPoint* application has great tools you can use to present facts and ideas to an audience. Let's begin by naming and saving Luis's presentation.

If you have an icon on your desktop for *PowerPoint*, just double-click it to open the application.

Creating, Naming, and Saving a New Presentation

Normal view
notes pane
Outline tab
presentation
slide
slide pane
Slides tab
thumbnail

Look carefully at the *PowerPoint* window. *PowerPoint* shares many window elements with *Word* and *Excel*, such as the Standard and Formatting toolbars and the menu bar. Many of the toolbar buttons and menus work the same in *PowerPoint* as they do in *Word* or *Excel*, including the **Open**, **Save**, **Print Preview** buttons and the **Save As** command on the **File** menu. Other toolbar buttons, commands, and features are designed specifically for working in *PowerPoint*.

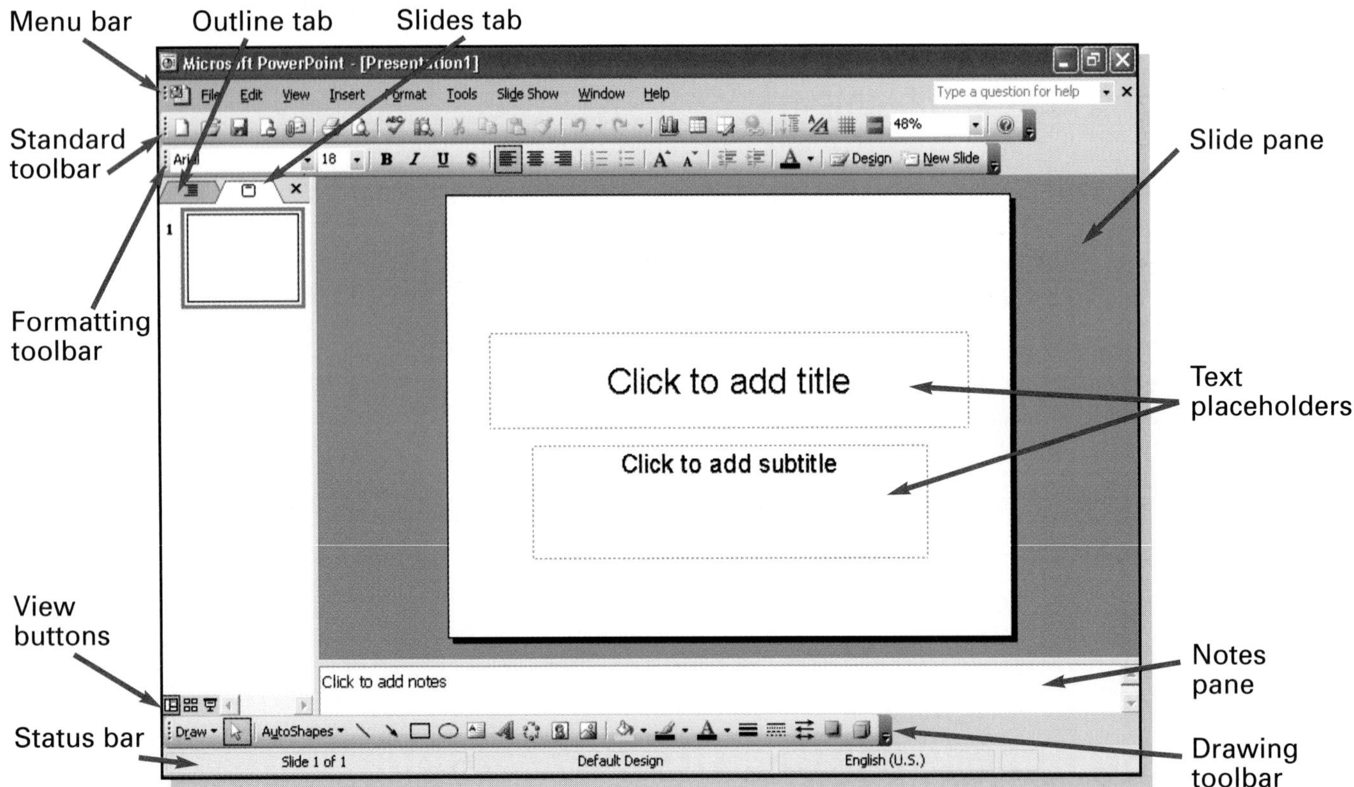

Here are Julie's notes about the world's great oceans.

The World's Oceans

Ocean Name	Area in Sq. Miles	Deepest Point in Feet
Pacific	60,060,700	36,198
Atlantic	29,637,900	30,246
Indian	26,469,500	24,460
Southern	7,848,300	23,736
Arctic	5,427,000	18,456

"Oceans and Seas," Infoplease.com. © 2003 Family Education Network. June 14, 2004. http://www.infoplease.com/ipa/A0001773.html (accessed January 13, 2006).

First, you will enter the title in cell A1 and then enter the column names and the data. Do not worry about how the text and numbers look in the cells. You will format the worksheet to make it easier to read and more attractive in the next Trail Marker.

Let's enter the worksheet title, column names, and the data.

1. Click cell **A1** to activate it and type **The World's Oceans**. Tap the ENTER key twice to activate cell **A3**.
2. Type **Ocean Name** and tap the Right arrow key. Type **Area in Sq. Miles** and tap the Right arrow key. Type **Deepest Point in Feet** and tap the ENTER key.

Now let's enter the names of the oceans. Remember, tapping the ENTER key after you type text or numbers enters the data in the cell and usually makes the *next cell in the column* the active cell.

3. Click cell **A4**; then type **Pacific** and tap the ENTER key. Type **Atlantic** and tap the ENTER key. Type **Indian** and tap the ENTER key. Type **Southern** and tap the ENTER key. Type **Arctic** and tap the ENTER key.

Nicely done! Now let's enter the square miles and feet data. Instead of typing the numbers using the top row of the keyboard, use the numeric keypad on the right side of your keyboard. It is much faster! As you type the square miles and feet data, do not type the commas. You will add the commas in the next Trail Marker.

Project 11

Presentations and Multimedia

Understanding Photosynthesis

Explorers' Guide

Data file: *none*

Objectives:

In this project, you will:

- create, name, and save a new presentation
- add and edit slide text
- insert new slides
- apply a design template
- use Slide Sorter view and run a slide show
- preview and print a presentation

Exploring on Your Own

additional practice in:

- creating, naming, and saving a presentation
- adding and editing slide text
- inserting new slides
- applying a design template
- using Slide Sorter view and running a slide show
- previewing and printing a presentation

Exploring Across the Curriculum

Internet/Web
Language Arts
Science
Getting Help
Your Personal Journal

Our Exploration Assignment:

Creating a slide show presentation about photosynthesis

Did you know plants use sunlight or artificial light to make their own food in a process called photosynthesis? Luis is preparing a presentation about photosynthesis. Help Luis with his presentation on photosynthesis by following the Trail Markers to create, name, and save a new slide show; add and edit slide text; insert new slides; apply a design template; view slides in Slide Sorter view; run a slide show; and then preview and print the slides.

4. Tap the NUM LOCK key, if necessary, to turn on the numeric keypad. The light near the NUM LOCK key will be turned on.
5. Click cell **B4**;, then type **60060700** and tap the Right arrow key. Type **36198** and tap the Down arrow key.
6. Continue to use the numeric keypad and the ENTER or arrow keys to enter the remaining square miles and feet data using Julie's notes as your guide. Save the workbook.

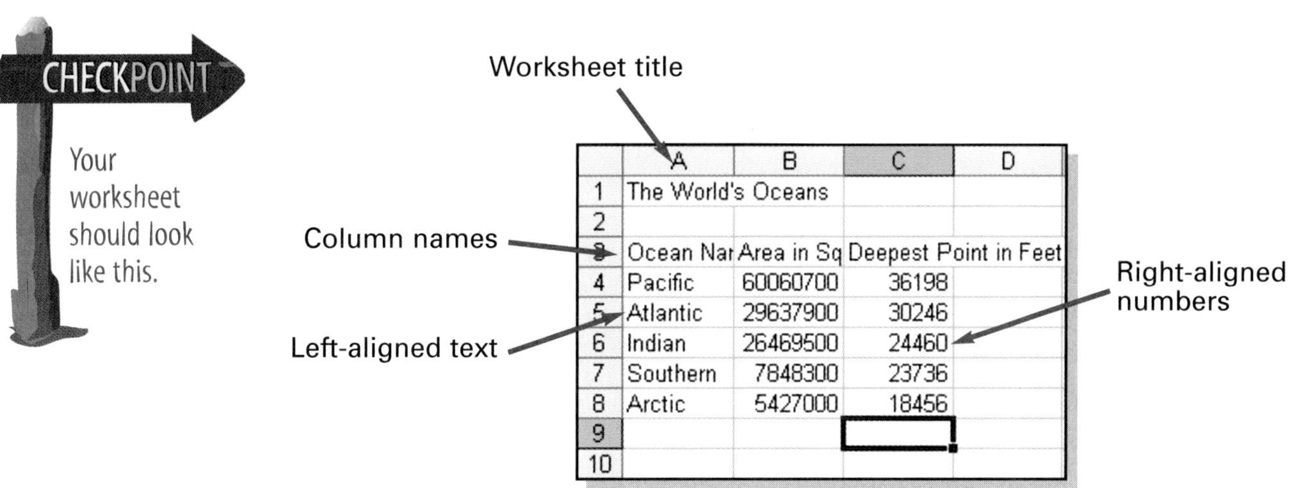

	A	B	C	D
1	The World's Oceans			
2				
3	Ocean Nar	Area in Sq	Deepest Point in Feet	
4	Pacific	60060700	36198	
5	Atlantic	29637900	30246	
6	Indian	26469500	24460	
7	Southern	7848300	23736	
8	Arctic	5427000	18456	
9				
10				

Tap the numbers on the numeric keypad just like you do on a calculator. You can also tap the ENTER key on the numeric keypad.

What a great job! You are ready to format the worksheet to make it easier to read.

TRAIL 4 MARKER

Formatting a Worksheet

merge
text wrapping

Formatting cell contents in *Excel* is much like formatting text in *Word.* You can change the font or font size and align the contents inside the cell using the same Formatting toolbar buttons you used in *Word.* But the *Excel* Formatting toolbar also has additional buttons designed to apply formatting to numbers or to center cell contents across a range.

Presentations & Multimedia

Unit 3

Welcome back! The Explorers Club is delving into the world of science and has many new interesting adventures planned for this session. Come with us to:

* **Understand Photosynthesis**
* **Investigate Volcanoes**
* **Describe the Scientific Method**
* **Make Sourdough Bread**
* **Explore the Mind of Leonardo**

Science comes alive when you create slide shows to present your information. You will learn how to use an application called *PowerPoint* to create slide shows that will capture the attention of your audience. *PowerPoint* has lots of templates that you can use or customize with your own color schemes and backgrounds. You will add animations and transitions, and insert sound, motion clips, and clip art to make your slides interesting and fun. You will also create audience handouts to accompany your slide show. You will even learn how to paste data from an *Excel* worksheet into a *PowerPoint* slide! Let's go!

Merging Cells, Wrapping Text, and Applying Font Styles

The **Merge and Center** button on the Formatting toolbar allows you to merge a range of cells into one cell and then center the contents of the upper-left-most cell in the range. To apply other formatting options, such as text wrapping inside cells, choose **Format** on the menu bar and choose **Cells** to open the **Format Cells** dialog box.

Let's make the *Five Great Oceans* worksheet easier to read and more attractive by centering the title text across the top of the worksheet, wrapping and centering the column names within each cell, applying the Bold font style to the title and column names, and applying the Italic font style to the ocean names.

Apply It!

Let's format the title text, column names, and ocean names.

1. Select the range **A1:C1** and click the **Merge and Center** and **Bold** buttons. The three cells in the range are merged into one cell and the worksheet title is bolded and centered in the cell.
2. Select the range **A3:C3**. Click the **Center** and **Bold** buttons.
3. Verify that the range **A3:C3** is still selected. Choose **Format** on the menu bar and choose **Cells** to open the **Format Cells** dialog box. Click the **Alignment** tab. Click the **Wrap text** checkbox to insert a check mark and click the **OK** button. The column names are wrapped in each cell and *Excel* automatically adjusts the row height.
4. Select the range **A4:A8** and click the **Italic** button. Press the CTRL + HOME keys and save the workbook.

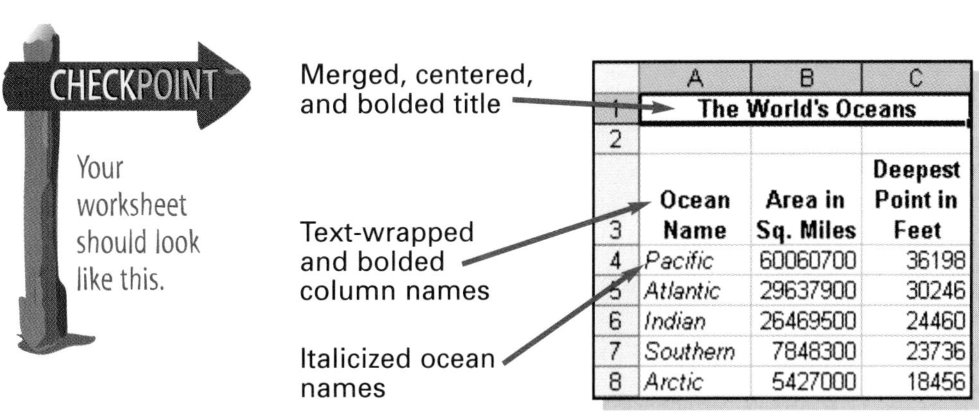

Fantastic! Let's add commas (thousand separators) to the square miles and feet data.

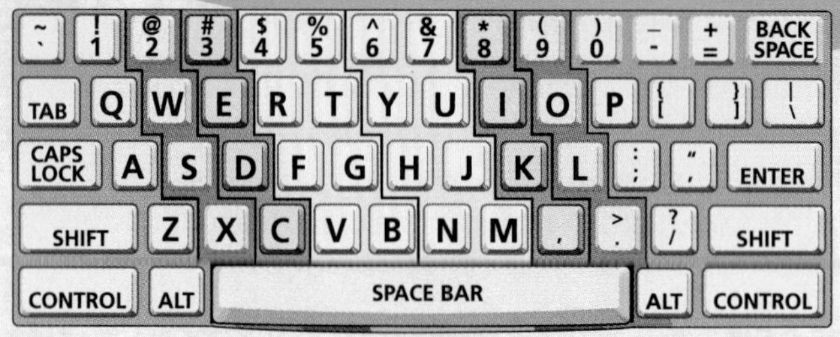

10a Build Skill

Key each line twice. Double-space between 2-line groups.

All the movement should be in the fingers; the hands and arms should not be moving as you key.

balanced-hand sentences

1 I may pay the maid when she signs the right forms.

2 Sign the form so the auditor may pay for the work.

3 It is their duty to fix the bicycle for the girls.

4 He may lend the map to us to do the work for them.

5 Send the forms to them at the address on the card.

6 If they do the work, he may spend the day with me.

7 The firm kept half of them busy with the hem work.

8 Ruth and I may handle the problems for their firm.

10b Build Skill: Paragraphs

Key the text at the right. Key the text again, trying to increase the rate at which you key the text.

Your reputation is what others think about the way you choose to live your life. It is all about your ethical and moral values. In other words are you fair, honest, and just in your dealings with other people? A good reputation is priceless. Your reputation should be one of your most prized possessions.

A good reputation requires time, effort, and discipline to develop and protect. However, a bad reputation can be acquired in a short period of time. It can result from just one misdeed and can be a heavy burden to carry the rest of your life. What are you doing to build and protect your reputation?

Applying the Comma, Currency, or Percent Styles

The *Excel* Formatting toolbar also has **Comma Style**, **Currency Style**, and **Percent Style** buttons. Use these buttons to format a range of numbers with dollar signs, commas, percent signs, and decimal places. You can increase and decrease the number of decimal places in the cells by clicking the **Increase Decimal** or **Decrease Decimal** buttons.

Let's apply the Comma Style with no decimal places to the square miles and feet data.

1. Select the range **B4:C8** and click the **Comma Style** button. ,

   Thousands separators and two decimal places are added to the numbers in the range.
2. Click the **Decrease Decimal** button twice. .00→.0 The two decimal places are removed.
3. Press the CTRL + HOME keys. Save the workbook.

CHECKPOINT

Your completed worksheet should look like this.

Numbers formatted with Comma Style and no decimal places

	A	B	C
1	The World's Oceans		
2			
3	Ocean Name	Area in Sq Miles	Deepest Point in Feet
4	*Pacific*	60,060,700	36,198
5	*Atlantic*	29,637,900	30,246
6	*Indian*	26,469,500	24,460
7	*Southern*	7,848,300	23,736
8	*Arctic*	5,427,000	18,456

Excellent! Now you need to let *Excel* automatically adjust the column widths to fit the cell contents.

Exploring Across the Curriculum

Science: Research and Write

Easter Island, sometimes called the Navel of the World, lies about 2,300 miles off the western coast of Chile. Use classroom, library, or online resources and data in the *Oceania10* workbook to learn about Easter Island. Who first settled the island and when? What is known about their language and customs? How did the settlement impact the ecology of the island? What mysterious feature of Easter Island continues to puzzle scientists? What is the status of Easter Island today? Take notes about what you learn from your research. Create a new *Word* document and type your notes as a properly formatted three-level outline.

Getting Help

Type **data table** in the **Ask A Question** box and tap the ENTER key. Research data tables and how to show or hide a data table on a chart. Then using what you have learned, open the *Oceania10* workbook, select a chart, and show and hide a data table on the chart. Close the workbook without saving it.

Your Personal Journal

Open your personal journal document. Insert today's date and two blank lines. Think about what you have learned about the continent and islands of Oceania. Choose one island that you would like to visit. Write a descriptive paragraph about the island's scenery. Use exact words that help you visualize the island's natural beauty. Spell-check, save, and close your journal.

Online Enrichment Games (Fun Stuff)  www.lwcgreen.keyboarding.com

Resizing Columns and Rows

To change the column width or row height, drag a column or boundary with the resizing pointer. As you drag the boundary, a ScreenTip shows the current column width or row height.

A quick way to resize a column is to double-click a column's right boundary with the resizing pointer. *Excel* then resizes the column automatically to fit the contents of the longest cell.

You can change column widths by choosing **Format** on the menu bar, pointing to **Column**, and choosing **Width**.

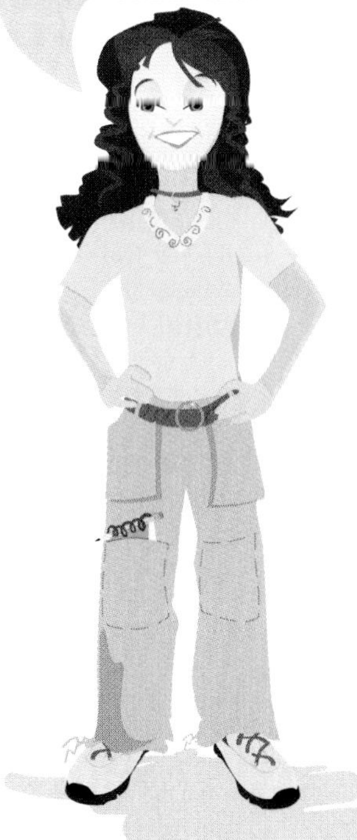

Apply It!

Let's let *Excel* automatically resize columns A–C to fit the cell contents.

1. Drag across the column headings *A:C* to select all three columns. Move the mouse pointer to the boundary between the column **C** and column **D** headings.
2. Double-click the boundary between the column **C** and column **D** headings to have *Excel* automatically resize the columns. Press the CTRL + HOME keys and save the workbook.

CHECKPOINT
Your worksheet should look like this.

Columns sized to fit cell contents

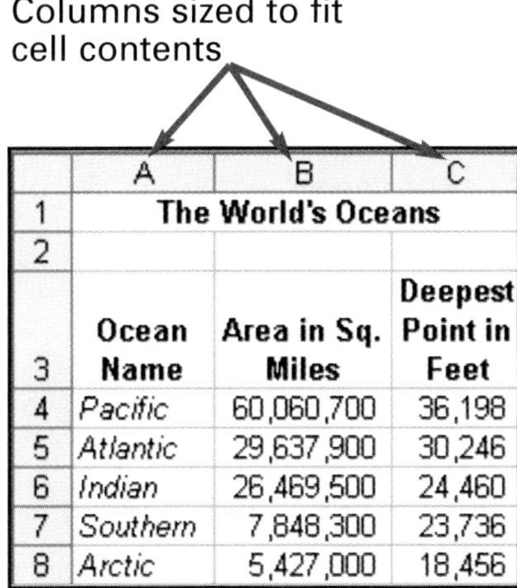

	A	B	C
1	The World's Oceans		
2			
3	Ocean Name	Area in Sq. Miles	Deepest Point in Feet
4	Pacific	60,060,700	36,198
5	Atlantic	29,637,900	30,246
6	Indian	26,469,500	24,460
7	Southern	7,848,300	23,736
8	Arctic	5,427,000	18,456

Good work! Placing your data in a worksheet allows you to use *Excel*'s powerful data analysis tools. For example, let's see how easy it is to reorganize the data on the *Five Great Oceans* worksheet using *Excel*'s sorting features.

Exploring Across the Curriculum

Internet/Web

The island in Oceania that has the smallest population also has one of the most famous histories. Open your Web browser and use a favorite to view the Learning with Computers Web page (www.lwcgreen.keyboarding.com). Click the **Links** option. Click **Project 10**. Click the **CIA World Factbook** link and use the website to learn more about Pitcairn Island. Use the Google link to search for additional information about the original European settlement of Pitcairn Island. Take notes about what you learn from the websites and the data in the *Oceania10* workbook.

Then create a new *Word* document and save it as *Pitcairn Island10*. Write a multi-page bound report with a cover sheet describing the European settlement of Pitcairn Island. Use endnotes to cite your sources. Save and close the document.

Language Arts: Words to Know

Look up the meaning of the following names, phrases, and terms using a classroom, library, CD-ROM, or online encyclopedia or dictionary.

atoll	coral	endemic	extinction
indigenous	subtropical	temperate	volcanic

Create a new workbook. Save the workbook as *definitions10*. Rename the Sheet1 sheet tab as **Definitions**. Enter the title **Oceania Definitions** in cell A1. Merge and center the title across the range **A1:B1**. Enter **Term** as the column name in **A3**. Enter **Definition** as the column name in **B3**. Bold the title and column names. Center the column names in the cells.

Enter the terms in the range **A4:A11**. Enter the definitions in the range **B4:B11**. Use the resizing pointer to automatically fit the cell contents for columns A and B. Save and close the workbook.

Explore More

Sorting Data

Sorting means to put text and numbers in ascending order (from A to Z or 0 to 9) or descending order (from Z to A or 9 to 0). To quickly sort data by a single column, activate a cell in a column *inside the data range* you want to sort and click the **Sort Ascending** or **Sort Descending** button.

ascending order
descending order

Let's sort the data in the range A3:C8 in ascending order by ocean name and then in descending order by area.

1. Click cell **A4** and click the **Sort Ascending** button. *Excel* selects all the data in the range A3:C8 and sorts it in ascending order by ocean name. Each ocean's area and depth data is rearranged along with its name.

	A	B	C
1	The World's Oceans		
2			
3	Ocean Name	Area in Sq. Miles	Deepest Point in Feet
4	*Arctic*	5,427,000	18,456
5	*Atlantic*	29,637,900	30,246
6	*Indian*	26,469,500	24,460
7	*Pacific*	60,060,700	36,198
8	*Southern*	7,848,300	23,736

2. Click cell **B6** and click the **Sort Descending** button. *Excel* selects all the data in the range A3:C8 and sorts it in descending order by area—its original order. Press the CTRL + HOME keys and save the workbook.

Your worksheet looks great! Let's preview and print it!

Exploring on Your Own

Math in Action

Finding the Slope of a Line

In math, the slope is a number that tells you how steep a line is. To calculate the slope of a line, pick two points on the line. The slope equals the vertical change (the change in *y*) divided by the horizontal change (the change in *x*). To find the vertical change, you will subtract the *y*-coordinates of the two points (shown in red). To find the horizontal change, you will subtract the *x*-coordinates.

The projected population growth of Hawaii between the years 2005 and 2020 is shown in the graph below. The years are the *x*-coordinates, and the population numbers are the *y*-coordinates. Here is how to find the slope of the line between the years 2005 and 2010:

$$\text{slope} = \frac{\text{change in } y}{\text{change in } x} = \frac{(1{,}367{,}000 - 1{,}304{,}000)}{(2010 - 2005)} =$$

$$\frac{63{,}000 \text{ people}}{5 \text{ years}} = \frac{12{,}6000 \text{ people}}{\text{year}}$$

This positive slope tells you that the population was going up at a rate of 12,500 people per year. If the slope were negative, it would indicate that the population was decreasing over time.

Now you try it!

What is the slope of the line between 2015 and 2020 for Guam? What is the slope of the line for the population of American Samoa between 2010 and 2015?

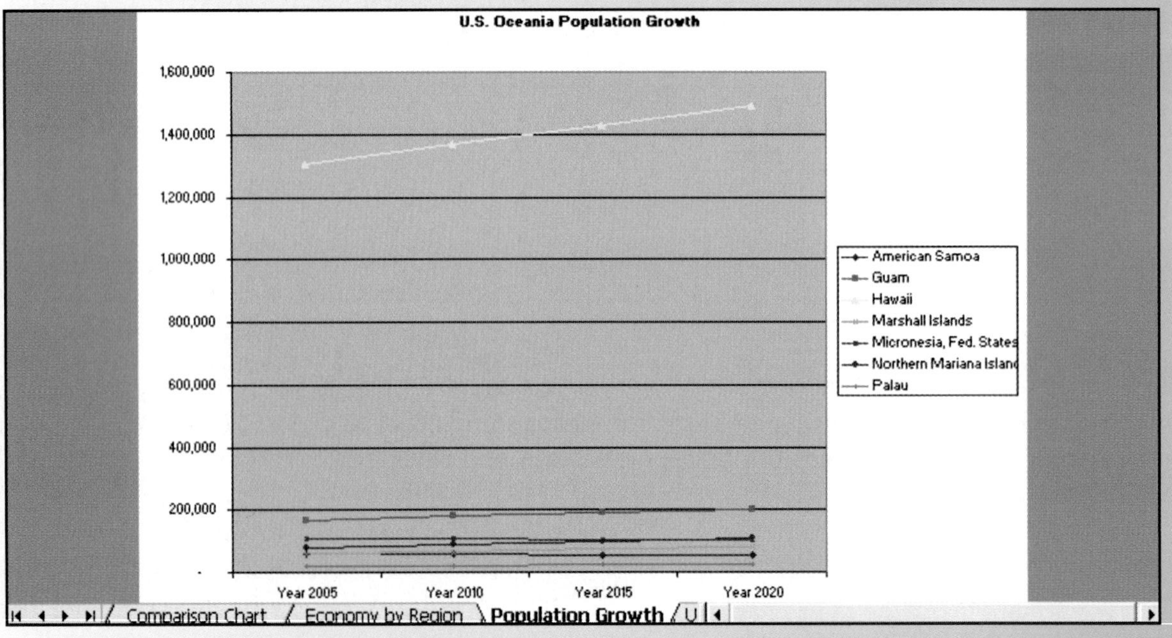

TRAIL 6 MARKER

Previewing and Printing a Worksheet

Use the same menu commands or toolbar buttons to preview and print a worksheet as you used to preview and print a *Word* document. However, unlike a *Word* document, it is usually better to preview a worksheet *before* you change its page layout. To change a worksheet's page setup options as you preview it, click the **Setup** button on the Print Preview toolbar to open the **Page Setup** dialog box.

Use options in the **Page Setup** dialog box to change the margins, center data both horizontally and vertically on the page, resize data by scaling it up or down to fit better on the page, set page orientation, print worksheet gridlines, print column and row headings, and add headers and footers.

Click the **Header/Footer** tab in the **Page Setup** dialog box to add headers and footers. *Excel* includes some common headers and footers that you can select and insert. Click the **Header** or **Footer** button drop-down arrows to see them. If you want to use specific text in the header or footer, click the **Custom Header** or **Custom Footer** buttons and then type text or insert a date or a page number.

Because the *Five Great Oceans* worksheet data covers a small area of the worksheet, let's scale it to print larger on the page, change the page orientation to Landscape, center the data horizontally and vertically on the page, and add a custom header and a predefined footer. ***Remember to ask your teacher before you print any worksheets in this unit!***

You can also view the **Header/Footer** tab in the **Page Setup** dialog box by choosing **View** on the menu bar and choosing **Header and Footer.** Try it!

Let's preview the *Five Great Oceans* worksheet, change page setup options, and then print the worksheet.

1. Click the **Print Preview** button.
2. Click the **Setup** button and then click the **Page** tab in the **Page Setup** dialog box. Setup...
3. Type **300** in the **Adjust to** text box to scale the data 300% larger, and click the **Landscape** option.
4. Click the **Margins** tab and click the **Center on page Horizontally** and **Vertically** check boxes to center the data between the margins.
5. Click the **Header/Footer** tab and click the **Custom Header** button to open the **Header** dialog box. This dialog box has three header areas for a left-aligned header, a center-aligned header, and a right-aligned header. Find the ten formatting buttons above the header areas.

Exploring on Your Own

You have learned several new skills in this project. Now blaze your own trail by practicing these skills on your own! Open the *Oceania10* workbook and insert a new worksheet named *Independent Islands*. Click the *Oceania* sheet tab. Sort the data by Country Association in ascending alphabetical order. Then insert temporary subtotals for the size, population, imports, and exports data for each region by country of association.

Copy the range **B4:L5** on the *Oceania* worksheet and paste it on the *Independent Islands* worksheet beginning in cell **A1**. Copy the range **B12:L18** on the *Oceania* worksheet and paste it on the *Independent Islands* worksheet beginning in cell **A6**. Delete column E, the per capita GDP data. Resize the columns or rows as necessary to create an attractive and easy-to-read worksheet. Remove the temporary subtotals from the *Oceania* worksheet and return the data to its original order.

Click the *Independent Islands* worksheet and create two charts. First, use the Chart Wizard to create an embedded pie chart with the subtype of your choice to show the percentage of each island's population to the total population. Reposition and resize the embedded chart below the data. Move the legend below the pie chart and resize it to fit across the bottom. Then use the F11 key to create a column chart on its own chart sheet that compares the import and export data for the independent islands. Name the chart sheet *Independent Economy*. (*Hint:* Your chart data selections will be nonadjacent ranges that include the column names and the columns that contain the data to be charted.)

Format one chart to change data marker colors and add data labels and a chart title. Insert any clip art you want on the worksheet. Use the drawing tools to draw and format an AutoShape with text or a text box on the chart sheet. Save and close the workbook.

Reading in Action

Using Prefixes and Root Words

Knowing the meaning of prefixes and root words can help you figure out the meanings of words. For example, knowing that the prefix *in-* means "not" and that the Latin root word *temperare* means "to moderate" can help you figure out that the word *intemperate* means "not moderate" or "excessive." Use the meaning of the prefixes and root words to help you define the words in the next column. Use a dictionary if you need help.

export import semi-arid subtropic

Prefix	Root Word
ex meaning "out"	+ *portare* meaning "to carry"
im meaning "into, toward"	+ *portare* meaning "to carry"
semi meaning "half, partly"	+ *aridus* meaning "dry"
sub meaning "under"	+ *tropicus* meaning "of the solstice"

Explore More

6. Type your name in the left-aligned header area and tap the TAB key twice to move the insertion point to the right-aligned header area. Click the **Insert Date** button above the header area. Click the **OK** button to close the **Header** dialog box.
7. Click the **Footer** button drop-down arrow and click the *oceans7.xls* filename from the list of predefined footer options. Click the **OK** button to close the **Page Setup** dialog box.

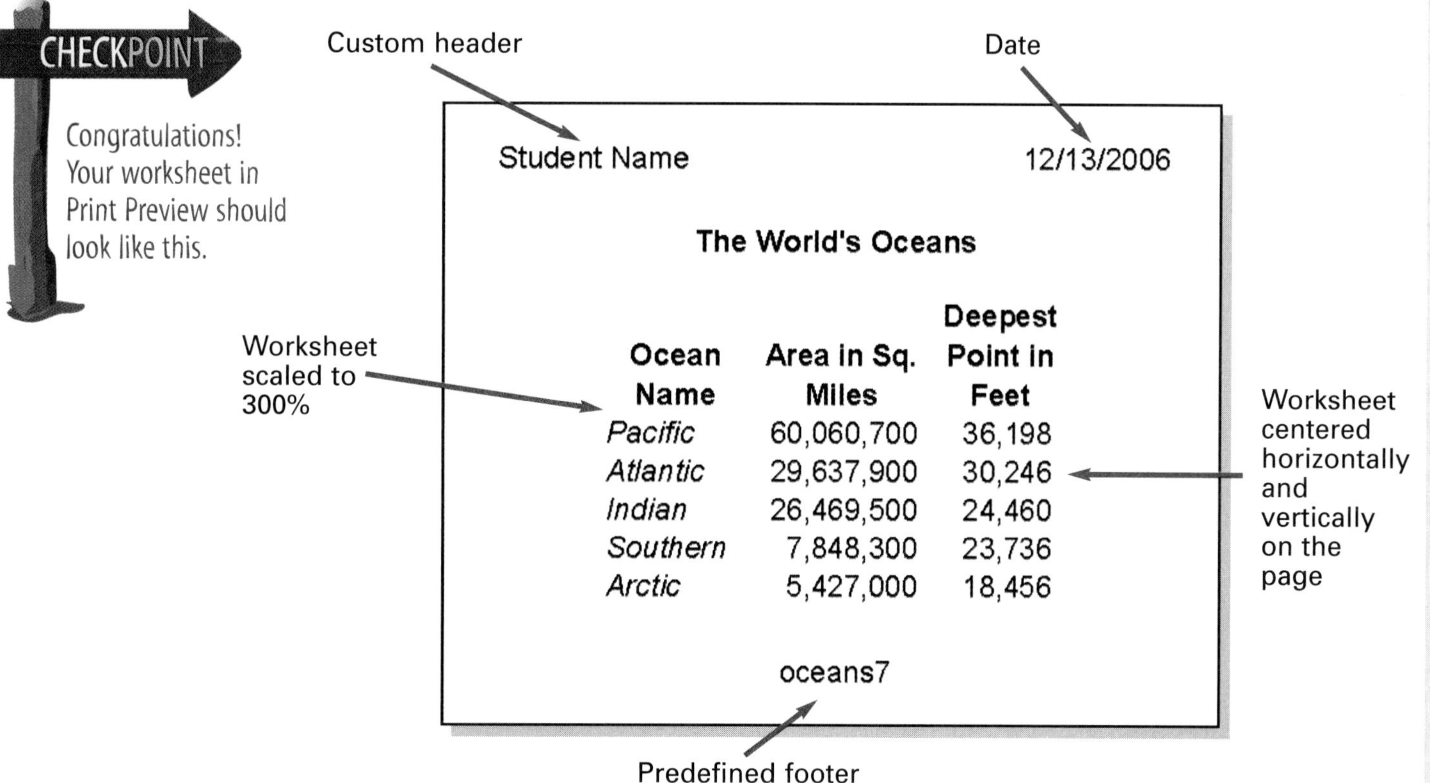

8. With permission, click the **Print** button. Print... Then save and close the workbook and close the *Excel* application.

Project | *Skills Review*

You learned a lot in this project! We are very impressed with your progress. Let's take a few minutes to review the skills that you learned.

Add and remove temporary subtotals	Choose **Data** on the menu bar and choose **Subtotals**.
Start the Chart Wizard	Select the data range or ranges and then choose **Insert** on the menu bar and choose **Chart**.
Change chart options	Choose **Chart** on the menu bar and choose **Chart Options**.
Display the Chart toolbar	Choose **View** on the menu bar, point to **Toolbars**, and choose **Chart**.
Select a chart object	Chart Area
Open the chart object's formatting dialog box	Right-click the chart element and choose **Format** (chart element). Double-click the chart element.
Change the chart type	Choose **Chart** on the menu bar and choose **Chart Type**.
Create a default column chart on its own sheet	Tap the F11 key.
Remove worksheet gridlines	Choose **Tools** on the menu bar, choose **Options**, and click **View** tab.

Project | *Skills Review*

You learned a lot in this project! We are very impressed with your progress. Let's take a few minutes to review the skills that you learned.

Activate a cell	Tap or press the ENTER, TAB, SHIFT + TAB, or arrow keys
Merge a range of cells and center the first cell's contents across the range	Choose **Format** on the menu bar and choose **Cells**.
Align cell contents within the cell	Choose **Format** on the menu bar and choose **Cells**.
Apply the Bold, Italic, or Underline font styles	Choose **Format** on the menu bar and choose **Cells**. B I U
Apply currency, percent, comma, and decimal formatting to numbers	Choose **Format** on the menu bar and choose **Cells**. $ % ,
Save a workbook	Choose **File** on the menu bar and choose **Save As** or **Save**.
Sort worksheet data	Choose **Data** on the menu bar and choose **Sort**.
Preview and print a worksheet	
Change page setup options	Setup...

Let's remove the gridlines and insert a map picture.

1. Click the *Map of Oceania* sheet tab, choose **Tools** on the menu bar, and choose **Options** to open the **Options** dialog box. Then click the **View** tab, if necessary, click the **Gridlines** checkbox to remove the check mark, and click the **OK** button. The gridlines are removed from the worksheet.
2. Display the Drawing toolbar, if necessary, and click the **Insert Picture From File** button. Open the folder that contains your data files and double-click the *oceania.jpg* filename to insert a picture of the Oceania map. Drag the map down about 1 inch and to the right about 0.5 inch and deselect it.

Fantastic! Now let's add a notation to the U.S. Oceania Population Growth chart and cite the source of the map clip art using the drawing tools.

3. Click the *Population Growth* chart sheet. Draw the non-line AutoShape *of your choice* below and to the right of the Hawaii line on the chart. Right-click the AutoShape and choose **Add Text**. Type **Hawaii has the largest population growth!** and tap the ESC key. Fill the AutoShape with the yellow color. Reposition it and resize it, if necessary. Deselect the AutoShape.

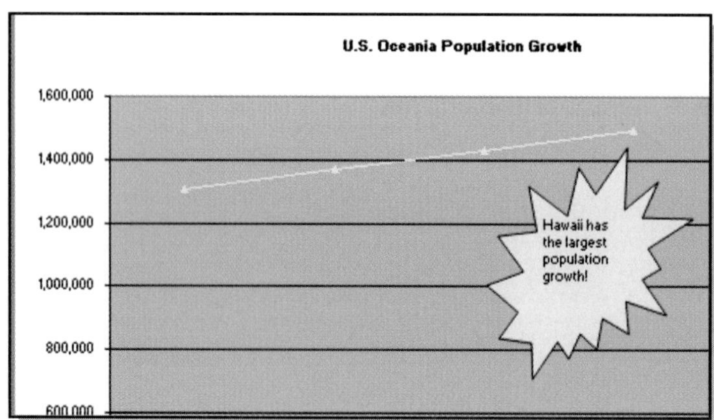

4. Click the *Map of Oceania* sheet tab and draw a text box above the map. Type the following citation in the text box.

   "The World Factbook," ***CIA*****, May 11, 2004,** **http://www.cia.gov/cia/publications/factbook/reference_maps/oceania.html (accessed today's date).**

5. Resize the text box as necessary. Format the URL with the blue font color and italicize the CIA website name. Then save and close the workbook.

You can preview and print a chart on its own sheet just as you do a worksheet. To preview and print an embedded chart without the accompanying worksheet, first select the embedded chart.

Exploring on Your Own

You have learned several new skills in this project. Now blaze your own trail by practicing these skills on your own! Open the *oceans7* workbook. Click the *Sheet2* tab to activate the worksheet. Change the sheet tab name to **Ocean Facts**. Use the following notes to add a title, column names, and data to the worksheet beginning in cell A1.

Ocean Facts

Ocean	Larger than U.S.	Coastline in Miles	Economy
Pacific	15.0 times	84,301	fishing, oil, gas
Atlantic	6.5 times	69,514	fishing, oil, gas
Indian	5.5 times	41,339	fishing, oil, gas
Southern	2.0 times	11,615	fishing
Arctic	1.5 times	28,205	fishing, sealing, oil, gas

Merge and center the title over columns A:D. Center the column names, wrap the column names in the cells, and apply the Bold style to the title and column names. Italicize the ocean names. Right-align the cells that contain the size comparison to the U.S. Apply the Comma Style with no decimal places to the miles data. Fit the column widths to the cell contents. Sort the data in ascending alphabetical order by ocean name.

Preview the worksheet and open the **Page Setup** dialog box. Change the page orientation to Landscape and change the scale to 200% so that the data will print larger on the page. Center the data horizontally and vertically on the page. Add your name and today's date as a custom header and the filename as a predefined footer. With your teacher's permission, print the worksheet. Save and close the workbook.

Explore More

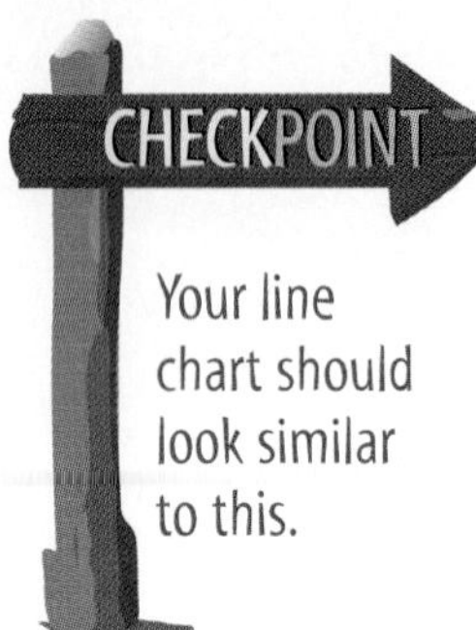

CHECKPOINT
Your line chart should look similar to this.

Line chart

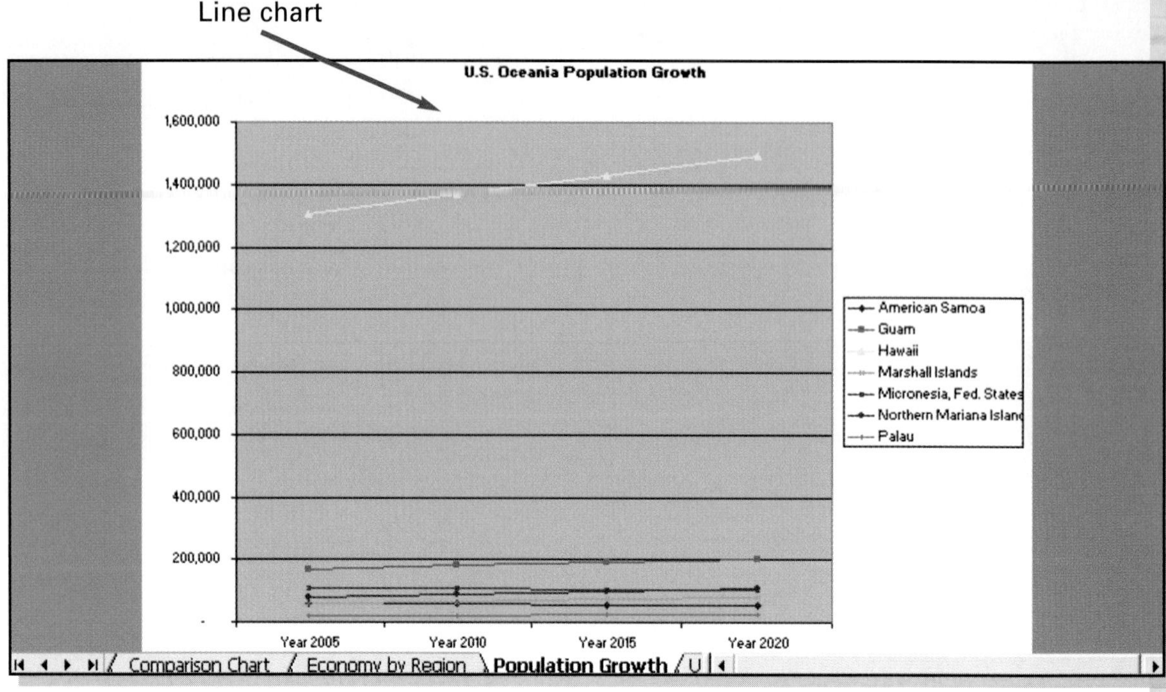

Well done! Now let's insert a map of Oceania on the *Map of Oceania* worksheet and add a text box to cite our sources.

Inserting a Picture and Using the Drawing Tools

You insert graphic images such as clip art or pictures on a worksheet just like you do in a *Word* document. Before you insert a graphic into a worksheet, you can change the worksheet so that you do not see the gridlines around the cells. Let's turn off the view of gridlines in the *Map of Oceania* worksheet to make it easier to see the map.

Exploring on Your Own

Reading in Action

Using Word Derivations

The formation of a word from another word or word root is called a derivation. The Atlantic Ocean was named after Atlas, a strong giant from Greek mythology who supported the heavens with his head and hands. Use a dictionary or what you already know about related words to find the word derivations of the Arctic, Pacific, Indian, and Southern oceans.

Ocean	Derivation and Meaning
Arctic	
Pacific	
Indian	
Southern	

Math in Action

Using Proportions

Earth is covered by about 140,000,000 miles^2 of water, which is 71 percent of Earth's total surface. How large is Earth's surface? Use proportions to solve the problem.

Let s = the total surface area of Earth

Since 140,000,000 is 71 percent of Earth's surface area, we can state the following proportion:

$\frac{140000000}{s} = \frac{71}{100} = (140{,}000{,}000 \times 100) \div 71s$

$= 197{,}183{,}090\ s$

Earth's surface area is approximately 197,000,000 miles^2.

Now you try it!

The United States covers 3,500,000 miles^2, about 6.1 percent of Earth's land surface area. Use proportions to find the surface area of all the land on Earth.

The United States is about 11.8 percent the size of the Atlantic Ocean. Use proportions to find the surface area of the Atlantic Ocean.

Creating and Formatting a Line Chart

line chart

A line chart is used to compare data over a period of time. You can create a line chart on its own chart sheet by using the Chart Wizard or by tapping the F11 key. When you use the F11 key, *Excel* creates a default column chart so you will need to change the chart type to a line chart.

Let's compare the population growth of islands in Oceania by creating a column chart using the F11 key and then change it to a line chart. The data is on the *U.S. Oceania* worksheet.

1. Click the *U.S. Oceania* sheet tab, select the range **A5:E12**, and tap the F11 key. *Excel* creates a default column chart on its own sheet. Rename the chart sheet **Population Growth**.
2. Choose **Chart** on the menu bar and choose **Chart Options**. Click the **Titles** tab, type **U.S. Oceania Population Growth** in the **Chart title** text box, and click the **OK** button. Tap the ESC key to deselect the chart title object.
3. Click the **Chart Type** button drop-down arrow on the Chart toolbar and click the **Line Chart** option (the fourth option in the first column).

You can also change the chart type by choosing **Chart** on the menu bar and choosing **Chart Type**.

Excel changes the column chart to a line chart with the island names on the category (x) axis and the data in the *columns* orientation. However, we want the years on the category (x) axis and the data in the *rows* orientation.

4. Click the **By Row** button to change the orientation of the data to rows instead of columns. Save the workbook.

Exploring Across the Curriculum

Internet/Web

You can learn about potential marine science or maritime careers on the Web. Open your Web browser and use a favorite to view the Learning with Computers Web page (www.lwcgreen.keyboarding.com). Click the **Links** option. Click **Project 7**. Click the links to research possible marine science or maritime careers and average annual salaries. Take notes on at least five different marine science or maritime careers that interest you.

Then create a new workbook and save it as *careers7*. Rename the *Sheet1* sheet tab **Salaries**. Enter **Maritime and Marine Science Careers** in cell A1. Merge and center the title across the range *A1:C1* and then bold it. Enter the column headings **Career** in cell A3, **Annual Salary** in cell B3, and **Description** in cell C3. Enter the career name, annual salary, and description data from your notes, beginning with cell A4. Italicize the career names and format the salary data with the Currency Style and no decimal places. Size the columns appropriately to view the contents of all the cells. Sort the data in descending order by salary. Preview the worksheet and change the page setup options to place the data attractively on the page; then (with permission), print the worksheet. Save and close the workbook.

Language Arts: Words to Know

Look up the meaning of the following terms using a classroom, library, CD-ROM, or online encyclopedia or dictionary.

tides	ocean	hydrosphere	sea
harbor	wave	hydrothermal vent	oceanography

Create a new workbook. Save the workbook as *definitions7.* Rename the *Sheet1* sheet tab as **Definitions**. Enter the title **Ocean Definitions** in cell A1. Merge and center the title across the range *A1:B1.* Enter **Term** as the column name in A3. Enter **Definition** as the column name in B3. Bold the title and column names. Center the column names.

Enter the terms in the range *A4:A11.* Enter the term definitions in the range *B4:B11.* Use the resizing pointer to automatically fit the cell contents for columns A and B. Sort the data in ascending alphabetical order by term. Save, preview, set page setup options, and (with permission) print the worksheet. Close the workbook.

Explore More

Let's change the data series colors and add data labels.

1. Show the Chart toolbar, if necessary. Click the **Chart Objects** button drop-down arrow and click **Series "Melanesia Total"** to select the data series. Chart Area Each data marker in the series now has a selection indicator indicating the entire data series is selected.
2. Click the **Format Data Series** button to open the **Format Data Series** dialog box.
3. Click the **Patterns** tab, if necessary, and click the **dark blue** color in the Area color grid. Click the **Data Labels** tab and click the **Value** checkbox to insert a check mark. Click the **OK** button. Tap the ESC key to deselect the data series.
4. Using steps 1–3 as your guide, change the **Series "Polynesia Total"** and **Series "Micronesia Total"** to the colors of your choice and add data labels.
5. Choose **View** on the menu bar and choose **Sized with Window** to turn off the view.

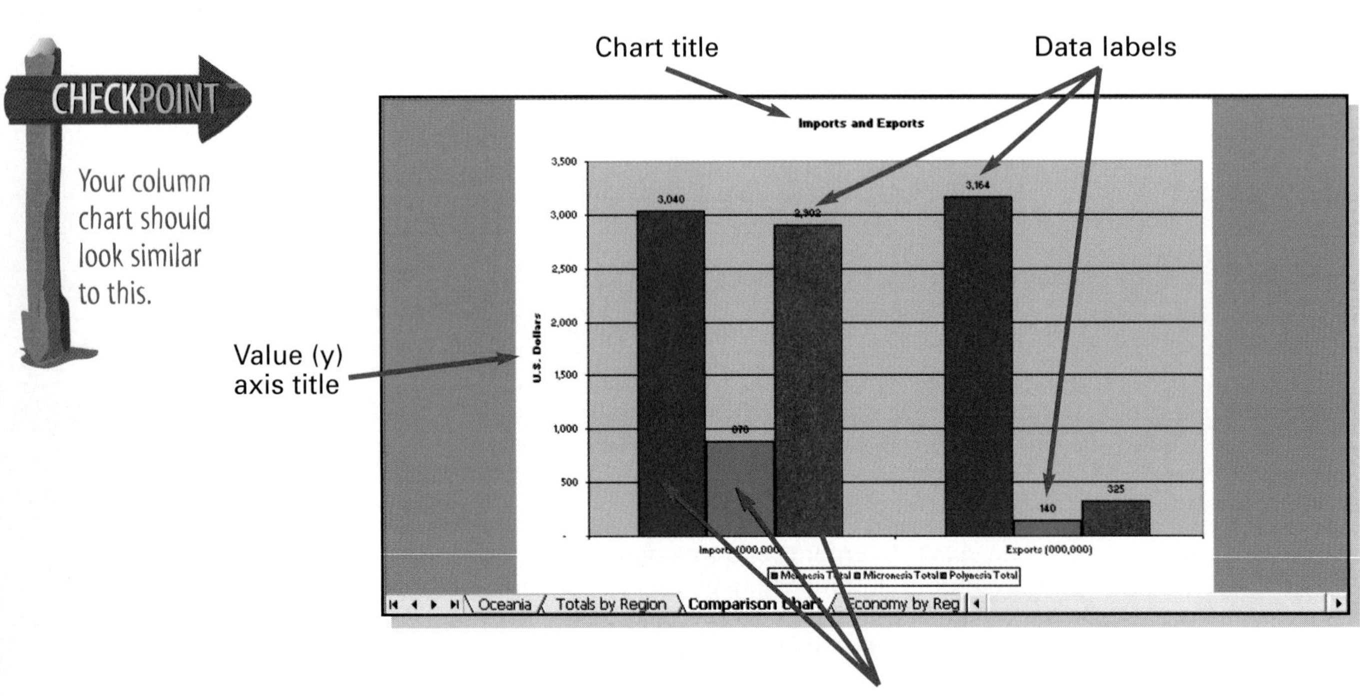

Well done! Another way to illustrate data is to compare the changes in the data over time.

Exploring Across the Curriculum

Science: Research and Write

Use classroom, library, CD-ROM, or online resources to learn more about the world's five oceans. Where are they located? What seas make up each ocean? What climatic conditions influence each ocean? What are the environmental issues affecting each ocean? What unique characteristics set each ocean apart from the other four oceans? What is the controversy surrounding the Southern Ocean? Take notes about what you learn.

Then create a new *Word* document and save it as *oceans report7.* Use the *oceans7* workbook data and your research notes to write a correctly formatted *bound* report about the world's five oceans. Include at least two report pages. Use endnotes to cite your sources and add a cover sheet to your report.

Getting Help

Getting Help

Type **insert cells** in the **Ask A Question** box on the menu bar and tap the ENTER key. Research how to insert cells, rows, and columns. Type **delete cells** in the **Ask A Question** box on the menu bar and tap the ENTER key. Research how to delete cells, rows, and columns. Then open the *oceans7* workbook you created in this project and practice what you learned. Close the workbook *without saving it.*

Your Personal Journal

Open your personal journal document. Insert today's date and two blank lines. Choose a marine science or maritime career that interests you. What qualities, talents, skills, and experience do you have that you could use in this career? Write a personal job profile, explaining work-related experiences you have had and your special qualities or qualifications that would help you in this career. Update your journal with one or two paragraphs answering these questions. Spell-check, save, and close your journal.

Online Enrichment Games (Fun Stuff)  www.lwcgreen.keyboarding.com

2. Choose **View** on the menu bar and choose **Sized with Window**. The chart objects appear larger and slightly out of proportion. *Don't worry! You will turn off the **Sized with Window** view after you format the chart.*

The column chart compares imports and exports for each region. You want to compare imports for all three regions and exports for all three regions. To do this, you need to change the way *Excel* reads the data from columns to rows. Then, you can format the chart to add a chart title and to reposition and resize the legend.

3. Click the **By Row** button on the Chart toolbar.
4. Choose **Chart** on the menu bar, choose **Chart Options**, and click the **Titles** tab. Type **Imports and Exports** as the chart title and type **U.S. Dollars** as the value (y) axis title. Click the **Legend** tab and click the **Bottom** option button for placement. Then click the **OK** button and tap the ESC key to deselect the chart object.

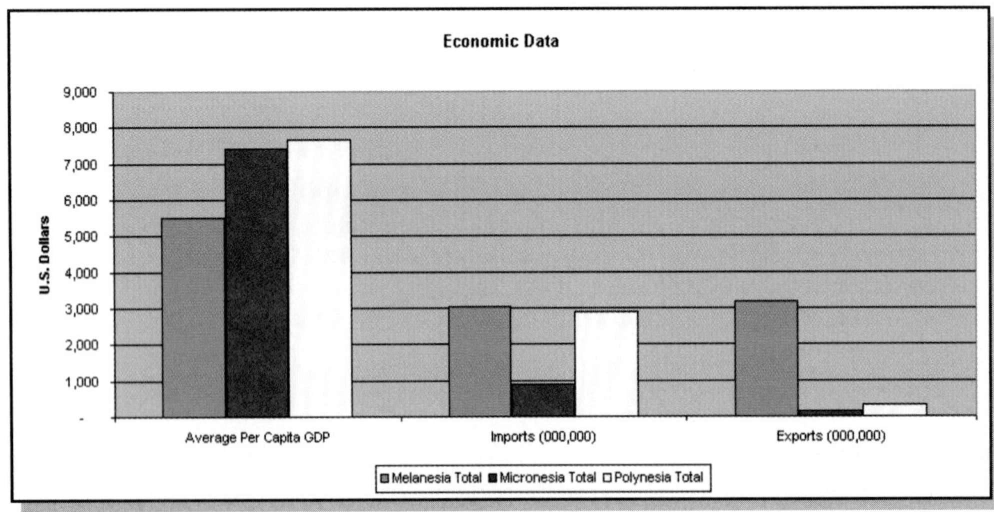

Now let's edit the chart using the Chart toolbar.

7a Review q, comma, z, colon

Key each line twice. Double-space between 2-line groups.

q

1 aq aq|qaq qaq|Jq Jq|Kq Kq|Lq Lq|Yq Yq|Uq Uq|Pq Pq;

2 quit quit|quake quake|quick; quick|banquet banquet

comma

3 k, k,|,k, ,k,|,D ,D|,C ,C|,W ,W|,Q ,Q|,T ,T|,V ,V,

4 Juan, Ellen, and James|Maria, Carlos, and Courtney

z

5 az az|zaz zaz|Uz Uz|Nx Nz|Pz Pz|Yz Yz|Mz Mz|Oz Oz;

6 zap zap|jazz jazz|ZIP ZIP|lazy lazy|quartz quartz;

colon

7 ;: :;|p:p p:p|:R: :R:|W:Q: W:Q:|p:C: p:C:|Z:T: Z:T

8 To: From: Date: Subject: To: Jane From: Sam

Reach down to the comma without moving your hands towards your body.

7b Technique: Space Bar

Key each line twice single-spaced; double-space between 2-line groups.

1 Chase

2 Chase can

3 Chase can take

4 Chase can take the

5 Chase can take the game

6 Chase can take the game home

7 Chase can take the game home with

8 Chase can take the game home with him

9 Chase can take the game home with him next

10 Chase can take the game home with him next week.

gwam 20" | 3 | 6 | 9 | 12 | 15 | 18 | 21 | 24 | 27 | 30 |

TRAIL 3 MARKER

Creating and Formatting a Column Chart

bar chart
category (x) axis
column chart
gridlines
plot area
value (y) axis

A column chart is used to compare two or more data series. In the chart we will create, data for imports and exports will be represented by vertical columns in the chart's plot area. Each data series—each region—appears in a different color. All the data markers for one data series—all the imports or exports for each region—appear in the same color. The plot area has two axes: a vertical axis, called the value (y) axis, and a horizontal axis, called the category (x) axis. The value (y) axis shows the numbers, or values (in U.S. dollars), over which the data is to be charted. The category (x) axis shows the names of the categories—imports and exports—being charted. Gridlines that help you see each data marker's position appear across the plot area at the value (y) axis.

The data markers are set horizontally as bars instead of vertically as columns in an *Excel* bar chart.

A quick way to create a column chart on its own chart sheet is to select the data and tap the F11 key. Then you can edit the chart with menu commands and toolbar buttons. It is easier to format a chart on its own sheet if you first view the chart sized to fit better in the *Excel* window.

Let's create a column chart *on its own chart sheet* that compares imports and exports by region for three regions of Oceania: Micronesia, Polynesia, and Melanesia.

1. Click the *Economy by Region* sheet tab to view the worksheet and select the nonadjacent ranges **A5:C5** and **A7:C9**. This selection excludes the Australasia data. Tap the **F11** key to create the chart on its own sheet. Name the chart sheet **Comparison Chart**.

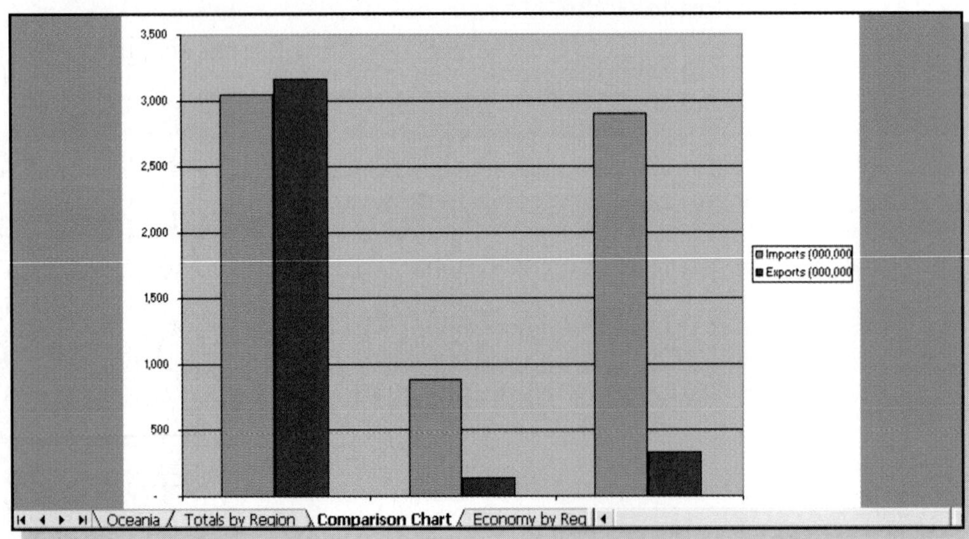

Project 8

Worksheets

Identifying Biosphere Reserves

Explorers' Guide

Data file: *biosphere*

Objectives:

In this project, you will:

- use the **Format Cells** dialog box
- edit data
- insert columns and rows
- fill a range and sort on three columns
- filter, copy, and paste data
- use functions

Exploring on Your Own

additional practice in:

- using the **Format Cells** dialog box to format text
- editing data
- inserting columns and rows
- filling a range and sorting on three columns
- filtering, copying, and pasting data
- using functions

Exploring Across the Curriculum

Internet/Web
Geography
Language Arts
Getting Help
Your Personal Journal

Our Exploration Assignment:

Updating and analyzing biosphere data

The Explorers Club is learning about the importance of conserving the world's natural resources. Ray has organized data about U.S. biosphere reserves in a workbook. He needs your help to update a worksheet and then answer some questions about the data. Follow the Trail Markers to apply formatting using the **Format Cells** dialog box, insert columns and rows, fill a range, edit data, filter data, and use functions to answer questions about data.

3. Right-click the legend's black boundary and choose **Format Legend** to open the **Format Legend** dialog box. Click the **Patterns** tab, if necessary. Click the **Custom** option button in Border group; then click the **Color** drop-down arrow, and click the **red** color on the Border color grid.

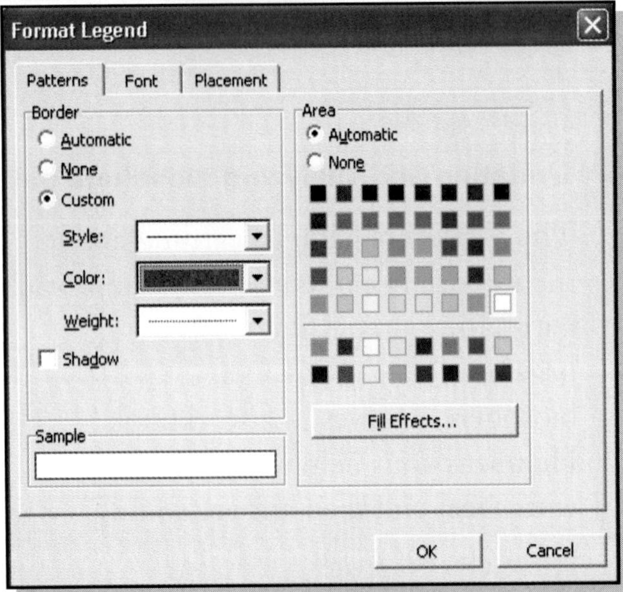

4. Click the **Placement** tab, click the **Bottom** option button, and click the **OK** button. Deselect the chart and save the workbook.

Your formatted embedded pie chart should look similar to this.

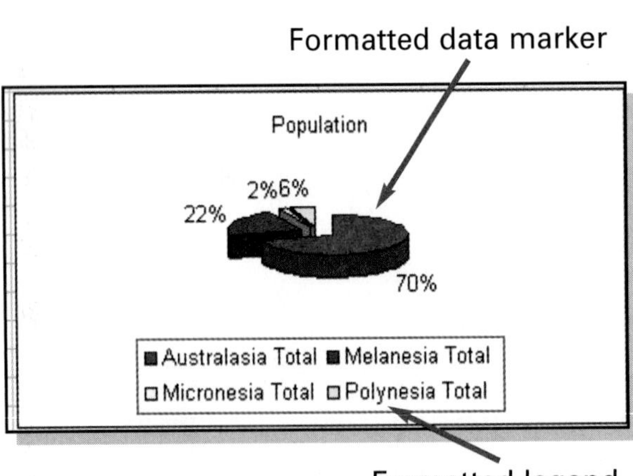

What a super-looking chart! Now let's create another chart. This time, we will create a column chart that looks at the relationship between imports and exports by three Oceania regions.

Starting Out!

Begin by opening Ray's workbook and saving it with a new name.

1. Open the *biosphere* workbook. Save the workbook as *biosphere8.* Click the **U.S. Biosphere Reserves** sheet tab, if necessary, to make it the active worksheet.

Super! Let's update the *U.S. Biosphere Reserves* worksheet and then analyze the data to answer Ray's questions about U.S. biosphere reserves.

Ergonomics *TIP*

Do you have tight shoulders and stiff fingers after working awhile at your computer? Roll your shoulders forward and back and flex your fingers several times. That's better! Now you are relaxed and ready to get back to work!

TRAIL 1 MARKER

Using the Format Cells Dialog Box

When you type a date into a cell, *Excel* will recognize that you are typing a date. *Excel* automatically formats it depending on how the date text was entered in the cell. Here are some examples of *Excel*'s automatic date formatting.

If you enter:	*Excel* formats the date as:
Jan 5 or January 5	5-Jan
Jan 5, 2006 or January 5, 2006	5-Jan-06
1/5/06	1/5/2006

Remember! To *enter* text or numbers in a specific cell, follow the three-step process: activate the cell, type the text or numbers, activate another cell.

To change the format of a date in a selected cell, open the **Format Cells** dialog box, click the **Number** tab, and choose a **Date** option.

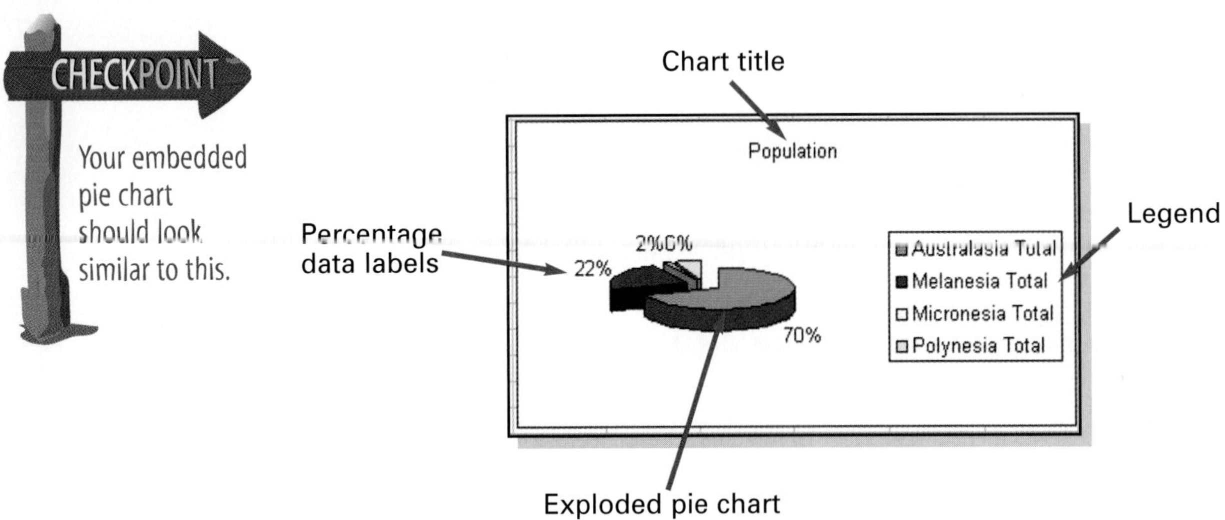

To format the embedded pie chart, first click the chart to select it. The menu bar changes when you select the chart—the **Chart** menu is added and other menus are modified to include commands for creating and editing charts. The Chart toolbar also appears. You can use the buttons on the Chart toolbar, the commands on the Chart menu, or a shortcut menu to format parts of the chart, such as the legend and the labels.

You can use Chart Tips to view different chart objects. Just move the mouse pointer over a chart to see the Chart Tips. Try it!

Let's format the embedded chart by changing a data marker's color, repositioning the legend, and changing the legend's border color.

1. Click the **3-D exploded pie chart** inside the embedded chart to select the data series. Click the **Australasia** data marker to select just that data marker. The black selection indicators on the boundary of the Australasia slice indicate that only that data marker is selected.
2. Right-click the selected **Australasia** data marker to show the shortcut menu *for the selected data marker*, and choose **Format Data Point** to open the **Format Data Point** dialog box. Click the **Patterns** tab, if necessary, and click the **red** color on the Area color grid. Then click the **OK** button. The **Australasia** data marker is now red.

Let's enter and format a date.

1. Enter today's date in the mm/dd/yy format in cell **A2**. Click cell **A2** and press the CTRL + 1 keys to open the **Format Cells** dialog box. Click **Date** in the **Category** list in the **Number** tab, if necessary, and click the sample date **March 14, 2001** in the **Type** list.
2. Click the **OK** button. The date is reformatted with the month spelled out and the year in four digits.

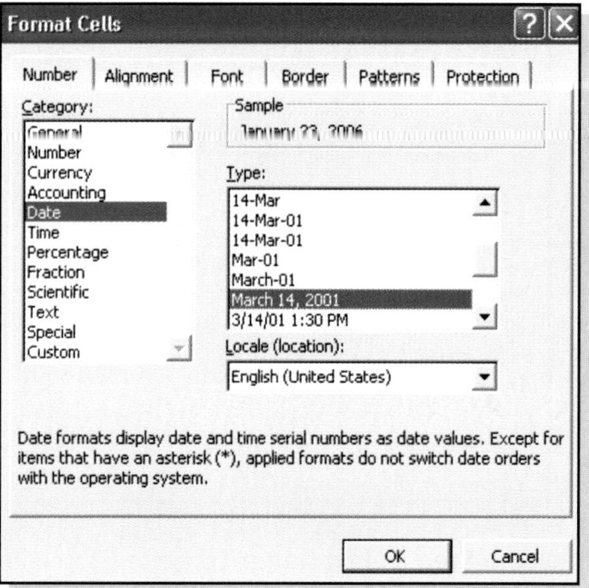

Good job! Now let's format the title and the date.

The **Format Cells** dialog box has many format options. Let's open the **Format Cells** dialog box again. This time, we will merge and center both the title in cell A1 and the date in cell A2 across a range and change the font to Times New Roman 12 point bold all at one time.

Let's open the Format Cells dialog box to format the contents of cells A1 and A2.

1. Select the range **A1:E2** using the SHIFT + click method. Press the CTRL + 1 keys to open the **Format Cells** dialog box. Click the **Font** tab. Click **Times New Roman** in the **Font** list; click **Bold** in the **Font** style list; and click **12** point in the **Size** list.

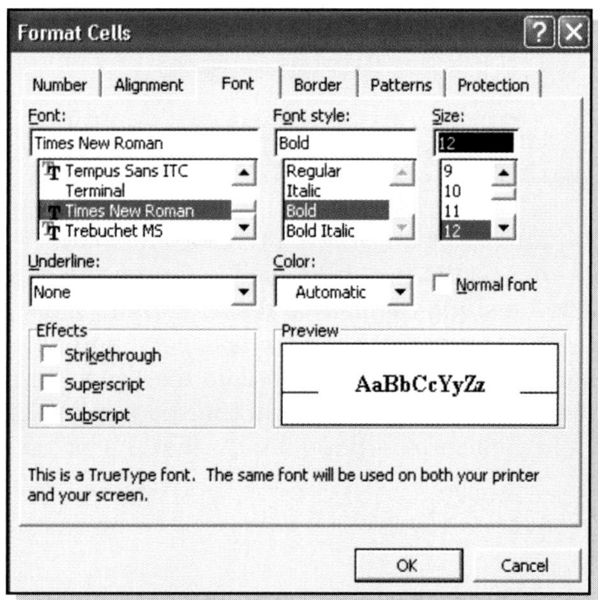

4. Click the **Next** button to go to Step 2. You can change the data to be charted in this step. The selected data is correct, so click the Step 2 **Next** button to go to Step 3. You can add or remove chart options in Step 3. Click the **Data Labels** tab and click the **Percentage** checkbox.

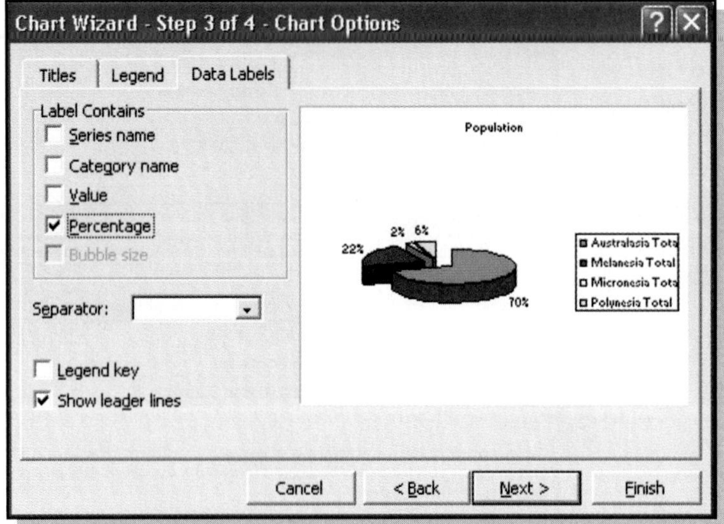

5. Click the Step 3 **Next** button to go to Step 4 and choose how to insert the chart—either as an embedded chart or a chart on its own chart sheet. Click the **As object in** option button, if necessary, to embed the chart on the *Totals by Region* worksheet.

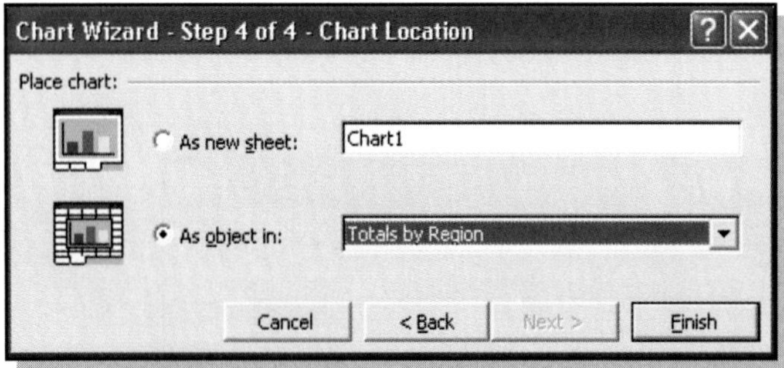

6. Click the **Finish** button. Click anywhere in the white chart background area—*not* on the pie chart itself—to drag the chart to the range **E3:J14**. Use the sizing handles to resize it to fit. Then click anywhere outside the embedded chart to deselect it and save the workbook. Each slice in the pie chart is a data marker that represents the population for one Oceania region. All four data markers represent the single data series—population—that makes up the entire pie.

2. Click the **Alignment** tab. Click the **Horizontal** text alignment drop-down arrow and click **Center Across Selection**.
3. Click the **OK** button. Save the workbook.

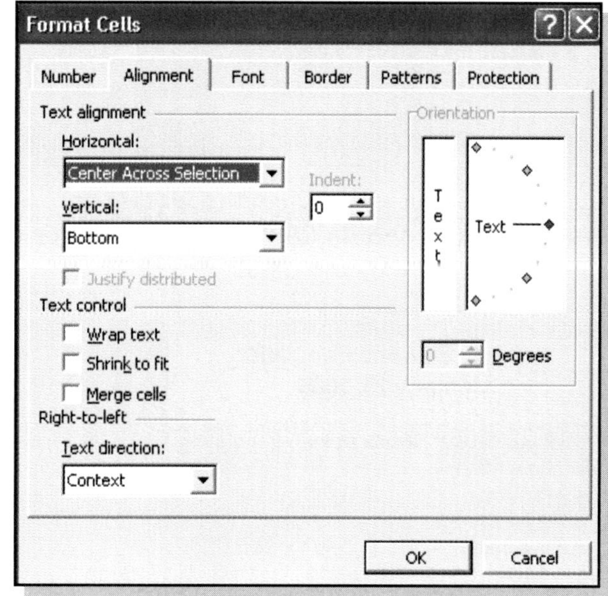

Your worksheet's title and date should look similar to this.

Formatted title and date

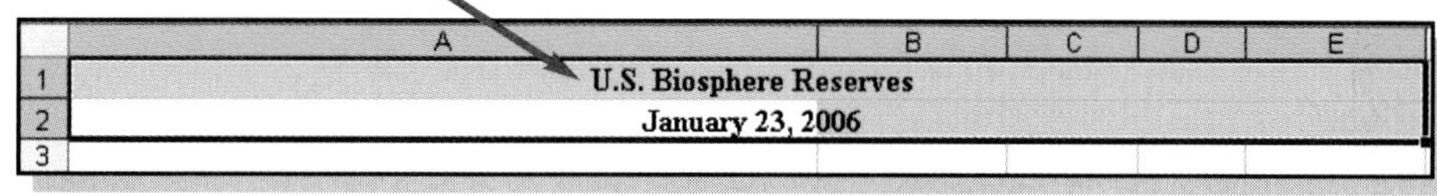

Fantastic! Next, let's edit the data.

The **Format Painter** button on the Formatting toolbar in *Excel* works just like it does in *Word*. Use it to paint formats from one cell to another cell or range. Try it!

Let's create an embedded pie chart of Oceania's population by region.

1. Click the *Totals by Region* sheet tab to view the worksheet. Select the nonadjacent ranges **A4:A8** and **C4:C8**. These two ranges include the data and the text that describes the data.

	A	B	C
1	Oceania Size and Population		
2	January 28, 2006		
3			
4	Region	Size in sq km	Population
5	Australasia Total	7,955,530	23,906,961
6	Melanesia Total	540,820	7,241,059
7	Micronesia Total	3,199	543,858
8	Polynesia Total	15,402	1,911,237
9	Grand Total	8,514,951	33,603,115

2. Click the **Chart Wizard** button on the Standard toolbar to start the Chart Wizard.
3. Click the **Pie Chart type** and click the **second subtype** option in the second row. This creates an exploded 3-D pie chart. Click the **Press and Hold to See Sample** button and hold down the mouse button to view a sample of the chart.

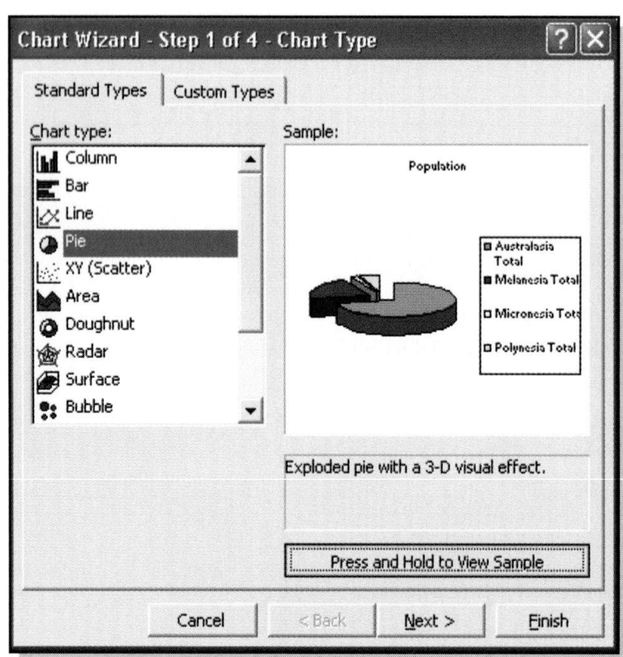

Another way to start the Chart Wizard is by choosing **Insert** on the menu bar and choosing **Chart**.

Editing Data

Excel gives you four ways to edit cell contents. After you click a cell, you can:

1. Simply enter new text or numbers in the cell.
2. Click the Formula Bar with the I-beam and edit the cell contents in the Formula Bar.
3. Double-click the cell and edit the cell contents directly in the cell.
4. Tap the **F2** key to open the cell and position the insertion point in the cell.

You can also use the I-beam to select text or numbers in the Formula Bar or in the active cell and then type new text or numbers. If you want to cancel your data entry before you tap the ENTER or TAB keys, tap the ESC key!

Let's edit the *U.S. Biosphere* worksheet using the four methods.

1. Use the numeric keypad to enter **1976** in cell **D7**. The new year (1976) replaces the old year (1986).
2. Double-click cell **E14**. Use the arrow keys to move the insertion point in front of the cell's contents (*NPS*). Tap the DELETE key twice to remove the *NP* characters; then type **F** and tap the ENTER key. The text *FS* replaces the original text *NPS* in cell E14.
3. Click cell **A16**. Move the I-beam to the Formula Bar and click between the two *e* characters in *Reerve* to position the insertion point. Type **s** and tap the ENTER key. The word *Reserve* replaces the characters *Reerve*.
4. Click cell **B30** and tap the **F2** key at the top of your keyboard. Drag with the I-beam to select the word *Oregon,* type **Kansas**, and tap the ENTER key. The word *Kansas* replaces the word *Oregon* in cell B30. Press the CTRL + HOME keys and save the workbook.

Great job! Now let's insert rows and columns.

To delete the contents of a selected cell or range, tap the DELETE key. To clear a cell of only its contents, only its formatting, or both, choose **Edit** on the menu bar, point to **Clear**, and choose an option.

TRAIL 2 MARKER

Creating and Formatting a Pie Chart

chart
chart area
chart objects
chart sheet
chart title
Chart Wizard
data labels
data marker
data point
data series
embedded chart
legend
pie chart

Turning data into a chart, or graph, helps you understand the data. You can create many different types of charts, such as pie, column, and line charts. Each type of chart is used to show a different type of relationship. Each chart type also has several subtypes from which to choose. *Excel* has special terms for each part of a chart.

Chart Object	Description
Chart area	The background for the chart
Chart title	Text title of the chart
Data point	A number in the worksheet that is converted into a column, point on a line, or pie slice in the chart
Data marker	A column, point on a line, or pie slice that represents the numbers, or data points, in the worksheet
Data labels	Text labels that identify the data markers on the chart
Data series	All the related data markers in a chart
Legend	Names or words and colors that identify each data series

To create a chart, first select the data and the text that will appear in the chart, and then click the **Chart Wizard** button on the Standard toolbar to start the Chart Wizard. The Chart Wizard is a four-step process you follow to: select the chart type; verify the data to be charted; add titles, legend, and data labels; and insert the chart. Charts can be inserted on a separate chart sheet or on the same worksheet as the data. A chart that is inserted on the same worksheet is called an embedded chart.

A pie chart is a good way to show data as percentages. To select the data for a pie chart, you must select both the cells that contain the data *plus* the row and column names that identify the data.

Let's create an embedded pie chart to show the relationship of each Oceania region's population to the total Oceania population. Remember to use the CTRL key to select nonadjacent cells. After you create the chart, use drag and drop to move it to a new location.

TRAIL 3 MARKER

Inserting Columns and Rows

Columns and rows can be inserted in a worksheet where you need them or deleted if you no longer need them. To insert or delete columns or rows, right-click the selected column or row headings and choose **Insert** or **Delete** on the shortcut menu.

To insert columns or rows, you can also choose **Insert** on the menu bar and choose **Columns** or **Rows**. To delete selected columns or rows, choose **Edit** on the menu bar and choose **Delete**.

Let's use the shortcut menu to insert a new column to the left of column A and five new rows below the data.

1. Right-click the **column A heading** and choose **Insert**. A new, blank column A appears and all the remaining columns move to the right. Enter **Number** in cell **A4**.
2. Scroll to view the bottom of the data and select rows **52–56** by dragging across the row headings. Right-click the selected row headings and choose **Insert**. Five blank rows are inserted and the remaining rows move down. Press the CTRL + HOME keys and save the workbook.

When you delete columns, the remaining columns move to the left. When you delete rows, the remaining rows move up to take their place.

Nice job! Now let's add unique identifying numbers to each row of data using AutoFill, and then sort the data.

Let's collapse and expand the list using the outlining buttons and then copy the subtotals and grand total and paste them into another worksheet for later use. Then remove the temporary subtotals.

1. Click the **level 2** button at the top of the outlining pane to view only the subtotals and grand total. Click the **level 1** button at the top of the outlining pane to view just the grand total. Click the **level 3** button at the top of the outlining pane to view all the data.
2. Select the range **C8:E8** and then use the CTRL key to select the nonadjacent ranges **C14:E14**, **C22:E22**, and **C35:E36**. Click the **Copy** button. Then click the *Totals by Region* sheet tab, click cell **A5**, and click the **Paste** button. The subtotals and grand total are pasted in the worksheet. The formulas are pasted as *values*. Deselect the range.

	A	B	C
1	Oceania Size and Population		
2	January 28, 2006		
3			
4	Region	Size in sq km	Population
5	Australasia Total	7,955,530	23,906,961
6	Melanesia Total	540,820	7,241,059
7	Micronesia Total	3,199	543,858
8	Polynesia Total	15,402	1,911,237
9	Grand Total	8,514,951	33,603,115

Now that you have pasted the region subtotals and grand total on another worksheet, you can remove the temporary subtotals and outlining pane from the *Oceania* worksheet.

3. Click the *Oceania* sheet tab. Click any cell inside the list, if necessary, choose **Data** on the menu bar, and choose **Subtotals**. Click the **Remove All** button. The subtotals, grand total, and outlining pane are removed from the worksheet.
4. Sort the # column in ascending numerical order to return the worksheet to its original order.

Nice work! Now you are ready to create a chart using the worksheet data.

Filling a Range and Sorting on Three Columns

AutoFill
fill handle

Ray wants to sort the biosphere data by administrator, then by size, and finally by reserve name. This is a complex, three-column sort. Before you sort a large amount of data, it is a good idea to make certain that you can return the data to its original order.

A good way to make sure you can return data to its original order is to add a unique sequential identifying number to each row. Then, no matter how you sort the data, you can always return it to its *original order* by sorting the identifying numbers in ascending numerical order. You can use AutoFill to add these numbers to each row. The AutoFill feature can be used to fill a range of cells with years (2006, 2007, 2008), the names of the months (January, February, March), dates (January 2 to January 8), or a series of numbers (1, 2, 3).

First, enter a year, month name, day of the week, date, or number in a cell. If you want to fill a range with years or another series of numbers that increase in increments of 1 (2006, 2007 or 1, 2, 3), press and hold down the CTRL key. Then drag the fill handle—the small black square in the lower-right corner of an active cell—to an adjacent cell or cells. As you drag across empty cells, you will see a ScreenTip indicating what will be filled in each cell. Releasing the mouse button fills the cells. To fill a range with the names of the months or days of the week, *do not* press and hold the CTRL key as your drag the fill handle.

You can also use the fill handle to fill a range with dates, such as Jan 1, Jan 8, Jan 15, or numbers, such as 1, 3, 5, 7, and so forth, that increase by more than 1. Check out online **Help** to learn how to do this and more fill handle tricks!

Apply It!

Let's fill the range A5:A51 with a series of incremental numbers by using AutoFill.

1. Enter **1** in cell **A5**. Click cell **A5** and move the mouse pointer to the fill handle; press and hold down the mouse button and the CTRL key. The mouse pointer changes shape to a small black crosshair pointer with a tiny plus sign in the upper-right corner.

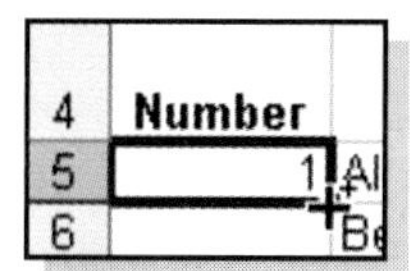

2. Drag down to cell **A51**. Release the mouse button first and then the CTRL key. A series of numbers from 1 to 47 fills the cells in the range A5:A51. Press the CTRL + HOME keys and save the workbook.

CHECKPOINT

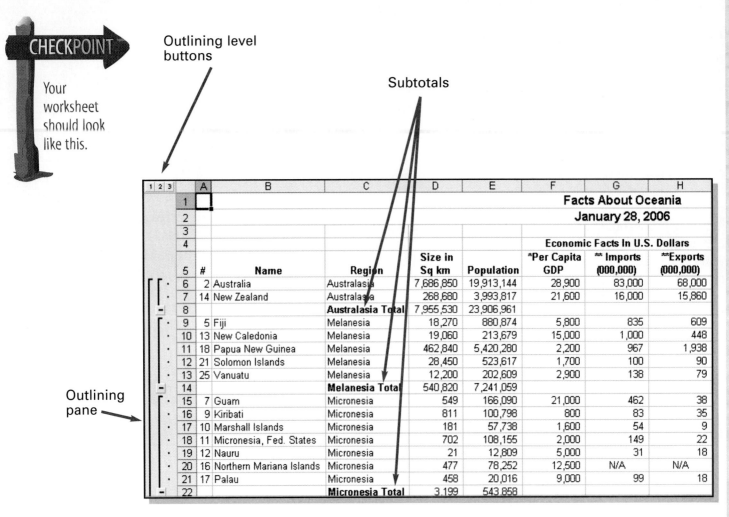

Your worksheet should look like this.

Outlining level buttons

Subtotals

Outlining pane

Facts About Oceania

January 28, 2006

#	Name	Region	Size in Sq km	Population	*Per Capita GDP	** Imports (000,000)	**Exports (000,000)
					Economic Facts In U.S. Dollars		
2	Australia	Australasia	7,686,850	19,913,144	28,900	83,000	68,000
14	New Zealand	Australasia	268,680	3,993,817	21,600	16,000	15,860
		Australasia Total	7,955,530	23,906,961			
5	Fiji	Melanesia	18,270	880,874	5,800	835	609
13	New Caledonia	Melanesia	19,060	213,679	15,000	1,000	448
18	Papua New Guinea	Melanesia	462,840	5,420,280	2,200	967	1,938
21	Solomon Islands	Melanesia	28,450	523,617	1,700	100	90
25	Vanuatu	Melanesia	12,200	202,609	2,900	138	79
		Melanesia Total	540,820	7,241,059			
7	Guam	Micronesia	549	166,090	21,000	462	38
9	Kiribati	Micronesia	811	100,798	800	83	35
10	Marshall Islands	Micronesia	181	57,738	1,600	54	9
11	Micronesia, Fed. States	Micronesia	702	108,155	2,000	149	22
12	Nauru	Micronesia	21	12,809	5,000	31	18
16	Northern Mariana Islands	Micronesia	477	78,252	12,500	N/A	N/A
17	Palau	Micronesia	458	20,016	9,000	99	18
		Micronesia Total	3,199	543,858			

Notice the level 1, 2, and 3 outlining buttons at the top of the outlining pane. These buttons expand or collapse the worksheet to show you all the rows (3), the subtotals and the grand total (2), or just the grand total (1). Clicking a minus sign (−) in the Outlining pane collapses a group of rows and clicking a plus sign (+) expands a group.

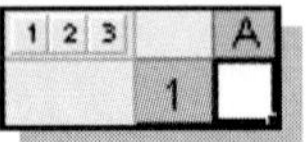

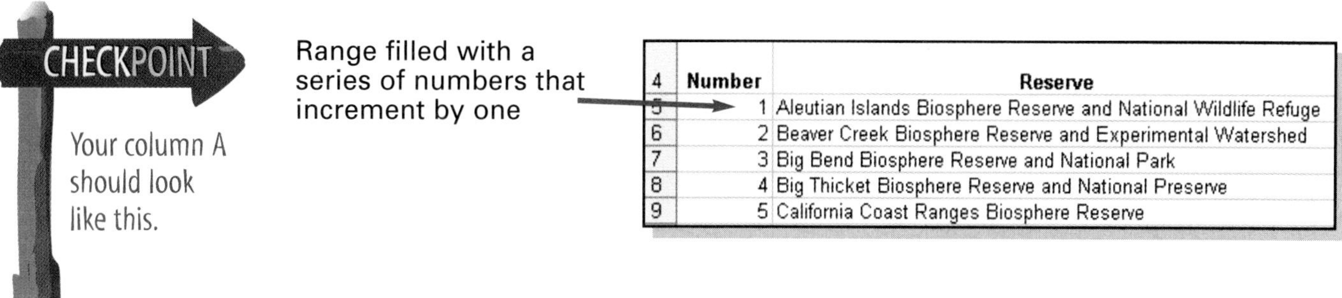

4	Number	Reserve
5	1	Aleutian Islands Biosphere Reserve and National Wildlife Refuge
6	2	Beaver Creek Biosphere Reserve and Experimental Watershed
7	3	Big Bend Biosphere Reserve and National Park
8	4	Big Thicket Biosphere Reserve and National Preserve
9	5	California Coast Ranges Biosphere Reserve

Now let's sort the data. A three-column sort is performed by setting sort criteria in the **Sort** dialog box. In the **Sort** dialog box, you can select the columns to sort; which column to sort first, second, and third; and whether to sort in ascending or descending order.

Let's sort the data in ascending order by administrator, then in ascending order by size, and, finally, in ascending order by reserve name.

1. Click in any cell in the data below the column names. Choose **Data** on the menu bar and choose **Sort** to open the **Sort** dialog box.
2. Click the **Sort by** drop-down arrow and click ***Federal Administrator** in the list. Click the related **Ascending** option button, if necessary.
3. Click the first **Then by** drop-down arrow and click **Size in Sq. Miles** in the list. Click the related **Ascending** option button, if necessary.
4. Click the second **Then by** drop-down arrow and click **Reserve** in the list. Click the related **Ascending** option button, if necessary.
5. Click the **OK** button.

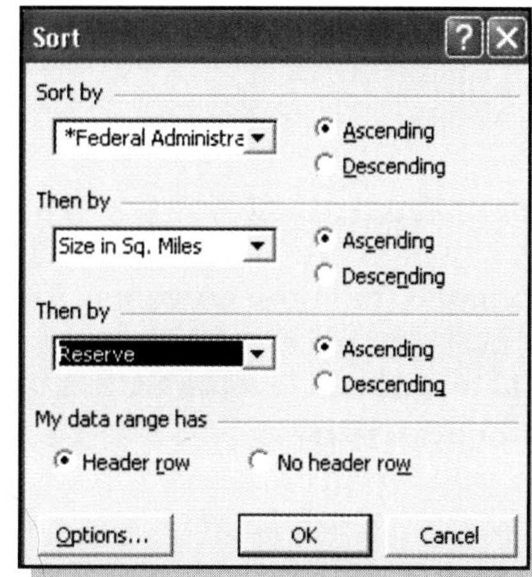

Let's sort the data by region and then insert subtotals.

1. Sort the Region column in ascending alphabetical order. Then choose **Data** on the menu bar and choose **Subtotals** to open the **Subtotal** dialog box. *Don't forget! Before you can sort or filter a list or insert subtotals, the active cell must be inside the list below the column names.*
2. Click the **At each change in** drop-down arrow and click **Region**. This tells *Excel* when to insert the subtotals. Click the **Use function** drop-down arrow and click **Sum** because you want to add subtotals.
3. Scroll the **Add subtotal to** list and click the **Size in Sq km** and **Population** checkboxes. These check marks tell *Excel* what data to use in the subtotal calculations. Remove any check marks from the other **Add subtotal to** list checkboxes, if necessary. By default, the **Replace current subtotals** and **Summary below data** checkboxes should already contain check marks.

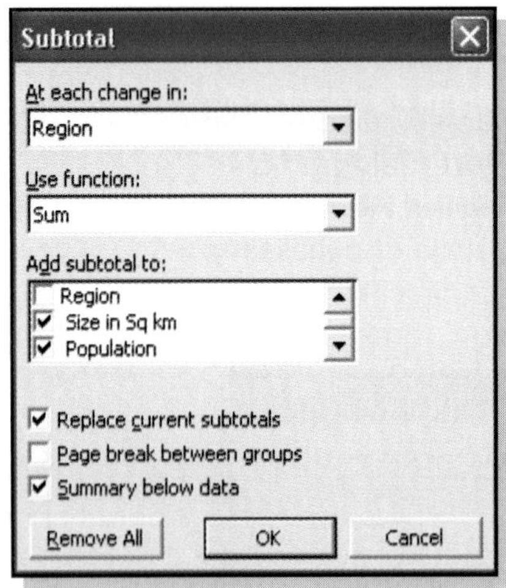

4. Click the **OK** button. Resize column C to fit the contents. The subtotals are inserted and the outlining pane appears on the left side of the worksheet. Click cells **D8** and **E8** to view the SUBTOTAL formulas. Then press the CTRL + HOME keys.

CHECKPOINT

Your sorted data should look like this.

Data in order by administrator, then by size, and then by reserve

	A	B	C	D	E	F
1		U.S. Biosphere Reserves				
2		January 24, 2006				
3						
4	Number	Reserve	State or Territory	Size in Sq. Miles	Year Named	*Federal Administrat
5	42	Stanislaus-Tuolumne Biosphere Reserve and Experimental Forest	California	2	1976	FS
6	38	San Joaquin Biosphere Reserve and Experimental Range	California	7	1976	FS
7	12	Coram Biosphere Reserve	Montana	12	1976	FS
8	23	Hubbard Brook Biosphere Reserve and Experimental Forest	New Hampshire	12	1976	FS
9	28	Luquillo Biosphere Reserve	Puerto Rico	13	1976	FS
10	21	H. J. Andrews Biosphere Reserve and Experimental Forest	Oregon	25	1976	FS
11	7	Cascade Head Biosphere Reserve and Experimental Forest	Oregon	27	1976	FS
12	37	San Dimas Biosphere Reserve and Experimental Forest	California	27	1976	FS
13	16	Fraser Biosphere Reserve and Experimental Forest	Colorado	36	1976	FS
14	14	Desert Biosphere Reserve and Experimental Range	Utah	87	1976	FS

To quickly return the data to its original order, simply sort the row of identifying numbers in column A in ascending order.

6. Click any cell in column A inside the data and then click the **Sort Ascending** button to return the data to its original order.

Terrific! The data is back in its original order. Ray has some questions about the data. Let's find the answers by filtering the data.

TRAIL 5 MARKER

Filtering, Copying, and Pasting Data

AutoFilter
filter
list

A filter is a set of criteria you apply to worksheet data to allow you to view and work with a portion of the data. For example, suppose you want to see only the reserves that were named in 1986 in the *U.S. Biosphere* worksheet. You can filter the data so that *Excel* shows those rows only and hides all the rows where the date in the *Year Named* column is not 1986.

In the previous project, you learned that data should be arranged in a specific way in your worksheet so that you can sort it. Data to be filtered should be organized similarly. This type of data arrangement is called a list.

To filter a list, turn on *Excel's* AutoFilter feature by first clicking in any cell inside the data to be filtered. Then choose **Data** on the menu bar, point to **Filter**, and choose **AutoFilter**. The AutoFilter feature adds drop-down arrows to all the column names. Click a drop-down arrow to see a list of all the entries in the column. Click a specific entry to filter the list based on that entry.

Starting *Out*!

Begin by opening Julie's workbook and saving it with a new name.

1. Open the *Oceania* workbook, save it as *Oceania10*, and click the *Oceania* sheet tab, if necessary.

Great! Let's start by sorting the data on the *Oceania* worksheet. Then we will insert temporary subtotals of the size and population data for four Oceania regions.

Ergonomics *TIP*

Is it hard to see your monitor's screen because of the glare from uncovered windows? Minimize the glare by covering those windows with blinds or curtains.

TRAIL 1 MARKER

Adding and Removing Temporary Subtotals

subtotal

Julie wants to know the total size and the total population for each of these Oceania regions: Polynesia, Melanesia, Micronesia, and Australasia. Look carefully at the *Oceania* worksheet. You can sort the data by regions. Then you can find the subtotals for the size and population data for each region.

You already know how to insert a new row and use the SUM function to calculate totals. These totals become a permanent part of the worksheet. But Julie plans to sort and filter this data in a number of ways, so she does not want to add permanent totals. Good news! You can insert *temporary* subtotals for a sorted list using the Subtotal feature. Then you can easily remove the subtotals when you no longer need them.

To insert temporary subtotals, first activate a cell inside the list and then choose **Data** on the menu bar and choose **Subtotals**. Then set the subtotal criteria—to tell *Excel* which data and function to use and when to use it—in the **Subtotal** dialog box. *Excel* outlines a worksheet containing subtotals and provides outline level buttons (1, 2, 3, +, and −) that you can use to expand or collapse the outline.

You can move, copy, and paste cell contents in a worksheet or between worksheets just like you did in *Word* by clicking the **Cut, Copy,** and **Paste** buttons or commands.

To scroll sheet tabs, click a first sheet, previous sheet, next sheet, or last sheet tab scrolling button to the left of the workbook's sheet tabs.

Ray wants to insert two worksheets—one that lists U.S. biosphere reserves that were named in 1986 and one that lists California reserves that are managed by the Forest Service. Let's filter the list on the *U.S. Biosphere Reserves* worksheet two times to find this data, and then copy and paste the data on the new worksheets.

To insert a new worksheet in the workbook, right-click a sheet tab and click **Insert** on the shortcut menu. Then double-click the Worksheet icon in the **Insert** dialog box.

Let's filter the data; then copy the filtered data and paste it on a new worksheet.

1. Click any cell in the data below the column names. Choose **Data** on the menu bar, point to **Filter**, and choose **AutoFilter** to turn on the AutoFilter feature. The AutoFilter drop-down arrows appear to the right of each column name.

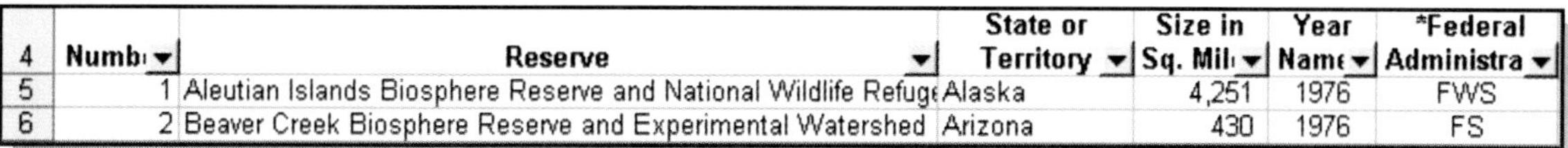

4	Numb	Reserve	State or Territory	Size in Sq. Mil	Year Name	*Federal Administra
5	1	Aleutian Islands Biosphere Reserve and National Wildlife Refuge	Alaska	4,251	1976	FWS
6	2	Beaver Creek Biosphere Reserve and Experimental Watershed	Arizona	430	1976	FS

2. Click the **Year Named** column AutoFilter drop-down arrow and click **1986** in the list.

Excel hides all the rows in the data except the rows that have *1986* in the *Year Named* column. The drop-down arrow for the filtered column is blue. Select the range **A1:F21** and click the **Copy** button. *Excel* copies all the rows in the range *except* the hidden rows.

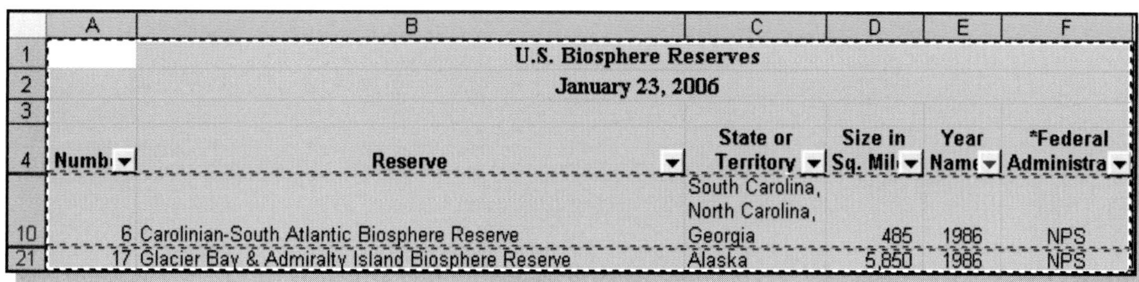

	A	B	C	D	E	F
1		U.S. Biosphere Reserves				
2		January 23, 2006				
3						
4	Numb	Reserve	State or Territory	Size in Sq. Mil	Year Name	*Federal Administra
10	6	Carolinian-South Atlantic Biosphere Reserve	South Carolina, North Carolina, Georgia	485	1986	NPS
21	17	Glacier Bay & Admiralty Island Biosphere Reserve	Alaska	5,850	1986	NPS

Project 10
Worksheets

Journeying to Oceania

Data file: *Oceania, oceania.jpg*

Objectives:

In this project, you will:

- add and remove temporary subtotals
- create and format a pie chart
- create and format a column chart
- create and format a line chart
- insert a picture and use the drawing tools

Exploring on Your Own

additional practice in:

- adding and removing temporary subtotals
- creating and formatting pie and column charts
- inserting a picture and using the drawing tools

Exploring Across the Curriculum

Internet/Web
Language Arts
Science
Getting Help
Your Personal Journal

Our Exploration Assignment:

Use subtotals and charts to analyze data about countries of the South Pacific

Oceania includes the continent of Australia and the islands that stretch across the South Pacific, from New Zealand to Easter Island off the coast of Chile in South America. Julie has found some interesting data about Oceania and now she needs your help to analyze it. Follow the Trail Markers to add, copy, paste, and remove temporary subtotals; create and format a pie chart, a column chart, and a line chart; insert clip art; and use the drawing tools.

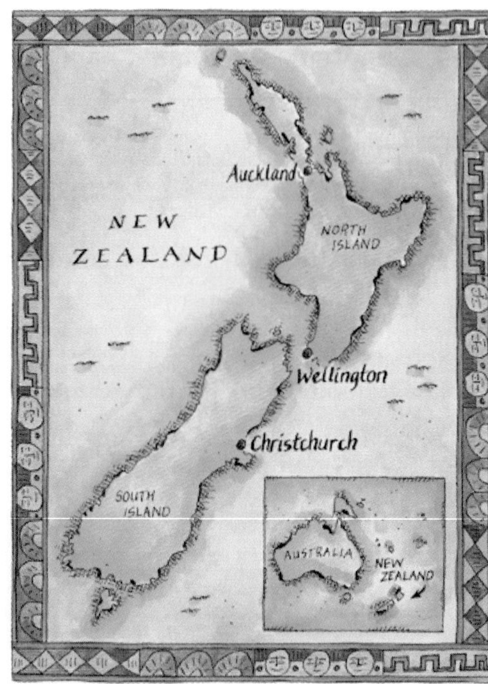

3. Right-click the *U.S. Biosphere Reserves* sheet tab and click **Insert** on the shortcut menu. Double-click the Worksheet icon in the **Insert** dialog box to create a new worksheet.
4. Rename the new sheet tab **Reserves Named in 1986**. Click cell **A1**, if necessary, and click the **Paste** button to paste the copied data to the new worksheet. Deselect the range and resize the columns as necessary.

	A	B	C	D	E	F
1		U.S. Biosphere Reserves				
2		January 23, 2006				
3						
4	Number	Reserve	State or Territory	Size in Sq. Miles	Year Named	*Federal Administrator
5	6	Carolinian-South Atlantic Biosphere Reserve	South Carolina, North Carolina, Georgia	485	1986	NPS
6	17	Glacier Bay & Admiralty Island Biosphere Reserve	Alaska	5,850	1986	NPS

5. Click the *U.S. Biosphere Reserves* sheet tab. Tap the ESC key to remove the copied data from the Office Clipboard, and deselect the range. Click the **Year Named** AutoFilter drop-down arrow, and click (**All**) to remove the filter from the data.

You can filter more than one column at a time. Let's filter the list to show all the biosphere reserves in California that are administered by the Forest Service (FS).

6. Click the **State or Territory** AutoFilter drop-down arrow and click **California**. Click the ***Federal Administrator** AutoFilter drop-down arrow and click **FS**. *Excel* hides all the rows except those where the state or territory is *California* and the federal administrator is the *Forest Service*.

	A	B	C	D	E	F
1		U.S. Biosphere Reserves				
2		January 23, 2006				
3						
4	Numb	Reserve	State or Territory	Size in Sq. Mil	Name	*Federal Administrat
41	37	San Dimas Biosphere Reserve and Experimental Forest	California	27	1976	FS
42	38	San Joaquin Biosphere Reserve and Experimental Range	California	7	1976	FS
46	42	Stanislaus-Tuolumne Biosphere Reserve and Experimental Forest	California	2	1976	FS
52						

Keyboarding Project 9

9a Build Skill

Key each line twice. Double-space between 2-line groups.

Quickly space after each word and immediately begin keying the next word.

balanced-hand sentences

1 Both of us may wish to bid for the antique mantle.
2 Lana is to pay the firm for the bodywork they did.
3 They may sign the amendment to handle the problem.
4 The eight haughty men may make a problem for them.
5 They both may make their goals if they work at it.
6 Vivian may go with the six busy maids to the lake.
7 Orlando may make the men pay for the burnt chairs.
8 The map may aid them when they do the work for us.

9b Build Skill: Paragraphs

Key the two paragraphs. Key them again at a faster rate.

Americans remember and recognize those who have dedicated their lives to making our country a better place to live with monuments. During his inaugural address, President Reagan referred to the monuments of several of those great Americans.

"Directly in front of me, the monument to a monumental man, George Washington, father of our country. A man of humility who came to greatness reluctantly. He led America out of revolutionary victory into infant nationhood. Off to one side, the stately memorial to Thomas Jefferson. The Declaration of Independence flames with his eloquence."

7. Copy the filtered data and paste it on a new worksheet named *California FS Reserves*. Deselect the range and resize the columns as necessary. Then return to the *U.S. Biosphere Reserves* worksheet, tap the ESC key, and deselect the range.
8. Choose **Data** on the menu bar, point to **Filter**, and choose **AutoFilter** to turn off the AutoFilter feature and view all the rows. Resize any columns, if necessary, to see all the data.

Excellent! Let's continue to answer Ray's questions, this time using functions.

TRAIL 6 MARKER

Using Functions

AVERAGE
formula
function
MAX
MIN
SUM

A formula is an equation you enter in one cell to perform a calculation on the contents of other cells. A function is a built-in *Excel* formula. You can use a function to perform common calculations, such as adding up a range of numbers or finding the largest number in a range.

When you use a function, you *must* include the function's name and a set of parentheses. The cell or range of cells containing the data the function uses for its calculations goes inside the parentheses. The most commonly used functions are SUM, MIN, MAX, and AVERAGE.

AVERAGE	Calculates the average value of the cells in a range
MAX	Finds the largest value of the cells in a range
MIN	Finds the smallest value of the cells in a range
SUM	Calculates the total value of the cells in a range

Here is an example of a formula that uses the SUM function: =SUM(D5:D51). The equal sign tells *Excel* that you are using a calculation; SUM names the function you are using; (D5:D51) means that you are adding all the values beginning in cell D5 and ending in cell D51. To add the values in the range, first click an empty cell where you want the total to appear. Then type the formula and tap the ENTER, TAB, or arrow key. The total appears in the cell.

Exploring Across the Curriculum

Math: Creating a Personal Budget

Open the *budget9* workbook and click the *My Personal Budget* sheet tab. Use the worksheet to create your own personal budget for an entire year by quarter. Insert or delete budget categories as necessary. Estimate how much money you will earn for the year, how much you will save, and how you will spend the money you do not save.

Add borders and shading to the Savings Assumption data. Then enter your estimates for all categories except Savings. Enter a formula to calculate your savings each quarter as a percentage of your total revenues (H9). Enter formulas to calculate Qtr 1 Total Revenues, Total Expenditures, and Surplus or (Deficit). Edit the Savings formula to make the savings percentage cell reference an absolute reference. Then copy all the Qtr 1 formulas to Qtr 2–4. Use the **AutoSum** button to calculate all the annual totals. Perform a what-if analysis to determine the effect on your budget if you increase or decrease your quarterly savings. Save and close the workbook.

Getting Help

Type **insert a date** in the **Ask A Question** box to research ways to insert the current date and time in a cell using keyboard shortcut keys. Then open a workbook and practice what you learned. Close the workbook without saving it.

Your Personal Journal

Open your personal journal document. Insert today's date and two blank lines. Write one paragraph about what you spend your money on and how much money you save each month. Then write a second paragraph about goals you have, such as saving money for a vacation, college education, or a new computer. Explain how a personal budget can help you attain your goals. Spell-check, save, and close your journal.

Online Enrichment Games (Fun Stuff)  www.lwcgreen.keyboarding.com

An even easier way to insert a formula that contains the AVERAGE, MIN, MAX, or SUM function is to click the **AutoSum** button drop-down arrow on the Standard toolbar and click a function name from the list. The **AutoSum** button inserts the equal sign (=), the function name, and the range of values to be used in the calculation enclosed in the parentheses. But be careful using the **AutoSum** button—the **AutoSum** button *guesses* at the range to use in a function's calculations! This *guess* is based on how the data is arranged above or to the left of the cell containing the function. Sometimes, the **AutoSum** button guesses incorrectly; then you must edit the function to correct the range. Always verify the function's range when you use the **AutoSum** button.

Instead of typing a function's range, you can select the range with the mouse pointer. Try it!

Ray wants to find the answers to three questions about biosphere size. Help Ray find the answers to his questions by using functions. The biosphere size data in square miles is in the range D5:D51.

Let's add Ray's questions to the worksheet and then find the answers using functions.

1. Enter **How many square miles are in U.S. biosphere reserves?** in cell **B53**. Click cell **D53**, type **=SUM(D5:D51)**, and tap the ENTER key. The total square miles appears in cell D53.

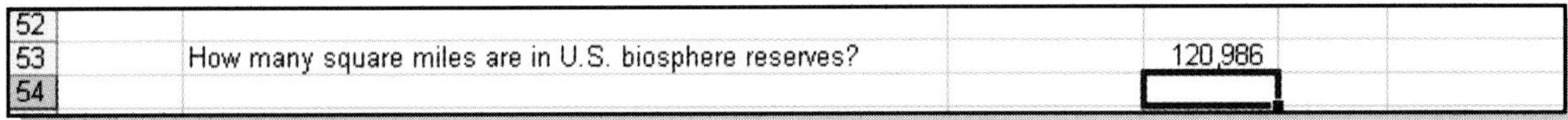

2. Enter **What is the largest biosphere area?** in cell **B54**. Click cell **D54**, click the **AutoSum** button drop-down arrow, and click **Max**. The formula containing the MAX function and a guessed range appears in the cell. Because of the empty cell D52, the **AutoSum** button incorrectly guesses that the range containing the data to use in the MAX calculation is only cell D53. You must correct the range to D5:D51.

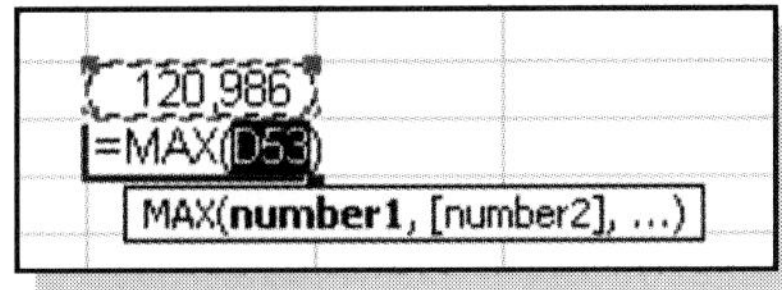

3. Type **D5:D51** and tap the ENTER key. Cell D54 now contains the largest value in the range.

Exploring Across the Curriculum

Internet/Web

You can learn more about budgeting and creating a personal budget by using the Web. Open your Web browser and use a favorite to view the Learning with Computers Web page (www.lwcgreen.keyboarding.com). Click the **Links** option. Click **Project 9**. Click the links to learn more about managing money and credit and creating a personal budget. Take notes about what you learn.

Then create a new *Word* document, save it as *money9*, and set the appropriate margins for an outline. (See the outline example in Appendix A, if necessary). Type the title **MANAGING MY MONEY** at the top of the page and tap the ENTER key twice. Type your notes as outline topics and then use *Word*'s Outline Numbered list feature to format your notes as a three-level outline. Change all level 1 topics to UPPERCASE. Double-space the outline. Save and close the document.

Language Arts: Words to Know

Look up the meaning of the following names and terms using a classroom, library, CD–ROM, or online encyclopedia or dictionary.

budget	assumption	what-if	expenditure
revenue	expense	surplus	deficit

Create a new workbook. Save the workbook as *definitions9*. Rename the Sheet1 sheet tab as **Definitions**. Enter the title **Budget Definitions** in cell A1. Enter the system date and time in cell A2 using the NOW function. Use the **Format Cells** dialog box to merge and center the title across the range A1:B2. Enter **Term** as the column name in A4. Enter **Definition** as the column name in B4. Bold the title and column name. Center the column names in the cells.

Enter the terms in the range A5:A12. Enter the term definitions in the range B5:B12. Use the resizing pointer to automatically fit the cell contents for columns A and B. Sort the terms and definitions in ascending alphabetical order by term. Save and close the workbook.

Explore More

4. Enter **What is the smallest biosphere area?** in cell **B55**. Click cell **D55**, click the **AutoSum** button drop-down arrow, and click **Min**. Again, the **AutoSum** button incorrectly guesses the range. Type **D5:D51** to correct the range and tap the ENTER key. Cell D55 now contains the smallest value in the range.

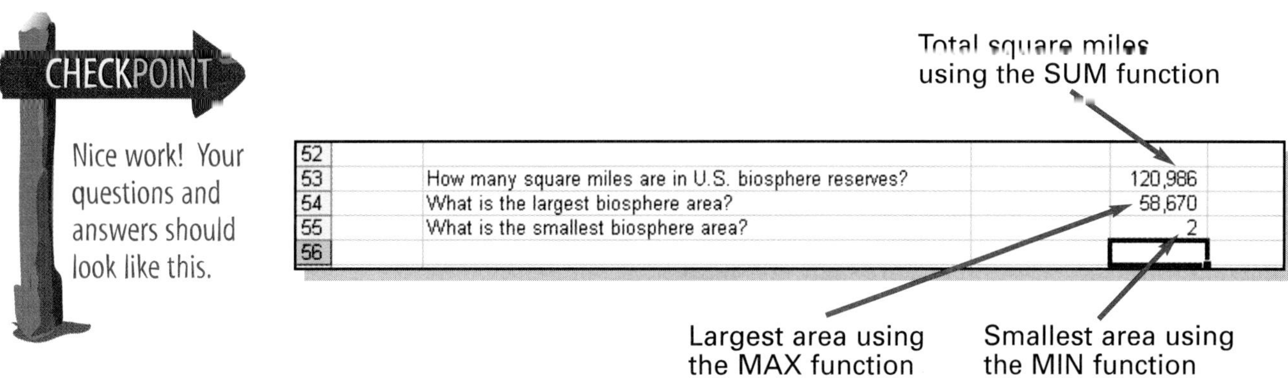

52		
53	How many square miles are in U.S. biosphere reserves?	120,986
54	What is the largest biosphere area?	58,670
55	What is the smallest biosphere area?	2
56		

5. Save and close the workbook.

Project *Skills Review*

You learned a lot in this project! We are very impressed with your progress. Let's take a few minutes to review the skills that you learned.

Open the Format Cells dialog box	Press the CTRL + 1 keys.
Insert or delete rows or columns	Choose **Insert** on the menu bar and choose **Rows** or **Columns**. Right-click one or more column or row headings and click **Insert** or **Delete**. Choose **Edit** on the menu bar and choose **Delete**.
Fill a range of cells with a data series	Drag the active cell's or range's fill handle.
Filter data	Choose **Data** on the menu bar, point to **Filter**, and choose **AutoFilter**.
Use functions	Σ ▾

Exploring on Your Own

Reading in Action

Using Latin Root Words

Use the meaning of the Latin root words to help you write definitions of the words shown on the right.

deficere	to be wanting	deficit
re + *venire*	to come back, return	revenue
ex + *pendere*	to weigh out, expend	expenditure

Math in Action

Finding the Percent of Change

Businesses create budgets to help them keep track of how much money they can spend on what they need. Your business has budgeted \$3,000 for supplies for one month. If \$3,600 is spent on supplies, by what percent will you have to increase your budget?

To find the percent of increase, find the amount of change from your budget to the actual cost, and then divide it by the budgeted amount. Convert the decimal as a percent.

$\$3,600 - \$3,000 = \$600$

$\frac{\$600}{\$3000} = 0.2 = 20\%$

You will have to increase the budget by 20 percent to pay for the supplies.

Now you try it! Find the percent of change for the following:

- A business has a monthly budget of \$40,000 but has expenses of \$44,000.
- A business has a monthly budget of \$50,000 but has expenses of \$30,000.

Exploring on Your Own

Open the *biosphere8* workbook and click the *NPS Biosphere Reserves* sheet tab. Enter today's date in cell A3 and format it as *month spelled out/day/year in four digits*. Select the range A1:D3 and open the **Format Cells** dialog box. Change the font to Times New Roman 12 point bold, and change the horizontal alignment to **Center Across Selection**. Edit the data in the following cells: Change B6 to **Big Bend**; change A21 to **Haleakala**; and change D21 to **29,094**.

Insert a new column to the left of column A and insert four new rows, 37–40, below the data. Enter **Number** in cell A5 and the number **1** in cell A6. Use the **Format Painter** button to copy the formats from cell B5 to cell A5. Use the fill handle to fill the range A6:A36 with numbers 1–31. Then sort the data first by state, then by acreage, and then by park name using the **Sort** dialog box. Use column A to return the data to its original order.

Use AutoFilter to filter the data to show only those biosphere reserves in Texas. Then copy the data, insert a new worksheet named *Texas Biosphere Reserves*, and paste the data in the worksheet. Resize the columns. Return to the *NSP Biosphere Reserves* worksheet, deselect the range, and turn off the AutoFilter. Enter the following questions in cells B38, B39, and B40: **What is the total biosphere acreage managed by the National Park Service? What is the size of the largest biosphere? What is the size of the smallest biosphere?**

Enter a formula to calculate the total biosphere acreage using the SUM function in cell E38. Use the **AutoSum** button and MAX and MIN functions to answer the remaining two questions. Place your answers in cells E39 and E40. (Remember to edit the function's range, if necessary.) Save and close the workbook.

Reading in Action

Restating Informational Text

After you read an informational passage, restate the main ideas and details in your own words.

Biosphere reserves are areas of terrestrial and coastal/marine ecosystems. Ecosystems contain many different living organisms, which interact with the physical environment.

Sentence 1 could be restated as "Biosphere reserves are areas of land and sea on Earth where living things live together with their environment."

Now restate sentence 2.

Math in Action

Using a Conversion Factor

There are 640 acres in 1 square mile. The Champlain-Adirondack biosphere reserve is 15,405 square miles. What is the size of the biosphere reserve in acres?

$15{,}405 \text{ miles}^2 \times \frac{640 \text{ acres}}{1 \text{ mile}^2} = 9{,}859{,}200 \text{ acres}$

Now you try it! The San Dimas Biosphere Reserve and Experimental Forest is 27 square miles. How many acres are in the San Dimas Biosphere Reserve?

Exploring on Your Own

You have learned several new skills in this project. Now blaze your own trail by practicing these skills on your own!

Open the *budget9* workbook and click the *Explorers Club Budget* worksheet. Use the TODAY function to insert the current date in cell A3. Use the **Format Cells** dialog box options to center the date in cell A3 across the range A3:F3, change the font size to 12, apply the Bold font style, and format the date with the month spelled out, the day, and the year in four digits.

Add a thick border and gray shading to the candy sales data in the range H8:I13 using toolbar buttons. Indent the categories below the Revenues and Expenses row names.

Enter formulas to calculate the following for Qtr 1:

Candy sales (B8)	Number of packages (H10) times the sales price per package (I10)
Total Revenues (B10)	Sum of all first quarter revenues (B7:B9)
Cost of candy (B14)	Candy sales times the cost percentage (H13)
Total Expenses (B18)	Sum of all first quarter expenses (B13:B17)
Surplus or (Deficit) (B20)	Revenues remaining after all expenses are paid (B10, B18)

Edit the Candy sales and Cost of candy formulas to make the appropriate cell references absolute references. Then use the fill handle to copy the Qtr 1 formulas to Qtr 2–4.

Use the **AutoSum** button to calculate the totals for each row. Then perform a what-if analysis to determine *what* happens to the budget *if*:

- Qtr 1 car wash revenues are $200.
- Qtr 3 garage sales revenues are $150.
- The number of packages of candy to be sold each quarter is 100.
- The sales price per package is $6.
- The candy cost percentage is 90 percent.
- Educational programs expenses are $200 per quarter.

Save and close the workbook.

Explore More

Exploring Across the Curriculum

Internet/Web

More than 90 countries around the world are partners in UNESCO's Man and the Biosphere program (MAB). You can learn more about this program and international biosphere reserves on the Web. Open your Web browser and use a favorite to view the Learning with Computers Web page (www.lwcgreen.keyboarding.com). Click the **Links** option. Click **Project 8**. Click the link to learn more about MAB and international biosphere reserves. Leave your browser and the UNESCO MAB website open.

The Web

Create a workbook and save it as *SA biosphere8.* Name the Sheet1 tab **SA Biosphere Reserves**. Add a title and today's date. Add the following column headings: **Reserve**, **Country**, **Size in Hectares**, and **Year Named**. Work back and forth between the UNESCO MAB website and the worksheet to find information about the biosphere reserves in South America and record that information on the *SA Biosphere Reserves* worksheet.

Use the **Format Cells** dialog box to format the worksheet. Insert columns and rows as necessary. Use the fill handle to add a sequential identifying number to each row of information you enter. Sort the data by country, size, and reserve name; then use the sequential identifying number to return the data to its original order.

Use AutoFilter to filter the data to show all biosphere reserves in Bolivia. Copy the data and paste it on a new worksheet named **Bolivian Reserves**. Then turn off AutoFilter.

Record the following questions in the *SA Biosphere Reserves* worksheet: **What are the total hectares for all the biosphere reserves in South America? What is the size of the largest biosphere reserve? What is the size of the smallest biosphere reserve?** Use SUM, MAX, and MIN functions to find the answers. Save and close the workbook.

Geography: Research, Organize, and Draw

Draw a map of the United States. Then, using classroom, library, or online resources, together with the data on the *NPS Biosphere Reserves* worksheet in the *biosphere8* workbook, indicate on the U.S. map the approximate location of each biosphere reserve managed by the National Park Service.

Geography

Explore More

Project | *Skills Review*

You learned a lot in this project! We are very impressed with your progress. Let's take a few minutes to review the skills that you learned.

Add a date that automatically updates using a function	Use the TODAY or NOW functions.
Add borders and shading to cells	Press the CTRL + 1 keys.
Indent cell contents or remove the indent	
Enter formulas	Type an equal sign (=), use the mouse pointer to select the cell references, type the calculation operator, tap the ENTER or TAB keys.
Copy or paste formulas	Choose **Edit** on the menu bar and choose **Copy** or **Paste**. Drag the fill handle.
Mark a cell reference as an absolute reference before copying a formula	Type **$** before the column letter and row number. Tap the **F4** key once.
Perform a what-if analysis	Use cell references instead of actual values in a formula. Change cell values and *Excel* automatically recalculates all related formulas.

Exploring Across the Curriculum

Language Arts: Words to Know

Look up the meaning of the following terms using a classroom, library, CD-ROM, or online encyclopedia or dictionary.

biodiversity	biosphere reserve	conservation	ecosystem
environmental	habitat	hectare	sustainable

Create a new workbook. Save the workbook as *definitions8*. Rename the Sheet1 sheet tab as **Definitions**. Enter the title **Biosphere Definitions** in cell A1 and today's date in cell A2. Use the **Format Cells** dialog box to merge and center the title and date across the range A1:B2 and to change the font to Times New Roman 12 point bold.

Enter **Term** as the column name in cell A4. Enter **Definition** as the column name in cell B4. Bold the column names. Center the column names in the cells. Enter the terms in the range A5:A12. Enter definitions for the terms in the range B5:B12. Use the resizing pointer to automatically fit the cell contents for columns A and B. Save and close the workbook.

Getting Help

Getting Help

Type **filling data adjacent cells** in the **Ask A Question** box on the menu bar and tap the ENTER key. Research different ways to use the fill handle to fill data in adjacent cells. Create a blank workbook. Practice the different fill methods you researched. Close the workbook without saving it.

Your Personal Journal

Open your personal journal document. Insert today's date and two blank lines. Think about what you have learned about international biosphere reserves. Why are these reserves important? Write a persuasive paragraph in which you give two or three strong reasons for protecting biosphere areas. Support each reason with specific details. Spell-check, save, and close your journal.

Online Enrichment Games (Fun Stuff)  www.lwcgreen.keyboarding.com

Because you used cell references instead of actual values in each of your formulas, performing Luis's what-if analysis is easy. Each time you change the contents of a cell, *Excel* automatically recalculates the formulas that reference that cell *plus* any TODAY or NOW function in the worksheet. Simply enter the amounts of the new contribution, T-shirt sales estimates, and cost of T-shirts percentage, and let *Excel* do the rest!

Let's see *what* happens to the budget *if* three budget estimates are changed.

1. Enter **250** in cell **D8**. All the formulas that are related to the contents of cell D8 recalculate, including Total Contributions for Qtr 3 and the year, Total Nature Society contributions for the year, Total Revenues for Qtr 3 and the year, and the Surplus or (Deficit) totals for Qtr 3 and the year.
2. Enter **90** in cell **H13** and **80** in cell **H16**. All of the formulas that are related to the contents of cells H13 and H16 recalculate. Scroll the worksheet to see the changes.
3. Enter **500** in cell **D8**, **75** in cell **H13**, and **90** in cell **H16** to return the estimates to their original values. Save and close the workbook.

8a Review ?, CAPS LOCK, TAB, BACKSPACE

Key each line twice. Double-space between 2-line groups.

Technique Tip

Keep your eyes on the textbook as you key.

?

1 ;:? ;:? ;:? Who? What? When? Where? Why? How?

2 Are you going? What day is it? Where is the dog?

caps lock

3 The CAPS LOCK is located to the LEFT of the A key.

4 I belonged to FBLA before joining PHI BETA LAMBDA.

tab

5 TAB→ Rick TAB→ Lexi TAB→ Barb TAB→ Rico ENTER

6 TAB→ Jake TAB→ Sally TAB→ Ben TAB→ Maria ENTER

backspace

7 abbackspacebcbackspacecdbackspacedebackspaceefbackspacefgbackspace

8 ghbackspacehibackspaceijbackspacejkbackspaceklbackspacelmbackspace

8b Technique: Shift Keys

Key each line twice single-spaced; double-space between 2-line groups.

1 aA bB cC dD eE fF gG hH iI jJ kK lL mM nN oO pP qQ

2 Rr Ss Tt Uu Vv Ww Xx Yy Zz AbC DeF GhI JkL MnO PqR

3 Monday, Tuesday, Wednesday, Thursday, and Saturday

4 October, November, December, January, and February

5 James R. Draxler; Amy C. Weaver; Kent G. Abernathy

6 The mayors of San Francisco and Los Angeles spoke.

7 The Yankees play the Mets on Tuesday or Wednesday.

8 Hank and Sally saw Mount Rushmore in South Dakota.

9 San Jacinto and San Luis Obispo are in California.

CHECKPOINT

Your worksheet should look like this.

Completed budget worksheet

	A	B	C	D	E	F
5		Qtr 1	Qtr 2	Qtr 3	Qtr 4	Total
6	**Revenues**					
7	Contributions					
8	Nature Society	$ 500	$ 500	$ 500	$ 500	$ 2,000
9	XYZ Corporation	300	300	300	300	1,200
10	Friends of West Meadov	150	150	150	150	600
11	Total Contributions	950	950	950	950	3,800
12	Other Revenues					
13	T-shirt sales	750	750	750	750	3,000
14	Bake sales	100	75	100	75	350
15	Total Other Revenues	850	825	850	825	3,350
16	Total Revenues	$ 1,800	$ 1,775	$ 1,800	$ 1,775	$ 7,150
17						
18	**Expenses**					
19	Educational programs	$ 250	$ 200	$ 350	$ 300	$ 1,100
20	Cost of T-shirts	675	675	675	675	2,700
21	Wildflower seeds	50	-	50	-	100
22	Grass seeds	-	25	-	25	50
23	Dr. Montague (Vet)	75	75	75	75	300
24	Maintenance	750	750	500	250	2,250
25	Total Expenses	$ 1,800	$ 1,725	$ 1,650	$ 1,325	$ 6,500
26						
27	**Surplus or (Deficit)**	$ -	$ 50	$ 150	$ 450	$ 650

Fantastic! Your worksheet looks great! But what will happen if some of the budget estimates are changed? Let's see.

TRAIL 5 MARKER

Performing a What-if Analysis

what-if analysis

When you create a budget using data based on expectations of future events, you may have to modify the budget as new information is received and expectations change.

For example, Luis now has new information that suggests three budget estimates should be changed: (1) the Qtr 3 contribution from the Nature Society may be $250; (2) the estimated number of T-shirts to be sold each quarter may be 90; and (3) the cost of T-shirts may be 80 percent of sales. To understand how making these three changes will affect the budget, Luis wants you to perform a what-if analysis—*what* will happen *if* a number is changed.

Project 9
Worksheets

Budgeting for a Wildlife Preserve

Explorers' Guide

Data file: *budget*

Objectives:

In this project, you will:

- use a function to insert a date
- apply borders and shading and indent cell contents
- enter basic formulas
- copy and paste formulas
- perform a what-if analysis

Exploring on Your Own

additional practice in:

- using a function to insert a date
- applying borders and shading and indenting cell contents
- entering basic formulas
- copying and pasting formulas
- performing a what-if analysis

Exploring Across the Curriculum

Internet/Web
Language Arts
Math
Getting Help
Your Personal Journal

Our Exploration Assignment:

Creating a budget

The Explorers Club has volunteered to work with students at the local high school to turn a small meadow into a wildlife preserve. Luis is creating an annual budget for the new wildlife preserve. Would you like to help? Great! Just follow the Trail Markers to use the TODAY function to enter a date for a worksheet; add cell borders and shading; indent cell contents; enter, copy, and paste formulas; and then perform a *what-if analysis* on the budget data.

Let's calculate the totals for each row using the AutoSum button.

1. Select the range **B8:F11** and then use the CTRL key to select the following nonadjacent ranges: **B13:F16**, **B19:F25**, and **B27:F27**.

	A	B	C	D	E	F
5		**Qtr 1**	**Qtr 2**	**Qtr 3**	**Qtr 4**	**Total**
6	**Revenues**					
7	Contributions					
8	Nature Society	$ 500	$ 500	$ 500	$ 500	
9	XYZ Corporation	300	300	300	300	
10	Friends of West Meadov	150	150	150	150	
11	Total Contributions	950	950	950	950	
12	Other Revenues					
13	T-shirt sales	750	750	750	750	
14	Bake sales	100	75	100	75	
15	Total Other Revenues	850	825	850	825	
16	Total Revenues	$ 1,800	$ 1,775	$ 1,800	$ 1,775	
17						
18	**Expenses**					
19	Educational programs	$ 250	$ 200	$ 350	$ 300	
20	Cost of T-shirts	675	675	675	675	
21	Wildflower seeds	50	-	50	-	
22	Grass seeds	-	25	-	25	
23	Dr. Montague (Vet)	75	75	75	75	
24	Maintenance	750	750	500	250	
25	Total Expenses	$ 1,800	$ 1,725	$ 1,650	$ 1,325	
26						
27	**Surplus or (Deficit)**	$ -	$ 50	$ 150	$ 450	

2. Click the **AutoSum** button face to insert the SUM function in each blank cell. Each row in the selected ranges is added horizontally and the results and formulas entered in the blank cells. Press the CTRL + HOME keys and save the workbook.

Starting Out!

Begin by opening Luis's workbook and saving it with a new name.

1. Open the *budget* workbook and save it as *budget9*.

Let's add a date that automatically updates to the current date on the *West Meadow Budget* worksheet.

Ergonomics TIP

Do your feet reach the floor? If not, be sure to use a footrest when sitting in your computer chair.

Using a Function to Insert a Date

TRAIL 1 MARKER

system clock

In the last project, you learned how to enter and format a date. Once inserted, that date never changes. But sometimes you may want the date to change each time the workbook is opened or each time formulas on the worksheet are recalculated. You can do this with the TODAY or NOW functions. These functions use your computer's system clock. The TODAY function inserts today's date. The NOW function inserts today's date and time. You can see the current time on the right side of the task bar. To see the current date in a ScreenTip, point to the current time on the task bar.

To enter the TODAY or NOW functions, type an equal sign (=), the name of the function, and a set of parentheses. The parentheses remain empty—you *do not* type or select a range of cells inside them—but the parentheses must be included!

If you forget to include a set of parentheses for the TODAY or NOW functions, you will see the #NAME? error message in the cell. This means that *Excel* does not recognize the function without the empty parentheses.

Let's insert today's date in cell A3.

1. Enter =**TODAY**() in cell **A3**. *Don't forget to type the set of parentheses!*
2. Select the range **A3:F3** and open the **Format Cells** dialog box. Center the date across the selection, change the font size to 12 point, apply the Bold font style, and change the date format to month spelled out, day, and year in four digits.

Great! Now let's make the worksheet easier to read by adding an outline border and gray shading to a range of cells and by indenting row names.

Let's copy the formulas.

1. Click cell **B11** and drag the fill handle to cell **E11**. Click cell **C11** and view the copied formula with relative references in the Formula Bar.
2. Click cell **B13** and drag the fill handle to cell **E13**. Click cell **C13** and view the copied formula with absolute references in the Formula Bar.
3. Click cell **B15** and drag the fill handle to cell **E15**. Click cell **B16** and drag the fill handle to cell **E16**. Click cell **B20** and drag the fill handle to cell **E20**. Click cell **B25** and drag the fill handle to cell **E25**. Click cell **B27** and drag the fill handle to cell **E27**. Press the CTRL + HOME keys and save the workbook.

Your worksheet should look like this.

	A	B	C	D	E
5		**Qtr 1**	**Qtr 2**	**Qtr 3**	**Qtr 4**
6	**Revenues**				
7	Contributions				
8	Nature Society	$ 500	$ 500	$ 500	$ 500
9	XYZ Corporation	300	300	300	300
10	Friends of West Meadov	150	150	150	150
11	Total Contributions	950	950	950	950
12	Other Revenues				
13	T-shirt sales	750	750	750	750
14	Bake sales	100	75	100	75
15	Total Other Revenues	850	825	850	825
16	Total Revenues	$ 1,800	$ 1,775	$ 1,800	$ 1,775
17					
18	**Expenses**				
19	Educational programs	$ 250	$ 200	$ 350	$ 300
20	Cost of T-shirts	675	675	675	675
21	Wildflower seeds	50	-	50	-
22	Grass seeds	-	25	-	25
23	Dr. Montague (Vet)	75	75	75	75
24	Maintenance	750	750	500	250
25	Total Expenses	$ 1,800	$ 1,725	$ 1,650	$ 1,325
26					
27	**Surplus or (Deficit)**	$ -	$ 50	$ 150	$ 450

Copied formulas

Super! Now let's calculate the row totals in column F. Instead of entering individual formulas using the SUM function, use the **AutoSum** button. After you select all the data to be added plus blank cells to contain the SUM function, *Excel* can automatically insert the totals in multiple blank cells at one time.

Applying Borders and Shading and Indenting Cell Contents

You can use borders and shading to draw attention to worksheet data. To add a border, click the **Borders** button drop-down arrow on the Formatting toolbar and click a border style. To add shading, click the **Fill Color** button drop down arrow on the Formatting toolbar and click a color on the color grid.

You can apply borders and shading with options in the **Border** and **Patterns** tabs in the **Format Cells** dialog box.

Let's add borders and shading to the range H10:I16.

1. Select the range **H10:I16** using the SHIFT + click method.
2. Click the **Borders** button drop-down arrow and click the **Thick Box Border** option on the grid.
3. Click the **Fill Color** button drop-down arrow and click the **Gray-25%** color on the grid. This is the last color in the second row from the bottom on the color grid. Press the CTRL + HOME keys and save the workbook.

Range formatted with thick border and gray shading

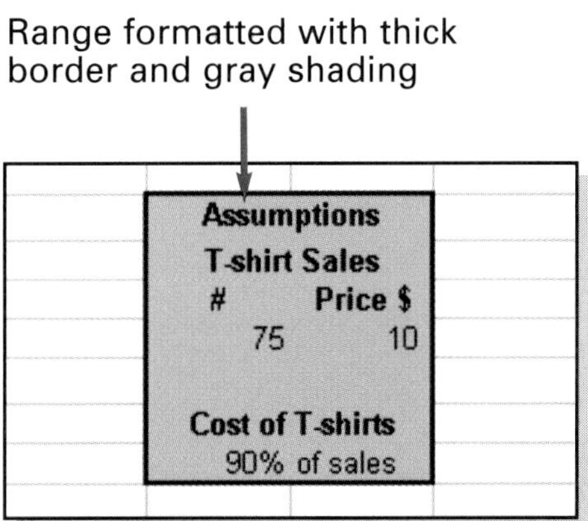

The row names in the worksheet identify categories, subcategories, subtotals, and totals. Make the row names easier to read by indenting the subcategory and subtotal text below each main category. Indent cell contents from the left side of the cell by clicking the **Increase Indent** button on the Formatting toolbar. To remove indents, click the **Decrease Indent** button.

Sometimes you do not want *Excel* to change a row or column reference when you copy and paste a formula. For example, in the *West Meadow Budget* worksheet, the number of T-shirts sold is always found in cell H13; the cost per T-shirt is always found in cell I13; and the T-shirt costs percentage of sales is always found in cell H16. When you copy formulas containing these cell references, you want the cell references to remain H13, I13, or H16. This is called copying and pasting with absolute references—cell references that *do not* change when copied and pasted.

To indicate an absolute reference, you insert a dollar sign ($) before the column letter and row number in the cell reference. An example of absolute references is the formula =H13*I13. The dollar sign ($) tells *Excel* not to change the column or row references when the formula is copied to the left or right in the same row or up or down in the same column. To add dollar signs to a cell reference, type the dollar signs or tap the **F4** key.

Let's edit two formulas to change relative references to absolute references.

1. Click cell **B13**. Use the I-beam pointer to select the entire formula in the Formula Bar; then tap the **F4** key one time to add the $ to both cell references.

2. Tap the ENTER key. The formula in cell B13 now includes two absolute references. Click cell **B20**. Click in the Formula Bar at the end of the H16 reference and tap the **F4** key one time.

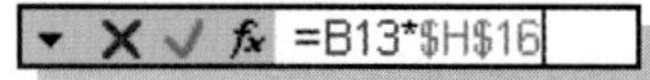

3. Tap the ENTER key. The formula in cell B20 now includes one absolute reference.

Nicely done! Now you are ready to copy the formulas.

Let's indent the row name subcategories and subtotal text.

1. Click cell **A7** and then use the CTRL key to select cells **A11**, **A12**, **A15**, and the range **A19:A24**. Click the **Increase Indent** button one time.
2. Select the range **A8:A10** and then use the CTRL key to select the range **A13:A14**. Click the **Increase Indent** button twice. Press the CTRL + HOME keys and save the workbook.

CHECKPOINT

Your indented row names should look like this.

Indented row names

6	**Revenues**	
7	Contributions	
8	Nature Society	$ 500
9	XYZ Corporation	300
10	Friends of West Meadow	150
11	Total Contributions	
12	Other Revenues	
13	T-shirt sales	
14	Bake sales	100
15	Total Other Revenues	
16	Total Revenues	
17		
18	**Expenses**	
19	Educational programs	$ 250
20	Cost of T-shirts	
21	Wildflower seeds	50
22	Grass seeds	-
23	Dr. Montague (Vet)	75
24	Maintenance	750
25	Total Expenses	

Super! Next, let's enter the formulas to calculate T-shirt sales and costs, subtotals, and totals.

TRAIL 3 MARKER

Entering Basic Formulas

budget
calculation
operator

Do you have a part-time job such as babysitting or mowing the lawn? And do you plan how much of the money you earn will be saved for future use and how much you can spend now on clothes, CDs, movies, and other items? Perhaps you even plan how much money you will earn and spend over the entire year. This plan is called a budget.

CHECKPOINT

Your Qtr 1 calculations should look like this.

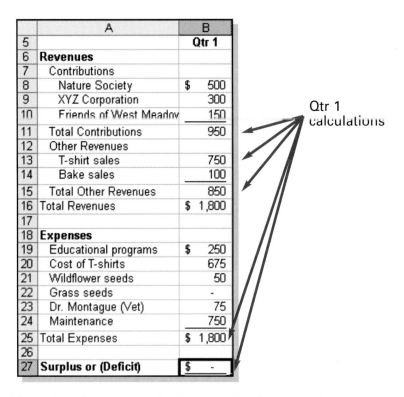

	A	B
5		Qtr 1
6	**Revenues**	
7	Contributions	
8	Nature Society	$ 500
9	XYZ Corporation	300
10	Friends of West Meadov	150
11	Total Contributions	950
12	Other Revenues	
13	T-shirt sales	750
14	Bake sales	100
15	Total Other Revenues	850
16	Total Revenues	$ 1,800
17		
18	**Expenses**	
19	Educational programs	$ 250
20	Cost of T-shirts	675
21	Wildflower seeds	50
22	Grass seeds	-
23	Dr. Montague (Vet)	75
24	Maintenance	750
25	Total Expenses	$ 1,800
26		
27	**Surplus or (Deficit)**	$ -

Qtr 1 calculations

Excellent! You could continue by entering the formulas for the remaining quarters. But it is much easier to copy the formulas you created for Qtr 1 to the remaining quarters and then use the **AutoSum** button to enter formulas for the totals in column F.

TRAIL 4 MARKER

Copying and Pasting Formulas

relative reference
absolute reference

Excel has special rules for copying and pasting formulas. When you copy a formula in one cell and paste it in the cell to the right, *Excel* automatically changes the column references. For example, the formula =B13+B14 appears as =C13+C14 when you copy and paste it in the next cell to the right. This is called copying and pasting with **relative references**—cell references that automatically change to reflect the formula's new position in the worksheet. *Excel* also changes row references when formulas are copied and pasted up or down to cells in the same column. By default, *Excel* copies and pastes formulas with relative references.

Use the **Copy** and **Paste** button or commands to copy and paste formulas anywhere in the worksheet. Use the fill handle to copy formulas into adjacent cells.

Look carefully at the *West Meadow Budget* worksheet. It contains estimates of what money will be available (revenues) and what money will be spent (expenses) to maintain the West Meadow Wildlife Preserve for an entire year. Any money left over after paying expenses will be a budget surplus. But if expenses are greater than the revenues, then there will be a budget deficit, and more money will be needed to maintain the wildlife preserve.

When you type or edit a formula, *Excel* color codes the cell reference borders. This gives you a visual clue about where the cells are located in the worksheet.

The estimates of revenues and expenses are based on the assumptions that over the next year:

- Money will be received (revenues) from contributions, the sale of T-shirts, and bake sales.
- Money will be spent (expenses) on educational programs, purchasing the T-shirts, wildflower and grass seeds, vet visits for injured birds and small mammals, and maintaining the meadow.

The *West Meadow Budget* worksheet already contains some data and formatting. But the formulas to calculate the T-shirt sales and costs, subtotals, and totals have not been entered. To enter a formula in a cell, type the equal sign, then select cell references, and type the calculation operator (+, −, *, or /) needed to perform the calculation. To calculate the totals, you can use the **AutoSum** button to insert the SUM function.

Instead of entering values in the formulas, you will enter the cell references that contain those values. Look carefully at the range H10:I16 in the *West Meadow Budget* worksheet to locate the estimates for T-shirt sales and costs. Then review the Qtr 1 column to locate each of the following cell references:

- Total Contributions in cell B11 and the individual contributions in the range B8:B10
- T-shirt sales in cell B13
- Total Other Revenues in cell B15
- Total Revenues in cell B16
- Cost of T-shirts in cell B20
- Total Expenses in cell B25 and individual expenses in the range B19:B24
- Surplus or (Deficit) in cell B27

To avoid typing errors, use the mouse pointer to select cells as you build the formulas and use the asterisk (*), plus sign (+), and minus sign (−) keys on the numeric keypad. Ready? Let's do it!

Let's enter the Qtr 1 formulas.

1. *Calculate Qtr 1 Total Contributions.* Click cell **B11** and type =**SUM**(and then drag to select the range **B8:B10**. Tap the ENTER key. *Excel* adds the closing parenthesis and enters the formula in the cell. Click cell **B11** again. Cell B11 contains the result of the calculation—950—and the Formula Bar shows the actual formula, =SUM(B8:B10).
2. *Calculate Qtr 1 T-shirt sales.* Click cell **B13** and type an equal sign (=). Then click cell **H13**, type an asterisk (*), click cell **I13**, and tap the ENTER key. Click cell **B13** again. Cell B13 contains the result of the calculation—750—and the Formula Bar shows the actual formula.
3. *Calculate Qtr 1 Total Other Revenues.* Click cell **B15** and type an equal sign (=). Then click cell **B13**, type a plus sign (+), click cell **B14**, and tap the ENTER key. Click cell **B15** again. Cell B15 contains the result of the calculation—850—and the Formula Bar shows the actual formula.
4. *Calculate Qtr 1 Total Revenues.* Click cell **B16** and type an equal sign (=). Then click cell **B11**, type a plus sign (+), click cell **B15**, and tap the ENTER key. Click cell **B16** again. Cell B16 contains the result of the calculation—$1,800—and the Formula Bar shows the actual formula.
5. *Calculate Qtr 1 Cost of T-shirts.* Click cell **B20** and type an equal sign (=). Then click cell **B13**, type an asterisk (*), click cell **H16**, and tap the ENTER key. Click cell **B20** again. Cell B20 contains the result of the calculation–675—and the Formula Bar shows the actual formula.
6. *Calculate Qtr 1 Total Expenses.* Click cell **B25** and type =**SUM**(and then select the range **B19:B24**. Tap the ENTER key. Click cell **B25** again. Cell B25 contains the result of the calculation—$1,800—and the Formula Bar contains the actual formula.
7. *Calculate Qtr 1 Surplus or (Deficit).* Click cell **B27** and type an equal sign (=). Then click cell **B16**, type a minus sign (−), click cell **B25**, and tap the ENTER key. Click cell **B27** again. Cell B27 contains a dash representing 0 (zero) formatted with the Currency Style, and the Formula Bar shows the actual formula. Save the workbook.

Three-Level Outline

A three-level outline has main topics, subtopics, and details that support a subtopic. Subtopics are indented under the main topic. Details are indented under subtopics. Each outline level is numbered or lettered according to a set system. The most common system is Roman numerals (I, II, III) for main topics; uppercase letters (A, B, C) for subtopics; and Arabic numerals (1, 2, 3) for details.

An outline should have 2-inch top, left, and right margins and a 1-inch bottom margin. Its title should be centered between the left and right margins. A short outline should be double-spaced.

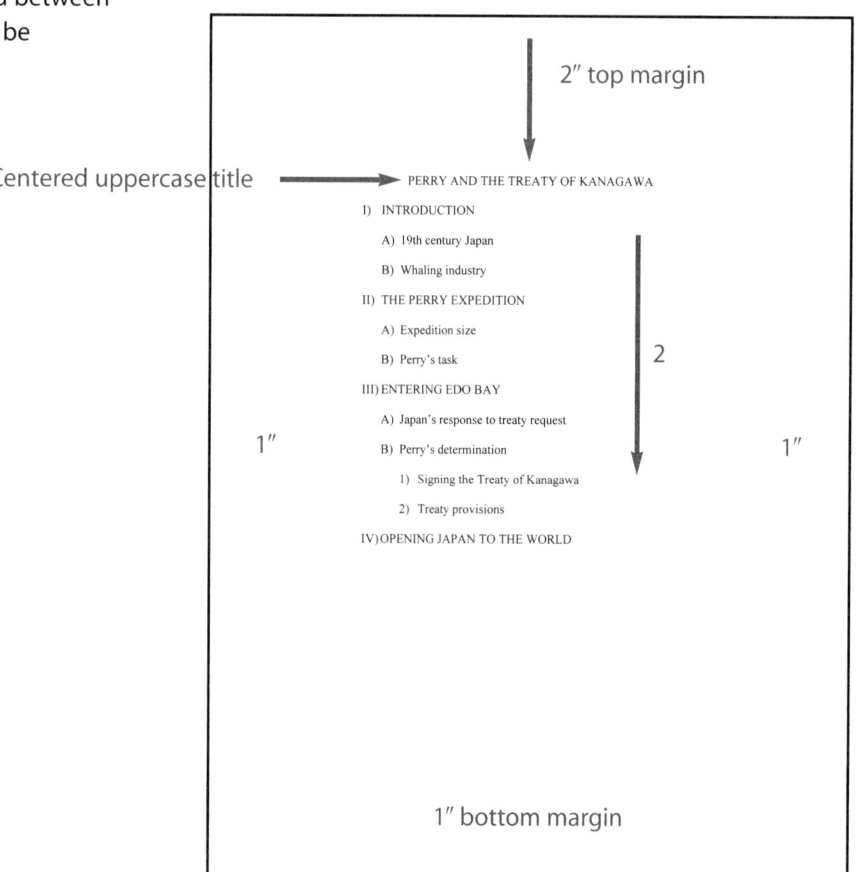

2″ top margin
Centered uppercase title
PERRY AND THE TREATY OF KANAGAWA
I) INTRODUCTION
A) 19th century Japan
B) Whaling industry
II) THE PERRY EXPEDITION
A) Expedition size
B) Perry's task
III) ENTERING EDO BAY
A) Japan's response to treaty request
B) Perry's determination
1) Signing the Treaty of Kanagawa
2) Treaty provisions
IV) OPENING JAPAN TO THE WORLD
2
1″
1″
1″ bottom margin

Exploring Across the Curriculum

Science: Talk About Science

You have probably conducted many scientific experiments. Can you explain one? Explain the steps of a scientific experiment. Begin with a hypothesis. Apply the Bold style to the hypothesis. Use bullets for the steps. Explain the results. End with the conclusion and apply the Italic style to the conclusion. Remember to speak carefully! Add a few words to the speech dictionary to help eliminate errors.

Getting Help

Click the **Help** button on the Language bar to learn how to format a title for a report. Create a new document and add a title. Then follow the steps given in the Help menu to format it. Close your document without saving it.

Your Personal Journal

Open your personal journal document. Insert today's date and two blank lines. Dictate how you feel about using speech recognition tools. Was using the tools easier than typing the words? Would you like to use speech recognition again? Support your answer with specific details.

Online Enrichment Games (Fun Stuff)  www.lwcgreen.keyboarding.com

Unbound Single-Page Report

An unbound single-page report has a 2-inch top margin, a 1-inch bottom margin, and 1-inch left and right margins. The main heading is in uppercase characters and centered horizontally at the top of the document. A quadruple space (three blank lines) separates a main heading from the body text.

Lines may be single- or double-spaced. Paragraphs are double-spaced. Side headings are underlined and have a double space above and below.

With single spaced body paragraphs, each paragraph begins at the left margin. With double-spaced body paragraphs, each paragraph is indented 0.5 inch from the left margin.

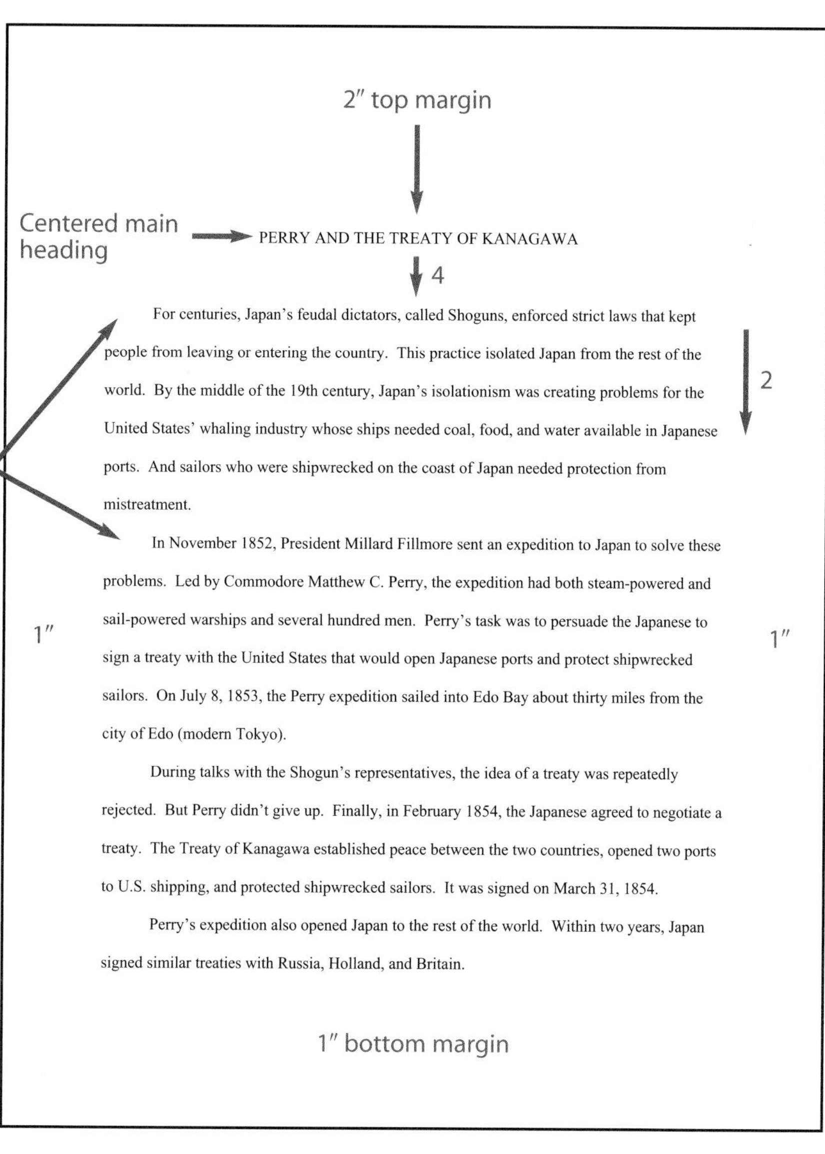

2″ top margin
Centered main heading
PERRY AND THE TREATY OF KANAGAWA
4
Indented body text paragraphs
2
1″
1″
For centuries, Japan's feudal dictators, called Shoguns, enforced strict laws that kept people from leaving or entering the country. This practice isolated Japan from the rest of the world. By the middle of the 19th century, Japan's isolationism was creating problems for the United States' whaling industry whose ships needed coal, food, and water available in Japanese ports. And sailors who were shipwrecked on the coast of Japan needed protection from mistreatment.
In November 1852, President Millard Fillmore sent an expedition to Japan to solve these problems. Led by Commodore Matthew C. Perry, the expedition had both steam-powered and sail-powered warships and several hundred men. Perry's task was to persuade the Japanese to sign a treaty with the United States that would open Japanese ports and protect shipwrecked sailors. On July 8, 1853, the Perry expedition sailed into Edo Bay about thirty miles from the city of Edo (modern Tokyo).
During talks with the Shogun's representatives, the idea of a treaty was repeatedly rejected. But Perry didn't give up. Finally, in February 1854, the Japanese agreed to negotiate a treaty. The Treaty of Kanagawa established peace between the two countries, opened two ports to U.S. shipping, and protected shipwrecked sailors. It was signed on March 31, 1854.
Perry's expedition also opened Japan to the rest of the world. Within two years, Japan signed similar treaties with Russia, Holland, and Britain.
1″ bottom margin

Exploring Across the Curriculum

Internet/Web

TheWeb

Use search engines and directories to find out about improvements in speech recognition software. Visit the following websites to learn more:

www.speakingsolutions.com/news/art19.htm

www.ScanSoft.com

www.Microsoft.com/speech

www.IBM.com/speech

Language Arts: Words to Know

Language Arts

Look up the meaning of the following terms using a classroom, CD-ROM, or online encyclopedia or dictionary.

oral tradition	journalist	transcriptionists
historian	transcription	

Create a new document. Use your speech recognition tools to write each word and definition. Save the document as *definitions B*.

Social Studies: Research, Write, and Map It!

Social Studies

Research a historical event. Write two or three paragraphs about this event, including details that answer the questions *who, what, when, where, why*, and *how*. Give the report a title and use voice commands to format the document.

Explore More

Unbound Multi-page Report

An unbound multi-page report has a 2-inch top margin on the first page; a 1-inch top margin on the remaining pages; and a 1-inch bottom margin and 1-inch left and right margins on all pages. The main heading is in uppercase characters and centered horizontally at the top of the first page. A quadruple space (three blank lines) separates a main heading from the body text.

Body text paragraphs may be single-spaced or double-spaced. Paragraphs are double-spaced. Side headings are underlined and double-spaced.

When paragraphs are single-spaced, each paragraph begins at the left margin. When paragraphs are double-spaced, each paragraph is indented 0.5 inch from the left margin.

The first page usually does not have a page number; but if it does, the page number is centered at the bottom of the page. The page number on the remaining pages is in the upper-right corner of the page.

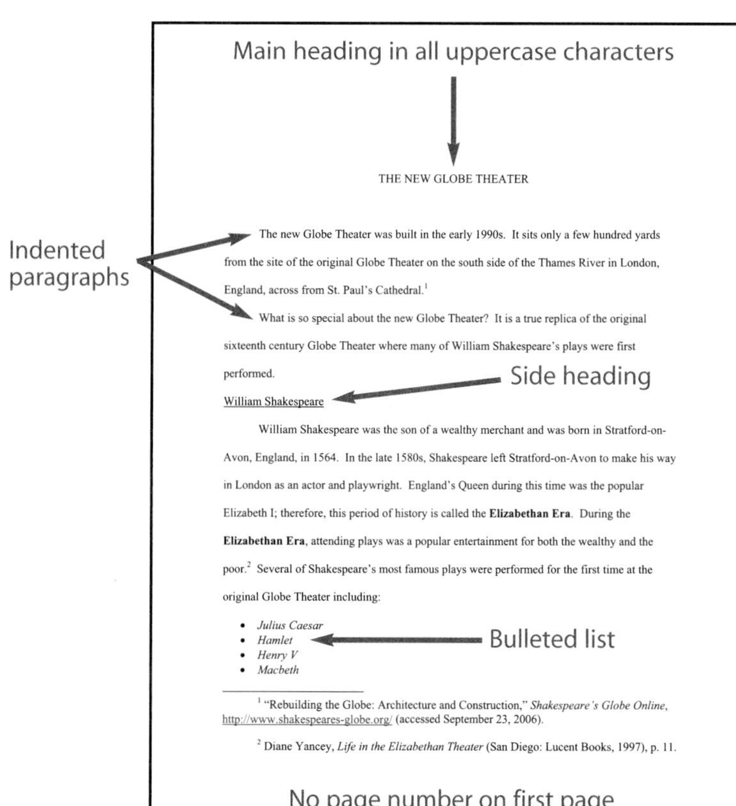

THE NEW GLOBE THEATER

The new Globe Theater was built in the early 1990s. It sits only a few hundred yards from the site of the original Globe Theater on the south side of the Thames River in London, England, across from St. Paul's Cathedral.[1]

What is so special about the new Globe Theater? It is a true replica of the original sixteenth century Globe Theater where many of William Shakespeare's plays were first performed.

William Shakespeare

William Shakespeare was the son of a wealthy merchant and was born in Stratford-on-Avon, England, in 1564. In the late 1580s, Shakespeare left Stratford-on-Avon to make his way in London as an actor and playwright. England's Queen during this time was the popular Elizabeth I; therefore, this period of history is called the **Elizabethan Era**. During the **Elizabethan Era**, attending plays was a popular entertainment for both the wealthy and the poor.[2] Several of Shakespeare's most famous plays were performed for the first time at the original Globe Theater including:

- *Julius Caesar*
- *Hamlet*
- *Henry V*
- *Macbeth*

[1] "Rebuilding the Globe: Architecture and Construction," *Shakespeare's Globe Online*, http://www.shakespeares-globe.org/ (accessed September 23, 2006).

[2] Diane Yancey, *Life in the Elizabethan Theater* (San Diego: Lucent Books, 1997), p. 11.

Page number

1″ top margin

2

The Original Globe Theater

Before 1576, plays were performed by traveling actors in the private homes of the wealthy, town halls, and inn courtyards.[3] By 1599, when the original Globe Theater was built, open-air theaters were very popular. Two other open-air theaters, the Rose and the Swan, were also located on the south bank of the Thames near the Globe Theater.

No one knows just what the original Globe Theater looked like. But past documents, maps, and the remains of other **Elizabethan Era** buildings give us a clue. It was likely built in a circle using wood and plaster. The stage jutted out into an uncovered courtyard where the poor stood—rain or shine—to watch the play. Side gallery seating areas for the wealthy were covered by a thatched roof. The original Globe Theater accidentally burned to the ground in 1613. It was rebuilt in 1614 and thrived until 1642 when the Puritan government closed it.[4]

The New Globe Theater

The new Globe Theater is also an open-air arena built of wood and plaster with seating areas covered with a thatched roof. Special permission was needed to restore the theater's thatched roof because of the possible fire hazard. A sprinkler system and extra exits are the chief differences between the original Globe Theater and the new Globe Theater.

Several of Shakespeare's plays are performed during each summer season. School children attend the special educational programs at the theater. Thousands of visitors also tour the Shakespeare Globe Exhibit at the theater each year.

[3] Christopher Martin, *Shakespeare* (Vero Beach: Rourke Enterprises, Inc., 1988), p. 35.

[4] Peter Chrisp, *Shakespeare* (New York: Dorling Kindersley Eyewitness Books, 2002), p. 35.

Exploring on Your Own

You have learned many new skills in this project. Now put your skills to work by transcribing an oral history. Interview a family member, a relative, a friend or a teacher about an event in history he or she experienced. Take notes and then turn your notes into one or two paragraphs about this event.

Open *Word* and create a new document. Name the document *oral history*. Open your Language bar. Using your speech tools, read aloud your paragraphs. Format your writing by applying Bold, Italic, and Underline font styles to specific words, such as the names of the people and places in your oral history. You may want to do a bulleted list too! Use your keyboard to correct any mistakes.

Cover Sheet for Unbound Multi-page Report

A cover sheet or title page gives the report title in all uppercase letters centered 2 inches from the top of the page. The writer's name and school or organization is centered and double-spaced in mixed case letters approximately 5 inches from the top of the page. The date of the report is centered approximately 9 inches from the top of the page.

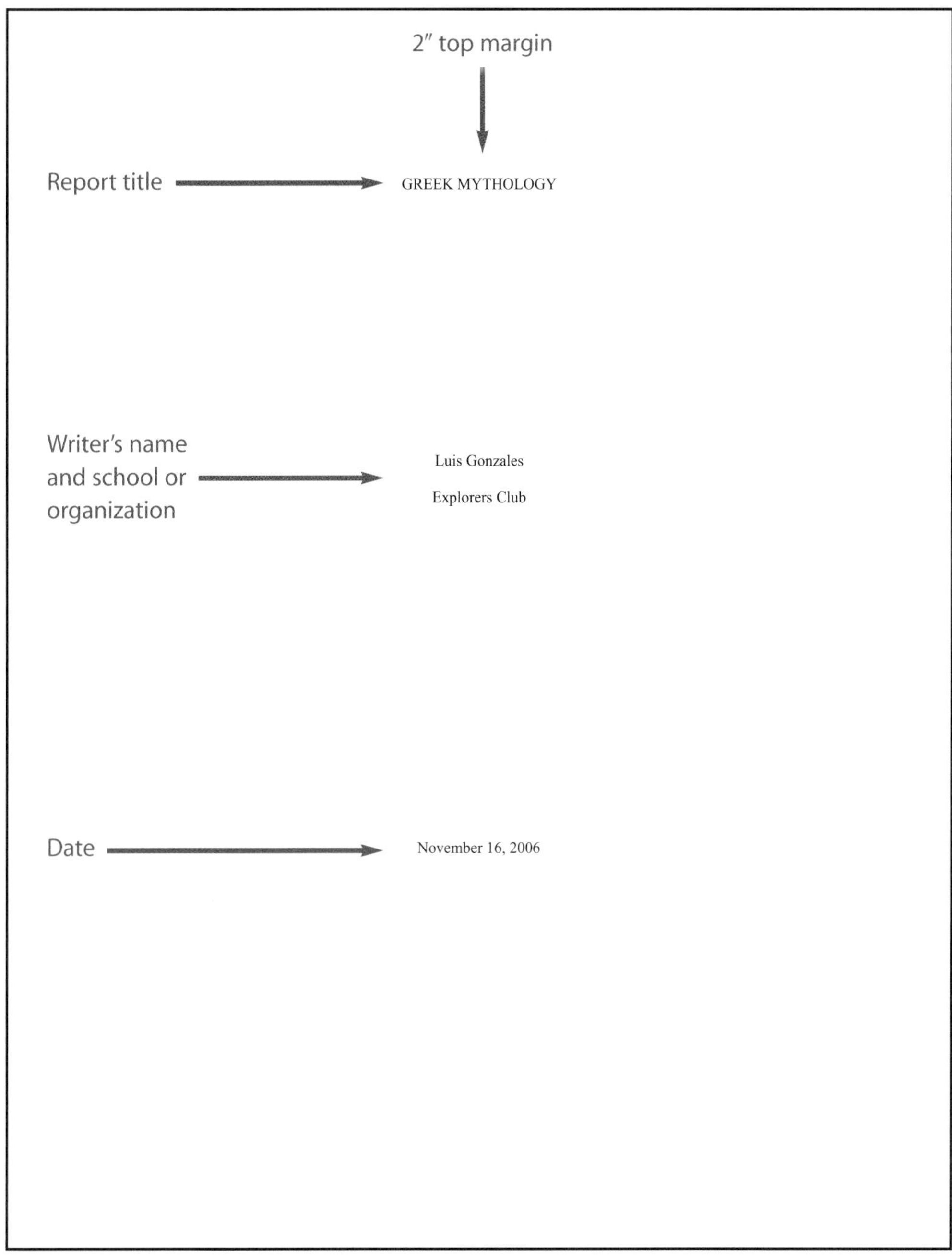

Project | *Skills Review*

You learned a lot in this project! We are very impressed with your progress. Let's take a few minutes to review the skills that you learned.

Place your headset in the proper position.	The speaking portion of your microphone should be three-quarters of an inch away from your lower lip. The headset should fit comfortably and should be in the same position every time you speak to your computer.
Train your speech software.	Read your initial training story clearly. Speak the way you intend to talk to your computer.
Dictate text.	Dictation
Dictate commands.	Voice Command
Add a name or troublesome words.	Add/Delete Word(s)
Format documents.	In Voice Command mode, say various formatting commands like BOLD, ITALIC, and UNDERLINE.

Endnotes

Each reference is indicated by a superscript number. The endnote citations are placed on a separate page at the end of the report.

The endnotes page has the same margins as the first page of the report and the main heading ENDNOTES centered at the top of the page.

The page number appears in the upper-right corner of the page.

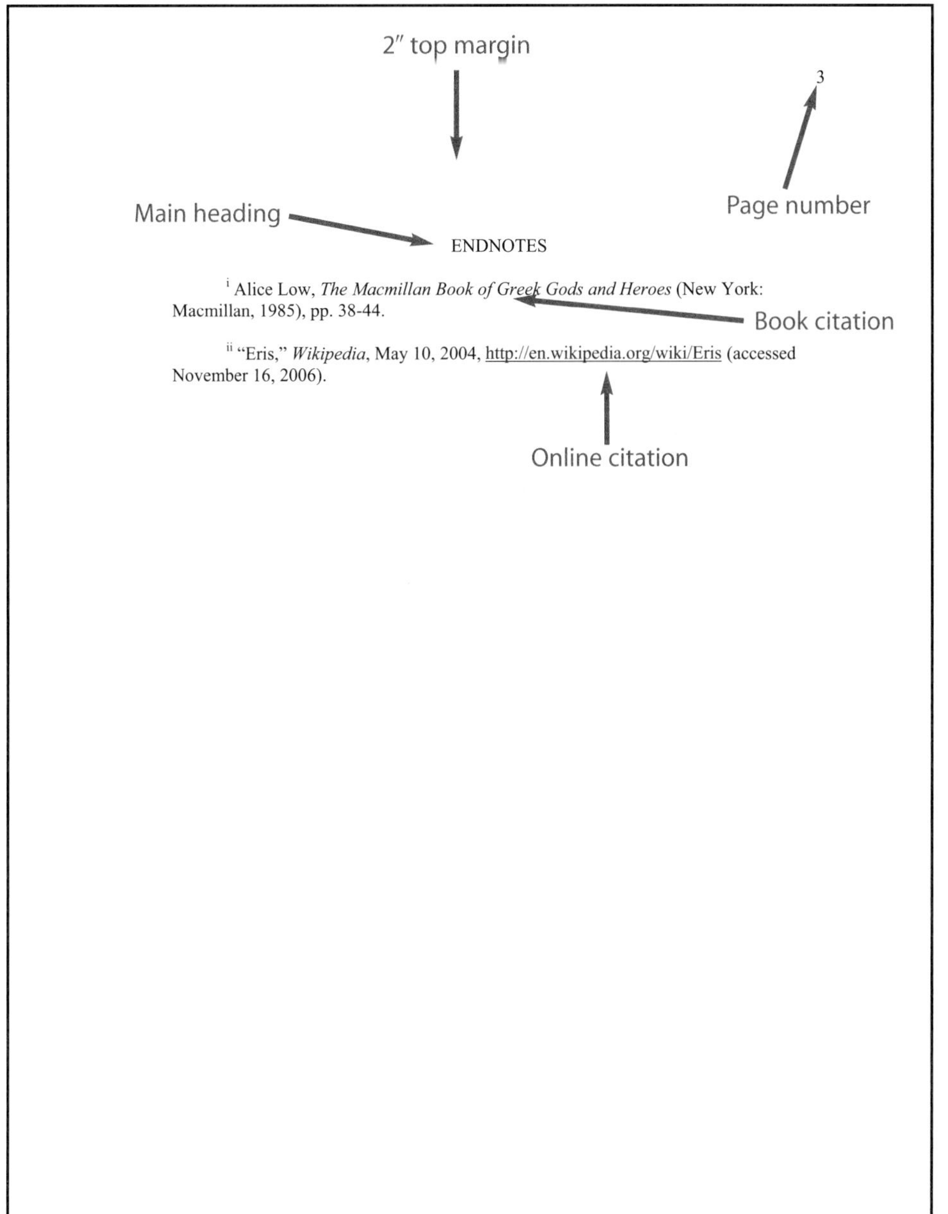

2″ top margin
3
Page number
Main heading
ENDNOTES
i Alice Low, The Macmillan Book of Greek Gods and Heroes (New York: Macmillan, 1985), pp. 38-44.
Book citation
ii "Eris," Wikipedia, May 10, 2004, http://en.wikipedia.org/wiki/Eris (accessed November 16, 2006).
Online citation

Your combined dictation exercises should look similar to this.

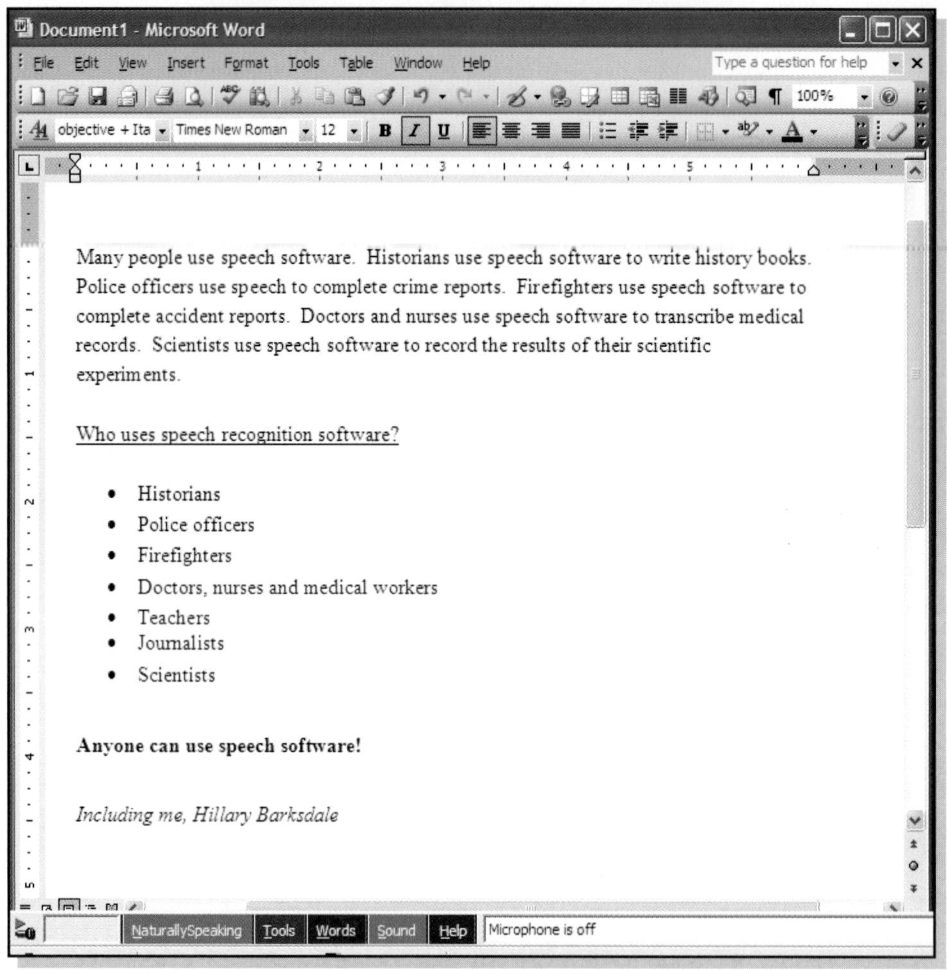

Congratulations! You really have learned how to use your speech recognition tools effectively.

Footnotes

Each reference is indicated by a superscript number. The footnote citations are placed at the bottom of the page where the referenced text appears.

THE NEW GLOBE THEATER

The new Globe Theater was built in the early 1990s. It sits only a few hundred yards from the site of the original Globe Theater on the south side of the Thames River in London, England, across from St. Paul's Cathedral.[1]

Note reference mark

What is so special about the new Globe Theater? It is a true replica of the original sixteenth century Globe Theater where many of William Shakespeare's plays were first performed.

William Shakespeare

William Shakespeare was the son of a wealthy merchant and was born in Stratford-on-Avon, England, in 1564. In the late 1580s, Shakespeare left Stratford-on-Avon to make his way in London as an actor and playwright. England's Queen during this time was the popular Elizabeth I; therefore, this period of history is called the **Elizabethan Era**. During the **Elizabethan Era**, attending plays was a popular entertainment for both the wealthy and the poor.[2] Several of Shakespeare's most famous plays were performed for the first time at the original Globe Theater including:

Note reference mark

- *Julius Caesar*
- *Hamlet*
- *Henry V*
- *Macbeth*

Note separator line

---

[1] "Rebuilding the Globe: Architecture and Construction," *Shakespeare's Globe Online*, http://www.shakespeares-globe.org/ (accessed September 23, 2006).

[2] Diane Yancey, *Life in the Elizabethan Theater* (San Diego: Lucent Books, 1997), p. 11.

Footnotes

8. Say the following:

   NEW PARAGRAPH
   Including me, <say your name>!

9. Save your changes by saying **SAVE**.

You can add any words that your computer has difficulty transcribing to your dictionary. Just follow the same steps you took to enter your name in the dictionary.

Good work! Now that you understand how to use your voice to position your I-beam pointer to specific words or places in your document, let's go to specific words and add formatting.

Let's practice formatting a document using voice commands.

1. Using voice commands, move your insertion point down to the word *Historian*.
2. Create a bulleted item by saying **BULLETS**.
3. Say **MOVE DOWN** to move to **Police officers** and say **BULLETS**.
4. Say **MOVE DOWN** to move to **Firefighters** and say **BULLETS**.
5. Say **MOVE DOWN** to move to **Doctors, nurses and medical workers** and say **BULLETS**.
6. Say **MOVE DOWN** to move to **Teachers** and say **BULLETS**.
7. Say **MOVE DOWN** to move to **Journalists** and say **BULLETS**.
8. Say **MOVE DOWN** to move to **Scientists** and say **BULLETS**.
9. Say **MOVE** DOWN to move to the paragraph that says, **"Anyone can use speech software!"** Say **SELECT PARAGRAPH**. Make this line bold by saying **BOLD**.
10. Say **MOVE DOWN** to move to the last paragraph that says, **"Including me, (say your name)!"** Say **SELECT PARAGRAPH**. Italicize this paragraph by saying **ITALIC**.
11. Say **MOVE UP** to move to the paragraph that says, **"Who uses speech recognition software?"** Say **SELECT PARAGRAPH**. Underline this line by saying **UNDERLINE**.
12. Save your changes.

Sample Citations

Book with one author

[1]Alice Low, *The Macmillan Book of Greek Gods and Heroes* (New York: Macmillan, 1985), pp. 38-44.

Book with two authors

[1]Margot Morrell and Stephanie Capparell, *Shackleton's Way: Leadership Lessons from the Great Antarctic Explorer* (New York: Viking, 2001), p. 32.

Book with four or more authors

[1]David Smithson, et al., *Qin Shi Huandi and the Warring States* (New York: Wilson & Sons, 2000), p. 52.

Journal or Magazine Article

[1]Mark F. Davis, "Perry and the Shogun," *Seafarers Journal*, March 16, 2006, p. 43.

Encyclopedia or Reference Book

[1]*Compton's Encyclopedia*, Vol. 24 (Chicago, IL: Encyclopædia Britannica, Inc., 2004), p. 325.

Web Page, Online Journal, Magazine, or Newspaper

[1]"Rebuilding the Globe: Architecture and Construction," *Shakespeare's Globe Online*, http://www.shakespeares-globe.org/ (September 23, 2006).

Proofreaders' Marks

Proofreaders' marks are used to mark corrections in keyed or printed text that contains problems and/or errors. As a keyboard user, you should be able to read these marks accurately when revising or editing a rough draft. You also should be able to write these symbols to correct the rough drafts that you and others key. The most-used proofreaders' marks are shown below.

Mark	Meaning	Mark	Meaning
‖	Align copy; also, make these items parallel	#>	Insert space
¶	Begin a new paragraph	∨ (')	Insert apostrophe
Cap ≡	Capitalize	stet	Let it stand; ignore correction
⁀	Close up	lc	Lowercase
ℓ	Delete	⊔	Move down; lower
<#	Delete space	⊏	Move left
No ¶	Do not begin a new paragraph	⊐	Move right
∧	Insert	⊓	Move up; raise
∧ (,)	Insert comma	O sp	Spell out
⊙	Insert period	∿ tr	Transpose
∨ ("")	Insert quotation marks	___	Underline or italic

Let's teach your speech software how to say your name.

1. Click **Tools** and then choose **And/Delete Word(s)** from the Language bar.

2. Enter your name into the **Word** text box.
3. Click the **Record Pronunciation** button and say your name aloud.

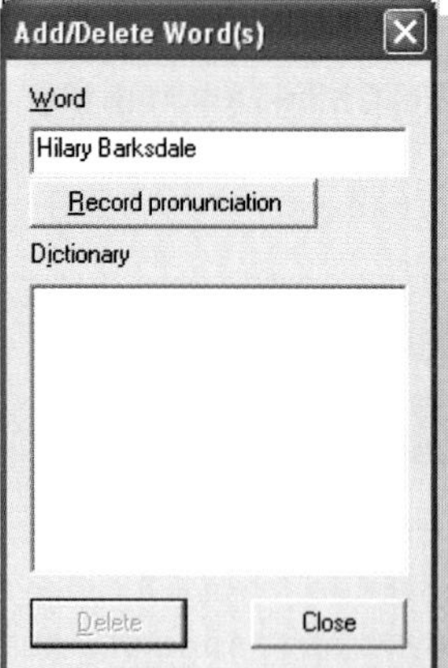

4. Your name will appear in the Dictionary list. Double-click your name to hear a digitized voice repeat your name.
5. Close the **Add/Delete Word(s)** dialog box by clicking the **Close** button.
6. Open your *transcription practice* document.
7. Move to the end of your document by saying **MOVE TO END OF DOCUMENT**.

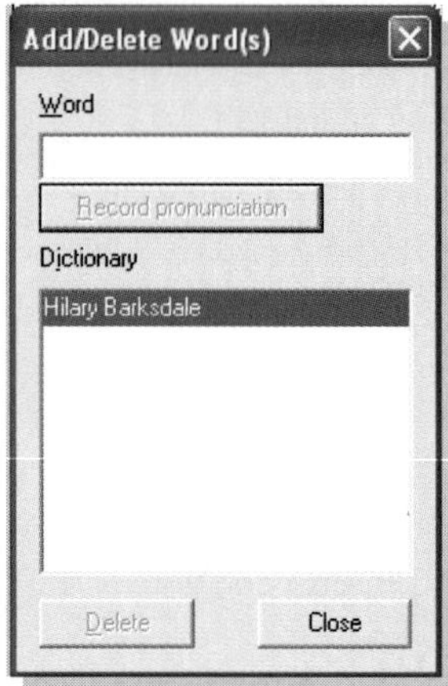

Envelope for a Personal-Business Letter

An envelope has a return address and a delivery address. The delivery address has special formatting. It should be typed in all uppercase without punctuation.

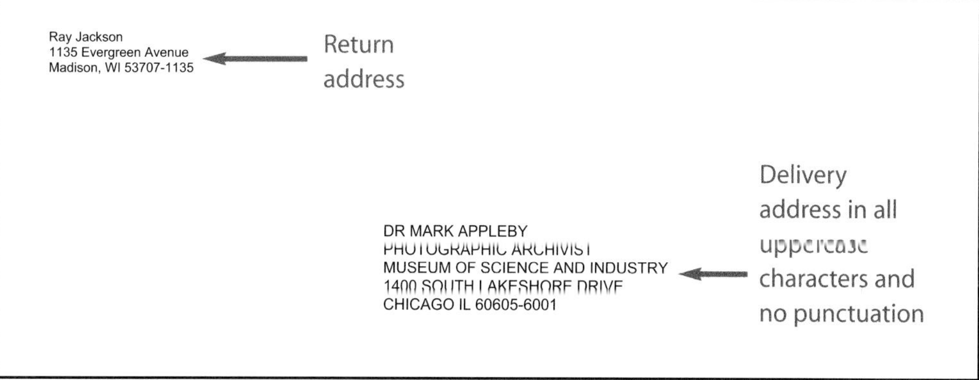

Personal-Business Letter in the Block Format

A personal-business letter is a formal letter written about a personal topic. A personal-business letter contains a return address, a date, a letter address, a salutation, a body, a complimentary close, and the writer's name.

Personal-business letters are usually typed in the block format. In block format, all the parts of a letter begin at the left margin.

Personal-business letters have a 2-inch top margin, a 1-inch bottom margin, and 1-inch or 1.25-inch left and right margins.

A colon is typed after the salutation. A comma is typed after the complimentary close.

2″ top margin

Return address →
1135 Evergreen Avenue
Madison, WI 53707-1135

Date →
December 1, 20--

↓ 4

Letter address →
Dr. Mark Appleby
Photographic Archivist
Museum of Science and Industry
1400 South Lakeshore Drive
Chicago, IL 60605-6001

↓ 2

Salutation →
Dear Dr. Appleby:

↓ 2

Body →

As I mentioned during our telephone conversation, my Explorers Club is learning about Antarctica and I am preparing a report about the Antarctic expeditions of Sir Ernest Shackleton. I would like permission to view the museum's special collection of Shackleton expedition photographs. I will be in Chicago on Saturday, December 9, and would like to view the photographs in the afternoon between 1 and 3 p.m.

I am very interested in viewing the following photographs:

Description	Expedition
Shackleton, Scott, and Wilson	1901 National Antarctic
Shackleton, Wild, and Adams	1909 *Nimrod*
Endurance and pack ice	1914 *Endurance*
Endurance crew on icebound ship	1914 *Endurance*
Icebound *Endurance* at night	1914 *Endurance*
Shackleton and pet dog	1921 Shackleton-Rowett

Please contact me by e-mail at Ray.Jackson@xeon.net to confirm this date and time.

Complimentary close →
Sincerely yours,

↓ 4

Writer's name →
Ray Jackson

1″ or 1 $\frac{1}{2}$″ left and right margins

Let's practice moving around a document using voice commands.

1. Make sure your Language bar is open. Use your mouse to move your insertion point to the very beginning of your document.
2. Click the **Microphone** button on the Language bar.
3. Click the **Voice Command** button or say **VOICE COMMAND**.
4. Say the following voice commands. Wait for each command to execute before saying the next command.

   MOVE TO END OF DOCUMENT
   MOVE TO BEGINNING OF DOCUMENT
   MOVE TO END OF DOCUMENT
   PAGE UP
   PAGE DOWN
   PAGE UP
   PAGE DOWN

5. Practice moving one line at a time:

   GO UP
   UP
   GO UP
   GO DOWN
   DOWN
   GO DOWN

6. Practice moving one or more characters at a time:

   GO LEFT
   GO LEFT
   LEFT
   GO RIGHT
   RIGHT
   GO RIGHT

7. Move from the beginning to the end of a line with the following commands:

   GO END
   GO HOME

That was easy! Next, let's teach your computer how to say your name.

Personal-Business Letter in Modified-Block Style

A personal-business letter in modified-block style is similar to a business letter that is written in block style. It also contains a return address, a date, a letter address, a salutation, a body, a complimentary close, and the writer's name.

Personal-business letters in modified-block style are usually typed with the date and the closing lines of the letter beginning near the horizontal center of the page instead of at the left margin. The first line of each paragraph may begin at the left margin or indented 0.5 inch.

Personal-business letters in modified-block style have a 2-inch top margin, a 1-inch bottom margin, and 1-inch or 1.25-inch left and right margins.

A colon is typed after the salutation. A comma is typed after the complimentary close.

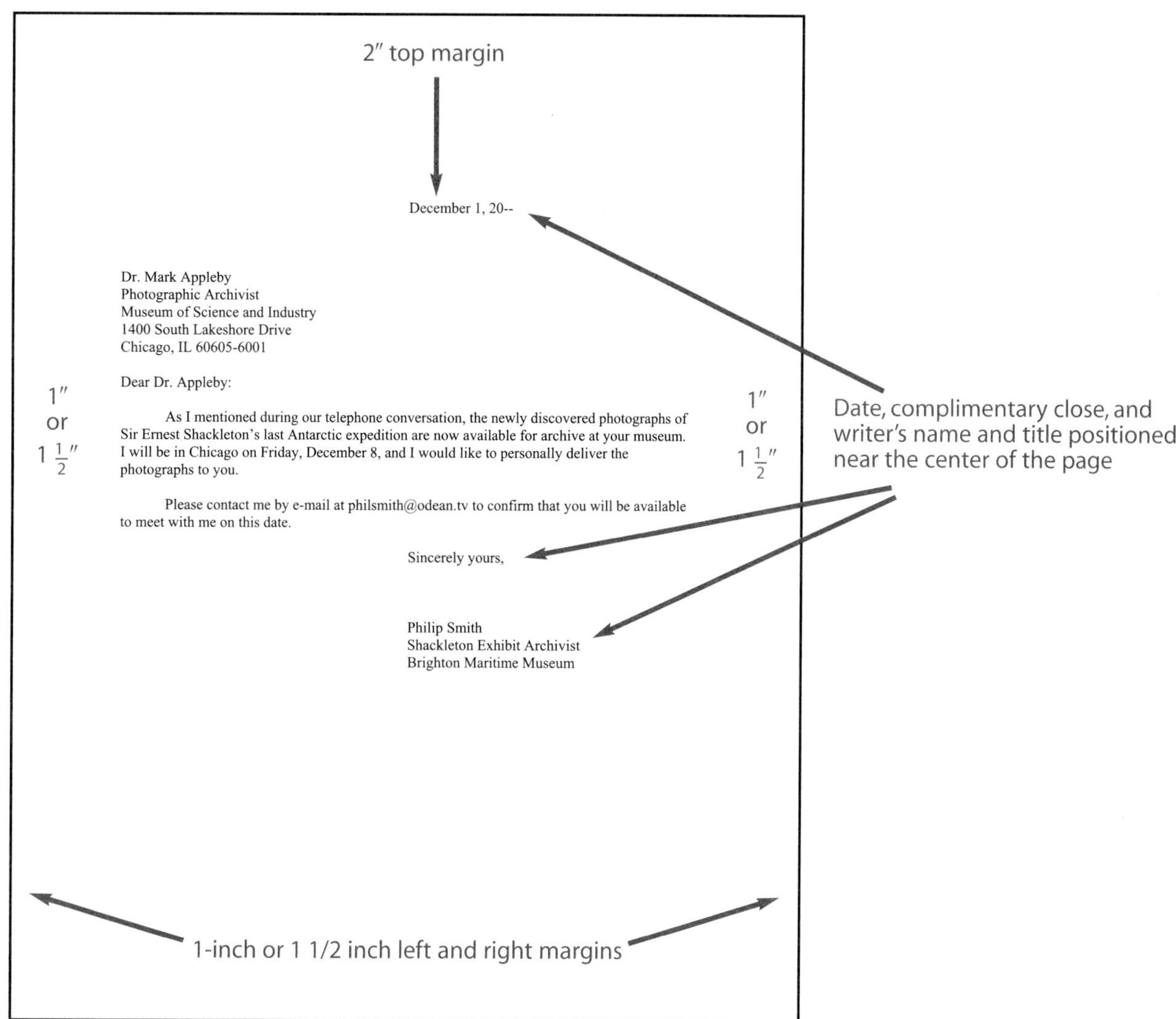

December 1, 20--

Dr. Mark Appleby
Photographic Archivist
Museum of Science and Industry
1400 South Lakeshore Drive
Chicago, IL 60605-6001

Dear Dr. Appleby:

As I mentioned during our telephone conversation, the newly discovered photographs of Sir Ernest Shackleton's last Antarctic expedition are now available for archive at your museum. I will be in Chicago on Friday, December 8, and I would like to personally deliver the photographs to you.

Please contact me by e-mail at philsmith@odean.tv to confirm that you will be available to meet with me on this date.

Sincerely yours,

Philip Smith
Shackleton Exhibit Archivist
Brighton Maritime Museum

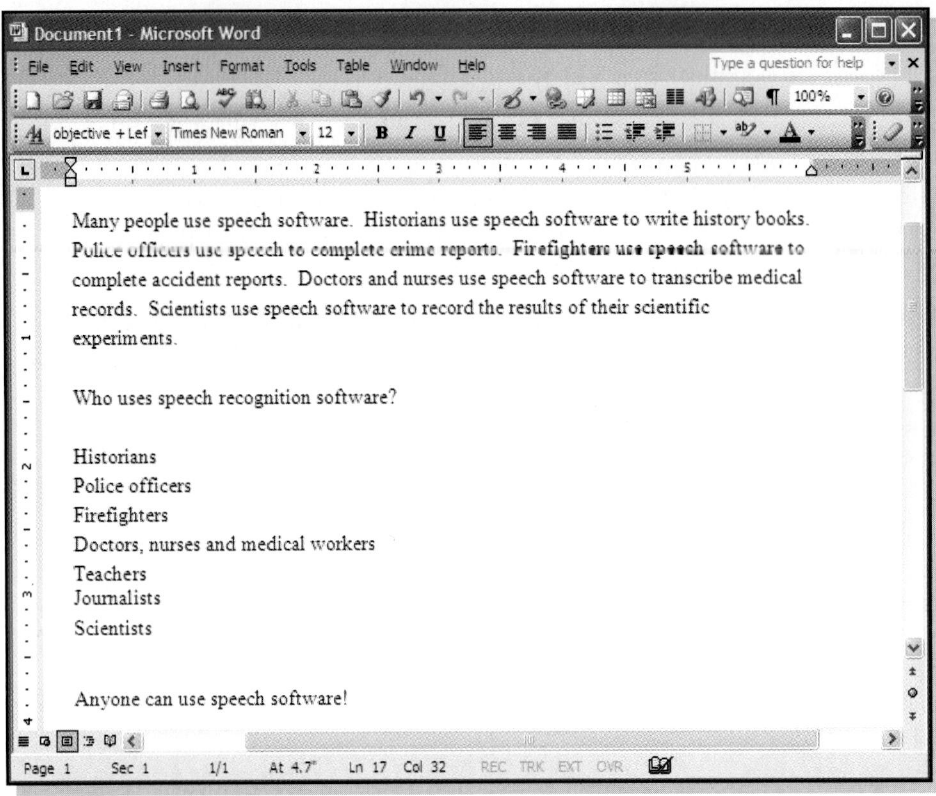

Nice job! Now let's make your text look more attractive by adding formatting.

Formatting Documents with Your Speech Recognition Software

formatting

Formatting is the art of making a document look good. You will add bullets and apply Bold, Italic, and Underline styles to some of the text in your *transcription practice* document. You will need to learn a few formatting commands to do this. You can also give commands to your computer to position your I-beam pointer.

When giving voice commands, it is important to pause for a second before you say each command.

Appendix B

Explorers' Guide

Data file: *none*

Objectives:

In this project, you will:

- train your speech recognition software
- manipulate the Language bar
- speak voice commands to your computer
- dictate and transcribe with your speech recognition software
- format documents with speech recognition software

Exploring on Your Own

additional practice in:

- using speech recognition tools
- practicing dictation skills
- writing by speaking clearly
- transcribing personal histories

Exploring Across the Curriculum

Internet/Web
Language Arts
Social Studies
Science
Getting Help
Transcribe Your Personal Journal

Using Speech Recognition Tools

Our Exploration Assignment:

Use speech recognition tools to dictate text into a computer

Julie is learning how to use speech recognition tools to speak to a computer. The computer then turns her spoken words into typed text. You can learn along with Julie! The first step is to train your computer to recognize your voice. Then follow the Trail Markers to switch between the Voice Command and Dictation modes, give voice commands to your computer, dictate words and sentences, and use voice commands to navigate within a document and format the document. Finally, you will create an entry in your personal journal using speech recognition tools!

Let's transcribe using a variety of punctuation marks.

1. Switch to Dictation mode by clicking the **Dictation** button or by saying **DICTATION**.
2. Say the following. Do not forget to say the punctuation marks.

NEW PARAGRAPH
Who uses speech recognition software?
NEW PARAGRAPH

Historians	**NEW LINE**
Police officers	**NEW LINE**
Firefighters	**NEW LINE**
Doctors, nurses and medical workers	**NEW LINE**
Teachers	**NEW LINE**
Journalists	**NEW LINE**
Scientists	

NEW PARAGRAPH
Anyone can use speech software!
NEW PARAGRAPH

3. Turn off your microphone by saying **MICROPHONE**.
4. Use your keyboard to correct any errors.
5. Save your file.

Starting *Out*!

Before you can use speech recognition software, you must have a **noise cancellation headset**. The headset cancels out background noise so the computer can focus on the words you say.

There are two types of noise cancellation headsets. An **analog headset** plugs directly into your computer's soundcard. A **USB headset** plugs into any USB port on your computer.

analog headset
noise cancellation headset
USB headset

Many high-quality headsets have mute buttons and volume controls. A mute button turns the microphone off. (The word *mute* means to silence or to shut off the microphone.) Follow these steps for placing the headset properly for good speech recognition:

- Position your headset comfortably on your head.
- Position the microphone three-quarters of an inch to the side of your lower lip.
- Do not move your headset around. Leave it in the same position every time you use your speech recognition software.

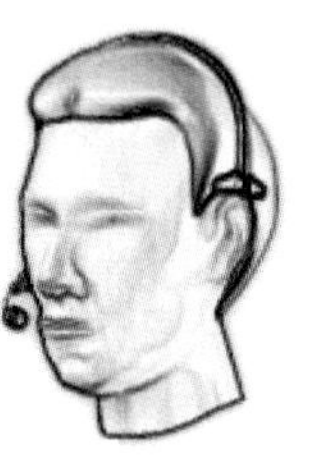

Ergonomics *TIP*

If you plan to speak for a long time to your computer, keep a water bottle handy. Taking constant sips of water will help prevent getting a dry, irritated throat.

Do you have your headset ready? Make sure the microphone is on before you start to speak. Adjust your volume as needed. Great! Now you are ready to train your speech recognition software.

The SCRATCH THAT command is very useful. If you stumble over a sentence, take a breath and say SCRATCH THAT. You can also say SCRATCH THAT more than once if you need to.

4. Say just the parts of the sample sentences given below and then erase them:

   NEW PARAGRAPH

Historians use speech	**SCRATCH THAT**
Police officers use speech	**SCRATCH THAT**
Firefighters use speech	**SCRATCH THAT**
Scientists use speech	**SCRATCH THAT**
Doctors, nurses and medical workers	**SCRATCH THAT, SCRATCH THAT**
Anyone can use speech software	**SCRATCH THAT, SCRATCH THAT**

5. Your screen should now be clear. Say your first paragraph again. If you stumble or make a mistake, use the SCRATCH THAT command to erase and start again.

   Many people use speech software. Historians use speech software to write history books. Police officers use speech software to complete crime reports. Firefighters use speech software to complete accident reports. Doctors and nurses use speech software to transcribe medical records. Scientists use speech software to record the results of their scientific experiments.

6. How many mistakes did you make? Use your keyboard to correct any errors.
7. Switch to Voice Command mode by saying **VOICE COMMAND** or by clicking the **Voice Command** button.
8. To save your work, say **FILE**. When the File menu opens, say **SAVE AS**. Type *transcription practice* in the **File name** text box. Say **SAVE** to save the file.

Next, let's practice dictating sentences and text that have different punctuation marks.

Training Your Speech Recognition Software

You will need to train your computer to understand your way of speaking and your accent.

Let's begin by training your computer to understand your voice. Open *Word* and locate your speech recognition tools.

1. Open *Microsoft Word*. Choose **Tools** and then choose **Speech**.

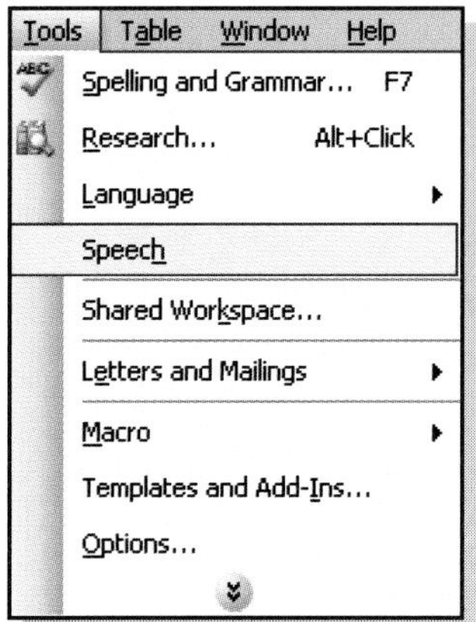

2. If this is the first time that speech software has been used on your computer, click the **Next** button and proceed to Step 5. Otherwise, the Language bar will appear on your screen. Choose **Tools** on the Language bar, and then choose **Options**.

Let's transcribe a simple paragraph using speech recognition.

1. Click the **Microphone** button on the Language bar.
2. Switch to Dictation mode by clicking the **Dictation** button or by saying **DICTATION.**
3. Say the following paragraph. Do not forget to say the period at the end of each sentence.

   Many people use speech software. Historians use speech software to write history books. Police officers use speech software to complete crime reports. Firefighters use speech software to complete accident reports. Doctors and nurses use speech software to transcribe medical records. Scientists use speech software to record the results of their scientific experiments.

4. Choose the entire document by saying:

   VOICE COMMAND
   EDIT
   SELECT ALL
   DELETE (or say **BACKSPACE**)

5. Turn off your microphone by saying **MICROPHONE.**

That was easy! Let's dictate some more sentences in a new *Word* document.

Let's use the SCRATCH THAT command to eliminate words.

1. Open a new, blank document in *Word.*
2. Click the **Microphone** button on the Language bar.
3. Switch to Dictation mode by clicking on the **Dictation** button or by saying **DICTATION.**

3. The Speech Properties dialogue box will open. Select **New** to create a new user profile. (Each user of the computer should create his or her own user profile.)

4. The Profile Wizard dialogue box will open. Enter a name for the profile and click the **Next** button.

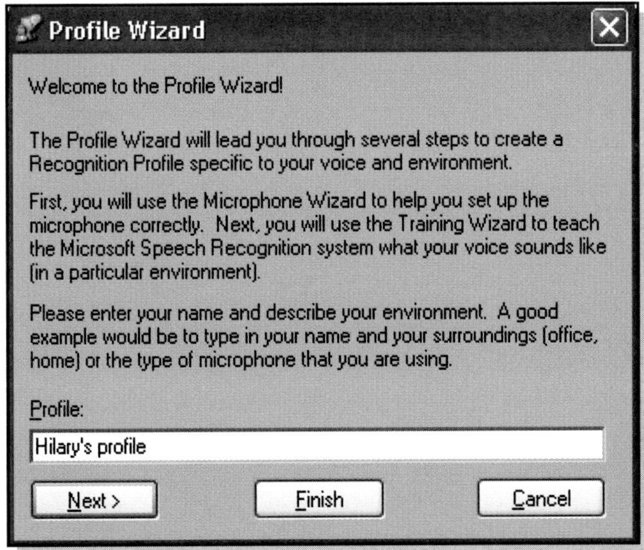

Great job! Make sure you can control your microphone and switch between Voice Command and Dictation modes easily. Practice some commands on your own. See what you can do with your voice in *Word*. In the next Trail Marker, you will learn how to talk to your computer and how to transcribe your words into typed text.

Make sure you turn off your microphone when you are not working with speech recognition.

Dictating and Transcribing with Your Speech Recognition Software

enunciating

Speaking clearly, or **enunciating**, is the key to dictating and transcribing. Speak in a normal way. Do not yell or shout at the microphone. Do not speak too slowly or too quickly. Speaking quickly can cause your words to run together. Speaking too slowly can also cause mistakes.

Some speech recognition programs will insert your punctuation for you. However, with *Microsoft Speech Recognition*, you should say each punctuation mark, including all commas, as well as the periods, question marks, and exclamation points at the end of sentences.

Here are some important commands that you will use often.

NEW LINE	Starts text on the next line; similar to tapping the ENTER key
NEW PARAGRAPH	Inserts a return and adds a line of space
SCRATCH THAT	Erases mistakes or allows you to change your wording

Make sure you speak clearly. Say each word as if you were talking to a young child.

5. Read the instructions that appear on the screen. When you are ready, click **Next**. Then speak into your microphone and read the phrase shown on your screen. The microphone meter level will move between the yellow, green, and red zones. When you can keep the meter level consistently in the green zone, click **Next**.

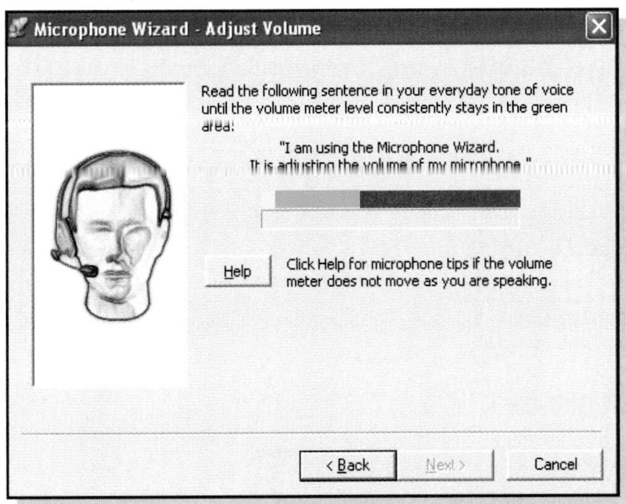

6. Continue reading each screen carefully and following the instructions. When the system asks you to speak, say the phrase that appears on your screen. Then click **Finish**.

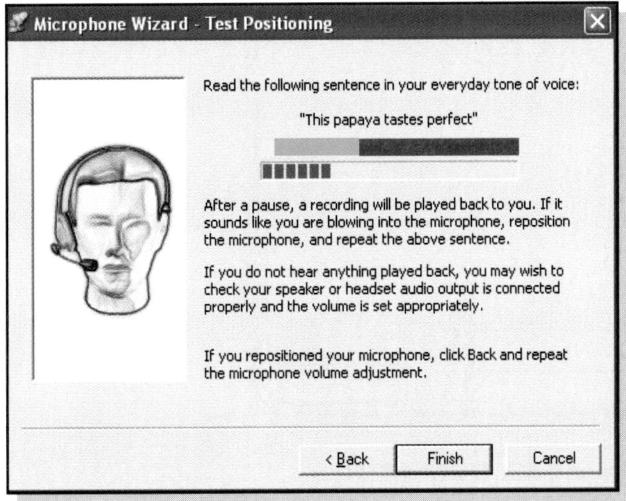

Note: In some versions of *Microsoft*'s speech recognition software, you must tell the program if you are male or female and then provide your age. Click **Next** after entering this information.

Let's use the voice command mode like a mouse to navigate dialog boxes.

1. Switch to Voice Command mode with your voice by saying **VOICE COMMAND**.
2. Open the **File** menu by saying **FILE**.
3. Open the **Open** menu by saying **OPEN**.

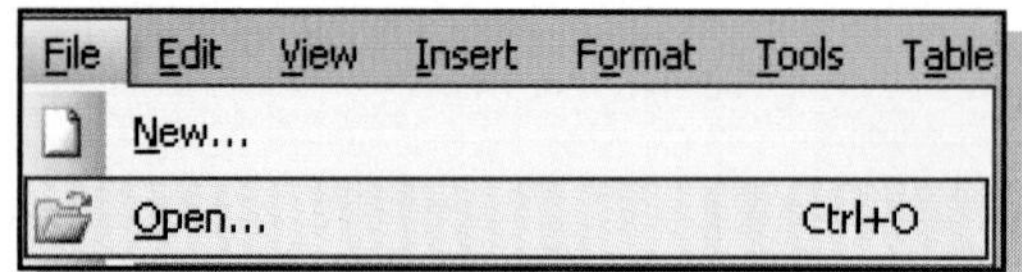

4. Switch to the Desktop view by saying **DESKTOP**.

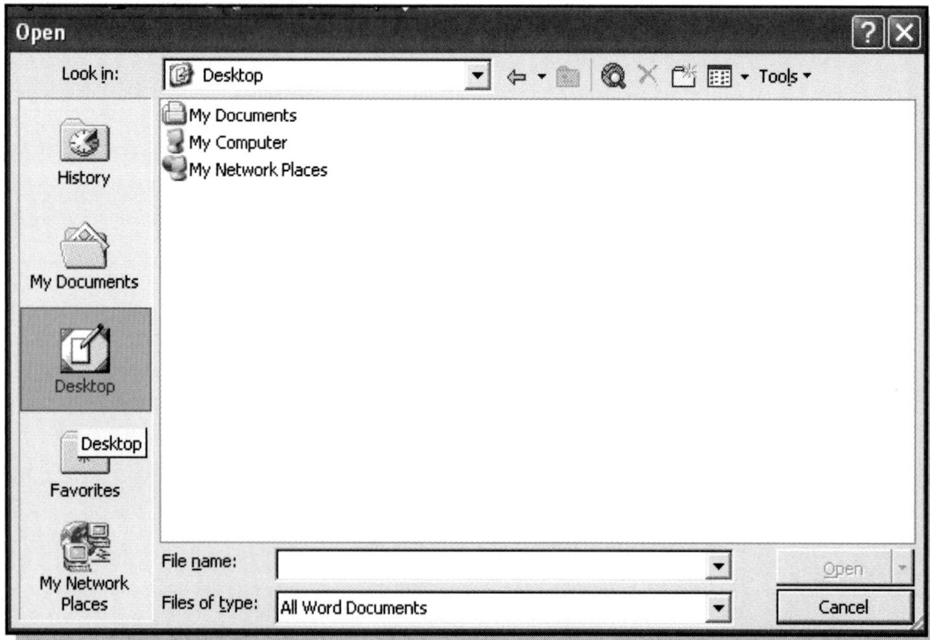

5. Switch to the My Documents view by saying **MY DOCUMENTS**.
6. Switch to the Desktop view by saying **DESKTOP**.
7. Close the **Open** dialog box by saying **CANCEL**.
8. Turn off your microphone by saying **MICROPHONE**.

7. Read the information on the screen and click **Next**. Listen to the sample sentence when this screen appears.

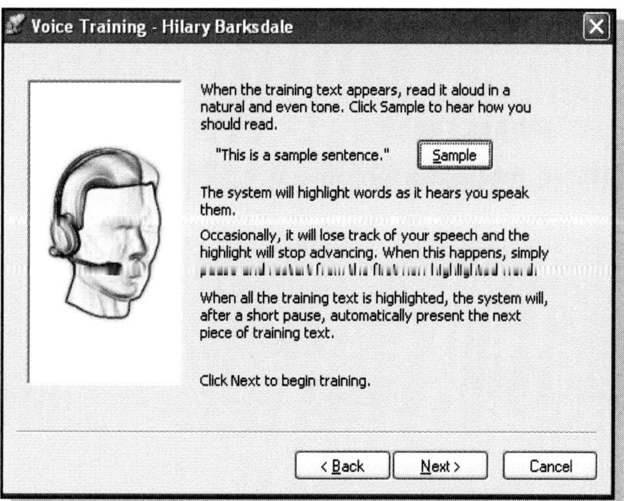

Listening to the sample will help you understand how you should speak to your computer. Then click **Next** to start the training session.

8. Read aloud the sentences that appear on the Voice Training screen. The software will track your progress in the Training progress bar. If you do not read every word clearly, the system will stop and make you read the sentence again.

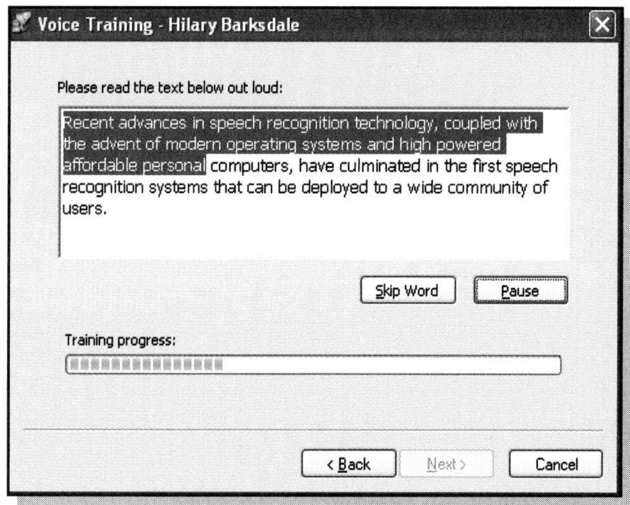

Let's use the Voice Command mode like a mouse to open menus.

1. Turn on the microphone by clicking the **Microphone** button on the Language bar.
2. Switch to Voice Command mode with your voice by saying **VOICE COMMAND**.
3. Open the **File** menu by saying **FILE**.

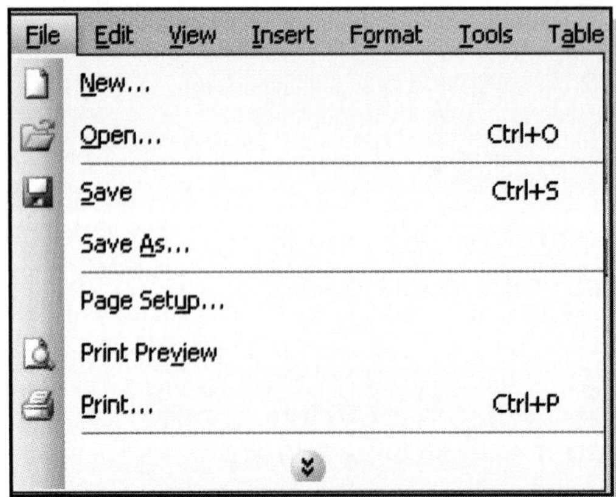

4. Close the menu by saying **ESCAPE**.
5. Open the **Edit** menu by saying **EDIT**.
6. Close the menu by saying **ESCAPE**.
7. Open the **View** menu by saying **VIEW**.
8. Close the menu by saying **ESCAPE**.
9. Open the **Help** menu by saying **HELP**.
10. Close the menu by saying **ESCAPE**, **ESCAPE**.

9. After you have finished reading, click the **Finish** button.

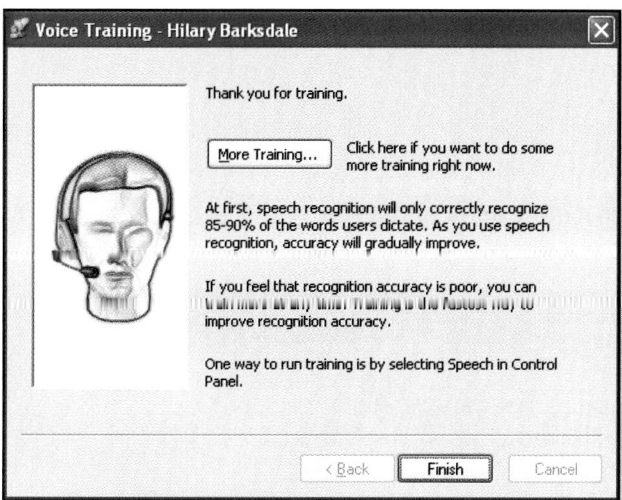

10. If this is the first time the training has been completed, the *Office* Speech Training Video appears. Watch and learn from the video and get ready for your next lesson.

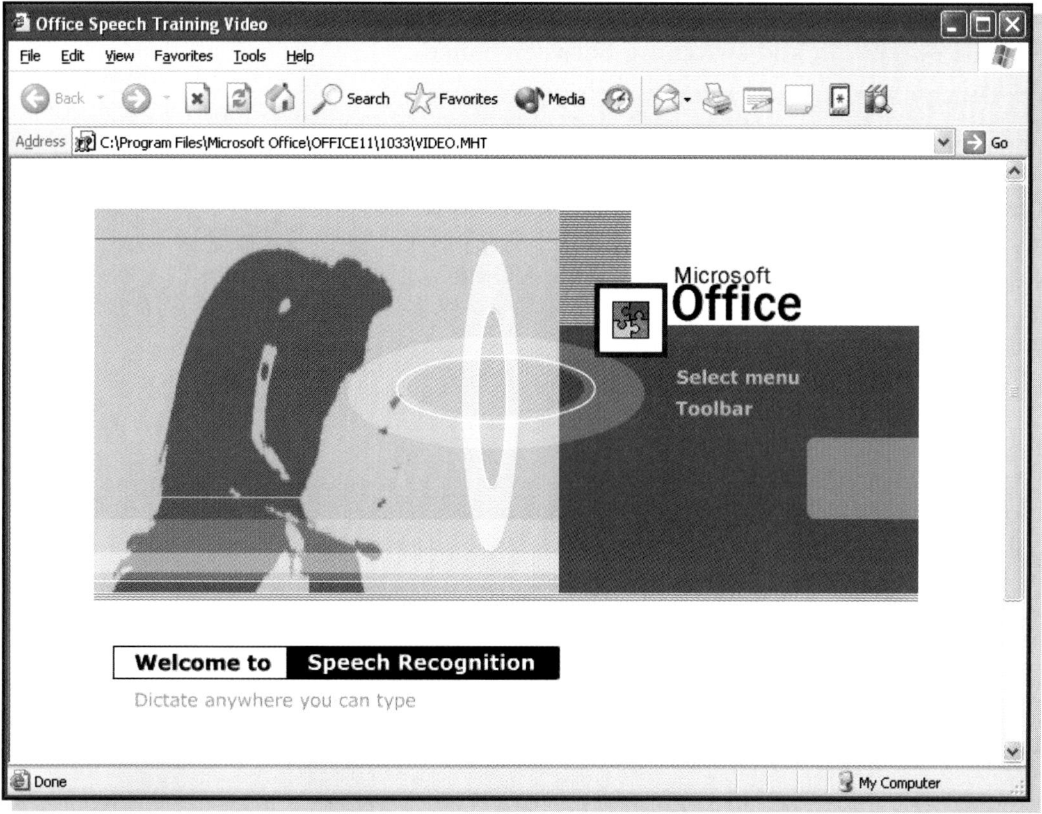

TRAIL 3 MARKER

Speaking Voice Commands to Your Computer

Dictation mode
Voice Command mode

Microsoft speech recognition has two different ways of working. One way of working allows you to give voice commands to your computer without having text appear on the screen. This is called Voice Command mode. To use Voice Commands, turn on the microphone and choose the **Voice Command** button.

The second way of working is called Dictation mode. You can use dictation mode to transcribe or type. All you have to do is talk and your words will be typed on the screen. You will learn to use Dictation mode in Trail Marker 4.

Practice turning your microphone on and off and switching between Voice Command and Dictation modes.

1. Open the Language bar.
2. Click the **Microphone** button on the Language bar.
3. Click the **Voice Command** button to switch to Voice Command mode.
4. Click the **Dictation** button to switch to Dictation mode.
5. Switch to Voice Command mode with your voice by saying **VOICE COMMAND**.
6. Switch back to Dictation mode by saying **DICTATION**.
7. Switch back to Voice Command mode once again by saying **VOICE COMMAND**.
8. Turn off your microphone by saying **MICROPHONE**.

The Voice Command mode allows you to use your voice instead of your mouse to open menus on the toolbar and to choose options in dialog boxes.

Use Screen Tips to find the **Voice Command** and **Dictation** buttons. The **Voice Command** and **Dictation** buttons disappear from the Language bar when the microphone is off. You can also turn off the microphone by clicking the **Microphone** button.

If the computer does not recognize a particular word you are saying, click the **Skip** button. Click **Pause** if you need to take a break.

If you have additional time, choose the option that allows you to read additional training stories. This will make your speech recognition system even more accurate. Otherwise, click **OK**.

Now let's locate and manipulate your *Microsoft Office* speech recognition tools.

TRAIL 2 MARKER

Manipulating the Language Bar

Language bar

The speech recognition tools are found on the Language bar. This bar displays all the tools you will need for both speech and handwriting recognition. You can move the Language bar anywhere on the screen by dragging the move handle on its left-hand side.

Apply It!

Let's open and examine some of the features of the Language bar.

1. Click **Tools** and choose **Speech** to open the Language bar.
2. Move the Language bar to the center of your screen by dragging the move handle on its left side.
3. Your Language bar may show many more buttons than you need for speech recognition. Reset the buttons by clicking the **Options** button in the right corner of the Language bar. (If necessary, use the Screen Tips to locate the Options button.) Then choose **Restore Defaults**.

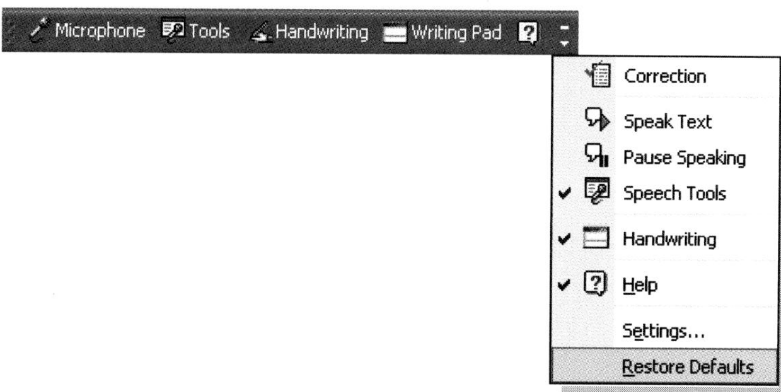

4. Click the **Minimize** button to minimize the Language bar. A box will appear telling you that the Language bar will be placed in the taskbar. Click **OK** to continue.

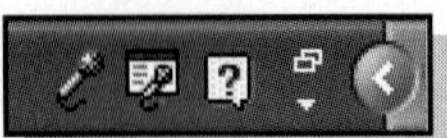

5. Look for the Language bar in the *Windows* taskbar. Restore the Language bar. Click the **Restore** button (or choose **Tools** and then choose **Speech**).
6. Use the move handle on the left side of the Language bar to drag the Language bar up to the title bar of *Word*.

Check to be sure that your personal speech recognition user file has been selected. Click the **Tools** button on the Language bar. Move down and select **Current User**. Your user filename will likely be the same as your *Windows* login name.

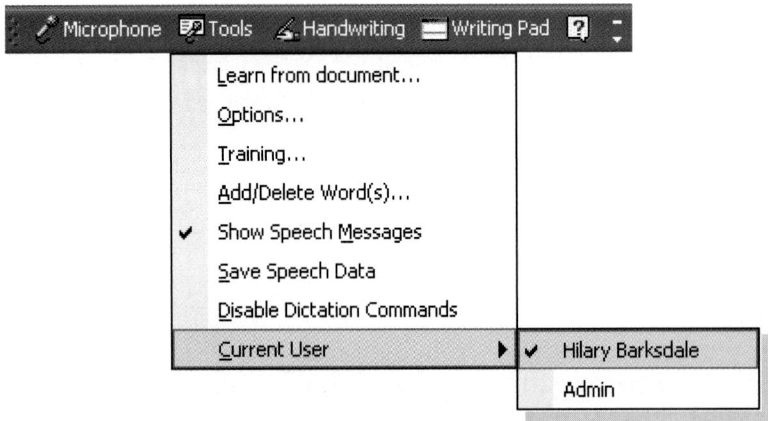

Super! Now let's start using *Microsoft* speech recognition!

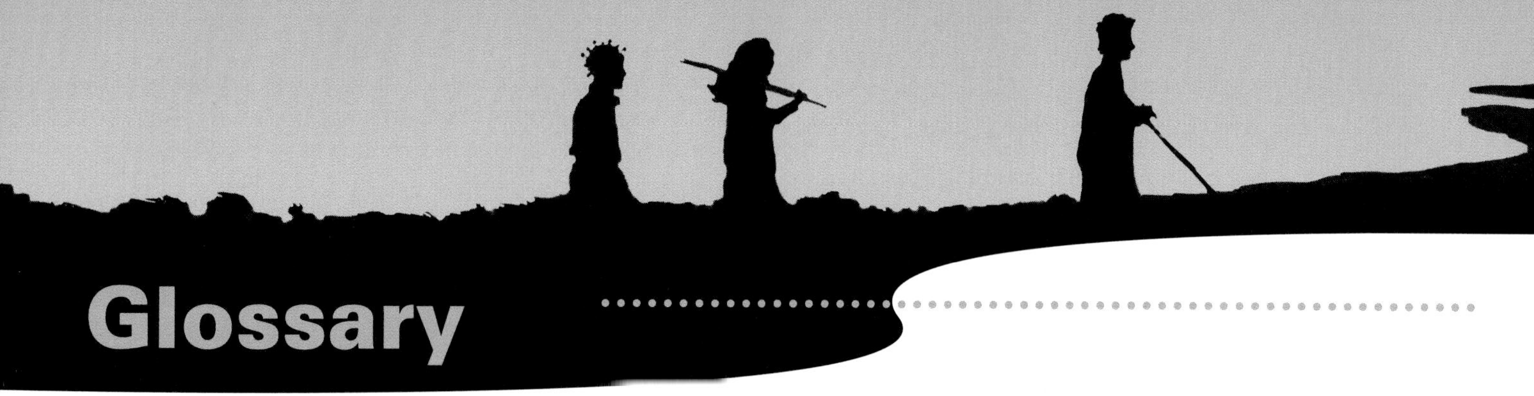

Glossary

A

absolute reference a cell reference that *Excel* cannot change when it copies and pastes a formula

action button a predesigned button icon to which you can add hyperlinks

active cell in *Excel*, the worksheet cell with the dark border that is ready for data entry

Address bar in *Windows Explorer* or *Internet Explorer*, the area in which you type a Web page URL or an e-mail address

align to position graphics, text boxes, and drawing objects horizontally and vertically in relation to each other on a slide

animation scheme animation effects and slide transitions combined into a single predefined scheme to be applied to one or more slides

antonym a word that has the opposite meaning of another word

application software software used for a specific task, such as word processing

ascending order A to Z or 0 to 9

AutoFill the *Excel* feature that allows you to place numbers, dates, or text combined with numbers in a range of cells

AutoFilter the *Excel* feature used to display rows in a list based on specific criteria

AutoForm an *Access* feature that allows the user to quickly create a database form that lists all the fields in a record

AutoNumber a unique identifying number automatically assigned to each record in a database

AutoReport a feature in *Access* that lets a user quickly create a simple report of all the records and all the fields in a selected table

AutoShape a predefined shape you draw with the mouse pointer

AVERAGE the *Excel* function that calculates the average value in a range of cells

B

bar chart a chart with horizontal data markers used to compare two or more data series

Blank the slide layout that has no placeholders

block format a letter format in which all the letter parts start at the left margin

body text in paragraphs that make up a letter's message

border formatting added to the outline of an object or text

bound report a multi-page report with the pages bound generally at the left or right margins

browser home page the default Web page that appears when you start your Web browser

budget a financial plan based on expectations of future events

bulleted list a list of words, phrases, or sentences preceded by a bullet graphic; an unordered list

C

cable insulated wire that connects the computer parts together

calculation operator the plus (+), minus (−), multiplication (*), or division (/) symbols in a formula needed to perform a calculation

Caption property the field property that specifies the text that appears in a datasheet or form instead of the field name

category (x) axis shows the names of the categories being charted; categories appear horizontally at the bottom of the chart

CD a device for reading and storing data

cell the intersection of a column and row in a *Word* table

cell the intersection of a column and a row in an *Excel* worksheet

cell reference a cell's row heading number and column heading letter in an *Excel* worksheet

Center tab a tab stop that centers heading text over tabbed columns

character formatting formatting applied to individual text characters

chart a picture, or graph, of worksheet data

chart area the background area of a chart

chart objects different parts of a chart such as its title, legend, or data markers

chart sheet a separate sheet in a workbook that contains a chart

chart title a chart's title text

Chart Wizard a step-by-step process to create a chart

click to point to a specific area on the screen and press the left mouse button once

Click and Type a *Word* Print Layout feature that allows you to double-click anywhere on the page to position the insertion point

Click and Type pointer the mouse pointer with a Click and Type formatting symbol

clip art predesigned pictures or drawings that can be inserted into a document

Close button button in the upper-right corner of a window that you click to close the window

color scheme the background, font, and graphic colors used in a *PowerPoint* design template

column a vertical arrangement of cells in a *Word* table

column a vertical arrangement of cells in a worksheet

column chart a chart with vertical data markers used to compare two or more data series

column heading letters from A to IV that appear across the top of a worksheet

complimentary close the words that come before the signature of a letter, such as *Sincerely yours*

computer ergonomics the way people sit at, place, and use the computer to avoid injury

Content group a group of slide layouts whose placeholder contains icons for creating different types of content

content placeholder a placeholder that contains icons used to create different types of slide content

copying and pasting duplicating text and inserting it into a new location

CPU the computer's "brain" that controls the interaction between hardware and software

custom animation animation effects applied to individual slide elements

cutting and pasting removing text and placing it in a new location

D

data file an electronic file you open and edit

data labels text labels that identify the data markers on a chart

data marker a column, slice, bar, or dot on a chart that represents the numbers, called data points, in a worksheet

data point a number in a worksheet cell that is converted to a column, point on a line, or pie slice in a chart

data series all the related data markers in a chart

Data Type property the field property that specifies the type of data that can be stored in a database table's field

database a file used to organize data in a structured way

database object a table, form, or report object stored in a relational database, such as an *Access* database file

Database window a smaller window inside the *Access* window that shows the contents of a database file, the Database window toolbar, and shortcuts to create tables, forms, and reports

datasheet a sheet with rows and columns, similar to an *Excel* worksheet, that displays data in an *Access* database

Datasheet view the view used to display an *Access* table datasheet

date a letter's date with the month spelled out

Decimal tab a tab stop that aligns numbers on the decimal point in tabbed columns

Default Value property the field property that specifies the text or value that automatically appears in each record

delivery address the name and address on an envelope of the person to whom a letter is sent

demote to move outline text down one level in the outline

descending order Z to A or 9 to 0

design template a color-coordinated predefined format for fonts, colors, or clip art applied to one or more slides of a presentation

Design view the view used to create an *Access* database table by manually specifying fields and field properties

desktop the background on the monitor's screen that appears when you start your computer

dialog box a small box that presents options you can set while performing a task in an application

disk drive hardware used to read, write, and store information on a disk

distribute to arrange slide objects an equal distance apart on the slide

dotted line insertion point the insertion point's appearance during a drag and drop action

double-click to point to a specific area on the screen and press the left mouse button twice very quickly

drag to press and hold down the left mouse button and move the mouse pointer across the screen

drag and drop using the mouse pointer to duplicate or reposition selected text

Drawing Canvas a *Word* drawing feature that helps you keep multiple drawing objects together

drawing object an object you draw with the mouse pointer

drop cap an uppercase letter enlarged and positioned at the left margin to create a special effect

E

electronic database a database file stored on electronic media

e-mail electronic messages or mail sent over the Internet

e-mail address the address at which a person receives electronic mail

e-mail etiquette rules for good behavior when sending e-mail

embedded chart a chart placed as a floating object on the same worksheet as the data

embedded workbook object data from an *Excel* worksheet pasted onto a *PowerPoint* slide and edited with *Excel* features

endnote a source reference that appears on a separate page at the end of a report

enter data to type text or numbers in a cell and then tap the ENTER, TAB, or arrow keys

F

favorite a link you can click to view a Web page that you visit frequently

field contains specific data for each record in a table; represented by a column in a datasheet

Field Name property the field property that specifies the name of a field

field properties multiple criteria (or characteristics) that define a field

Field Properties pane the *Access* table Design view pane used to set various field properties, such as Field Size or Caption

field selector the column heading button on a table datasheet used to select a column or show the field name or caption; the row heading button in the Fields pane in Design view used to select a field

Field Size property the field property that specifies how many characters can be typed in a field

Fields pane the *Access* table Design view pane used to type the name of the field and set the Data Type property

file a document you open or create and save on your computer

fill handle the small black square in the lower-right corner of a worksheet cell used to copy cell contents to adjacent cells

filter a set of criteria applied to worksheet data; to display a portion of data having the same content

filter to show only those records that have the same content in a specific field

filtering by selection to specify the filter criteria by moving the insertion point into the field that contains the value to be filtered

First Line Indent marker an indent that moves only the first line of a paragraph inward from the left margin

floating object a text box, picture, or drawing that can be positioned in front of or behind text

folder an electronic version of a paper folder in which you can organize and store your computer files

font typeface; the way letters and numbers look

font effect special text effects available in the Font dialog box

font size the size of a font, generally measured in points

font style Bold, Italic, or Underline formatting; used to add emphasis to text

footer text, page numbers, and dates that appear at the bottom of a page

footnote a source reference that appears at the bottom of the same page as the information

form a database object used to enter or edit data

Form view the *Access* view that displays a database form in which to edit a record or create a new record

Format Painter in *Office*, a feature that allows you to copy or paint formats from formatted text to unformatted text

formatting mark a nonprinting character inserted in a *Word* document to control the position and formatting of printed text

Formatting toolbar a toolbar that contains buttons used to change the look, shape, or position of text and numbers

formula an equation entered in a cell that performs a calculation on the numerical contents of other cells

Formula Bar the area below the Formatting toolbar that shows the contents of the active worksheet cell

function a formula created by *Excel* to perform a common calculation

G

Go button a button in the *Internet Explorer* window you click to load a Web page

gridlines dark horizontal lines that help you see each data marker's position in a chart's plot area

gutter an additional 0.25-inch margin added for the binding to the left or right margin for a bound report

H

handout master the *PowerPoint* master document that controls the placement of placeholders on audience handouts

handouts slide miniatures printed in a variety of formats

Hanging Indent marker an indent that moves all the lines of a paragraph inward from the left margin except the first line

hard page break a manual page break inserted by the typist

hardware computer parts that you can see and touch

header text, page numbers, and dates that appear at the top of a page

home cell cell A1; the first cell in the upper-left corner of the worksheet

home page the primary Web page at a website

host name the computer on which a recipient's electronic mail box is stored

hyperlink text or a picture that is linked to another Web page

I

I-beam pointer the mouse pointer's shape when placed in a text area; used to position the insertion point in the text area

icon small graphic symbol used to represent electronic files, folders, or software applications

indent to move one or more lines inward from the margins

indentation text moved inward from the left or right margins

inline an object positioned in the same line as text

insertion point the small, black vertical line that indicates the typing position in a document

Internet a worldwide network that connects computers

Internet Explorer a commonly used Web browser

K

keyboard hardware that contains a set of keys you tap to insert text and numbers or to perform special tasks

keyboard shortcut a set of keystrokes used to perform a task

L

Landscape orientation a printed page that is wider than it is long

Left Indent marker an indent that moves all the lines of a paragraph inward from the left margin

Left tab a tab stop that indents text from the left margin or left-aligns text in tabbed columns

legend labels and colors that identify each data series

letter address the name and address of the person to whom a letter is addressed

line chart a chart used to compare data over time

line spacing the amount of white space between lines of text

link hyperlink; text or a picture that is linked to another Web page

list brief itemized text usually preceded by a bullet graphic or a number

list an arrangement of worksheet data in which each row has the same type of data in each column; a header row with column names that defines data in the column so that the list can be sorted and filtered

loop to play a music clip or slide show continuously from beginning to end

lowercase letters or characters that are not capitalized

M

main heading the title of a report

margin the amount of white space at the top, bottom, left, and right sides of a page

MAX the *Excel* function that calculates the largest value in a range of cells

Maximize button a button in the upper-right corner of a window you click to size the window to cover the screen

menu bar a toolbar that contains drop-down menus

merge to combine multiple cells into one cell

MIN the *Excel* function that calculates the smallest value in a range of cells

Minimize button a button in the upper-right corner of a window you click to hide the window; a button appears on the taskbar

monitor computer hardware with a screen that displays the documents you create

motion clip animated clip art added to a slide

mouse a pointing device used to perform a task such as clicking or dragging

movie file a video file or motion clip added to a slide

My Computer folder a *Windows* folder that displays system icons for files and folders stored on the computer

My Documents folder a *Windows* folder in which you can store your electronic files

N

Name Box the area to the left of the Formula Bar that shows the cell reference of the active cell

navigation button a button in the lower-left corner of an *Access* table datasheet or form used to navigate between records

newspaper column a column of text that flows downward to the bottom of the column and then up to the top of the next column like a printed newspaper page

Next page section break a break that creates a new document section and a new page at the same time

Normal view in *Word*, the editing view in which the top and bottom sides of a page are not visible

Normal view in *PowerPoint*, the default view in which you create and edit slides

note reference mark a tiny number or symbol that appears next to referenced text

note separator line a line that separates footnotes from a report's body text

notes page individual pages for each slide that show speaker notes and a slide miniature

notes pane the area of the *PowerPoint* window in Normal view in which you can type speaker notes or additional content

notification area tray at the bottom of the screen; displays the current time, as well as small icons for system software and programs running in the computer's background memory

nudging the process of moving an object slightly with an arrow key

null screen the window that appears when *Word*, *Excel*, or *PowerPoint* applications open with no open document, workbook, presentation, or database file

numbered list a list of words, phrases, or sentences preceded by a number in sequence; an ordered list

numeric keypad the set of keys to the right of the main body of the keyboard used to enter numbers

O

Office Clipboard a special place in the computer's memory that stores copied or cut items

ordered list a list of words, phrases, or sentences preceded by a number in sequence; a numbered list

outline text structured with main topics, subtopics, and details

Outline numbered list *Word* feature used to create a multiple-level outline

Outline tab the area of the *PowerPoint* window in Normal view in which you can view, edit, and create slides in an outline format

P

page orientation specification for printing a page horizontally or vertically

paragraph formatting formatting that is applied to complete paragraphs; changes to text layout, such as indenting and aligning text lines and setting line spacing

paragraph heading short underlined phrase followed by a period that introduces a paragraph

pencil symbol symbol in the record selector in a table datasheet that indicates changes to a record are not saved

personal-business letter a formal letter written about a personal topic

pie chart a chart used to show each value as a percentage of the total value

placeholder an area or box on a slide presentation that can contain text, clip art, or other content

plot area the area of a chart in which the data markers appear

point to place the mouse pointer on a specific area of the screen

point a font measurement

Portrait orientation a printed page that is longer than it is wide

presentation a *PowerPoint* file that contains one or more slides

primary key a special field that contains the unique identifier for each record in a table

Print Layout view in *Word*, the editing view in which the top, bottom, left, and right edges of a page are visible

Print Preview in *Word*, the view that displays a document as it will look when it is printed

printer a device that prints a hard copy of electronic documents

promote to move outline text up one level in the outline

proofreaders' marks special symbols that note errors or changes to a proofread document

proofreading reading a document to look for errors or formatting changes

Q

query an *Access* object that looks at the records in a table and displays only those records that meet specific criteria

R

range a group of adjacent worksheet cells written with the first and last cell reference separated by a colon, such as A1:B3

record all the data for one specific item; represented by a row in a table datasheet

record selector the row heading button in Datasheet view used to select a record

Recycle Bin folder a folder that temporarily stores electronic files deleted from a computer's hard drive

relational database a single file that contains multiple related items called objects

relative references cell references that *Excel* can change when it copies and pastes a formula into a new position on a worksheet

report a database object used to preview and print data

Restore Down button a button in the upper-right corner of a window that resizes the maximized window to a smaller size

return address a letter sender's name and address

Right Indent marker an indent that moves all the lines of a paragraph inward from the right margin

Right tab a tab stop that aligns dates and other text at the right margin or right-aligns text in tabbed columns

right-click to point to a specific area on the screen and press the right mouse button once

right-pointing arrow symbol the symbol in the record selector in Datasheet view that indicates the current record

rotate handle a point on a selected AutoShape you can drag with the mouse pointer to change the shape's rotation

row a horizontal arrangement of cells in a *Word* table

row a horizontal arrangement of cells across a worksheet

row heading numbers 1 through 65536 that appear down the left side of the worksheet

ruler a vertical or horizontal tool used to identify typing position in a document

S

salutation a letter's greeting line

screen the viewing area on a computer monitor

ScreenTip a small yellow box that contains the name of a window element; it appears when the mouse pointer is placed on a window element

scroll bar a vertical or horizontal tool you can use to view different parts of the open document, workbook, presentation, or database object

scroll box a small box on the vertical or horizontal scroll bars you can drag up or down with the mouse pointer

section break a break that creates areas of a *Word* document that can have text in columns or margins that are different from the other pages

select to drag the I-beam over text or click the text to make it available for editing

shading background color added to text within borders

sheet tab the tab at the bottom of a worksheet that shows the worksheet's name

shortcut menu a brief menu of commands that appears when you right-click an icon or different areas of the screen

side heading short underlined phrase that begins at the left margin and introduces a section of a report

Simple Query Wizard a step-by-step process to create a simple query that lists specific fields from a table in a datasheet.

sizing handle black square or white circle on the boundaries of selected pictures or drawings; used to resize objects

slide an individual page in a *PowerPoint* file that can contain text, graphics, video, audio, and animation

slide layout in *PowerPoint*, predefined boxes, called placeholders, used to organize presentation data that appears on a slide

slide master a special hidden slide that contains all the design elements from the applied template and controls the appearance of all the slides except the title slide

slide pane the area in the *PowerPoint* window in Normal view in which you add content to slides

slide show display of each slide so that it covers the entire screen

Slide Show view shows how the slides will look when projected in the slide show

Slide Sorter view the view in which you can see all the slides in the presentation at one time as thumbnails

slide timings the preset amount of time between slides as they advance automatically during a slide show

slide transitions special motion effects that appear as one slide leaves the screen and another one appears during a slide show

Slides tab the area of the *PowerPoint* window in Normal view in which you can see slide thumbnails

soft page break an automatic page break created by *Word* when a text page is full

software instructions used by a computer to operate its hardware or perform tasks such as word processing

sound file music or other sounds added to a slide

source the origin of facts and ideas used in a report

speaker notes information added to a slide that is not visible to the audience but can be used to prompt the presenter

Standard toolbar a toolbar that contains buttons for commonly used tasks such as opening, saving, or printing a document, workbook, or presentation

Start button located on the desktop; opens the Start menu, which lists the applications on a computer

status bar a bar at the bottom of an application window that contains information about the open document as well as the position of the insertion point

storage devices external or internal hardware for storing and reading data

style a collection of formats saved with a name and applied all at once to text

subtotal a temporary column sum, average, or other calculation created with the *Excel* Subtotal feature

SUM the *Excel* function that calculates the total value of a range of cells

Summary Slide a Title and Text slide that lists the title text of selected slides

symbol a special font character inserted in a document to represent items, such as physical things, trademarks, or copyrights

synonym a word that has the same or similar meaning as another word

system clock an internal computer clock that tells the date and time

system software software needed by a computer to operate

T

tab formatting mark a formatting mark inserted in a document when you tap the TAB key

tab indicator the button to the left of the horizontal ruler used to set custom tab stops

tab stop an icon on the horizontal ruler that indicates a specific typing position

tabbed column column of text created with tab stops and tab formatting marks and aligned at a tab stop

table a grid of vertical columns and horizontal rows

table an *Access* database object that contains data

Table Wizard a step-by-step process to create a new database table from the fields in a sample table

taskbar an area at the bottom of the *Windows XP* or *Windows 2000* window that displays buttons for open documents and applications

taskbar button a button on the taskbar that represents a minimized application or document

Text and Content group a group of slide layouts that combine text placeholders with a content placeholder

text box a moveable container for text or pictures

text wrapping formatting text to wrap to multiple lines within a cell

thesaurus a collection of synonyms and antonyms for specific words; a built-in feature in *Word*

thumbnail a tiny version of a slide

Title and Text the slide layout that has title and bulleted-list placeholders

title bar the blue bar along the top of an application or operating system window that contains the window's Minimize, Restore Down, and Close buttons and the name of the open application, document, or folder

title master a special hidden slide that contains all the design elements from the applied template and controls the appearance of the title slide

Title Slide the slide layout that has title and subtitle placeholders; usually the first slide of the presentation

triple-click to point to a specific area on the screen and press the left mouse button rapidly three times

typeface font; the way letters and numbers look

U

unbound report a short, one-page report that has a 2-inch top margin and 1-inch side and bottom margins

Uniform Resource Locator the address of a Web page, or URL

unordered list a list of words, phrases, or sentences preceded by a bullet graphic; a bulleted list

uppercase letters or characters that are capitals

URL the address of a Web page

USB flash drive portable hardware device for storing data

user name the name of the person using an electronic mail box

value (y) axis shows the numbers or values over which the data is to be charted; values appear vertically on the left side of the chart

V

View button a button in the lower-left corner of the *Word* window used to change the editing view

W

Web World Wide Web; a special part of the Internet in which computers called servers store documents called Web pages

Web browser the application software used to load and view Web pages

Web page a document containing text, pictures, sound, and animation linked to other Web pages with hyperlinks

website a collection of related Web pages

what-if analysis a method of analyzing the results of a formula by changing the variables used in the formula's calculations

window a rectangular area on the screen in which you can see and work in an application or a document

WordArt predesigned text formats used to create interesting and colorful text objects

wordwrap the process by which text automatically moves to the next line when there is no more room at the right margin

workbook a single *Excel* file that contains multiple worksheets

worksheet a grid of columns and rows in which you can enter data and formulas

World Wide Web a special part of the Internet in which computers called servers store documents called Web pages

writer's name the name of the person who is writing a letter

Index